Pelevin and Unfreedom

SRLT

NORTHWESTERN UNIVERSITY PRESS
Studies in Russian Literature and Theory

SERIES EDITORS
Caryl Emerson
Gary Saul Morson
William Mills Todd III
Andrew Wachtel
Justin Weir

Pelevin and Unfreedom

Poetics, Politics, Metaphysics

Sofya Khagi

NORTHWESTERN UNIVERSITY PRESS / EVANSTON, ILLINOIS

Northwestern University Press
www.nupress.northwestern.edu

Printed in the United States of America

10 9 8 7 6 5 4 3 2 1

Library of Congress Cataloging-in-Publication Data

Names: Khagi, Sofya, author.
Title: Pelevin and unfreedom : poetics, politics, metaphysics / Sofya Khagi.
Other titles: Studies in Russian literature and theory.
Description: Evanston, Illinois : Northwestern University Press, 2021. |
    Series: Northwestern University Press Studies in Russian literature and
    theory | Includes bibliographical references and index.
Identifiers: LCCN 2020031189 | ISBN 9780810143029 (paperback) |
    ISBN 9780810143036 (cloth) | ISBN 9780810143043 (ebook)
Subjects: LCSH: Pelevin, Viktor—Criticism and interpretation. | Liberty in
    literature. | Social control in literature.
Classification: LCC PG3485.E38 Z748 2021 | DDC 891.73/5—dc23
LC record available at https://lccn.loc.gov/2020031189

To my daughter, Amaliya

Contents

Acknowledgments

I would like to thank my colleagues at the Department of Slavic Languages and Literatures at the University of Michigan, Ann Arbor—I am lucky to have such a stimulating place to work. I am especially grateful to Herb Eagle, my mentor of many years, for his wise guidance and exceptional kindness, and to Michael Makin for his insights and encouragement. I am profoundly grateful to Stephanie Sandler of Harvard University for guiding me all these years in and after graduate school, and always being ready to provide astute advice and friendly support. I would like to express my warm appreciation to Irene Delic of Ohio State University and Kathleen Parthé of the University of Rochester (my undergraduate teacher of Russian literature) for being generous long-term mentors and friends. I am indebted to Richard Lee Pierre and Terre Fisher at the University of Michigan for their superb editorial work on my manuscript. At Northwestern University Press, I am thankful to Gary Saul Morson for his endorsement of my project (my second book with Northwestern University Press), to Trevor Perri and Patrick Samuel for guiding me through the intricacies of the publication process, and to the three anonymous reviewers for suggesting ways to enrich my work. I would like to thank my parents, Khaya and Kasriyel Khagi, for always being by my side with love, strength, and support. This book is dedicated to my daughter, Amaliya: she gave me the whole world and a pair of skates besides.

✿ ✿ ✿

I would also like to thank the editors and publishers of those periodicals in which several parts of this book were previously published as articles. I have revised the material for this book in light of Pelevin's later works and critical essays that have appeared since my articles were published.

"Alternative Historical Imagination in Viktor Pelevin." *Slavic and East European Journal* 62, no. 3 (Fall 2018): 483–502. Used with permission from The Ohio State University.

"From Homo Sovieticus to Homo Zapiens: Viktor Pelevin's Consumer Dystopia." *The Russian Review* 67, no. 4 (October 2008): 559–79. Used with permission from John Wiley & Sons.

"Incarceration, Alibi, Escape? Victor Pelevin's Art of Irony." *Russian Literature* 76, no. 4 (November 2014): 381–406. Used with permission from Elsevier.

"The Monstrous Aggregate of the Social: Toward Biopolitics in Victor Pelevin's Work." *Slavic and East European Journal* 55, no. 3 (Fall 2011): 439–59. Used with permission from The Ohio State University.

"One Billion Years after the End of the World: Historical Deadlock, Contemporary Dystopia, and the Continuing Legacy of the Strugatskii Brothers." *Slavic Review* 72, no. 2 (Summer 2013): 267–86. Used with permission from Cambridge University Press.

Abbreviations of Works by Pelevin

AV   *Ananasnaia voda dlia prekrasnoi damy.* Moscow: Eksmo, 2010.

CP   *Chapaev i pustota.* Moscow: Vagrius, 1996.

DPP(NN)   *Dialektika perekhodnogo perioda iz niotkuda v nikuda.* Moscow: Eksmo, 2003.

EV   *Empire V / Ampir V: Povest' o nastoiashchem sverkhcheloveke.* Moscow: Eksmo, 2006.

G'П'   *Generation 'П.'* Moscow: Vagrius, 1999.

LTC   *Liubov' k trem cukerbrinam.* Moscow: Eksmo, 2014.

SF   *Sinii fonar'.* Moscow: Alfa fantastika, 1991.

SKO   *Sviashchennaia kniga oborotnia.* Moscow: Eksmo, 2004.

SU   *Shlem uzhasa.* Moscow: Otkrytyi mir, 2005.

VPE   *Vse povesti i esse.* Moscow: Eksmo, 2005.

Pelevin and Unfreedom

Fifty Shapes of Grid

—Why has our planet been selected?
—It has not been selected. It was created as a
prison from the start.
—Victor Pelevin, *Empire V*

VICTOR PELEVIN is one of the most significant post-Soviet writers, as well as the most extensively translated one in the English language. Pelevin has been highly visible on the post-Soviet cultural scene since he became a spokesman for the generation that came of age in the 1990s, grappling with life in a disintegrating empire. He has perfected his own unique kind of socio-metaphysical fantasy that blends hilarious parody with black absurdist plot twists, and integrates meticulous observations of the everyday with the occult and the surreal. Pelevin has been compared to masters of socio-metaphysical fantasy like Gogol, Kafka, and Borges, and has been celebrated over the past two decades for being the most "zeitgeisty" of contemporary writers—as well as for his uncanny prescience. He has captured Brave New Russia with unprecedented acuity—and may have succumbed to its corrupt realities. The debates around his prolific output have proved some of the most heated in post-Soviet cultural circles.[1]

There has been a boom in scholarly treatments of Pelevin's work in recent years, not to mention the countless reviews in both print and online media. However, there has also been a tendency either to collapse the wide range of his attitudes toward literary production to a form of postmodernism, or to enlist or dismiss him in accordance with narrow ideological agendas. Moreover, his latest output has received less critical attention than earlier works such as *Chapaev and the Void* (*Chapaev i pustota*, 1996; translated into English as *Buddha's Little Finger*) and *Generation 'П'* (1999). Reviews of his recent work have been marred by ideological or personal views that cause their authors to miss the ambiguities and subtleties of Pelevin's work.

Pelevin is a challenging author because of all the tricks he deploys in his texts, the complexity of his narratives, and the general elusiveness of their meaning. His exuberant fantasies harbor a rich potential for interpretation. Ironies and paradoxes saturate his work, making its meaning highly unstable.

Pelevin is information-oriented, globally savvy, and a razor-sharp thinker, and he also possesses an uncanny degree of cultural reflexivity (including hyper-auto-reflexivity).[2] He is more resistant to critical analysis than one might think, and my project takes him seriously without discounting the role of gleeful play in his writing.

This study aims to give the philosophical and aesthetic complexities of Pelevin's writing their due and to address the full evolution of his work, from the early post-Soviet years to Putin's Russia. The fact that Pelevin has been a prominent cultural presence for a quarter of a century provides the historical perspective necessary to assess his stature and endurance. To this end, I perform close readings of his texts, look at his dialogue with theory, and bring into focus the broader patterns of thought that unify his extensive body of work.

In this book, I try to understand a significant portion of Pelevin's body of work by exploring his critique of post-Soviet and global postmodern contemporaneity. Pelevin is such a significant writer at this moment because he shows us that we live in a world where freedom has been made impossible. He is popular because he is fun to read, but he has in mind much more than entertainment. If we focus too much on the gleeful distractions of his work, we miss the deadly serious and devastating critique that he has launched of the contemporary world. My study aims to restore critical balance and to show how much this writer has to teach us—about society, bondage, and possible avenues of liberation.

The core theoretical concern of my study is the philosophical problem of (un)freedom in Pelevin's work. His oeuvre and worldview take shape around Dostoevsky-like obsessive reflections on how freedom is perverted in contemporary social conditions. A determinedly anti-authoritarian writer, he never takes for granted what he terms "collective visualizations"—divergent ideologies, alternative mythologemes, and common-sense assumptions. The deconstruction of Soviet ideology in Pelevin's early work (an easy enough target in light of the collapse of the Soviet Union) gave way to a decades-long scrutiny of global techno-consumerism.[3] Since the 1990s, the quandaries of the global, postmodern, techno-consumer realm have constituted an ever-present locus of his thought. From Pelevin's perspective, the world of the present, by means of hyper-commodification and technological manipulation, promotes human degradation, historical deadlock, and cultural and spiritual collapse.

As Pelevin pithily observes in his anti-techno-consumerist manifesto *Generation 'П'*: "Man has a natural right to freedom" (*GП* 110).[4] In his universe, freedom of thought and action is the most valuable thing humans possess, and is to be striven for against all biological and social odds. Pelevin's protagonists, like the eponymous Pyotr Pustota, are continuously on the run from imprisonment. In rare cases they succeed, and this is indeed reward-ing. More often, Pelevin's characters are denied this crucial right.

From novel to novel, from the volatile 1990s to the crisis- and violence-fraught current decade, Pelevin models detailed systems of unfreedom. The modeling unfolds organically across his writing—in divergent configura-tions, from different angles, and with varying degrees of success—but always around the same core set of inquiries. There is a specific structural rhythm to a typical Pelevin narrative. As he works with a cluster of key motifs such as hyper-consumerism, dehumanization, techno-control, illusions, and the lies of language, pulp culture, and critical theory, he builds upon his preceding works and introduces new insights in successive texts.

While many writers do this, Pelevin's oeuvre possesses a much higher-than-average degree of connectivity, both within a given text and between successive texts. If one may indulge in a classical analogy, a Tolstoyan laby-rinth of linkages is apparent in his work. Individual narratives are connected in a stereoscopic manner, in which the same subjects are viewed at different angles to impart multidimensionality to their representation. It is as if, in an almost Einsteinian manner, Pelevin plays with relativity and positions.

More importantly, successive narratives offer seemingly distinct socio-metaphysical models which, in fact, refer back to and grow out of the pre-ceding paradigms. From novel to novel, Pelevin builds his Chain of Being—which in his case is reconceived as a Chain of Unfreedom. Each successive model lifts yet another veil of Maya, exposes yet another scheme hidden behind the one previously portrayed. The novels form a kind of *matryoshka* in reverse, exposing levels of enslavement in a seemingly infinite series: A coerced by B in turn manipulated by C in turn puppeteered by D, and so on. Underlying all these schemes is the ever-present hyper-commodification and hyper-technological transformation of existence that results in dehumani-zation and social degradation.

I demonstrate that the divergent levels of Pelevin's texts—poetics, politics, and metaphysics—are coordinated to produce a playful, paradoxi-cal, yet thorough and ultimately unforgiving diagnosis of contemporary society. Pelevin holds up a mirror to his readers to show how social control effectively masquerades as freedom, how people freely accept (and actually welcome) enslavement by the system, and how received markers of freedom (like the free market) are in fact misguided or illusory.

Isaiah Berlin's well-known characterization of Dostoevsky versus Tol-stoy observes that there are writers who are preoccupied with a particular set of problems and who pursue them doggedly throughout their work (hedge-hogs), and writers with wider, more all-encompassing interests (foxes). Like his illustrious predecessor Fyodor Dostoevsky, Pelevin is definitely a hedge-hog. He outlines the how's and why's of unfreedom with a doggedness that reminds one of a science textbook. As in Dostoevsky's case, contemporary events are especially germane to Pelevin's art. His forte has to do with what in Russian is termed *aktual'nost'*—an unrivaled ability to keep his finger on the pulse of the time. He zeroes in and extrapolates on the most characteristic and alarming trends of an epoch before they get noticed by the majority who "live and die" in it.[5] He is uncannily attuned to the Mandelstamian "noise of time," which morphs into Don DeLillo's white noise.[6] And with time, the issues Pelevin engages become clearer and more conspicuous. Whether x-raying the seismic events of the early post-Soviet 1990s, the deceptive stability of the 2000s, or the apocalyptic feel of the present, he diagnoses social diseases, carrying them through to (il)logical conclusions. The more those spot-on trends are pushed to the absurd, the sharper Pelevin's diagnosis of reality shines through.

Why is Pelevin preoccupied with unfreedom in an age when the starkest totalitarian regimes have receded into history? Although straightforward dictatorships like Nazism or Stalinism are matters of the past, the present state of humankind represents the suppression of freedom to an unheard-of extent. Unlike the crudely carceral twentieth-century totalitarian states, the global techno-consumer system provides a more comfortable and therefore more efficient modus operandi for controlling the human subject. And since those subjects are content with their cozy imprisonment, the status quo suppresses the populace all the more effectively.[7] This is exactly the sort of paradox that Pelevin is fond of.

For Pelevin, the unfreedom of contemporaneity goes all the way to the obliteration of the human subject as such. One may be tortured into loving Big Brother, as in George Orwell's *1984* (1948). One may reject freedom because a voluntary and conscious choice is too much of a burden, as in Dostoevsky's "Grand Inquisitor" chapter in *The Brothers Karamazov* (1880). Or one may envision a scenario in which the subject no longer mourns the loss of freedom—and this is one of Pelevin's key points—because there remains no one to mourn or for that matter to even recognize the loss. With its comfortable self-occluding bondage, the system destabilizes (or obliterates altogether) the very status of the human being as an agent of free will, reason, and ethics.

Pelevin satirizes Russia's grotesque infantile capitalism, a raw form of commodified existence, but his critique—and this is worth emphasizing—is aimed at the entirety of the global techno-consumer status quo.[8] He sheds light on the painful and disruptive transition from failed Soviet modernity to post-Soviet postmodernity, presenting vivid snapshots of the turbulent years following the dissolution of the Soviet empire with its disintegrating economy, multiple military conflicts, and ecological degradation. But his pessimistic reflections on the human condition resonate well beyond post-Soviet space. This Russian writer engages in dialogue with techno-consumer critiques worldwide on his own idiosyncratic terms.

As Fredric Jameson asserts in *Archaeologies of the Future: The Desire Called Utopia and Other Science Fictions* (2005), Pelevin's oeuvre cuts deeper into the sources of commodification and spectacle society than, for example, that of Philip K. Dick or Ursula Le Guin (82). This claim does make sense. Growing up as a child in the Soviet Union, the Russian writer may have become aware at some point that the socialist utopian vision was a sham. That disillusion came heavy, and the capitalism that succeeded it presents itself as a huge demonic force—life reduced to the accumulation and spending of money, devoid of any kind of ethical imperative.

With Russia crashing into global techno-consumer postmodernity, Pelevin's works bring home global predicaments in an exemplary fashion. Unlike Western fiction and theory's portrayals of established commodified society, Pelevin captures the violent and grotesque replacement of the Soviet way of life by an alien order of commodities. The writer and the people of his generation fall through the cracks between the two realms, their Soviet childhood and youth and their post-Soviet adulthood. He reflects on major historical changes and simultaneously on the self. It is no surprise, then, that Pelevin dissects the Brave New status quo with productive estrangement, as well as a good deal of revulsion.

My approach to Pelevin's oeuvre is twofold: to consider it thematically, as well as look at its development over the course of the last quarter-century or so. When his work first appeared in the late 1980s and early 1990s, it was something of a phenomenon thanks to its cutting-edge combination of Buddhist spirituality, postmodernist style, and all-encompassing irony toward the social establishment, whether liberal or conservative. In that sense Pelevin was true to the general zeitgeist. Dissident authors of the late twentieth century such as Venedikt Erofeev, Andrey Sinyavsky-Tertz, Vladimir Voinovich, and Vasily Aksyonov—whose prominence on the post-Soviet literary scene was the result of perestroika and glasnost—along with conceptualists (Dmitry Prigov, Lev Rubinshtein) and postmodernists like Vladimir Sorokin, also reveled in the absurd, savored the grotesque, and lampooned the political. But even against this broadly experimental landscape, Pelevin still stood out as a stark iconoclast.

Decades after the fall of communism and after the heyday of postmodernism, Pelevin is again reinventing himself. Here I posit an ethical turn in Peleviniana—his intermittent but palpable shift from the metaphysical solipsism and social disenchantment in the classics of the 1990s like *Chapaev and the Void* to a growing ethical concern for others. This shift does not hinder but hinges on individual freedom, since a strong mental interiority is necessary if there is to be an ethical perspective in a universe of coercion.

APPROACHES AND CONTROVERSIES

While I orient myself toward the singular problem of (un)freedom, I also address some of the most contested issues in Pelevin studies, including his relationship to postmodernism, pop culture, and ethics. Though Pelevin is a virtuoso at deploying postmodern devices, he critiques postmodernism as a social and cultural phenomenon. An aggregate of pop culture, Pelevin's text does not merely transcribe information, but manipulates pulp worlds to serve the ends of meta-critique. As an alternative to the monetary *perpetuum mobile* of commodified society, Pelevin posits freedom as an ethical necessity, and later shifts his emphasis to ethics.

This study connects with, amplifies, and challenges previous interpretations of Pelevin's work. I am indebted to a number of scholars and critics for their insights into Pelevin's art—especially Mark Lipovetsky, Aleksandr Genis, Keith Livers, Irina Rodnianskaia, Sergei Kostyrko, Dmitry Bykov, Eliot Borenstein, Angela Brintlinger, Edith Clowes, and Alexander Etkind. It speaks to the richness of Pelevin's art that contrastive readings of his oeuvre abound, and I will address some of their controversies in this book.

I am also interested in putting Western and Russian readings of Pelevin in dialogue with each other—including what I would label schematically as the debate between "Westernizers," who read Pelevin as a textbook postmodernist, and "Slavophiles," who read him as a traditionalist—though of course we should not oversimplify this. The representatives of these two approaches tend to ignore each other. So reviews in *Novyi mir* of Pelevin's novels, for example, call extensively upon Mikhail Bulgakov and keep silent about Jean Baudrillard. And vice versa, articles in *Narrative* or *New Literary Observer* are heavy on Western theory while leaving Bulgakov out of the discussion. To me, work in the spirit of Elbe Day—with a cross-pollination of readings that dismisses neither one of the B's—appears the more rewarding.[9]

I view Pelevin as a playful and ironic writer who employs postmodern devices of plot construction, language, and so on, yet still holds on to the idea of individual emancipatory potential, ethics, and even humanism. To suggest that Pelevin's texts cleave to a humanistic-ethical paradigm, even one heavily saturated with irony, is a risky endeavor, and one that may be taken as a sign of naïveté. Is not Pelevin, in a proper postmodern manner, merely playing with the reader, and would not the critic fall into his trap when seeking to extrapolate a message from his text? Doesn't Pelevin say to his readers: "There are no messages, I am just playing with you, and you are locked in the box with the game, participating in your own way"?

To address such potential objections, for one thing, the claim that Pelevin says to his readers "there are no messages" is torn by an internal ironic contradiction. If there are no messages, there can also be no message that "there are no messages." To put this slightly differently: it is not axiomatic that Pelevin is always-only-merely playing. One needs as much proof that he is reducible (expandable) to messages as that he is expandable (reducible) to sheer postmodern play. In literary scholarship, one generally deals not in proofs but in interpretations that are more or less compelling. Accordingly, this study does not aim to solve a Pelevin theorem, but to offer readings that may be generative in some useful way for readers.

Second, postmodernism itself is hardly confined to untrammeled play. Writers worldwide who are regarded as arch-postmodernists are concerned with things besides verbal and meta-literary games, and they advance critiques that are relevant to the way things are in the real world. Someone like Thomas Pynchon, for instance, while foregrounding how language is used and narrative is constructed, simultaneously conveys serious social critiques of modern American life. The same applies to prominent postmodern writers across the globe, including DeLillo, Tom Wolfe, Salman Rushdie, Italo Calvino, Margaret Atwood, Le Guin, and others.

Third, writers use postmodern devices of verbal play and plot construction to convey different kinds of meanings, and to tend to individual motifs and concerns. Pelevin, for one, is one of the most adroit post-Soviet users of postmodern themes, devices, and tropes. He is highly erudite and very familiar with (among other things) the post-structuralist critique of the Enlightenment initiated by Friedrich Nietzsche and exemplified by Michel Foucault, who assert the historicity of human experience, question the universality of knowledge and moral action, and expose the linkages between metaphysics and violence, education and power. That said, from my perspective, Pelevin's texts convey their own messages—including, but not confined to, the requisite postmodern "there is no message" or "the medium is the message," and privileging certain forms of spiritual questing (such as Buddhism) and serious ethical inquiry.

Even though laughter and irony may be perceived as more stylish in the current climate, Pelevin's work both laughs at the absurd facets of techno-consumerism, neoliberalism, and globalization—and condemns them. There is a limit to the instability here—his texts are serious, in particular when we deal with their crystal-clear and persistent assertions about what's wrong with the current way of life. As opposed to what the *texts* articulate, it is harder to figure out what the authorial attitude to the depicted phenomena entails. Whether the writer himself responds with laughter to obtuseness and ignorance as well as with sympathy to the exploited and the trapped (the familiar Gogolian "humane passage" dilemma) is harder to ascertain, since literary scholars are no clairvoyants.[10]

I accept Pelevin's invitation to participate in my own way, and read him as a social-cultural diagnostician who exposes the brainlessness and brutality of this world. The satirical thrust of his art is apparent, and not only apparent but cutting-edge contemporaneous. Pelevin demonstrates the dangers inherent in commodified society, technological progress, neoliberalism, biopolitics, pulp culture, and so on. He has a set of ideas about what's wrong with the world, and he pursues them. Disabusing people of the fakery in their lives (and not only in the news) is an important task, and he performs it well.

My strong focus on the social aspects of Pelevin's art entails a certain degree of attention to the esoteric (occult, Buddhist) layers of his texts insofar as they form part of his social critique. So, for example, a peculiar blending of ancient myths, world religions, and spot-on topical details (a prominent feature of Pelevinian poetics) raises his indictment of contemporary techno-consumerism to a higher metaphysical level. And so do his references to Buddhism, which envisions all material phenomena as empty, and functioning only to erect an illusory yet well-nigh impenetrable dungeon around the human subject.

Outside post-Soviet space, I examine Pelevin's oeuvre in dialogue with postmodernism, science fiction, utopia/dystopia, alternative history, posthumanism, and philosophical prose in world literature. Since Pelevin works within the post-Soviet context but also incorporates Western reference points, he has a global take on these issues. I suggest international parallels in Anglo-American, Latin American, French, Italian, Czech, Polish, and Baltic fiction: Thomas Pynchon, Jorge Luis Borges, Franz Kafka, Aldous Huxley, George Orwell, Karel Čapek, Ray Bradbury, Stanislav Lem, Ursula Le Guin, Philip K. Dick, William Gibson, Douglas Coupland, Chuck Palahniuk, Frédérick Beigbeder, Michel Houellebecq, Umberto Eco, and Ricardas Gavelis, among others. Pelevin's familiarity with their writings is evident from his work. In many instances he is directly referencing (and arguing with) the authors in question. In other instances, his writing does not necessarily display typological parallels of marked intertextuality, suggesting that a general zeitgeist is producing these resonances.

Equally, I engage Pelevin's texts in dialogue with modern critical theory (the Frankfurt school, neo-Marxism, post-structuralism). He alludes to theorists, mocks them, and frequently spins out his own artistic theorizing. Something like a Foucauldian (or Žižekian, Derridean, or Baudrillardian) reading of Pelevin would therefore miss much of his reflexivity, ingenuity, and sarcasm. I treat Pelevin's thought and theory as equals rather than using theory as a prism to read this writer, and I take care to observe both their points of contact and divergences. By this approach, I hope to cultivate a productive relationship between literary and theoretical practices. My objective thereby is to illuminate Pelevin's contributions to ongoing cultural and political debates both within and outside the post-Soviet space.

THE SPRINGBOARD OF THEORY

Pelevin's oeuvre is heavily informed by Western intellectuals' critique of techno-consumerism—ranging from early visionary works like Walter Benjamin's *The Work of Art in the Age of Mechanical Reproduction* (1936) and José Ortega y Gasset's *The Revolt of the Masses* (1932) to in-depth critical engagements by the Frankfurt school (Herbert Marcuse, Theodor Adorno, Max Horkheimer), to late twentieth-century work by the likes of Fredric Jameson, Michel Foucault, Jean Baudrillard, and Slavoj Žižek. Pelevin explicitly refers to various Western theorists, and draws on (seriously as well as parodically) major ideas and debates on commodification, technology, neoliberalism, biopolitics, posthumanism, postmodernism, and history. Let me sketch out the most relevant concepts and sources in order to contextualize Pelevin's thought.

The One-Dimensional Man

As Herbert Marcuse argues in *One-Dimensional Man: Studies in the Ideology of Advanced Industrial Society* (1964) and *A Critique of Pure Tolerance* (1965), the presence of an advanced industrial society suggests by no means a weakening of political power, but rather a different model of operation under which—unlike totalitarian and despotic governments—control is implemented through daily routine as the media mediates between the masters and the populace. This novel power model is "a comfortable, smooth, democratic *unfreedom* . . . a token of technical progress" (Marcuse, *One-Dimensional Man*, 1). It implies a voluntary acceptance of repression. The democratic majority, conditioned by a monopolistic or oligopolistic administration, are unable to determine their lives for themselves. Whatever "improvement" may occur is likely to change in a direction favored by the powers that be.

In Marcuse's reading, in advanced industrial society the subject merges with its function, and politics merges with commerce. To circumscribe the individual within the social norm, concepts are redefined in operational terms, including the very concept of the subject, which is now identified with its function: "In the most advanced sector of functional and manipulated communication, language imposes in striking constructions the authoritarian identification of person and function." Individuals "appear to be mere appendices or properties of their place, their job, their employer or enterprise," and are "introduced as Virginia's Byrd, U.S. Steel's Blough, Egypt's Nasser" (Marcuse, *One-Dimensional Man*, 92).

What Marcuse terms the "language of total administration" or "operational language" is the idiom employed by the media, politicians, publicity agents, the advertising industry, and the like that is first and foremost function-oriented. The objective is to induce people to do and buy (products as well as ideas). The media shapes the universe of communication in which one-dimensional (or technological) behavior gets enforced. Language "tends to express and promote the immediate identification of reason and fact, truth and established truth, essence and existence, the thing and its function," and it "orders and organizes, induces the people to do, to buy, and to accept." The grammatical subject "does not carry a meaning in excess of that expressed in the sentence," and the word "is expected to have no other response than the publicized and standardized behavior (reaction)" (Marcuse, *One-Dimensional Man*, 85–103).

The language of total administration ensures that the subject has no analytical means for critical thought, especially for questioning the system. It systematically promotes positive thinking and doing, identification and social unification. A contrast emerges between critical modes of thought, on the one hand, and technological behavior or social habits of thought where a concept is fully absorbed by a word, on the other. Operational language translates universal concepts into terms with specific referents. Such notions as "freedom," "equality," democracy," or "peace" come to imply a set of attributes that are invariably invoked when the noun is spoken via analytic predications such as "free enterprise," "free elections," and so on.

To ensure that the public is cognitively locked into the established system, the criteria for judging a given state of affairs are those imposed by the given state of affairs. This excludes judging the context in which the facts are made, and in which their meaning is determined. The governing noun is insulated from any of its contents that would disturb the accepted use of the noun. Speech moves in self-validating hypotheses, synonyms, and tautologies. A sentence becomes a declaration to be accepted, repelling demonstration, qualification, or negation of its codified meaning.

Marcuse's theory of "repressive tolerance" contends that the prevailing practice of toleration in advanced industrial society is a mask that covers oppressive political realities. The governed tolerate the government, which in turn tolerates the opposition within the framework determined by the constituted authorities. Tolerance of that which is radically evil (total resource extraction, exploitation of the weak, environmental pollution) "now may appear good because it serves the cohesion of the whole on the road to affluence and more affluence" (Marcuse, "Repressive Tolerance," 82–83). Toleration of deception in advertising and of the systematic brainwashing of the populace by publicity constitutes the essence of a system that fosters tolerance to perpetuate the struggle for existence.[11]

The Frankfurt school's analyses of techno-consumerism in the 1960s anticipate late twentieth-century critiques—for example, Fredric Jameson's discussion of the penetration of advertising, television, and the media throughout society in *Postmodernism, or, The Cultural Logic of Late Capitalism* (1991) and *The Cultural Turn* (1998), as well as Jean-François Lyotard's targeting of society under the sway of the technological impera- tive.[12] In *The Postmodern Condition: A Report on Knowledge* (1984), Lyotard points out the degradation of intellectuals to cogs-in-the-machine in techno- consumer society: "The transmission of knowledge is no longer designed to train an elite capable of guiding the nation towards its *emancipation*, but to supply the system with players capable of acceptably fulfilling their roles at the pragmatic posts required by its institutions" (48). Efficiency becomes society's primary goal. Technical devices "maximize output (the information or modifications obtained) and minimize input (the energy expended in the process)." Technology "is therefore a game pertaining not to the true, the just, or the beautiful, etc., but to efficiency" (44).[13]

Desert of the Real

Jean Baudrillard's notions of simulacra and consumer desire are ever-present in Pelevin. As Baudrillard argues in *Simulacra and Simulation* (1981), in the world of contemporaneity, semiotic systems with no relation to the real oust reality. While representation stems from the equivalence of the sign and the real (even if this equivalence is utopian, it is taken as axiomatic), simulation "stems from the utopia of the principle of equivalence, from the radical ne- gation of the sign as value, from the sign as the reversion and death sentence of every reference" (6). The successive stages of the image are as follows: (a) reflection of a profound reality, (b) masking a profound reality, (c) mask- ing the absence of a profound reality, (d) having no relation to a reality what- soever and being its own pure simulacrum.

As Baudrillard argues in *The Gulf War Did Not Take Place* (1995), the media blurs the boundaries between the real and the illusory—as in the virtual warfare of the Gulf War presented for the benefit of the popu- lace. The technical drive to create exact replicas of phenomena results in the emptying-out of an object's meaning and its replacement with a simulacrum (68). Digitized versions flourish by virtue of their proximity to the real and refuse to signify anything beyond this effect of simulation. The event disap- pears "into its own special effect" (Baudrillard, *The Illusion of the End*, 5).

Baudrillard associates media spectacle with the fetishization of com- modities under advanced capitalism and criticizes its hollowing-out of any genuine (ethical or political) commitment and of history itself. Everywhere, virtuality "eradicates what we could call, if it still meant anything at all, the

13

real movement of history" (*The Illusion of the End*, 4–5). The end of history is the stage when humans "become tiny mechanisms of spectacle and finally turn into celibate machines which exhaust their capabilities in an empty vortex, as in Duchamp's work" (4–5).

In *The Consumer Society: Myths and Structures* (1970), Baudrillard explores the self-perpetuating cycle of consumer desire. Under techno-consumerism, human desires are channeled into the act of selling and buying. Such channeling precludes other than consumerist pursuits. Advertising creates images of power and desire that stimulate one to crave more and more: this "carefully preserved mystique of individual satisfaction and choice . . . is the very ideology of the industrial system, justifying its arbitrary power and all the collective nuisances it generates: dirt, pollution, decultura-tion." The consumer "is sovereign in a jungle of ugliness where freedom of choice has been forced upon him" (72–73).[14] The media urge people to consume ever more and never be satisfied, the industrial system tolerates radical evil, and the freedom to buy constitutes an illusory locus of freedom.

In *Symbolic Exchange and Death* (1976), Baudrillard offers a dichotomy between societies organized around premodern exchange and societies organized around production exchange. In the machine of modern capital, nature no longer counts, and political economy survives only in a brain-dead state. Neither does the symbolic—gift and counter-gift, reciprocity and reversal, expenditure and sacrifice—any longer count in modern society (35).[15] As Baudrillard suggests, archaic mechanisms of gift, expenditure, sacrifice, and destruction resist neo-capitalist values of utility and monetary profit.

Baudrillard's assessment of contemporaneity is discouraging overall. As he puts it in *The Illusion of the End* (1994): "History, meaning, and progress are no longer able to reach their escape velocity" (4). The present, bereft of visionary ideas, revolves around repetition, simulation, and sanitization of the past; it entertains a death wish while endlessly deferring the end. "The perception and imagination of the future are beyond us" (*The Jean Baudrillard Reader*, 126). Nor will the end of times, whether disastrous or revelatory, ever arrive: "Everything will continue to take place in a slow, fastidious, recurring and all-encompassing hysterical manner—like nails continue to grow after death" (Baudrillard, "Hystericizing the Millennium," 1).

Biopolitics, Biopower

If Marcuse approaches modern society from the angles of one-dimensionality and repressive tolerance, and Baudrillard emphasizes the simulated aspects of modern (ir)reality, Michel Foucault critiques society from, among other things, a biopolitical angle. The closely related notions of biopolitics and biopower—the governance of a population understood at once as a biological species and a political-economic body—is associated primarily with Foucault's works, and specifically with his Collège de France lectures of 1975–79. Prior to these lectures, his *The Order of Things: An Archaeology of the Human Sciences* (1966) conceived of the community as a whole of individuals organically related to each other. *Discipline and Punish: The Birth of the Prison* (1975), in its turn, exposes a modern system of domination made all the more insidious because it is perceived not as oppression but as liberation.[16]

Following the publication of *Discipline and Punish*, Foucault's lectures at the Collège de France examine biopolitical modes of power which incorporate the living into state concerns: "the set of mechanisms through which the basic biological features of the human species became the object of a political strategy, of a general strategy of power." Starting from the eighteenth century, "modern Western societies took on board the fundamental biological fact that human beings are a species" (Foucault, *Security, Territory, Population*, 1). The state achieves the regulation of its subjects by mechanisms that seek the modification of the biological destiny of the species. Biopolitics aims at a multiplicity of humans, not to the extent that they are mere individual bodies, but to the extent that they form a global mass that is affected by processes of birth, illness, reproduction, and death (Foucault, *Society Must Be Defended*, 143).

The Posthumanism Debate

Along with his biopolitical critique, Foucault advances charges against traditional humanism. As he formulates it in *The Order of Things*: "It is comforting, however, and a source of profound relief to think that man is only a recent invention, a figure not yet two centuries old, a new wrinkle in our knowledge, and that he will disappear again as soon as that knowledge has discovered a new form" (xviii). Foucault argues that man as the object of study was born during the age of the Enlightenment, and if those arrangements were to disappear, man would disappear, too (*The Order of Things*, 357). Following Nietzsche, thinkers like Foucault, Lyotard, and other Western critics have called humanism both obsolete and insidious and problematized it as a construct used as a cover for capitalism, Western imperialism, patriarchy, and other concepts and entities.[17]

Not all Western critics, however, have unequivocally welcomed posthumanism—the various theories that are critical of traditional humanism. Unlike his earlier works, Lyotard's *The Inhuman: Reactions on Time* (1991) considers both the pros and cons of inhumanity taking over: "What if human beings, in humanism's sense, were in the process of becoming inhuman (the first part)? And (the second part), what if what is proper to humankind were to be inhabited by the inhuman?" (2). Lyotard further asks: "What else remains as 'politics' except resistance to this inhuman? And what is left to resist with but the debt which each soul has contracted with the miserable and admirable indetermination from which it was born . . . , which is to say, with the other inhuman?" (*The Inhuman*, 7).

After Francis Fukuyama published "The End of History?" (1989) and *The End of History and the Last Man* (1992), in which he argued that the collapse of communism signaled the global victory of liberal democracy, he reconsidered his earlier thesis.[18] In *Our Posthuman Future: Consequences of the Biotechnology Revolution* (2002), Fukuyama views recent advances in the life sciences as capable of transforming humankind in fundamental ways. The book's objective is "to argue that Huxley was right, that the most significant threat posed by contemporary biotechnology is the possibility that it will alter human nature and thereby move us into a 'posthuman' stage of history" (6). For Fukuyama, human nature shapes and constrains the possible kinds of authoritarian political regimes, and therefore a "technology powerful enough to reshape what we are will have possibly malign consequences for liberal democracy and the nature of politics itself" (7). Fukuyama understands posthumanism in the classic negative (Huxleyan) sense: people "no longer struggle, aspire, love, feel pain, make difficult moral choices, have families, or do any of the things that we traditionally associate with being humans. They no longer have the characteristics that give us human dignity" (7).

Why accept Fukuyama's appeal to human nature as the bedrock of moral, social, and political freedom when the very definition he presents of human nature may be outdated? Yet, as Tony Davies points out, it would be unwise to abandon the ground occupied by the traditional humanisms because "the *freedom* to speak and write, to organize and campaign in defense of individual or collective interests, to protect and disobey: all these can only be articulated in humanist terms" (*Humanism*, 131–32).[19]

Subverting Opposition

In one more insight of the Frankfurt school, advanced industrial society seamlessly absorbs oppositional forces. As Marcuse argues, the power that society acquires over its subjects is absolved by its efficacy and productiveness: "It assimilates everything it touches, it absorbs the opposition, it plays with contradiction, it demonstrates its cultural superiority" (*One-Dimensional Man*, 84).

The status quo neutralizes forces of dissent not via punishment (in contrast to totalitarian structures), but by reabsorbing them in the techno-consumer apparatus. It enforces total homogeneity and neutralizes ("non-violently") anyone diverging from the norm. Genuine (self)-marginalization is impossible, and the tolerance of opposition, paradoxically, serves to contain qualitative change. Marcuse offers a dichotomy between genuine political resistance and self-actualization, a personal letting-go, which leaves the mechanisms of repression in society intact. Self-actualization actually strengthens these mechanisms by substituting the satisfactions of private and personal (mock) rebellion for a collective and therefore authentic counteraction ("Repressive Tolerance," 107).

Slavoj Žižek likewise differentiates between genuine rebellion and rebellion co-opted by the status quo. Discussing David Fincher's film *Fight Club* (1999), based on Chuck Palahniuk's novel, he distinguishes between redeeming political violence and acting out that merely confirms one's entrapment. In accordance with late-capitalist global commodification, violence—the very attempt to explode the universe of commodities—is offered as an experiential commodity. An act of transgression serves social cohesion by releasing pent-up aggression (Žižek, *The Sublime Object of Ideology*, 300).[20]

According to Fukuyama in *The End of History*, *Homo economicus* alone is inadequate as an explanation for how humans behave. He adds *Homo thymoticus*, the human being who strives to be recognized as a *free* being: "the Man of desire, Economic Man, will perform an internal 'cost-benefit analysis' which will always give him reason for working 'within the system.' It is only . . . the man of anger who is jealous of his own dignity and the dignity of his fellow citizens who is willing to walk in front of a tank" (*The End of History and the Last Man*, 80). Yet Fukuyama doubts the possibility of counteracting the system.

Freedom and Ethics

The suppression of freedom—collective and personal, political and spiritual, the freedom to act and think—is at the core of the critique of techno-consumerism. Furthermore, in the critical theory of the Frankfurt school, the advanced industrial status quo suppresses *freedom and ethics concurrently*. As Theodor Adorno argues in *Problems of Moral Philosophy* (1967), society draws on the human subject's entire resources in the work of survival and socialization. Reality possesses such an enormous power in the present, it demands so much adaptability from the human, that "in the endless curves of the social . . . , the possibility of *freedom* is decreased to such an extent that one can, even should, seriously raise the question of whether the categories of the *moral* still make any sense" (Adorno, *Probleme der Moralphilosophie*, 246).

While Adorno suggests that the total suppression of freedom precludes any meaningful discussion of moral categories, Marcuse sees the loss of ethical coordinates precluding an attitude critical of the regime and therefore any possibilities for liberation. Repressive tolerance neutralizes crucial opposites like truth and falsehood, right and wrong—which enable critical thinking. In media debates, the stupid or ignorant opinion is allotted the same amount of respect as the intelligent one. This toleration of nonsense is justified by the argument that nobody, either a group or an individual, is in possession of the truth. But, as Marcuse insists, emptying out the distinctions between truth and falsehood, right and wrong—via one-dimensional behavior, the language of total administration, and repressive tolerance— endangers freedom to an unprecedented extent:

> Tolerance cannot be indiscriminate and equal with respect to the contents of expression, neither in word nor in deed; it cannot protect *false words and wrong deeds* which demonstrate that they contradict and counteract the possibilities of *liberation*. Such indiscriminate tolerance is justified in harmless debates, in conversation, in academic discussion. . . . But society cannot be indiscriminate where *freedom* and happiness themselves are at stake. . . . A mental attitude which tends to obliterate the difference between *true and false, information and indoctrination, right and wrong* . . . asserts itself in the juxtaposition of gorgeous ads with unmitigated horrors, in the introduction and interruption of the broadcasting of facts by overwhelming commercials. ("Repressive Tolerance," 88, 97–98)

Marcuse is distinctly non-postmodern here. Far from necessitating relativism, critical thought searches in real history for the criteria of truth and falsehood, progress and regression. Confronted with a given society as an object of reflection, it judges, perceives the forces of domination, and demands social change. This way to freedom is closed off for the one-dimensional subject who, due to the dissolution of basic moral coordinates, is unable to recognize social flaws and demand change.

Notwithstanding the Frankfurt school's (post-Auschwitz) charges against humanism, Adorno and Marcuse connect free will and ethics, as well as reason, in a manner that draws on post-Enlightenment and post-Kantian traditions. It is reason that enables one to distinguish between good and evil, as well as making possible an independent choice between the two. In Kantian terms, the fundamental principle of morality is the law of an autonomous

will, and a moral requirement is based on a standard of rationality (the categorical imperative). The destruction of reason paradoxically takes place in
ultra-advanced technological societies, along with the destruction of free will
and morals.

RUSSIAN (UN)FREEDOM

Pelevin combines Western theoretical models with Russian ideas of (un)
freedom. In *Another Freedom: An Alternative History of an Idea* (2010),
Svetlana Boym distinguishes between *freedoms* in the plural—political freedoms, human rights, collective solidarities—and *freedom* in the singular—
religious, artistic, and existential inner freedom associated with introspec-
tion and imagination. The expression in the book's title, "another freedom,"
comes from Alexander Pushkin's "From Pindemonti" ("Iz Pindemonti," 1836),
the poet's response to Alexis de Tocqueville's first volume of *Democracy in
America* (1835). In this poem Pushkin mocks democratic freedoms, dismisses them in a Shakespearean idiom as "words, words, words," and praises
"another, better freedom" (*inaia, luchshaia svoboda*) that lies outside the
political and social realms in the exploration of natural beauty and the beauty
of art (Boym, *Another Freedom*, 84).

Boym suggests that the cross-cultural dialogue between Pushkin and
Tocqueville exceeds their personal idiosyncrasies and points to the dif-
ferent cultural and political conceptions of freedom in Russia, Europe, and
America:

> In Russia, freedom . . . is an object of a nostalgic or futuristic desire, not a
> set of rules for everyday behavior in the present. Liberation presents itself as
> trespassing, transgression or transcendence, not as a balancing act between
> play and responsibility at the boundary of the law. At the same time, an un-
> critical practice of *freedoms* in the plural, when conflated with the tyranny of
> the majority, might breed conformism and limit imagination. American de-
> mocracy cannot become a form of manifest destiny for the world. Freedom
> needs its otherness, its creative individual dimension reflected in literature,
> philosophy, and unconventional arts of living. . . . Perhaps what scared Push-
> kin most about democracy in America was not the fact that it did not work but
> the fact that it could. (*Another Freedom*, 94)

As we know now—in fact it did.

Russians, who are relative newcomers in this Brave New World—hardly
of democracy proper, but surely and ironically the recipients of its worst

aspects—often sound on edge when expostulating on the tyranny of the masses. At times a good deal of their inferiority complex seeps through: who are we—failures as we are in the socialist experiment and in the Cold War (the past), inept at capitalism-building (the present), in short all-round losers (*luzery*), even in the language battle—to presume to critique the "winning paradigm"? More often there is lots of resentment and revanchism: we, the "righteous ones," have been tricked by *Them*, and now there is no escape from this benighted world for anyone living in it. Frequently lacking on the Russian part is a calm, incisive, ironic perspective that is untainted by sentiments of inferiority and superiority or some uneasy intertwining of the two, a look that neither smiles ingratiatingly nor glares defiantly—but *scrutinizes—thinks*.

And this is precisely what Pelevin does best—if only because this Russian writer "in general likes to think [*emu voobshche nravitsia dumat'*]" (Kostyrko, *Prostodushnoe chtenie*). Contemporary theorists and Pelevin may rival each other in their ability to spin out sprightly aphorisms and paradoxes that capture the (non)sense of our time: "We 'feel free' because we lack the *very* language to articulate our unfreedom" (Žižek, *Welcome to the Desert of the Real*, 2). " 'Why has our planet been selected?' 'It has not been selected. It was created as a prison from the start' " (Pelevin, *EV* 320). More to the point, Pelevin's thinking can be as sharp and insightful as the best of theory. But he is also an artist with impressive imaginative powers—who, as he himself puts it, performs "somersaults of thought."[21] Theory and life become springboards from which to jump into art.

As Baudrillard, an astute interrogator of the contemporary condition, formulates it: "Nothing ever really takes place, since everything is already calculated, audited, and realized in advance" (*The Jean Baudrillard Reader*, 156–57). He observes: "Whether the universe is expanding to infinity or retracting toward an infinitely dense, infinitely small nucleus depends on its critical mass [that] defeats the initial energy and takes us down an inexorable path of contraction and inertia" (*Illusion of the End*, 5). The former pronouncement is amusingly Dostoevskian (though without acknowledging it). In the classic idiom of *Notes from Underground* (1864), Dostoevsky declares: "Everything will be so accurately calculated and designated that there will no longer be any actions or adventures in the world" (*Notes from Underground*, 26). The latter example of theory waxing poetic can be engagingly contrasted to Pelevin's poetry at its most cogent: "We are hanging in an expanding emptiness that, some say, has started shrinking" (*EV* 323). In the best Dostoevskian tradition, Pelevin's works provide scathing artistic perspectives on the world we live in. These issues will be explored in greater depth in the chapters to follow.

CHAPTER OUTLINE

My chapters do not follow a chronological structure, but commence with a close reading of *Generation 'П'*—Pelevin's key fin-de-siècle novel that sets up the power lines of his social and cultural diagnosis. While chapters 1 and 2 focus on this single text, in chapter 3 and all subsequent ones, I survey a number of texts to better chart specific themes. Chapters 1–2, 3–4, 5–6, and 7–8 are grouped under part I ("Techno-Consumer Dystopia"), part II ("Posthumanism"), part III ("History"), and part IV ("Intertext and Irony"), respectively. Since I analyze Pelevin's texts thematically, some passages in the books are referred to more than once and illuminated from various angles.

Chapter 1, "After the Fall," situates *Generation 'П'* within the dystopian tradition of world literature. I argue that Huxley's *Brave New World* (1932), in which total control is achieved by saturating the populace with products of mass culture that serve as tools of social conditioning, is the most fitting model for this Pelevin novel. I juxtapose Pelevin's interrogation of techno-consumerism with mid- to late twentieth-century Western critiques of postindustrial capitalism, most centrally Marcuse's concepts of the one-dimensional man and repressive tolerance, and post-structuralist theories of simulation and hyper-reality à la Baudrillard. Pelevin's novel ridicules the impact of Western consumerism on early post-Soviet Russia, as Soviet hegemony is replaced by the regime of global capital. I show how *Generation 'П'* refurbishes classic dystopian conventions (including Huxley's) by portraying a self-perpetuating dystopia that dismisses the saving qualities of art and erotic passion and implicates the entire populace in social deadlock.

Chapter 2, "Language Games," examines Pelevin's style as an off-shoot of his social critique. Much of the vibrancy of Pelevin's prose derives from its verbal play—his idiosyncratic metaphors, sprightly paradoxes and aphorisms, abundant use of jargon, and inventive bilingual and multilingual puns. Using *Generation 'П'* as my primary text again, I pay special attention here to the novel's explosive mixture of metaphysical and material terminology, high-tech and marketing jargon, puns, and bilingual and multilingual experiments. In my reading, language politics plays a key role in Pelevin's satire of cultural decline and hyper-consumerism in post-Soviet Russia. The newly adopted idioms of advertising and the media, computer terminology, and English and other foreign borrowings capture the seismic changes in the post-Soviet setting. The deformation of the Russian language reflects the deformation of the post-Soviet psyche. Pelevin's metaphysical-material metaphors, ontological concepts articulated via techno-consumer terminology, puns, and a Babel-like proliferation of tongues mimic the cultural disorientation and regression that are rampant in post-Soviet Russia and the world at large. Far from being trivial, the language games in *Generation 'Π'* foreground the novel's concerns with historical and social deadlock.

Chapter 3, "Biomorphic Monstrosities," knits together Pelevin's novels and short stories from around 1990 to the mid-2000s using the prism of biopolitics. Foucault's theory of biopolitics provides a helpful foil to Pelevin's fantasies. Pelevin persistently represents the social collective in biomorphic and zoomorphic terms. As I show, the trope of humanity as biomass, a zoomorphic community ripe for exploitation, has been a concern of his work from the very beginning of his career. The chapter follows this trope through several narratives, including *The Life of Insects* (1993), *Generation 'Π'* , *DPP(NN)* (2003), *The Sacred Book of the Werewolf* (2004), and *Empire V* (2006). Pelevin's biotic schemes express themselves in a stable associative chain: humans—animals—biomass—a source of energy (blood or oil)—money.[22] These schemes, I demonstrate, buttress his diagnosis of the collapse of spirituality and the hyper-consumerism and insidious modes of social regimentation in contemporary life.

Chapter 4, "Can Digital Men Think?" examines Pelevin's recurrent focus on mechanistic dehumanization (humans turned into machines), from "The Prince of Gosplan" (1991) through *The Helmet of Horror* (2005) and other works of the 2000s to *Pineapple Water for the Beautiful Lady* (2010) and *S.N.U.F.F.* (2011). Both scenarios of dehumanization—animalistic (humans turned animals/biomass) and mechanistic (humans turned automatons)— allow Pelevin to elaborate on the crucial issue of the lack of freedom in techno-consumer society. Animalistic and mechanistic scenarios alike offer examples of a posthumanism interpreted negatively, as the justification and spread of human degradation and dehumanization. In my reading, Pelevin probes the boundaries of what it means to be human, but, more importantly, he disparages what he perceives as the endangered status of the human being in today's world. From this perspective, even though the accusations against humanism are grave, there is an ethical necessity to save the concept of the human.

Chapter 5, "Not with a Bang but a Whimper," explores Pelevin's eschatology as a facet of his indictment of the contemporary condition, from "Hermit and Six Toes" (1990) to *S.N.U.F.F.* Notwithstanding all his humor and irony, Pelevin returns again and again to the gloomy themes of the apocalypse and the final judgment. I examine his distinctive end-of-the-world scenarios against the background of classic and modernist apocalyptic narratives, and argue that Pelevin's eschatological narratives, though playful, are thoroughly malignant, entropic, and non-redemptive. His perception of history as degraded is unredeemed by seeds of rebellion, a state of flux and possibility, or any millenarian promise. Conventional eschatology—an object of Pelevin's meta-reflection—for all its scares, is simply too human-centered and optimistic to capture the replacement of the human by the posthuman. In the grip of the techno-consumer apparatus, humankind loses its freedom of choice and its ability to distinguish between good and evil. Unfree and unselfconscious replicons oust the human subject as an agent of free will, reason, and ethics. The world ends not with a bang but a whimper in Pelevin's work—and is all the more disturbing precisely for that.

In chapter 6, "Butterflies in Sunflower Oil," I turn to a crucial aspect of Pelevin's historical imagination: his reworking of the alternative history genre, a popular subgenre of science fiction that explores "what if" scenarios at crucial points in history and presents outcomes other than those in the historical record. In my argument, as Pelevin plays with, and skewers, the memes of alternative history, he critically interrogates the contemporary popular mindset while pursuing his ongoing social and philosophical concerns. "The Crystal World" (1991), Pelevin's alternative historical imagination in a microcosm, frustrates an alternative historical scenario. In *Chapaev and the Void*, which also takes alternative history as the object of meta-reflection, the protagonist and other characters create timelines of their own—not communal alternative histories, but parallel realities formed by their individual consciousness, an approach inspired by the writer's interests in solipsism and Buddhism. In *Love for Three Zuckerbrins* (2014), Pelevin reinterprets the multiverse of alternative history as a constellation of individual ethics-dependent projections. What emerges is an unorthodox alternative to, and a critique of, the more established forms of alternative history fiction. Pelevin's version is predicated not on complicated time-travel technology or pragmatic reasoning, but on individual freedom and moral choice, thus returning historical questions to the larger ethical domain.

Chapter 7, "Somersaults of Thought," examines the ways Pelevin engages his literary predecessors to buttress his social critique. While his oeuvre, in a proper postmodernist manner, is suffused with intertextual play, I focus on two significant subtexts—Dostoevsky and the Soviet science-fiction cult novelists, the Strugatsky brothers. I contend that Pelevin draws on the nineteenth-century classic writer and the Soviet science fiction duo to dramatize his own increasingly dark vision of modernization, progress, and morality. Dostoevsky's exemplary indictment of materialism, rethought in light of more recent history, promotes Pelevin's own metaphysical critique of capitalism. Dostoevskian quandaries about freedom and its limitations, (un)predictability, free will, and natural determinism lie at the core of Pelevin's own thought. Whether freedom is an endowment, a torment, or a combination thereof, one's inalienable right to it has been effectively dispensed with in the contemporary world.

My analysis of Pelevin vis-à-vis the Strugatsky brothers revolves around what I see as his critique of postmodernism from the perspective of the Enlightenment. Pelevin continues in the tradition of the Strugatskys (among others) using science fiction for social critique—in his case, critique of a society collapsing into techno-consumerism and postmodernity. The Strugatskys' earlier discourse on modernity provides a blueprint for Pelevin's investigation of postmodernity. He parodies their high-minded futuristic fantasies, demonstrating how their projects have been embodied in the post-Soviet present, albeit in a cynical, perverted manner. But Pelevin directs his sharpest criticism not at his literary forebears but at his own generation, which has betrayed the humanistic ideals shaped in no small measure by these classics of Russian and Soviet literature. In the process, he reads the defeat of inner freedom by socially imposed unfreedom—whereas the Strugatskys tend to resolve the conflict as a victory of the former—not just in post-Soviet Russia, but in a broader techno-consumer postmodernity, and in so doing he displays the humanist's fears more than postmodernist skepticism.

Chapter 8, "The Total Art of Irony," investigates what I see as perhaps the most striking aspect of Pelevin's critique of the world we live in: namely, his implication of the authorial figure in the very same corrupt social context that gets anatomized in the texts. This chapter analyzes Pelevin's oeuvre by means of its ironic techniques—from *Chapaev and the Void* and *Generation 'П'* through *The Sacred Book of the Werewolf* and *Empire V* to *T* (2009) and *S.N.U.F.F.* Pelevin deploys a variety of strategies, from stable Augustan irony that exposes the follies of society and humans, to a less secure romantic irony that stresses the limits of language vis-à-vis life and selfhood and plays with paradoxes and self-refuting speech acts, to the volatile postmodern irony that destabilizes all kinds of discourses and envisions the subject itself as an effect of narration.

While both irony and self-irony run through Pelevin's works, it is the latter, I argue, that is pivotal to his poetics. Pelevin constructs ironic mechanisms by which the narrative turns on itself. He tosses off contradictions and paradoxes that evade resolution: cases of critical solipsism in which the protagonist's attempts to comprehend reality fall back upon himself, texts that accuse language of falsehood, and critiques of techno-consumer society that are themselves cogs in the machine of techno-consumerism. The result is a dizzying act of dissimulation, at once playful and earnest, that is destabilized by inner contradictions and directed at the ironist as much as at external targets and everyday concepts and values. Pelevin is a consummate postmodern ironist, but an affirmative dimension in his texts—one that invests them with a measure of ethical authenticity—may be suggested by his ironies themselves. His multiplication of ironies reflects authorial attempts to escape his own bounds, and is analogous to the key motif in his works— his protagonists' struggle to make a break, literal and figurative, from their caged existences. In Pelevin's universe, irony may allow a modicum of free space from encroaching social dogma.

In this book's conclusion, "A Christmas Carol with Qualifiers," I chart Pelevin's oeuvre in a wider post-Soviet context, from his groundbreaking writings of the perestroika era to his recent literary output, articulating the continuities and transformations of his art and reaffirming its significance. How can we enrich our readings of Pelevin's classics written in the heyday of postmodernism and during the initial volatile period after the dissolution of the Soviet Union? How has Peleviniana been evolving, and what is its current condition? Pelevin's multivolume project serves as a launch pad for a wide-ranging interrogation of postmodernism both as a literary style and a cultural-sociological phenomenon. He is a consummate performer of postmodernism—and simultaneously its acute critic who posits the problem of individual liberation from a carceral society as an ethical imperative. A trajectory emerges with his shift from a metaphysical experimentation, stressing solipsism and personal liberation, to a greater emphasis on ethical relationships to others.

Pelevin poses difficult and important questions about the nature of cultural production and its relationship to economics and politics. Just as post-Soviet fiction subjects all traditional social and moral norms to ridicule, it substitutes simulacra for reality as a new "norm" driven by market interests. What does it mean to be a writer in a culture where the most subtle and ironic critique of commercialism can (and indeed should) be turned into a commodity? Pelevin's art reflects and *reflects on* the pitfalls of our postmodern techno-consumer present.

PART I

Techno-Consumer Dystopia

After the Fall

> Buratino dug a hole in the ground and
> whispered three times: "Kreks, feks, peks." He
> put four golden coins inside, covered them
> with soil, took some salt from his pocket, and
> sprinkled it above. Then he took some water
> from a puddle into his palm, poured it over.
> And he sat waiting for when the tree would
> sprout.
> —Alexei Tolstoy, *The Little Golden Key, or The
> Adventures of Buratino*

VICTOR PELEVIN'S *Generation 'Π'* (1999), one of the most conspicuous Russian novels of its day, is a fin-de-siècle expression of dystopian imagination. With the advance of Mikhail Gorbachev's reforms in the mid-1980s, Russian writers engaged in increasingly open attacks on the mythology of a socialist utopia. It was during those years that the subgenre of dystopia again came to the fore in literary works. As the collapse of the Soviet empire seemed imminent, parodic treatments of the socialist experiment appeared, as well as more somber works concerned with the menace attending the breakdown of the Soviet state. Whether writing in a primarily satirical vein (for example, Vladimir Voinovich, Mikhail Veller, and Vasily Aksyonov) or in a more wistful spirit (the Strugatsky brothers in their later oeuvre), writers of the Gorbachev era sought to reinterpret the past and discern possible directions for the country's future. Such efforts continued after the fall of the Soviet Union.

Generation 'Π' marks a watershed in the development of the dystopian genre in Russia.[1] While dystopias written during perestroika, including Pelevin's own *Omon Ra* (1992) and his early short stories from the collection *The Blue Lantern* (*Sinii fonar'*, 1991), were mainly preoccupied with the deconstruction of the Soviet "utopia" and prognostications about the country's breakdown, *Generation 'Π'* was the first major post-Soviet work to come to grips with the impacts of consumer capitalism and global pop culture. In the aftermath of the Soviet Union's traumatic collapse, as the euphoria of the early 1990s evaporated in the face of harsh new economic realities and the no less tyrannical demands of the market replaced Soviet ideological control, attitudes toward the brave new order grew increasingly discomfited. Dystopian literature began to focus on the "consumer dream" as all that remained to Russian society.

Generation 'П' set the parameters for contemporary Russian techno-consumer critique and anticipated Pelevin's later works, as well as a veritable outburst of dystopic works produced in the first two decades of this millennium by Vasily Aksyonov, Dmitry Bykov, Garros-Evdokimov, Olga Slavnikova, Gary Shteyngart, Viacheslav Rybakov, Yulia Latynina, Dmitry Minaev, and others. Pelevin's modern classic both builds upon and subverts traditional dystopian paradigms by offering a multilayered critique that, despite its dutiful ironies and its demurral from any claims to authority, reveals a more thorough social skepticism than its more solemn generic forebears.[2]

FIELD OF MIRACLES IN THE COUNTRY OF FOOLS

Dystopian novels share several genre markers: the portrayal of an evil social structure; a defamiliarizing and/or fantastic element; entry into an exchange with the heritage of utopian/dystopian thought; and common themes like mind/body control, technology, the collective versus the individual, reason versus imagination and art, and urbanism versus nature.[3]

Among the best-known twentieth-century dystopias, Orwell's *1984* reacted largely to the totalitarianism of the Soviet and Nazi states, while Huxley's *Brave New World* focused mainly on consumerism, technological development, and "the psychological poverty of groups" (Freud, *Civilization and Its Discontents*, 74) in the North American jazz age.[4] Evgeny Zamyatin's *We* (*My*, 1920–21), a key Huxleyan and Orwellian predecessor, responded to both totalitarian Soviet tendencies and Western mechanized culture. Orwell's novel features extreme governmental tyranny, a penal system that employs physical and psychological torture, a ubiquitous police presence, a personality cult, and a meager quality of life. Huxley's novel is a denunciation of "greed and its ennoblement" (Huxley, *Aldous Huxley, 1894–1963*, 72).

Rather than relying on Orwell's archetypal indictment of the totalitarian state, Pelevin's *Generation 'П'* follows Huxley's portrayal of the world of Our Ford as he pursues his own post-Soviet consumerist critique. Vavilen Tatarsky, the hero of the novel, comes of age as the Soviet Union is disintegrating. As a youngster, he was an aspiring poet and a student at the Moscow Literary Institute. With the collapse of the country, he becomes, first, a lowly shop assistant, and later an advertising copywriter, whose job is to concoct Russian ads patterned on the latest American advertising techniques. By the novel's end, he presides over Russian advertising and has become a kind of media divinity. As Tatarsky prospers in the advertising business, there unfolds a savage Pelevinian spoof of Russia's transformation into a capitalist society. This society is a grotesque domain of drug dealers, the extravagant nouveau riche, a sinister corporate underworld, and mystifying political plots.

Like Huxley's novel, *Generation 'П'* is a scathing satire on cultural degradation and rampant consumerism. Pelevin's post-Soviet Russia has been overwhelmed by a sudden onslaught of Western goods and media. Amid the endless soap operas and meaningless advertising jingles, it is a surreptitiously totalitarian society in which total control is achieved not through crude force, but by saturating the populace with products of mass culture that serve as a subtle tool of social conditioning. The individual disappears in favor of a homogeneous, mind-numbed mass. There is no need to torture a Winston Smith into loving Big Brother, for post-Soviet Winston Smiths have neither the time nor the capacity for resistance, absorbed as they are in a relentless pecuniary cycle. No more Three-Minute Hates, torture chambers, and suppression of sex. Instead, crass materialism, mind-stultifying popular entertainment, the destruction of historical and cultural consciousness through kitsch, and rampant corruption are the pillars of this new society.

In this scheme, television plays a crucial role. The novel's epigraph from Leonard Cohen with its "hopeless little screen" initiates Pelevin's investigation of the impact of advanced media technologies on the modern human being (*G'П'* 7).[5] As explained in a mock-scholarly treatise attributed to the spirit of Ernesto Che Guevara, television transforms the populace into "Homo Zapiens" (from "zapping," changing channels to avoid watching advertisements), zombies manipulated by a global, profit-driven information space:

> The changes in the image produced by various techno-modifications can be correlated with a virtual psychological process in which the observer is forced to . . . manage his own attention as the makers of the program manage it. This psychological process creates its own virtual subject, which for the duration of the television program exists in the place of the individual. . . . Assuming the condition of Homo Zapiens, the viewer becomes a remotely controlled television program. (*G'П'* 104–7)

Human beings become cells of an organism known by the ancients as Mammon or "Oranus" (and in a more down-to-earth Russian version, *rotozhopa*).[6] The purpose of each human cell is to allow money to pass into and out of it. In the process of its evolution, Oranus develops a primitive nervous system, the media. This nervous system transmits "wow impulses" that control the activity of the monadic cells: oral (inducing a cell to digest money), anal (inducing it to eliminate money), and displacing (inhibiting all psycho-logical processes that might hinder an individual's identification with a cell of Oranus). After repeated exposure to television, the human mind commences to produce these impulses without external stimulation. Each monad is once and for all trapped in a cycle of consumption-excretion, a *perpetuum mobile* of consumer culture.

The human subject disappears through absorption into the sinister monetary collective. Since Oranus's cells no longer possess any inner being, all they can do is define themselves by possessing the products advertised on television. Genuine interiority is exchanged for an illusion of interiority, a so-called *identichnost'* (calqued after the English word "identity"). Money is viewed as an entity that removes humanity from humans and creates a primi-tive parasitical organism that is incapable of cognition or even self-awareness, a sort of perverted sub-personal rather than a supra-personal deity.

In "Che Guevara's" argument, the transformation of Homo Sapiens into Homo Zapiens constitutes an unprecedented rupture. For the first time in the history of humankind, the problem that repressive societies of the past had struggled with—the obliteration of the human individual—is effectively solved via the new "categorical imperative" to consume and eject money. A mocking combination of dialectical materialism, Buddhism, and a twentieth-century bourgeois critique of consumerism, Che Guevara's treatise adds Immanuel Kant to the picture as well. Che's meditations on the old-school dualism as engendered by the arbitrary division of the world into subject and object tap into Kant's classic reconsideration of the Cartesian dichotomy between the subject and object of knowledge in the *Critique of Pure Reason* (1781). The new system parodically outdoes Kant's Copernican revolution by dispensing with the subject of knowledge altogether.

Pelevin's exploration of the process through which Homo Sovieticus is transformed into Homo Zapiens is heavily informed by Western criticism (both fiction and theory) of the electronic age, with its mass conformity and boundless possibilities for the manipulation of consciousness. *Generation 'П'* falls in line with late twentieth-century European and American novels that, following Huxley, focus on the ennoblement of greed and covert varieties of control in contemporary society. These novels include Thomas Pynchon's *Vineland* (1990), Don DeLillo's *White Noise* (1985), Douglas Coupland's *Generation X: Tales for an Accelerated Culture* (1991) and *Microserfs* (1995), Chuck Palahniuk's *Fight Club* (1996), and others.[7]

Likewise, *Generation 'П'* responds to Western critical theory. Pelevin takes Baudrillard's ideas about simulated politics to their limits, and describes a Russia where reality has disappeared.[8] But where Baudrillard leaves room for a metaphorical reading of his provocative thesis about the Gulf War, with some provisional reality beyond the virtual warfare presented for the benefit of the populace, Pelevin's post-Soviet politicians are literally disembodied. *Generation 'Π'* neither parallels nor simplifies Baudrillard but, rather, literal- izes and pushes to the limit a critical notion. This is one of Pelevin's favorite devices and part of his more general proclivity for literalized idioms in the fantastic genre.[9] It turns out that the country's very government is virtual: its highest officials are digital dummies on television whose movements are scripted by copywriters. In this world, the Russian financial default of 1998 was brought on by a sabotaging copywriter who erased the entire virtual government.[10] Furthermore, in a play on the expression "critical days" from a 1990s Tampax ad, the financial crisis itself functions as a promotion for Tampax tampons.

Analogously, Pelevin pushes to the limit Marcuse's linkage of poli- tics with the media and the subject with his function in modern society. In *Generation 'Π'* the media literally equals politics, and the subject equals the goods. Media moguls create simulacra of politicians, and the consumer an- swers the question "Who am I?" with "I am the one who possesses X, Y, and Z." For Homo Zapiens "the only possible answer to the question 'Who am I?' is: 'I am the individual who drives such-and-such a car, lives in such- and-such a house, wears such-and-such type of clothes'" (*G'Π'* 113). As in Marcuse's theory of repressive tolerance, the prevailing practice of tolera- tion in advanced industrial society masks oppressive political realities such as neoliberal exploitation, the brainwashing of the populace by publicity, and the deceptions of the market. In Pelevin's novel the market complacently absorbs art and pseudo-art alike, fostering neutrality and destructive toler- ance. All kinds of opposition are subverted by the system and turned to its own benefit.

FROM HOMO SOVIETICUS TO HOMO ZAPIENS

While echoing Western critiques of techno-consumer society (Baudrillard, the Frankfurt school), *Generation 'Π'* simultaneously displays features that distinguish it from the by now familiar European and American analyses of ubiquitous consumerism and all-powerful technological control.

Importantly, Pelevin depicts not an established consumer society, but Russia's traumatic entrance into the world of commodities purveyed by mar- ket mechanisms. Much of the force of *Generation 'Π'* derives from its dra- matization of this cultural rupture. By portraying the violent imposition of an alien order of life, Pelevin makes the grotesqueries of commodified society stand out all the more acutely. In other words, although many traits portrayed are specific to Russian realities of the 1990s, the country's grotesque infantile capitalism is an exaggeration of, rather than a departure from, established commodified existence elsewhere.

The novel's beginning highlights social and cultural rupture.[11] The teasingly elegiac opening sentences refer to the "pre-fall" innocence of Homo Sovieticus that for generation 'П' has also coincided with the innocence of childhood: "Once upon a time in Russia there really lived a carefree youthful generation that smiled in joy at the summer, the sea and the sun and chose Pepsi" (*G'П'* 9). The phrase "Once upon a time" (*kogda-to*) gives Soviet life a distant-past, almost fairy-tale-like quality. The word "really" (*i pravda*) further strengthens the legendary feel of the statement. Within this very first sentence, elegy dissipates through a quick move from a prolonged "lived" (*zhilo*) to one-time acts of "smiled" (*ulybnulos'*) and "chose" (*vybralo*). The next sentence, "It's hard to figure out now why this happened," also conveys the feeling of the Soviet past's distant obscurity, an assertion incommensurate with the short time that has actually elapsed since the fall of the Soviet Union (*G'П'* 9).

In the novel, Russia's capital Moscow is poised precariously between its Soviet past and the rough capitalist reality of the present. Sleek new highrises, shopping centers, and villas of the nouveau riche intermingle with abandoned factories and decaying Soviet apartment blocks. The socialist ideology with its modernizing projects of technological development and social progress lies in ruins, metaphorical and literal. Garbage-strewn industrial zones, vestiges of the Soviet project, dominate the landscape. The authorial gaze lingers over these remnants of the Soviet world, presenting this wasteland as an archaeological ruin.

The archaeological remnants of an "ancient" empire do not reflect a real temporal lapse so much as the intense alienation of Homo Sovieticus from the post-Soviet way of life. The interweaving of Babylonian and Soviet mythologemes over the course of the narrative also communicates, among other things, the deceptive sense of a vast temporal span that separates post-Soviet times from Soviet ones. So, for instance, when looking at the "ziggurat" on Moscow's outskirts, Tatarsky thinks, "It must be one of those military construction projects begun in the seventies. . . . It might have been a thousand or even a full ten thousand years old" (*G'П'* 55).

In a twist on the narrative pattern in Thomas More's *Utopia* (1516), Tatarsky is a visitor from another place or time who encounters an amazing new realm, except in this case that realm is utterly dreary. Initially, his perception of the new way of life is estranged. Long a locus of naive dreaming in the Soviet psyche, the distant and forbidden world of free-market commodities turns out to be anything but a utopia. Pelevin, who was critical of Soviet mythology in his early works, here reflects on a value void that opens

with the deconstruction of the socialist utopia. The novel juxtaposes the re-
treating Soviet mentality and the new mindset in a way that does not favor
the latter.

Significantly, the transformation of Russia into a consumer society is
presented not merely as a displacement of one social system by another radically different one, but as an ontological and epistemological break, a break
in the structure of reality per se:

> The very space into which their gaze had been directed . . . began to curl back
> in on itself and disappear, until all that was left of it was a microscopic spot on
> the windscreen of the mind. . . . It was not possible to say that the world had
> changed in its essence because now it no longer had any essence. A frighten-
> ing uncertainty reigned over everything. (*G'П'* 14, 17)

Tatarsky and his compatriots are lost in a murky domain where the familiar
laws of space and time no longer apply. It is not that society is crumbling:
reality itself is crumbling in Russia. Pelevin amplifies the social through its
linkage with the ontological.

Generation 'П' reinforces this feeling of ontological/epistemological
confusion with its comment on the removal of Lenin's statues:

> But he was only replaced by a gray frightening murk. . . . The newspapers
> claimed that the whole world had been in this frightening murk for ages,
> which is why it is so full of things and money, and the only reason people can-
> not understand this is their "Soviet mentality." (*G'П'* 32)

Elsewhere, and now in Russia, commodities disguise metaphysical emptiness. The peculiar term "gray frightening murk" (*seraia strashnovatost'*)
echoes the "frightening uncertainty" (*strashnovataia neopredelennost'*) cited
above. The material is replaced by amorphous abstractness (the suffix *ovat*
is an ambivalent marker of an attribute's gradation), emphasizing the be-
fuddling nature of the new reality.

Lest one read *Generation 'П'* as an unambiguously nostalgic project, one
should note its persistent paralleling of the "loser" (the Soviet mythologeme)
and the "winner" (the consumer mythologeme). The displacement of one
pernicious ideological system by another, which probably possesses more
vitality, is formulated sardonically from the outset as the "historical victory
of the red [Coca-Cola] over the red [communism]" (*G'П'* 11). In the manner of Sots Art, Pelevin combines incompatible ideologies in order to comment on the misleading nature of all kinds of mythologemes. Not accidentally, the ancient tyrannical divinity Enkidu (in the Babylonian pantheon)
resembles Cardinal Richelieu (Catholicism) and Vladimir Lenin (socialism),

just as the soft drink logos of Coca-Cola and Coke seamlessly replace Soviet symbols.[12]

Tatarsky and his copywriter colleagues are the ideologues of the new dystopia, imposing the values of the market economy on a pliant populace just as their predecessors imposed the values of communism. His places of work, advertising agencies in the former Pravda complex, and later in a large Stalinist-style building from the 1940s, underscore this notion. To further drive the point home, Pelevin describes a Stalinist poster in which the hammer, the sickle, and the star are replaced with "Coca-Cola" and "Coke" so neatly that one does not notice the transformation. He also mentions that in Spanish the word for "advertising" is "propaganda."

According to the novel, however, there are crucial differences between the Soviet and the consumer mindset. Where the mentality of Homo Sovieticus had embraced eternity, Homo Zapiens has dispensed with it:

> Something also began happening to the very eternity to which Tatarsky had decided to devote his labors and his days. . . . It turned out that eternity existed only as long as Tatarsky sincerely believed in it and was nowhere to be found beyond the bounds of this belief. For him to believe sincerely in eternity, others had to share in that belief because a belief shared with no one is called schizophrenia. . . . He also understood something else: the eternity he used to believe in could exist only on state subsidies, or else—which is the same thing—as something forbidden by the state. (*G*Π 13–15)

Though these meditations on the disappearance of eternity from Russian life can be read as the post-Soviet intelligentsia's loss of faith in the values of culture, there is, as I see it, more at stake here.[13] As the former Soviet Union joined the family of market economies, the Russian logos came under assault. In one of his sprightly paradoxes, Pelevin suggests that eternity was nurtured by the autocratic system of the Soviet period. Indeed, peaks of culture often occur under tyrannical regimes. The Russian logos, in particular, derived much of its moral force (symbolic capital, if we put it in modern critical-pecuniary terms) from opposing the ignominy of the state. But *Generation 'Π'* shows that commodified society is much more destructive to culture than authoritarianism.

Since Russian artists have traditionally insisted on endorsing themselves in ethical and even religious terms, one is tempted to reinterpret the loss of eternity as a loss of faith in culture and, by proxy, religion. That art stands in for religion in modern times is a common enough notion in the West as well, articulated by Nietzsche, among others. The erasure of eternity in this novel, however, not only portends the defeat of culture, but portrays a total collapse of spirituality, including spiritual values traditionally unrelated to the Russian cultural or religious sphere and involving the less educated segments of the populace, as well as the intelligentsia. To look at the same issue from a different angle, the very tightness of the linkage between culture and religion in the Russian context implies that the de-sacralization of culture has grave spiritual implications for all aspects of life.

Other spiritual systems disappeared along with the Soviet world. Thus, Tatarsky's Buddhist friend Gireev "seemed like the final fragment of some lost universe—not the Soviet one because it did not have any wandering Tibetan astrologers, but some other world that had existed in parallel with the Soviet one and even in contradiction to it but had perished together with it" (*G'Π* 46). Buddhism proves as alien to Brave New Russia as do more traditional spiritual values.

Allusions to post-Soviet esoteric waves do not problematize but reinforce *Generation 'Π*'s diagnosis of the overall collapse of spirituality. In the novel's portrayal, post-Soviet esoterica is commodified and thus degraded. Picking up on the contemporary fascination with the occult, Pelevin mashes mystical practices against consumerist realities of the era. The Ouija board used to communicate with Che is, for example, bought in the shop "Path toward Oneself," which sells all kinds of occult paraphernalia.

In *Generation 'Π'* the Soviet mentality had once supported metaphysical idealism, and the destruction of that mentality means the destruction of a far from unproblematic but still spiritual worldview. Given Pelevin's intense subjectivism, the disappearance of faith in eternity equals the disappearance of eternity itself.[14] What matters is not whether eternity exists in the minds of people or whether it exists "as such," for nothing exists "objectively"—as Pelevin asserts throughout his oeuvre—what matters is the spirit-nurturing or spirit-stifling nature of myth shared by the community of believers.

If Homo Sovieticus harbors illusions about life, not necessarily in ideology-specific terms but in a more universal romantic sense, Homo Zapiens tends to have no illusions at all about his lot or the regime, but is nevertheless caught in his consumer dystopia as firmly as the naive Soviet man was in his web of Marxist Maya. As Dmitry Pugin, one of Tatarsky's employers, formulates a distinction between the old Soviet and the new consumer consciousness:

> In New York you realize especially clearly . . . that you can spend your entire life in some foul-smelling little kitchen, staring out into some shitty little yard, chewing on a lousy burger. . . . Right, there are many more stinking kitchens and shitty yards over here. But here you will never realize that that's where you will spend your whole life. Until you've spent it all, that is. And that, by the way, is one of the main features of the Soviet mentality. (*G'Π* 33–34)

Pelevin's post-Soviet heroes realize the vacuity of their existence and yet fully abide by the rules of the game. In the new society, technology brings vast possibilities of social control, and the success of society depends not so much on the power of ideological phantoms to dupe individual human beings as on the self-perpetuating power field of the entire structure in which humans/cells are functioning as they ought to, whether duped or not.

In the end, Russia's long-mythologized spiritual immunity to the idol Baal (the money god) is found wanting.[15] The former devotees of the spirit swiftly succumb to market realities. Pelevin's dedication, "to the memory of the middle class," refers to the degraded version of the intelligentsia under the new conditions (*G'П* 5). The "middle class in Russia is formed directly from the intelligentsia, which ceased thinking nationally and turned to the question of where it can get money" (*G'П* 255). The financial default of 1998 depicted at the end of the book undermines the emerging post-Soviet middle class. Simultaneously, the epigraph designates the Soviet intelligentsia as the middle class, presenting an ironic anachronism that exposes the power of new consumer paradigms to impose themselves on the past, effectively erasing the past's own values.

All values, including the most prized ones of the Russian national particularity, turn into market values under the new conditions. Indeed, it is precisely one's most cherished ideals, including the ideal of Russia's unique spiritual resistance to materialism, that sell particularly well. In Pelevin's sardonic observation, "That which is most sacred and exalted should be sold at the highest price possible because afterwards there will be nothing to sell" (*G'П* 30).

The idée fixe of Russian culture (Dostoevsky et al.), the "Russian idea" becomes a monetary auxiliary because some kind of national paradigm must accompany capital for capital to position itself on the international market. Since both prerevolutionary "Orthodoxy, Autocracy, and Nationality" and the Soviet "Victory of Communism" are passé, the media must come up with a clear and simple brand essence with which to garnish monetary transactions.[16] In *Generation 'П'* no such home paradigm can be found, and since alternatives that can genuinely oppose global consumerism and popular culture no longer exist, simulacra concocted by the media proliferate.

Pelevin's novel explores the interpellation and vulgarization of the local by the global in the global techno-consumer village. For the domestic market, the concept of nationhood as defined against the shortcomings of the Other can be a profitable strategy. An advertising concept for Russian Golden Yava cigarettes proposes using a bird's-eye view of New York, with a pack of Yava diving at the city like a nuclear warhead. The concept taps into the nostalgic imperial mentality that surfaced in the late 1990s, which gradually ousts the critical reevaluation of the Soviet past that was characteristic of the perestroika period. Pseudo-Slavophilism, manipulating a now fashionable glorification of prerevolutionary Russia, is another phony solution. This means packaging Western goods in a pulp-local style, as in an ad for Sprite: "In the springtime forest I drank my birch Sprite" (*G'П* 37).

Whether it is injured imperial sensibilities or a clichéd, obtuse presentation of traditional Russianness that are put on sale, Pelevin captures a key trait of the new society. Commodified versions of worldviews hollow them out, offering cheaper, profit-driven adaptations, and concealing their hollowed-out nature by transforming what should have been a full cognitive-emotional process into an auxiliary of acquisition. The signifiers of socialist ideology point to transcendental meanings, however unattainable; the signifiers of consumer culture bear no meaning at all except one of expenditure.

TRANSFORMING DYSTOPIAN PARADIGMS

Generation 'П' identifies a key postmodern political strategy: it is not necessary to apply brute force to suppress dissent, one need merely optimize its market value. This nonviolent interpellation of oppositional forces into commodified society is highlighted when, for instance, Tatarsky listens to Che Guevara's denunciation of capitalism, wearing the well-known rock band T-shirt with the revolutionary's face on it and the slogan "Rage against the machine."[17] Clearly, the Che Guevara of the novel has little to do with the Cuban communist. He is rather a second-order phenomenon, a flourishing Western leftist brand.

In fact, Che's subversive treatise itself inspires Tatarsky in his advertising concepts and helps him rise on the media ladder. Tatarsky's second Gap ad shows an Afghan War veteran throwing a stone at a shop window and shouting, "It was heavier under Kandahar!" (*G'П* 300).[18] Two ads for Nike, one playing on the mass suicide of members of the occult group "Heaven's Gate," and the other involving American prisoners in Vietnam, are examples of the many ads in the second half of the novel that effectively sell opposition (*G'П* 126).[19]

The nonviolent neutralization of dissent is one point of departure from twentieth-century dystopias. How else does *Generation 'П'* refurbish dystopian conventions? Part of this has to do with structural features, for instance, temporality, and in part the novel plays with key themes such as art, eroticism, the "world controller" figure, and so on.

The position of art in utopia/dystopia has been one of the genre's recurring concerns from Plato's *Republic* onward. Shakespeare figures in both *Brave New World* and *1984*, just as Pushkin does in *We*. The removal of the faculty of imagination signifies spiritual death for Zamyatin's protagonist.

Classic dystopias present genuine art as an aesthetic and ethical antidote to the snares of ideology as well as the products of ersatz culture.

Like Zamyatin, Huxley, and Orwell, Pelevin contemplates the baneful effects of social and technological development on artistic creativity, but unlike them, he homes in on art's subversion by kitsch. The humiliation of the artist in these new conditions is satirically worked out through the hamster Rostropovich (referencing, in a double lunge, the renowned cello player and the Soviet-period dissident) belonging to the media mogul Azadovsky, to whom the mogul awards medals of honor when in a benevolent mood. Tatarsky's early advertising concepts recycle famous literary quotations as "a relic white noise of the Soviet psyche"—as in "World Pantene-pro V! God bless!" a tawdry twist on "World conflagration in blood, God bless," from Alexander Blok's 1918 poem "The Twelve" (*G'П* 62). "White noise," a designation of meaningless auditory stimuli, and which is also the title of Don DeLillo's dystopic novel, suggests a loss of connection to pre-dystopian art.

Art is first co-opted into the system and then dispensed with altogether. The mounting tawdriness of the tasks to which it is put erodes its ability to function as a refuge from spiritual degradation. Simultaneously, the overselling of culture makes it no longer viable as a sphere of commerce. Observing a poster for a clothes boutique recycling romantic clichés, Tatarsky comments that "the human mind had sold this romanticism to itself far too many times to be able to do any more business on the last remaining noncommercial images" (*G'П* 69). Later advertisements replace classical allusions with references to New Russians, mafia, or pop culture. The reigning ersatz culture is merely another projection of Oranus, and a black money bag has become the main focus of the viewer's/reader's attention.

While eroticism functions as another subversive element in classical dystopian novels, in *Generation 'П'* sexuality is also channeled in ways that are beneficial to the system. Zamyatin's D-503 and Orwell's Winston Smith are propelled along the path of rebellion by their relations with I-330 and Julia, respectively; and Huxley's John the Savage is revolted by his realization of Lenina's emotional sterility. By contrast, Tatarsky's only erotic encounter is with a thousand-dollar prostitute who is indistinguishable in the darkness from Claudia Schiffer.

Like art, eroticism is translated into pecuniary lust. At the end of *Generation 'П,'* Tatarsky unites with Ishtar's golden idol, that is, on an abstract level, with the idea of money.[20] In the novel, commodities are no longer linked to specific functions, but operate in a mechanism of never-satisfied social desire that supplants other kinds of desire, including sexual ones. Sex is valued as symbolic of the vital energy of youth which can be converted into money, rather than vice versa. Che Guevara's description of oral, anal, and displaced "wow impulses" jokingly reinterprets the Freudian psychosexual model as the monetary model.

40

As Tatarsky works his way up the media ladder, he struggles—and ultimately fails—to comprehend what holds this twisted social structure together. Zamyatin's Benefactor and Huxley's World Controller explicate their benevolent rule over the selfish and infantile populace to the novels' rebellious protagonists (in terms heavily reminiscent of Dostoevsky's Grand Inquisitor). Orwell's O'Brien, likewise, explains to Winston the rule of Big Brother and the Inner Party, although in this case any pretense of benevolent parental care is dropped since Orwell's rulers exercise power for sheer power's sake. In *Generation 'П'* no Grand Inquisitor reveals himself.[21] Tatarsky's discovery that the media creates virtual reality does not explain the system's workings. The oligarchs determine Russian national policy and inform the media of the latest trends, but, in a circular illogic, these very same oligarchs are virtual dummies created by the media. Going beyond Kafkaesque irrationality, Pelevin's world is an illogical self-referential structure.

In this universe, ignorance is bliss and inevitability but it is also insurance (temporary) against removal from the board (permanent). Still later Tatarsky finds out that media moguls belong to a secret neo-Babylonian society whose purpose is to defend the world against the apocalypse that will be brought on by Ishtar's nemesis, the five-legged dog Pizdets. As Ishtar's new earthly consort, Tatarsky inquires again who rules over the world. The reply, as before, is not to pry into the issue if he wants to remain a "living god" for a reasonably long time. In the words of the jingle that accompanies Tatarsky on his path to the top, "This game has no name." The game's purpose and the will of its players both remain shrouded in (quasi)-mystery—since there is no answer to the question.

Ultimately, the system is viral and self-perpetuating, with copywriters pawning commodities off on people, and people pawning them off on each other, and back on the copywriters:

> People want to earn money to gain freedom or at least a bit of respite in their endless suffering. Everyone is trying to show that they have already gained one, and so all we do is swindle each other into buying black coats, cell phones, and cabriolets with leather seats. . . . Freedom is symbolized by an iron, or a tampon with wings, or lemonade. We sell [*vparivaem*] these to them from the screen, and they sell these to each other and to us, copywriters. This is like radioactive contamination when it is no longer important who blew up the bomb. (*G 'П'* 135)

Even those at the highest echelons of power live in the grip of consumerist simulacra and are unable to break away. The novel suggests, only to quickly dismiss, the conspiracy theories of which postmodernism is enamored. One of Pelevin's recurrent symbols, an eye in a triangle from the U.S. one-dollar bill, parodically references a Masonic and American "anti-Russian" conspiracy. But the text in the end rejects this conspiratorial explanation, pointing out that the eye sees nothing.

In *Generation 'Π,'* the failure to comprehend the status quo matches the failure to resist it. In the classical dystopian scheme, the protagonist, a sympathetic human being, rebels in a gallant but hopeless attempt to assert his and others' freedom, and is destroyed by the machinery of the state. As Edith Clowes formulates it in her work on Soviet meta-utopias of the 1950s through the 1980s: the best human being "comes to understand the meshing of social laws and ideals in his life and chooses to say no, not to be driven by the rat race for power and influence, and to live according to his conscience" (*Russian Experimental Fiction*, 24).[22] In his turn, Krishan Kumar suggests that a source of hope in dystopia may be found in a relatively free-thinking and independent upper stratum that society requires to handle the challenges it faces (*Utopia and Anti-Utopia in Modern Times*, 285).

By contrast, in the cynical world of *Generation 'Π,'* no human being exists who is ready to apply his understanding of ideology against this ideology. Tatarsky is swiftly assimilated. Under the comfortable modus operandi of techno-consumerism, subjects pretend that they want to escape but know for a fact that they do not. Not only is Tatarsky co-opted by the establishment, but his co-option intensifies once he has attained a commanding position in it. For obvious reasons, members of the upper stratum are especially intent on preserving the status quo. As Tatarsky becomes more closely acquainted with the power structure, he applies his familiarity with it to further his personal ascent. He views his work unsentimentally as a kind of prostitution, discerns the spurious nature of the new way of life, and yet applies all his energies to gaining a better position in the race for power.[23] No correlation between understanding and moral behavior obtains here. Moreover, if any knowledge is to be gained, it is only a limited and perverted kind of "enlightenment."

The novel dismisses the "innocent victim" status of the protagonist and suggests that all the population of Russia is at fault for the vile times into which the country has fallen: "The anti-Russian conspiracy exists without any doubt. The problem, however, is that all the adult population of Russia takes part in it" (*G'Π'* 11). The members of Generation 'Π,' a young, active part of the populace, are the first to blame. In the protagonist's realization (Tatarsky—the Tatar yoke), it is them, having fallen into unbridled egotism and greed, who are the apocalyptic dog Pizdets advancing on Russia and the world at large.[24]

That the whole of Russia, and generation 'Π' especially, are responsible for their land crashing into bankruptcy, chaos, and criminality is an idea that the text conveys on multiple levels. One is through al-Ghazali's poem "The Parliament of Birds," about thirty birds who flew off in search of the bird called Semurg only to learn that the word "Semurg" means "thirty birds." In mythological terms, as Ishtar's consort, Tatarsky dreams up this world, and the goddess of money herself obtains her vitality through his dreaming. His "ascent" up the ziggurat culminates in his descent into "hell" by the Ostankino television tower, to be anointed a living evil deity.[25] The "π" in Generation 'Π' suggests mediocrity: its value cannot be captured exactly, but its specificities become only more and more infinitesimal.[26] A pedestrian member of a pedestrian generation, Tatarsky turns into a petty demon who presides over Russia's witches' Sabbath.

Insofar as the existence that is depicted is unacceptable, the search for a different path is bound to present itself to the dystopian writer. Archetypal modernist dystopias envision a healthier alternative to the sterility of the state among the lowly "wild" masses outside the official sphere. Untouched by totalitarian conditioning, they are able to preserve the indispensable human qualities of free will and love. In this sense, Zamyatin's Mephies, Huxley's inhabitants of the savage reservation, and Orwell's proles offer a return-to-nature scenario not as a literal reversion to savagery but as a reawakening to the fullness of life, a regained ability to love, hate, and suffer. In the words of Huxley's John the Savage, one needs "God, poetry, real danger, freedom, goodness, sin" and "the right to be unhappy" (*Brave New World*, 288).

Pelevin's work toys with the possibilities of alternative social scenarios, but fails to imagine ways of escape from dystopia. Potential alternatives are promptly discarded. The narrative rejects a conservative "return to the roots" through a parody of contemporary Slavophilism—which is degraded into a virtual pseudo-Slavic commodity wrap-up. Pelevin's mockery of the leftist scenario is equally scathing. The liberal values of the 1960s, both in the Soviet Union and in the West, are seen to be naively idealistic. Tatarsky's given name, Vavilen, a combination of Vasily Aksyonov and Vladimir Lenin given to him by his father, is as inept stylistically as it is misguided ideologically:

> Tatarsky's father, it seems, found it easy to imagine a faithful disciple of Lenin gratefully learning from Aksyonov's liberated page that Marxism originally stood for free love, or a jazz-crazy aesthete suddenly convinced by a particularly protracted saxophone riff that communism would win. But it was not only Tatarsky's father who was like that. The entire generation of the fifties and sixties was the same. (*G'Π'* 12)

Given our knowledge of subsequent history, an attempt to reconcile communist ideals with the liberal Western values of the 1960s was bound to fail. What linked the *shestidesiatniki* ("Sixtiers," the young Soviet intelligentsia of the 1960s) and the Western hippies was their infantile idealism, their belief that a rebellion inspired by sex, rock, and marijuana could offer a serious challenge to the system. It could not—as Pelevin, in the vein of Marcuse and Žižek, stresses—because all self-actualization (a personal letting-go) does is reinforce societal mechanisms of repression by venting youthful energies in a private mock rebellion. A serious collective rejection of the system would have had to go beyond the campus-confined, Beatles and Bob Dylan–accompanied play of these flower children, however appealing such play may be.

In the eyes of generation 'П,' which has aged and hardened prematurely under duress, the Soviet *shestidesiatniki* and the Western youth counterculture of the 1960s alike engaged in an infantile opposition simply because the overflowing of youthful vitality sought some kind of outlet on both sides of the Iron Curtain. The members of generation 'П,' the children of these *shestidesiatniki*, are neither young (by experience, if not age) nor naive. Perhaps more to the point, they are hardly virile (unless they are copulating with money or money surrogates). Their game is a different one— with no name.

By the time generation 'П' matures, the leftist scenario has become just another brand in the world of brands. The novel ironizes not only consumer society, but also the leftist critique of society as exemplified by Che Guevara's mock-scholarly treatise. In an additional joke, Che's spirit informs Tatarsky that the study of television is prohibited in every country except Bhutan, where television is forbidden. Since the "fictitious" country of Bhutan is invented by one of Tatarsky's colleagues in the media, Che's critique is short-circuited again. One may flaunt a T-shirt with Che's pop-stylized face on it, or create an ad about smashing a shop window, shouting "It was heavier under Kandahar!" The stone hits the glass, the point hits home: not only does an act of transgression serve social cohesion by releasing pent-up aggression (Žižek), but it has an added benefit—the sales of T-shirts and Nike sneakers go up.

OBSCENE TRANSCENDENTAL

The dehumanizing effect of the new society is complete—the human has disappeared. If the classic dystopias present cautionary tales, positioning their societies in the future or in an imaginary locale (with Orwell placing it closest, only thirty-five years from the time of publication), Pelevin's narrative, set in the 1990s, is the book's recent past. The notion that the novel does not lay out an "if this transpires" scenario but describes existing conditions is further reinforced by the inconspicuousness of its fantastic elements. Only a few implausible details such as virtual politics seamlessly blend into post-perestroika realia, which are depicted with a journalistic topicality and precision of detail. *Generation 'Π'* is a realized dystopia.

Importantly, the mystical and the religious do not oppose the social in the text (as in classic dystopias), but instead reinforce it. The esoteric (Babylon) layer of *Generation 'Π,'* with its biblical connotations of greed and corruption, purposefully meshes with the earthly dystopia. In the novel's version of this mythology, the ancient Babylonians equated supreme riches and power with supreme wisdom. To obtain them, one must achieve sexual union with Ishtar's golden idol, winning the "great lottery." This means figuring out the three riddles of Ishtar, the answer to which is hidden in the words of the market songs that were sung in the bazaar at Babylon. This formula for success, the "golden idol," the "great lottery," and "market songs," all point to this myth's monetary obsessions. In his rise to the upper echelons of power, Tatarsky accomplishes all the above. His rise is simultaneously a mystical ascent along Ishtar's ziggurat. At the end, Tatarsky becomes the supreme creator of virtual reality and the husband of the golden goddess.

In *Generation 'Π,'* realia and *realiora* do not oppose but rather mirror each other. The monetary below echoes the monetary above.[27] When Tatarsky asks what's holding the whole structure together, he is forbidden to ever contemplate the issue. Exasperated by the whole procedure, he wonders:

> What bad bastard could have written this scenario [*kakaia gadina napisala etot stsenarii*]? And who's the viewer who sits and stuffs himself with pizza [*zhret svoiu piccu*] while he watches this screen [*gliadit na etot ekran*]? And most important of all, can it all really be happening just so some fat heavenly hulk [*zhirnaia nadmirnaia tushka*] can rake in something like money from something like advertising [*navarila sebe . . . deneg na chem-to vrode reklamy*]? (*G'Π'* 223)

This passage blends commercial, meta-literary, and metaphysical rhetoric. In Tatarsky's eyes, the noumenal is a revolting "fat heavenly hulk" that authors people's lives, amuses itself by the spectacle of this world, and collects its profits. The mercenary is a model of ontology and authorship. The evil demiurge and the author mirror the copywriter. The new society empties out metaphysics not by dismissing it as illusory, but by transposing the consumer paradigm onto the transcendental itself. The novel's esoteric layer buttresses Pelevin's assertion of social and spiritual deadlock. *Generation 'Π'* juxtaposes the phenomenal with the noumenal but, unlike in the more familiar symbolist scenarios, the noumenal is corrupted, and becomes a mere mirror image of the mundane.

In the novel the commodified dystopia, Che Guevara's treatise, and

45

Babylonian mythology are all coordinated. In Tatarsky's drug-induced hallucinations, a vision of the ancient Babylonian deity Enkidu replicates Che Guevara's image of Oranus. Like Oranus, Enkidu holds golden strings on which men are threaded, entering at the mouth and exiting from the anus. He is a fisherman who must gather all the people on his spindles of golden thread. The same deity as the biblical Baal presides over Tofet or Gehenna, where people are burned.[28] In earthly terms, Tofet/Gehenna is the modern media burning people in the fires of pecuniary desire. Inspired by his visions, Tatarsky begins his rise to the top. "Sacral" knowledge leads to worldly success. The myth does not permit him to transcend the earthly but, on the contrary, imprisons him in this society's monetary preoccupations. If modern theory, with a penchant for figuration that is more proper in MFA coursework, describes the metaphysical as symbolic capital, Pelevin makes crystal-clear his sardonic point: this dystopia's new religion is—*literally*—money.[29]

✵ ✵ ✵

While still searching for an authentic reality, Tatarsky comes up with the following notion:

> A wall on which a panoramic view of a nonexistent world is drawn itself does not change. But for a great deal of money you can buy a view from a window with a crudely painted sun, an azure bay and a calm evening. . . . Then perhaps the wall is drawn too? But drawn by whom and on what? (*G'П'* 73)[30]

In terms reminiscent of Plato's allegory of the Cave, Tatarsky views commodities as systems of false symbols that disguise human imprisonment. The painting on the wall and the window with the view in it (upgrades that one can acquire) are equally phony. Tatarsky's stark insight is that consumer mythologemes are actually simulacra of a second order, hiding the primary simulacrum—the illusion of the wall itself.

Such an understanding might potentially lead to an escape from the phony reality, but instead, by the conclusion of the book Pelevin's protagonist has become the ruler of Russia's virtual reality, and a virtual reality himself—the hero of multiple advertising clips. The latest hopelessly bewildered consort of Ishtar makes a meaningless swap of Pepsi for Coca-Cola, both equally brown and equally reminiscent of excrement and Nazism. He asks to take care of Rostropovich in a sardonic tribute to the fallen idols of culture and exits the book in a highly pastoral Tuborg beer commercial, in thirty all-too-reproducible copies.

Instead of being a terrifying narrative of triumphant totalitarianism, *Generation 'П'* emphasizes the farcical aspects of Brave New Russia. The novel offers its dystopian critique with a postmodern self-deprecating smile. Its allegiance to studied detachment and literary games, however, cannot hide its grim attitude toward social processes. The methods of a Huxleyan techno-consumer dystopia can be both more dangerous to the psyche and more politically insidious than the straightforward brutality of a traditional dictatorship. *Generation 'Π'* portrays a self-perpetuating dystopia that subverts the saving qualities of art and erotic passion, implicates all the populace in social impasse, fails to imagine ways of escape from the deadlock, and even develops its own monetary metaphysics. The book is a most hilarious product of hopelessness.

Language Games

> This might well seem an indiscretion,
> Description, though, is my profession;
> But *pantaloons, gilet*, and *frock*—
> These words are hardly Russian stock.
> —Alexander Pushkin, *Eugene Onegin*

MUCH OF THE VIBRANCY of *Generation 'П'* derives from its verbal play—puns, metaphors, paradoxes, and aphorisms, as well as bilingual and multilingual experimentation. These words and images capture the turbulence of turn-of-the-century Russia, and prove to be some of the most inventive in Pelevin's oeuvre. It is no surprise that aphorisms from *Generation 'П'* have entered the popular lexicon. Indeed, who won't recall "CHRIST THE SAVIOR RESPECTABLE LORD FOR RESPECTABLE LORDS" ("KHRISTOS SPASITEL' SOLIDNYI GOSPOD' DLIA SOLIDNYKH GOSPOD") when confronted with the pomp and hyper-materiality of Moscow's main cathedral?

As Irina Rodnianskaia observes in her review of Pelevin's later novel *S.N.U.F.F.*, Pelevin "is an aesthete, and he evaluates what exists by aesthetic criteria, like Konstantin Leont'ev and Vladimir Nabokov" (Rodnianskaia, "Somel'e Pelevin"). Yes and no, as I see it. If one falls back on a schematic division between writer-stylists (like Nabokov) and writer-ideologues (like Dostoevsky)—and most writers surely partake of both—Pelevin is closer to the latter. That is, while Pelevin is attentive to verbal makeup and makes lavish use of wordplay, his philosophical and ideological preoccupations drive his stylistic quests—not vice versa.

This chapter considers Pelevin's verbal play in the framework of *Generation 'П'*'s political and philosophical concerns. Critics have been quick to point out that *Generation 'П'* brims over with verbal play.[1] Where they split is how to interpret Pelevin's wordplay—whether in a positive or a negative light. If, as in Lev Rubinshtein's opinion, many of Pelevin's puns "without any doubt are fated to be cited nonstop," the Russian literary critic Andrei Nemzer, Pelevin's long-term nemesis, describes his style as "a Volapük of mediocre translations from English" ("Kak by tipa po zhizni"), and Mikhail Sverdlov terms it "a senseless conglomeration of the same [verbal] devices."[2]

Where I part from Nemzer and like-minded critics is in assessing Pelevin's stylistics as merely frivolous verbal juggling. I would argue, rather, that the verbal experimentation in *Generation 'Π'* is an integral part of the novel's cultural diagnosis. In other words, the novel's linguistic play exemplifies its concerns with historical and social deadlock. In Pelevin's satire of cultural decline and hyper-consumerism, language politics plays a central role. Rather than "degrading the spiritual to spiritual refuse" (Sverdlov), whether with deconstructive intent or for the sheer fun of it, *Generation 'Π'* both ridicules and indicts Brave New Russia as a space where hardly any vestiges of the spiritual remain. There is only "spiritual refuse."

In *Generation 'Π'* the transformation of the Russian language reflects the transformation of the post-Soviet psyche. The new idioms of advertising and the media, computer jargon, and English capture these seismic changes. Since Russian techno-consumer postmodernity is a state imported from the West, primarily the United States, the viral penetration of the Anglo-American idiom into Russian dramatizes the new mindset particularly well. Pelevin creates his own equivalent of Huxleyan verbal shorthand (and Orwellian Newspeak). His paranomastic constructions, distinctive metaphors, a peculiar mixture of metaphysical and material terminology, and translinguistic coinages embody the chaos and degradation rampant in post-Soviet Russian society and the global techno-consumer village at large.

NEWSPEAK, HUXLEYAN MNEMONICS, THE LANGUAGE OF TOTAL ADMINISTRATION, AND WORD AND SILENCE

Pelevin's representation and critical analysis of linguistic crisis in *Generation 'Π'* intersect with Marcuse and George Steiner's theories and Huxley and Orwell's artistic theorizing. Orwell's major concern in *1984* is the way language is corrupted for political ends. In Oceania language structures and thereby limits the ideas that individuals are capable of formulating. If the control of language were centralized in a political agency, Orwell suggests, such an agency could alter the very structure of thinking to make it impossible for one to even conceive a disobedient notion ("thoughtcrime"), since there would be no words to express one. Newspeak eliminates words like "freedom" and "individual" and eliminates opposites ("bad" becomes "ungood") in order to purge the emotion behind complex verbal constructions, and it encourages contrarian uses of language, as in the names of the four government ministries of Oceania (for instance, the Ministry of Peace wages war).

Both Orwell and Huxley are concerned with rhetoric that stymies

49

thought.[3] Whereas Newspeak eliminates words and muddles ideas, Huxley's dystopian idiom relies on mnemonic devices and jingles that hammer in advertisements and propaganda in tandem. In *Brave New World*, the populace is conditioned to communicate mechanically through an endless diet of brief, catchy, pun-based slogans. The objective here is less to dispense with politically undesirable words and meanings (as in *1984*) than to create a mental shorthand that confines cognition within the bounds of primitive publicity discourse. The results are more or less the same as in Orwell's novel.

Much of what Huxley as well as Orwell dramatize in their dystopias is what Marcuse theorizes in his analysis of the language of total administration (aka operational language) in advanced industrial society. Operational discourse uses a syntax in which no tension is left between the parts of a sentence—to militate against the development of meaning. Clichéd assertions and an overgrowth of synonyms and tautologies produce ideological incantations that disable any attempts at critical distancing. Elements of autonomy, discovery, demonstration, and critique recede before designation, assertion, and imitation. This idiom deprives language of the mediations proper to the process of cognition and evaluation. The linguistic structure lives only as a whole, and assertions are sealed off against potential questioning or opposition.

In operational language, the subject loses its meaning in excess of its function as defined by other parts of the sentence. In the classical philosophy of grammar, the grammatical subject of a sentence is related to its predicates but remains different from them, carrying more meaning than what is expressed in a given sentence. That is, the subject can enter into grammatical relationships with other parts of the sentence but is not identical to those relationships.[4] But in the language of total administration or operational discourse, the subject is fully defined by its predicates. It is no longer a substance that remains such in various states, conditions, and functions: it turns into a thing and a function itself.

Marcuse's critique of the language of total administration in advanced industrial society resonates in many respects with George Steiner's analysis of post–World War II Anglo-American idiom in *Language and Silence: Essays on Language, Literature and the Inhuman* (1967):

> What are the relations of language . . . to the great load of vulgarity, imprecision, and greed it is charged with in a mass-consumer democracy? . . . The language of the mass-media and of advertisement in England and the United States, what passes for literacy in the average American high school or the style of present political debate, are manifest proofs of a retreat from vitality and precision. The English spoken by Mr. Eisenhower during his press conferences, like that used to sell a new detergent, was intended nei-

ther to communicate the critical truths of national life nor to quicken the mind of the hearer. It was designed to evade or gloss over the demands of meaning. (26–27)

Like Marcuse, Steiner draws an analogy between the rhetoric employed by modern politicians and the advertising industry (with both pursuing the objective of brainwashing). Advertisements and propaganda alike aim at selling. Hence Steiner places Eisenhower's speeches and ads for a new detergent at the same discursive level.

Why and how does language get corrupted—so that it is no longer the means to thinking but a barrier to thought? Steiner zeroes in on stock metaphors, slogans, and jargon—as well as excessive foreign borrowings:

A language shows that it has in it the germ of dissolution in several ways. Actions of the mind that were once spontaneous become mechanical, frozen habits (dead metaphors, stock similes, slogans). Words grow longer and more ambiguous. Instead of style, there is rhetoric. Instead of precise common usage, there is jargon. Foreign roots and borrowings are no longer absorbed into the bloodstream of the native tongue. They are merely swallowed and remain an alien intrusion. All these technical failures accumulate to essential failure: the language no longer sharpens thought but blurs it. (*Language and Silence*, 96)

Using post–World War II Britain as his example, Steiner notes that American neologisms express novel economic and social realities, and become part of the new dream life and vulgate (the consumer dream). The question, then, becomes: what should a writer who feels that the condition of language is in question, that the word may be losing its humanistic value, do? Two courses are available: to render one's idiom that is representative of the general crisis, or to choose silence. The language politics in *Generation 'Π'* evokes Huxley's jingles and Orwellian Newspeak and dramatizes—in a comic and hypertrophied form—Marcuse's language of total administration.

METAPHYSICAL-MATERIAL METAPHOR

The prose style of *Generation 'Π'* is characterized by a mixture of metaphysical and material terminology, and especially of technological and commercial idioms. The passage in which Tatarsky imagines the divine as a copywriter spinning out dastardly scenarios of human life is a vivid example of this: it blends metaphysical and commercial terminology, and the evil demiurge is analogous to the copywriter.

51

Ontological concepts are likewise articulated via consumer terminology in the slogan "Time for rent, space for rent" on the novel's inside cover. The media business is one "in which the basic goods traded are space and time" (*G'Π* 131). The phrase "the final positioning" (given in English, and translated in a footnote as *okonchatel'noe pozitsionirovanie*) blends religious (apocalyptic) and advertising terms (*G'Π* 63). This same blending also occurs in Thomas Pynchon's *Vineland*, where characters "are trying to balance their karmic accounts" (173), or in Michel Houellebecq's metaphor of the world as a supermarket in *Extension du domaine de la lute* (1994).[5] In a parodic rewriting of science and philosophy (Einstein's theory of relativity) in monetary terms, cosmonauts fly to dollars, not to stars: "The nonlinear nature of time and space is expressed in the fact that we and Americans burn equal amounts of fuel and fly equal numbers of kilometers to arrive at absolutely different amounts of money" (*G'Π* 131–32). A confluence (or clash) of the material and the spiritual can be observed in the description of the Soviet-era bureaucrat "who took the crucial decision to sign the [Pepsi] contract [because] he simply fell in love with this dark fuzzy liquid with every pore of his soul" (*G'Π* 9).

Pelevin mixes up ontological and economic categories and, more broadly, imposes materialist, and even markedly vulgar meanings onto conventionally spiritual discourse. As a result, the lofty may be purged of meaning. Yet, as I see it, what takes place is not so much a deconstruction as a critical-satirical effect. Rather than voiding metaphysical categories by weighing them down with the base and material, the explosive joining of the two in the text exposes the effects of de-spiritualization. So, Tatarsky's vision of the divine reflects his inability to conceive the spiritual as anything but hyper-material. The fact that he equates God with money and advertising solipsistically speaks to Tatarsky's and his generation's loss of the spiritual; it does not contend that the spiritual is "phony" per se.

The depiction of people through monetary tropes dramatizes the total commercialization of life, where humans are as much for sale as the food they consume and the clothes they wear. As in Frédérick Beigbeder's world: "You are simply a product. Since globalization no longer considers people, you had to become a product for the society to be interested in you. Capitalism turns people into yogurts—perishable (i.e., mortal), zombified by the Spectacle, in other words, aimed at the destruction of their own kind" (*99 Francs*, 51). Analogously, the power of technology emerges through the consistent description of humans in technological (television or computer) terms: "Instantaneous and unpredictable techno-modifications switch the actual viewer to and fro. . . . HZ is simply the residual luminescence of a soul fallen asleep; it is a film about the shooting of another film, shown on a television in an empty house" (*G'Π* 106). The proliferation of monetary and techno-idioms in *Generation 'П'* reflects the priorities (idols) of Brave New Russia. People "weren't sniffing cocaine, they were sniffing money, and the rolled-up hundred-dollar bill required by the unwritten order of ritual was actually more important than the powder itself" (*G'П* 74).

TATARSKY'S ADVERTISEMENTS

Tatarsky's ads are where Pelevin's wordplay and critique emerge in full force. The brainwashing of the post-Soviet populace is achieved by the debasement of the Russian language and art in advertising jingles. These jingles suck in once-potent cultural statements and disgorge them as white noise. Tatarsky's ads exemplify Pelevin's multilayered ironic and social-critical observations on the absurdities (some ludicrous, some gloomy) of post-Soviet history.

A series of Tatarsky's Parliament cigarette ads provides a vivid example of Pelevin's critique. Beginning with the rather innocuous pun on parliament, "PAR KOSTEI NE LAMENT" ("Steam does not hurt bones"), Tatarsky moves to "PARLIAMENT—THE UN-YAVA," and then to "WHAT DOES THE NEXT DAY HAVE FOR US? PARLIAMENT. NEYAVA" (*G'П* 38).[6] As the protagonist progresses from what he perceives as less successful to more successful commercial scenarios for Parliament (a cigarette brand and simultaneously a key democratic institution), *Generation 'П'* meditates on the infelicities of post-Soviet reality. The change of the regime from socialism to "democracy" is no more than a change of goods (from the Soviet Yava brand of cigarettes to the Western Parliament brand).

Through the poet-turned-copywriter Tatarsky, who recycles high culture (Pushkin, Tchaikovsky) for tawdry purposes, *Generation 'П'* indicts recent post-Soviet history. The Parliament series culminate in an ad that Tatarsky takes particular pride in: the poster consists of a photograph of the Moscow River embankment taken from the bridge where tanks rumbled in October 1993. On the site of the Russian White House (the parliament building) we see a huge pack of Parliament cigarettes. Palms are growing around it. The slogan is a quote from Alexander Griboedov's canonical comedy *Woe from Wit* (1825): "TO US EVEN THE SMOKE OF THE FATHERLAND IS PLEASANT AND SWEET" (*G'П* 59; Griboedov, 472).[7]

Not only is Griboedov's canonical aphorism expressing love of country debased as a slogan for foreign cigarettes, but Pelevin invokes a highly controversial point in history, the shelling of the Russian parliament building in 1993.[8] Both classical culture and the violence of post-Soviet history are trivialized for the purpose of cigarette sales.[9] More importantly, "democracy" emerges via an attack on the parliament, a key democratic institution. As Tatarsky himself wryly concludes: "The entire history of parliamentarism in

Russia amounted to one simple fact—the only thing the word was good for was advertising cigarettes, and even there you could get by quite well without any parliamentarism at all" (*G'Π* 44).

In one more layer of Pelevinian irony and critique, the Russian White House itself is replaced on the poster by a pack of Parliament cigarettes surrounded by palm trees. What has arisen in the wake of the collapse of the Soviet Union is a third-world banana republic. The traditional archetype of Moscow as the "Third Rome" (*Tretii Rim*) reverses to "Third World" (*Tretii mir*), and the question presents itself: "Was it worth exchanging an evil empire for an evil banana republic that imports bananas from Finland?" (*G'Π* 18).

Beyond the notion that a product (Parliament cigarettes) is all that remains after the parliament building is shelled, *Generation 'Π'* imposes a new sardonic semantics onto the canonical Griboedov phrase. The post-Soviet man in fact enjoys "the smoke of the Fatherland," both in the sense of cigarette smoke and in the sense of endorsing (if not taking perverse pleasure in) violence (the smoke from the shelling).

The ironic contrast between Griboedov's classical pastoral and new sardonic meanings highlights the pathologies of 1990s history and pathological changes in the post-Soviet psyche. Pelevin (using a frequent device of his) imbues a familiar phrase with unexpected meaning in a pun-like manner by transferring the procedure by which puns operate onto intertext.[10] He does not recycle dead words as does Sots Art, nor does he resurrect them à la post-conceptualism and the "new sincerity"; instead, he imposes a new and unexpected meaning on them. Imbuing familiar expressions with a new sense thus both exploits the comic potential of the exercise and comments disparagingly on the climate of contemporaneity.

An advertisement for Smirnoff vodka that Tatarsky sees in the "Poor Folk" restaurant functions as a critique of the weakening of culture and the intelligentsia's degraded position in Russia, as well as the loss of Russian particularity. The poster features the nineteenth-century poet Fyodor Tyutchev wearing a pince-nez, with a glass in his hand and a rug across his knees. His sad gaze is directed out the window, and with his free hand he is stroking a dog sitting beside him. Peculiarly, Tyutchev's chair is not set on the floor, but hangs from the ceiling. The slogan reads: "UMOM ROSSIJU NYE PONYAT, V ROSSIJU MOJNO TOLKO VYERIT. SMIRNOFF" ("One cannot understand Russia with the mind, one can only believe in it. Smirnoff") (*G'Π* 77). In an additional ironic touch, Tyutchev's famous line is written in Russian transliterated into Latin characters.

That Tyutchev on the poster is positioned "head down-feet up" (*vverkh tormashkami*) is a fitting reflection of the perversion of the poet's idea in the advertisement. The original quote is Tyutchev's line "Russia is not to be understood by the mind" ("Umom Rossiiu ne poniat'," 1866) (Tiutchev, 102). So, Tyutchev's Slavophile panegyric to Russia promotes a foreign product, a vodka at that. And to top it off, the canonical claim to Russian unique-ness is transliterated into the Roman alphabet.[11] Read sarcastically, an inor-dinate consumption of hard liquor might be what is "unique" about Russia. Furthermore, it is under the effect of inebriation that Tyutchev experiences his visionary insight—not understanding Russia with the mind, but believ-ing in it. In a further joke, Tatarsky himself sees the poster (on the wall of a restaurant that bears the Dostoevskian name "Poor Folk") while high on co-caine. A twisted version of the Slavophile mythologeme of Russian unique-ness becomes both a commercial ad and a drug-induced hallucination.

Tatarsky's ad for Gap stores conveys the notion that Russian culture is approaching its nadir. Tatarsky proposes a poster of Anton Chekhov, first in a striped suit, and then in a striped jacket without trousers, the gap between his skinny bare legs taking the shape of a Gothic hourglass. Next, Chekhov is removed, and the poster features just the outline of the gap between his legs. The gap then becomes an hourglass, with almost all the sand fallen through to the bottom. The slogan reads: "RUSSIA WAS ALWAYS NOTORIOUS FOR THE GAP BETWEEN CULTURE AND CIVILIZATION. NOW THERE IS NO MORE CULTURE. NO MORE CIVILIZATION. THE ONLY THING THAT REMAINS IS THE GAP. THE WAY THEY SEE YOU."

Analogous to the Parliament and Smirnoff ads, the Gap advertisement exemplifies the commercial exploitation of culture and also functions as a meta-critique of that exploitation. The Gothic hourglass suggests that time is running out for Russian culture. Chekhov's bare legs, the space between them, and the semen-like sand that falls into the bottom half of the hourglass are at once comic and obscene. Culture, formerly the most vital aspect of Russian existence, now disintegrates in a void. The void that remains after both "culture" and "civilization" are dispensed with ("the only thing that re-mains is the gap") is how Russia now appears to its Western Other ("the way they see you").

The post-Soviet spiritual void is literally clothed in a commodity, whose very name exposes the emptiness that it hides. By actualizing the twofold meanings of "Gap," political and commercial, Pelevin makes literal Adorno and Horkheimer's contention in *Dialectic of Enlightenment* (1944) that com-modity culture conceals a void. This is the same void that gets revealed after the removal of Lenin's statues, those markers of the socialist myth: "The whole world had been in this frightening murk for ages, which is why the world is so full of things and money." In a world driven by things and money, everything can be turned to profit, including the death of culture. Here Ta-tarsky succeeds by selling Russia's cultural bankruptcy where before he suc-ceeded in selling its cultural riches.

The Gap text is written in English and translated into Russian in a footnote. The footnote adds an explanation of Pelevin's wordplay: *gap—razryv* ("rupture"), *Gap—set' universal'nykh magazinov* ("a chain of department stores") (*G'П'* 85). That the notion of Russia's cultural degradation emerges in an English-language advertisement for a clothing chain further underscores the irony and poignancy of the situation.

Tatarsky's forays into advertising culminate in his writing an ad for none other than God Himself—perhaps the novel's most striking dramatization of the hyper-materialization of contemporary consciousness. Since other copywriters wrongly "position" the Lord, Tatarsky promises to produce a fitting slogan for Him. He recalls a video clip calling for money to be donated to rebuild the Cathedral of Christ the Savior, in which a man driving a Zaporozhets (a small, cheap, Soviet-era car) donates a ruble, while a man driving a Mercedes gives a hundred dollars. Tatarsky decides that his "target group" should be the guys in the Mercedes, and he comes up with the following advertising scenario:

> Poster: a long white limousine with the Cathedral of Christ the Savior in the background. Its back door is open, and light is pouring out. A sandal appears from the light nearly touching the asphalt, and a hand on the door handle. The face is not seen. Only light, car, hand, and foot. Slogan: CHRIST THE SAVIOR. RESPECTABLE LORD FOR RESPECTABLE LORDS [KHRISTOS SPASITEL' SOLIDNYI GOSPOD' DLIA SOLIDNYKH GOSPOD]. (*G'П'* 159)

This seemingly frivolous advertisement works as critique on multiple levels. By its paronomasia, *solidnyi gospod'—solidnykh gospod*, the ad links Jesus Christ and New Russians (the post-Soviet nouveau riche, mostly criminals). Christ is further identified with the nouveau riche by his arrival in a luxury automobile. This ad draws on the idiom of elite real estate ads in the 1990s, which often featured the phrase "for respectable gentlemen" (*dlia solidnykh gospod*). The Cathedral of Christ the Savior (blown up under Stalin in the 1930s) has been rebuilt under Moscow Mayor Yuri Luzhkov in the 1990s as an opulent place of worship for the government and the rich.

Such an elitist, hyper-material image of Jesus of course stands in marked contrast to the Sermon on the Mount that promises the kingdom of God to "You poor . . . You that hunger . . . You that weep" (Luke 6:20–21). One is expected to consume Christian faith as one more product in the universe of products, thereby perverting Christianity's emphasis on the immateriality of faith. Even the divine is circumscribed and commodified. The glossy poster, the light, the arm, the foot, and the Mercedes limousine create a fixed image that sticks in the consumer's mind—as does the edifice of the cathedral. The phrase "Christ the Savior" simultaneously refers to (and thereby equates) Jesus and his respectable dwelling place. The grammatical subject (Jesus) does not carry a meaning in excess of that expressed in the sentence, just as the Lord does not transcend His representation (the cathedral). What, then, is Tatarsky selling here? The Lord (perverted), Luzhkov's cathedral, the Mercedes limousine, new Russians, or perhaps all of them in one beefy package?

WITH A BRIGHT FOREIGNER'S FONDNESS FOR PUNS

Pelevin's puns, both mono- and trans-lingual, are a marked feature of his poetics.[12] *Generation 'П'* features abundant, perhaps even obsessive, punning. If analyzed carefully, however, Pelevin's puns are by no means wordplay for the sake of wordplay. Most of the puns and paronomastic constructions participate meaningfully in the novel's overarching critique of contemporary culture.

As Roman Jakobson observes in "Linguistics and Poetics" (1960), similar phonemic sequences near each other tend to be drawn together in meaning. Puns and paronomasias, even if they present instances of patently false common etymology, encourage semantic linkage. So, for instance, in Edgar Allan Poe's poem "The Raven" (1845), the perch of the bird, "the pallid bust of Pallas," merges through sonorous paronomasia into one organic whole, and the bond between the sitter and its seat is fastened by paronomasia: "Bird or beast upon the . . . bust" (Jakobson, *Language in Literature*, 86). Jakobson points out the same effect in his "Linguistic Aspects of Translation" (1959): "If we were to translate into English the traditional formula *Traduttore, traditore* as 'the translator is a betrayer,' we would deprive the Italian rhyming epigram of all its paronomastic value. Hence a cognitive attitude would compel us to change this aphorism into a more explicit statement and to answer the questions: translator of what messages? Betrayer of what values?" (*Language in Literature*, 435).

The value of such puns explains their use in advertising. Puns are popular rhetorical figures in advertising jingles—which take advantage of their rhetorical impact.[13] *Generation 'П'* illustrates the linguistic and psychological strategies which advertising uses to manipulate the target audience into buying the product—specifically, through punning techniques. The novel offers examples and a meta-critique of advertising, and, by extension, of the phony media-driven world into which the post-Soviet populace has been thrust.

One of Tatarsky's early ventures into advertising, a bit for a Sprite campaign in Russia, ironically, taps into national particularity in order to customize the campaign for the target clientele. It turns on a pun: "SPRITE.

THE UN-KOLA FOR NIKOLA" ("SPRITE. NE-KOLA DLIA NIKOLY") (*G'II'* 36).[14] Translated into Russian, "Un-cola" becomes "Ne-Cola." The sound of the word is close to the old-fashioned Russian name Nikola. The associations aroused by the slogan are suitably pseudo-Slavonic, exploiting nationalistic consciousness. "Un-cola" sounds vaguely oppositional—suitable for a post-Soviet audience with anti-Western leanings. One turns quasi-local in order to sell Russians one more kind of American soft drink.

Based on phonic resemblances of the kind theorized by Jakobson, the "Un-cola" advertising slogan functions as a self-validating formulation—helping seal together an absurdity. Ne-kola (or Un-cola in English) uses the Orwellian prefix "un" to flatten out (un-think) thought. Perhaps most ludicrous is the slogan's dramatization of the subject's identification with the goods it consumes. As the bird and the beast are fastened together in Poe's "The Raven," "Un-cola for Nikola" forcefully binds man and drink, welding them together in a solid and familiar structure. Like Huxley's hypnopedic formulae in *Brave New World*, the ad zombifies as it is hammered and re-hammered into the consumer's mind.

Another instance of bilingual (Russian-English) punning occurs in Tatarsky's ad for a Sony television: "DID YOU THINK THERE WAS A VACUUM BEHIND THE ABSOLUTELY FLAT 'BLACK TRINITRON' SCREEN? NO! THERE'S A FLAME BLAZING THERE THAT WILL WARM YOUR HEART! 'THE SONY TOFETISSIMO.' IT'S A SIN" (*G'II'* 238–39). This slogan exemplifies Che Guevara's critique of the media as a purveyor of avarice and illusions—by selling those very illusions. "It's a sin" is written in English, and is translated in a footnote as *eto grekh*. Tatarsky incorporates his drug-induced insight into television as the modern version of hell—the Old Testament Gehenna or Tofet where people are burned in flames for their material lust. In Pelevin's wordplay, "Tofetissimo" echoes *tofet*, and "sin" is a bilingual pun on the Russian *son* ("dream").

The puns in *Generation 'II'* expose the least appealing traits of the early post-Soviet years—drabness, criminalization across society, and the commodification of life. Such puns work by blending a higher (conventional) and lower (unexpected) meaning of expressions—as in the case of the bilingual punning on the word "freelance." Tatarsky's work was "freelance—he translated this expression as *svobodnyi kopeishchik*, having in mind first of all the level of his pay" (*G'II'* 33). The English term "freelance" (derived from medieval mercenaries) used verbatim in the text cannot be translated literally into Russian. Tatarsky translates "lance" as *kop'e* ("spear") and, by means of phonemic similarity, moves from *kop'e* to *kopeika* (a kopeck—small change). Thus, from the neutral English word "freelance" he derives the derogatory and ironic (since from his own perspective it is not possible to be free without money) Russian term *svobodnyi kopeishchik* (free kopeck-earner).

In a similar procedure, as Tatarsky jots down ideas for future ads in his notebook, he reinterprets the phrase *veshchii Oleg* from Alexander Pushkin's "Song about the Prophetic Oleg" ("Pesnia o veshchem Olege," 1822) as meaning *veshch-ism* ("thing-ism"). In an obvious instance of falsifying its etymology, he invests the word with a new and parodic meaning based on its phonic characteristics. Pelevin's pun critically reflects on (and invites the reader to critically reflect on) *veshchism*, the driving force of contemporary culture.

THE LINGUA FRANCA OF AMERICAN ENGLISH

Pelevin's style incorporates up-to-date political and cultural realia, as well as computer, youth, gangster, and other kinds of contemporary slang, and a profusion of Anglo-Americanisms. As Tatarsky's advertising slogans demonstrate, Pelevin has at his command an explosive mixture of Russian and American English.[15] Deliberately creating a new hybrid lingo is an essential component of his farce. In Eliot Borenstein's formulation: These examples [of Soviet pulp] "pale in comparison to the memetic explosion that constitutes Western popular culture, whose ubiquity is facilitated by the political hegemony of the United States and the linguistic dominance of English" ("Survival of the Catchiest," 470). Mark Lipovetsky comments on the multilingualism in *Generation 'П'* as follows: "This novel is written in a fantastic mixture of Russian and English where one and the same text and even word acquires a double meaning because of its double status, that is, it immediately turns into a metaphor." Even a Russian text "simply written in Latin letters (something that happens all the time) immediately creates the second metaphorical layer of sense" (Lipovetskii, *Paralogii*, 449).

Pelevin begins his mixing up of Russian and Anglo-American in the novel's very title, which is a combination of the English "generation" (a nod to the Anglophone tradition of assigning a letter to a generation, as in "Generation X" and so on), and the Cyrillic letter П. The epigraph to the novel is in English as well: "I'm sentimental, if you know what I mean. . . ." This line, from a song by Leonard Cohen (from his album *The Future*, 1992), is translated into Russian in the footnote.

The first English phrase in the body of the text naturally comes from advertising: "tak nazyvaemuiu *target group*" ("the so-called *target group*"), with the English term set off in italics (*G'П'* 11). The phrase has not been translated into Russian since no established equivalent existed. The target group in question is late Soviet-era consumers of Pepsi-Cola, and the narrator finds it "somewhat disappointing to learn how the guys from advertising agencies on Madison Avenue conceptualize their audience"—namely, as apes (*GП* 11). On the same page where the term "target group" appears, the English words "copywriter" (*kopiraiter*) and "designer" (*dizainer*) appear, both transliterated into Cyrillic. The novel draws attention to the Anglo-American lexicon infiltrating post-Soviet Russian by noting that during Soviet times, even such a peaceful word as *dizainer* "seemed a dubious neologism existing in the great Russian language as a temporary worker [*po lingvisticheskomu limitu*]" (*GП* 12).

What ensues is the opening of physical and metaphorical borders, an influx of American idioms into the post-Soviet scene, and Pelevin's confrontation of the two different languages and their very different worldviews. The poet Tatarsky's initial experience with the influx of Americanisms is one of sadness and bewilderment. Russian "no longer matches, or matches only at certain ritual, arbitrary points, the changing landscape of fact" (Steiner, *After Babel*, 241). Both the changing landscape and the new idioms to describe it are difficult for the post-Soviet man to grasp. Certain Americanisms that Tatarsky comes across during his initial exposure to the media world— such as "draft podium"—prove incomprehensible. Since no Russian translation of the term is given, the reader's sense of estrangement matches that of the protagonist.

Tatarsky's becoming more comfortable with media and the advertising industry proceeds in parallel with his immersion in American English. Besides the Gap ad (written in English) and the Smirnoff ad (using the Roman alphabet), many American verbal imports enter the post-Soviet lexicon— such as "wow impulses" which, according to Che Guevara's mock treatise, the media transmits to control humankind:

> These impulses are of three types, which are called oral, anal, and displacing wow-impulses (from the commercial ejaculation "*wow!*"). The oral wow-impulse induces a cell to ingest money in order to eliminate its suffering as a result of the conflict between its self-image and the image of the ideal "super-self" created by advertising. . . . The anal wow-impulse induces the cell to eliminate money in order to experience pleasure from the coincidence of the above-mentioned things. . . . The displacing wow-impulse suppresses and displaces from the individual's consciousness all psychological processes that might hinder total identification with a cell of Oranus. . . . Man has long ceased being a wolf to man. Man is not even an image-maker, dealer, killer, or exclusive distributor to man. . . . Man is wow to man—and not even to man but to another wow. Projected onto the modern system of cultural coordinates, the Latin saying becomes: "*Wow Wow Wow!*" (*GП* 108–9, 118)

The obliteration of humankind is conceptualized as a regression from the Latin *Homo homini lupus est* ("Man is wolf to man") to *Wow Wow Wow!*

Written at first mention in English, the exclamation "Wow" is subsequently calqued as a Cyrillic "*vau*." And then "*imidzhmeiker, diler, killer i ekskliuziv-nyi distrib'iutor*," a sequence of American neologisms, have all been calqued into Russian. These are all business terms, and the human being himself is up for consumption—whether for sale or for murder. The inventory of foreign borrowings progresses mechanically, strung together on the basis of their formal similarity.[16] Swallowed in one big lump, they are hard to digest.

While the initial Latin conception, "man is wolf to man," is gloomy enough, and the "image-maker" string of notions is even more pessimistic, under current conditions humans (and their relationships to one another) get reduced to the more drastic triple *Wow*. The sequence of oral, anal, and displacing wow-impulses that flare up and fade away in one's consciousness cancel out human subjects proper, as well as circumscribing their stance toward one another. The triple Wow makes literal and extends *Homo homini lupus est*. Man is wolf to man not in any metaphorical sense of predatory animosity toward one's peers; rather, in the hyper-mediation of contemporaneity, the human being is literally reduced to a howl ("wow!").

As Che Guevara unfolds his theory of the annihilation of humankind by the techno-consumer machine, he engages more American neologisms to drive his points home. The oral wow-impulse corresponds to the internal auditor holding up the flag "loser" (written in English and translated into Russian as *neudachnik* in a footnote), while the anal wow-impulse corresponds to the internal auditor holding up the flag "winner" (translated as *pobeditel'*) (*GΠ* 116). Appropriately enough, the call to conform to the new upbeat outlook on life is articulated in the language that embodies the dominant cultural trend. Elsewhere in the book, it is mentioned how insulting it would be to be a "loser": "You promise to yourself that you will rip mountains of money out of this hostile void with your bare teeth, . . . and nobody will ever dare to call you that American word 'loser' [*amerikanskim slovom luzer*]" (*GΠ* 179).

Analogously, via Che Guevara, Pelevin meditates on the annihilation of the human subject by thinking about the American word "identity." "Identity" designates an illusory inner center:

> Identity is a false ego, which says everything there is to be said about it. In its analysis of the modern human condition, bourgeois thought regards the violent escape from identity back to one's ego as a tremendous spiritual achievement. Perhaps that is really the case, since the ego is nonexistent in relative terms, while identity is absolutely nonexistent. (*GΠ* 114)

The word "identity" marks the state in which genuine interiority is exchanged for an illusion of interiority (since the human being is absorbed into the monetary collective). Identity is circumscribed by consumption: "I am that one that eats X, wears Y, drives Z . . ." Elsewhere Pelevin's characters stumble on the unfamiliar term *iden-tich-nost'* (a calque on the American "identity")—a fashionable yet vacuous word.

To articulate his critique of global neoliberal society, Pelevin assigns lowering, mocking meanings to key Anglophone terms such as "liberal values" and "democracy." As Morkovin, who introduces Tatarsky to the advertising business, claims, *leve* ("money" in Russian criminal jargon) is an abbreviation for "liberal values." For Morkovin, people like himself and Tatarsky are oppressed and scared yet have "inalienable rights. And *leve*" (*G'П*' 22). In liberal-democratic society, every individual is supposed to possess civil rights. In the global neoliberal society that Pelevin conceives of in derogatory terms, money means freedom, and democracy, in its modern everyday usage, means the market.

As *Generation 'П'* demonstrates, in the world of contemporaneity, liberal values equate with monetary values. This is what Baudrillard describes as the transformation of the liberal tradition of individual choice into "the consumer being sovereign in a jungle of ugliness where freedom of choice has been forced upon him." Money or *leve* (criminal money) represents the social performance of the concept "liberal values"—a performance that subverts or at least significantly weakens the concept's essence.

Analogously, the word "democracy" in its current usage has not only been enclosed by an analytic predication (as in Marcuse's analysis of operational discourse), but has completely lost its proper meaning:

> The word "democracy" which is used so frequently in the modern mass media is by no means the same word that was widespread in the nineteenth and early twentieth centuries. These are so-called homonyms. The old word "democracy" was derived from the Greek "demos" while the new word is derived from the expression "demo-version." (*G'П*' 119)

The term "homonym" bares the device Pelevin employs frequently ("Gap"-"gap," *veshchii*, etc.).[17] What the average consumer understands by the much-abused term "democracy" in today's world is actually just a "demo," the demonstration of a product or service.

A seminal linguistic and cultural clash between the Russian and American cosmos takes place in *Generation 'П'* when Tatarsky is hired by Khanin in his advertising business. Pelevin stages the transformation of his protagonist from a naive and idealistic man of letters into a man of business by switching from Russian to Anglo-American. The passage explicitly foregrounds language dynamics:

"Will you come and work for me full time?"

Tatarsky took another look at the poster with the three palm trees and the Anglophone promise of eternal metamorphoses.

"As what?" he asked.

"*Krieitorom.*"

"Is that a creator [*eto tvortsom*]?" Tatarsky asked. "If translated?"

Khanin smiled gently.

"We don't need any fucking creators [*tvortsy*] here," he said. "*Krieitorom,* Vava, *krieitorom.*" (*G II* 91)

No established Russian calque for the writer of advertising slogans existed at this point (*kopiraiter,* also borrowed from English, is now typically used). To designate Tatarsky's future vocation, Khanin uses the English word "creator" directly transliterated into Cyrillic in the text. As one might expect at this point, Tatarsky translates "creator" straightforwardly as *tvorets,* and is promptly corrected by Khanin. Tatarsky still harbors artistic aspirations, but Khanin is in the artless word of business.

This instance (among others) of code-switching between Russian and American falls under a Bakhtinian understanding of languages as bound to ideological systems and worldviews.[18] By opposing the Russian meaning of *tvorets* to the Western notion of advertising copywriter, the passage expresses a social-cultural clash by means of a linguistic clash. No *tvortsy,* in the lofty Russian sense ascribed to this word, are needed in advertising— only pragmatic and cynical creator-copywriters. Indeed, Tatarsky's adaptations of American ads to Russian soil are a degraded version of the "writing for eternity" discussed at the novel's opening. The whole exchange, appropriately, takes place in front of an American advertising poster with palm trees and, as Tatarsky notices wistfully, an Anglophone (*angloiazychnym*) promise of eternal metamorphoses. This background further hints at the as-yet innocent protagonist's simultaneous crossing of linguistic and sociocultural boundaries.[19]

Assigning a markedly negative connotation in Russian to the neutral American term "creator-copywriter" not only suggests that language is culturally embedded, and that the cultural associations of words in Russia are often different from the same words in the United States, but conveys a negative assessment of Tatarsky's future job and the whole media business. That is, Pelevin's code-switching is as much evaluative as it is playful.

The "creator vs. *tvorets*" dichotomy comes through in another exchange between Khanin and Tatarsky that features transmesis (explicit discussion of translation in the text). As Khanin explains it, the expression "brand essence" is translated as *legenda* ("legend") in Russian. When Tatarsky finds this translation odd, Khanin replies: "What's to be done about it? This is Asia" (*G'П* 138). Here again Pelevin is tongue-in-cheek: the "Asiatic" (read: barbaric and naive) understanding of "brand essence" as "legend"—in the sense of cover-ups (as in spy and criminal circles)—in fact points to the wholesale deception at the heart of advertising—the leitmotif of *Generation 'П.'*

THE TOWER OF BABEL

The Babel-like confusion of tongues, especially Russian and today's lingua franca, American English, dramatizes Russia's crashing into global postmodernity. Tatarsky's career rise is a mystical ascent up Ishtar's ziggurat, which is simultaneously the Tower of Babel.[20] Babylon is alluded to in Tatarsky's first name, Vavilen (*Vavilon* is Babylon in Russian), and in Genesis 11:1–9, when God unleashes the confusion of tongues to punish human presumption for seeking to erect a pillar as high as the heavens. The proliferation of languages at the Tower of Babel results in the builders no longer understanding one another, which effectively undoes the project.

When Tatarsky visits Ishtar's ziggurat/Tower of Babel, his language disintegrates under the influence of hallucinogenic mushrooms. Attempting to ask for water, he utters: "Li'd winker drike I watof!" (*Mne by vopit' khotelos' pody* instead of *Mne by popit' khotelos' vody*) (*G'П* 50). The syllables that make up the words are jumbled up chaotically. Initially the first syllable of each word in the phrase is moved to another word. Next there is a full-on scramble: *mne by pokhit' dytelos' vokho.*

Tatarsky's loss of communicative capacity under the influence of drugs launches him into thinking about the biblical confusion of tongues:

> "Why, of course, it's the Tower of Babel!" he thought. "They probably drank that mushroom mixture and the words began to break apart in their mouths, just like mine. Later they began to call it the confusion of tongues. It would be more correct to call it "confusion of the tongue. . . . The confusion of tongues [*stolpotvorenie*] is pillar and creation [*stolp i tvorenie*]. The creation of the pillar [*tvorenie stolpa*], not erection but precisely creation. That is, the confusion of the tongue constitutes the creation of the tower. When the confusion of the tongue occurs, the Tower of Babel rises. Or maybe it doesn't rise, it's just that the entrance to the ziggurat opens up." (*G'П* 53–54)

Generation 'П' creatively reimagines the biblical story to make a statement about multilingualism in the global techno-consumer village. Instead of the classical Tower of Babel, the drugged Tatarsky experiences the confusion of *iazyk* in its twofold meaning of "language" and "tongue." The narrative resurrects the faded trope of *stolpotvorenie* (the Tower of Babel; metaphorically, a mess, chaos) by breaking the word apart into its two structural constituents, *stolp* and *tvorenie*. The text reinterprets *tvorenie* as a mystical creation rather than the physical erection of a tower, and switches cause and effect as we know them from the Genesis story. It is the confusion of the tongue/language that enables the creation of the tower, not vice versa.

In Pelevin's unorthodox rendition of the biblical story, the confusion of Tatarsky's tongue magically opens the entrance to the tower which, in a mythological conflation, is also the ziggurat of Ishtar, the goddess of money. As the hero enters an abandoned construction site from Soviet times, a confusion of tongues does occur: the gates carry an English sign, "This game has no name," and a voice adds in Russian, "With hanging gardens" (as in Babylon) (*G'П* 55–56). By this time Tatarsky is so used to Russian being subordinated to English that he actually thinks the Russian phrase is just a hallucination. Since the tower itself resembles a decaying military construction from the 1970s, the "winner paradigm" appears to have taken root right on the ruins of the Soviet project.

Tatarsky's *stolpotvorenie* (*tvorenie stolpa*) enables and foreshadows his subsequent rise to power over the course of the novel. In a hallucinogenic vision that might open the protagonist up to a higher reality (by his standards, a higher commodified realm), Tatarsky's ascent up the tower inspires him to conceive an early and successful Parliament ad, which gives him an initial career boost in the industry. The ascent to the top of the tower anticipates his eventual (if utterly pedestrian) union with the goddess of money.[21] The ascent up is also a descent into the pit of commercialization.

The Tower of Babel symbol, so popular among postmodern writers and theorists, emerges in *Generation 'П'* in a negative light.[22] Postmodern code-switching between languages does not result in greater cognitive or emotional freedom (the de-automatization of thought, creative-critical possibilities outside one's own native idiom), but in entropy. Where tyrannies often appear to be characterized by linguistic fundamentalism, postmodern market economies come packaged in verbal relativism and pluralism. In the latter case, any liberating potential may be trumped by "an equal distribution of heat." When one language and value system is judged to be no better and no worse than any other, aesthetic and ethical entropy ensues.

Even worse is the kind of crude linguistic imperialism that the lingua franca of Anglo-American business parlance performs in post-Soviet Russia. *Generation 'П'*'s "winner" idiom is neither British nor American English proper, but the much more restrictive, primitive, yet powerful rhetoric of advertising, media, and mass culture—Marcuse's language of total administration. Appropriately, the unfinished Soviet construction/Tower of Babel/

Ishtar's ziggurat that Tatarsky ascends features graffiti in Roman script, English obscenities, an empty pack of Parliament cigarettes, and other consumer waste littered on the floor.

In one more instance of mythological-religious associative linkage, *Generation 'П'* reinvents the Tower of Babel story as the story of Babylon in the biblical book of Revelation. The loss of linguistic and cultural particularities in post-Soviet Russia is the new Apocalypse. The hero's career rise in the media or, in mythical terms, his ascent up the Tower of Babel/Ishtar's ziggurat, culminates in his descent into a hundred-meter Inferno-like pit under the Ostankino television tower. Tatarsky's anointment as the consort of the goddess of money marks the triumph of the infernal Generation P(izdets).

❉ ❉ ❉

In the process of exploring early post-Soviet society in *Generation 'П,'* Pelevin foregrounds language politics. His verbal play is a vehicle for cultural diagnosis. The critical focus is the onslaught of global consumerism, the media, advertising, and technology, transmitted in the lingua franca of American English. The Russian language (and culture) stand little chance of resisting this onslaught.

As Pelevin and Marcuse demonstrate, the former narratologically, the latter theoretically, the language of advertising and the media, with its closing-off of the universe of discourse, is representative of the more general primitivization of language and thought in the global techno-consumer village. The objectives of this kind of discourse are efficacy and productivity—first and foremost, the efficient flow of commodities and capital. Tatarsky and his colleagues in the advertising industry are behaviorists par excellence. Their task is to induce a reaction (parodically stated, oral and anal) on the part of the target group. The syntax of abridgement employed in the idiom of advertising ("Parliament. Ne-yava"; "Ne-kola dlia Nikoly") militates against the development of meaning, potential doubt, or opposition. "Nikola" is induced to buy—among other ways, by pushing him (by linguistic paranomastic means) to identify with the product. Crucial concepts such as "democracy" have been loaded with ridiculous homonyms such as "demo-version." Of all people, Jesus is up for sale, packaged with a glossy image and a catchy impact line. And, in a species reduced to social behaviorism, words only elicit a maximally standardized reaction—the subhuman Wow Wow Wow!

PART II

Posthumanism

Biomorphic Monstrosities

> It was no four-sided cage with bars, but only
> three walls fixed to a crate, so that the crate
> constituted the fourth wall. The whole thing
> was too low to stand upright and too narrow for
> sitting down. So I crouched with bent knees,
> which shook all the time, and since at first I
> probably did not wish to see anyone and to
> remain constantly in the darkness, I turned
> towards the crate, while the bars of the cage
> cut into the flesh on my back.
> —Franz Kafka, "A Report to an Academy"

THIS CHAPTER LOOKS at Pelevin's biopolitics, a consistent portrayal of society in biomorphic and zoomorphic terms. My objective is twofold: to draw attention to the prominence of biomorphic and zoomorphic representations of the human collective in Pelevin's oeuvre, and to show that this imagery is a corollary of his central concern with dehumanization in the contemporary techno-consumer realm.

Pelevin's biopolitics expresses itself through a recurrent associative chain: humans—animals—biomass—a source of energy (blood or oil)—money. The portrayal of humans as biomass and of society in terms of biocoenosis (the interaction of organisms living in a specific habitat and associated by way of interdependence as evident in consumption links) are traits of his oeuvre from his early to more recent work.[1] To highlight the degradation of the individual and the collective, the consumer paradigm is presented in two forms: monetary or economic consumption, and the process of consumption in the state of nature.

Pelevin's fictional biopolitics shows similarities to Foucault's biopolitical theorizing.[2] In Foucault's diagrams of power relationships in the body politic, a sovereign power is replaced by a power based on discipline. The latter, in turn, is ousted by biopolitics or the apparatus of security operating not through punishment or correction, but through calculation and intervention. In Pelevin's biopolitical fantasies and Foucault's theory of biopolitics alike, humans are conceived of as biological organisms, and the social collective as a body of living matter that is maintained, increased, and managed by the status quo.

Pelevin's biotic structures are metaphors for consumerism and social degeneracy. Conversely, his bio-aggregates literalize the biomorphic metaphors underlying the rhetoric of Foucault's biopolitical writings. Foucault's "global mass that is affected by processes of birth, illness, reproduction, death, etc." and which constitutes the state becomes biomass, as Pelevin is fond of saying, "in the most literal sense" (*v samom priamom smysle*). However playfully, theory is taken to the limits, to come alive in fiction.[3]

In this chapter, after brief discussions of "Hermit and Six Toes" and *The Life of Insects*, works already informed by a biotic vision, I examine biocoenosis in *Generation 'П,'* focusing on the image of the bio-aggregate of Oranus. Subsequently I explore the consumption of the body politic in *DPP(NN)* and in *The Sacred Book of the Werewolf*, with the trope of oil entering the larger paradigm of hyper-consumerism. Next I discuss the "dairy industry" or enlightened vampirism in *Empire V/Ampir V*. In conclusion, I highlight the differences between more traditional zoomorphic narratives and Pelevin's biopolitical fantasies.

CHICKENS, INSECTS, HUMANS

Pelevin's early short story "Hermit and Six Toes" ("Zatvornik i shestipalyi," 1990) captures in a microcosm his key biopolitical motifs and, more generally, much of his cosmology. A story about broiler chickens bred at a chicken factory, it begins with a meeting between two social outcasts among the chickens, the enlightened Hermit and the deformed Six Toes. According to Six Toes, the world in which they live is enclosed in "the Wall of the World," governed by "Twenty Closest," and has, at its apex, the feeding trough and the drinking trough. But the wiser Hermit explains to his eager disciple that in reality their world is but one of seventy worlds traveling through space on a black belt in the universe called the "Lunacharsky Chicken Factory."[4] The end of the world is approaching fast, since the chickens are to be slaughtered in less than twenty-four hours.

"Hermit and Six Toes" envisions human existence as a biofactory and the social collective as biomass. The chicken collective, in which the birds compete for proximity to the troughs, ignorant of their impending slaughter, functions as a parable of carceral human society. The narrative proceeds in such a manner that nothing in it suggests initially that the protagonists are not human. Only gradually does the reader come to realize who and what is being depicted.[5] Even as this realization dawns, one perceives the chicken metaphysicians as grappling with human existential problems—freedom and imprisonment, deception and genuine enlightenment, and the awareness of death. In the finale of the story, the two protagonists manage to break the laws of their prison and fly away into freedom.

Like "Hermit and Six Toes," Pelevin's early novella *The Life of Insects* (*Zhizn' nasekomykh*, 1993) revolves around the trope of organisms consuming other organisms. This time around, the novella lays out a more extended zoomorphic parable. Set in a decaying post-perestroika Crimean resort, it is structured as a collection of seemingly unrelated but in fact interconnected episodes, each on the life of an anthropomorphized insect or group of insects. Several species are depicted—mosquitoes, dung beetles, ants, moths, flies, cicadas—all of them struggling to survive and succeed, searching for the meaning of life, consuming others and being consumed themselves.

The Life of Insects commences with a meeting of three mosquitoes—an experienced American businessman, Sam Sucker, and two aspiring Russian entrepreneurs, Arnold and Arthur—all of them on the lookout for easy money in the volatile post-Soviet market. As the narrative progresses, the literal "capitalist bloodsucker" (*kapitalist-krovopiitsa*) Sam seduces a young Russian ant-turned-fly named Natasha. In the course of their brief affair Sam sucks Natasha's blood, and soon enough she dies while trapped on flypaper. That Natasha is to be consumed by Sam is foreshadowed during their first encounter, when the mosquito notices the fly sitting on his plate, and mistakes her for a bit of dill. At the end of the novella, the same waitress who initially served food (and Natasha) to Sam disposes of her as waste.[6]

With the exception of the story about the moth Mitya, who attains literal and figurative enlightenment by rising above the chain of consumption and turning into a glowworm at the book's finale, the lives of the insects in the novella—Natasha's ant mother Marina, Natasha herself, the mosquitoes Sam, Arnold, and Arthur, the drug addicts Maxim and Nikita, and so on—illustrate the same relentless ethos of consumption. In this sense, the fly Natasha–mosquito Sam plotline is a typical one. The Darwinian vision of "eat or be eaten" runs throughout the story.

In Pelevin's mature novels, the "Lunacharsky Chicken Factory" will metamorphose into a global biotic community. "Hermit and Six Toes" and *The Life of Insects* lay the groundwork for the ideas that are fleshed out in later novels. The short story's portrayal of the universe as a bio-factory and slaughterhouse and the novella's "nature red in tooth and claw" theme inform subsequent texts, but with a significant divergence. Unlike the chicken heroes or Mitya the moth of Pelevin's youthful parables, the protagonists of his later works are mostly unable to either attain self-enlightenment or escape the bounds of their prison into freedom. The boundaries of the "bio-factory" are indeed hard to cross since the whole world turns out to be a bio-factory.

ORANUS AND THE EROSION OF THE SUBJECT

Generation 'П' portrays the social collective in animalistic terms. As early as the first chapter of the novel, Pelevin employs Darwinian tropes to characterize the violent and divisive transitions of the initial post-Soviet period. For example, a Pepsi-Cola advertisement portrays two apes, one drinking Coca-Cola and unable to perform the most primitive of actions, and the other drinking Pepsi and happily driving around in an expensive car in the company of pretty girls. It was "a bit of an insult to learn how the guys from the advertising agencies on Madison Avenue imagined their audience, the so-called target group. But one could hardly fail to be impressed by their deep knowledge of life" (*G'П'* 10–11).

The unfolding narrative develops these Darwinian motifs. The most efficient specimens in *Generation 'П'* are those who adapt to the rough-and-tumble post-Soviet environment faster than others. Given the struggle for existence, this flexibility leads to the proliferation of aggressiveness, callousness, cunning, and other behavioral patterns that allow one to prosper in a nature "red in tooth and claw." The novel's hero, Tatarsky, proves successful in part because he adapts quickly to new dominant behavioral patterns. The value of morals is ousted by the survival of the fittest. Behavior that does not foster the survival and the reproduction of the biological unit—for instance, the ethical norms of the intelligentsia—is evolutionarily discarded.[7]

Generation 'П' envisions the global social collective as a monstrous bio-aggregate that has trapped humans and eroded the human subject as such:

> Every man constitutes a cell of an organism which the economists of antiquity called Mammon. Study materials of the battlefront of complete and total liberation call it simply ORANUS [in Russian—*rotozhopa*]. . . . Each of the cells, that is, each human, in his economic function, possesses a kind of social-psychic membrane allowing one to let money (playing the role of blood or lymph in the organism of Oranus) in and out. (*G'П'* 108)

A primitive parasitic organism, Oranus-Mammon is unique in that, unlike common parasites, it does not benefit at the expense of a single host, but instead transforms multiple human hosts into its constituents.[8] Each human being becomes a cell of Oranus, with the sole purpose of allowing money to pass into and out of it.[9]

The aggregate of Oranus is a personification of bio-morphosis. Paradoxically, Oranus, an organism incapable of cognition or even self-awareness, occupies a much lower evolutionary position than each of its cells, and yet it can infiltrate a human being to the point that the person, an entity with high cognitive capacities, is obliterated altogether.[10] The absorption of human beings into the primitive, parasitical, self-perpetuating entity of Oranus is an event that has taken place for the first time in the history of mankind in modern techno-consumer society. People are transformed into a homogeneous biomass caught in a cycle of consumption and excretion, having abandoned complex cognitive processes for reflexes, and having accepted being driven by purely sensory stimuli. As biological existence is accentuated, the powers of reason and will weaken considerably or disappear altogether. The cells of Oranus may have a high reproductive capacity, but otherwise they are utter nullities—unthinking and appallingly homogeneous.

In its parody of the social superstructure, *Generation 'П'* reverses the scheme of rational self-interest outlined in classic free-market theory (Adam Smith's *The Wealth of Nations,* 1776). According to this theory, human behavior, based on a drive for profit, summarily advances the interests of society as a whole. Pelevin's novel presents humans benefiting neither themselves nor other members of society by earning money in a competitive market economy, but instead being caught in servitude to Oranus. If Oranus-*rotozhopa* does indeed provide for some semblance of safety and prosperity, it accomplishes this only at the level of human biomass, and at the cost of eliminating the individual. Even so, these human cells, enslaved to the collective, continue to assault one another.

Generation 'П' repeatedly evokes the aggregate of Oranus—in multiple hypostases of the Babylonian divinity Enkidu and the biblical deity Baal. In the latter part of the book, Oranus reappears as a fat heavenly hulk (*zhirnaia nadmirnaia tushka*), an animalistic entity that Tatarsky imagines to be governing all human existence. The ruler of the world is a loathsome zoomorphic creature that toys with humans, amuses itself with the spectacle of their fruitless striving, and feeds off its prey.

OIL PEOPLE, OIL MONEY

Both *DPP(NN)* and *The Sacred Book of the Werewolf* unfold the idea of an all-encompassing, all-consuming, evil, deity-like power, and add the theme of oil to it. This theme is not just about the global commodity of oil; it is also another form of bio-morphosis, in which people are subsumed into the economic aggregate. Just as the parasitic bio-aggregate of Oranus consumes humans, eroding the independent human subject, humans are likened to oil as the biomass—source of energy—money in the process of total commodification and resource extraction.

With his characteristic predilection for punning, Pelevin quips that the prefix "petro" (in Russian place-names like Petrodvorets and Petropavlovsk) derives not from Emperor Peter the Great but from *petro-leum* (*EV* 64). As is the case with most bon mots by this writer, this is no empty wordplay. The principle of cultural break still obtains, though the moment is different: from Peter I's reforms, breaking with the past and attempting to remold Russia swiftly as part of the West, to the former Soviet Union's no less violent entrance into the global commodified space of a market economy.

Pelevin's *DPP(NN): The Dialectic of the Transitional Period from Nowhere to Nowhere* (*Dialektika perekhodnogo perioda iz niotkuda v nikuda,* 2003) elaborates his portrayal of degraded society, focusing on the consumption of the body politic and the past, and petro-leum specifically. *DPP(NN)* is a volume made up of one novel, one novella, and five short stories. It opens with the novel *Numbers* (*Chisla*), which picks up the biotic vision of *Generation 'П.'* Styopa Mikhailov, the protagonist, learns that people of antiquity used to sacrifice bulls to the gods, and so he burns canned beef left over from Soviet times, whose smell puts him in mind of the fiery Gehenna. These animal sacrifices evoke the humans turned into animalistic monads in the service of Oranus, and the fiery Gehenna echoes Enkidu's reign in the Tofet/Gehenna references in *Generation 'П.'* The burning of animals/humans (ritual sacrifice) alludes to oil and bio-morphism via oil. Simultaneously, the opening of *Numbers* initiates the problematic of consumption of the past to be developed over the course of the book. For Styopa, "grayish beef from strategic Soviet resources is but packaging left from a living force dispersed long ago" (*DPP(NN)* 9–10).[11]

The novella "The Macedonian Critique of French Thought" ("Makedonskaia kritika francuzskoi mysli") develops one more key element in Pelevin's biopolitical chain—a source of energy to be hunted for, specifically, petroleum.[12] The epigraph to the story reads: "The smell of petroleum prevails throughout." The narrative focuses on the life of Kika Nafikov, the Europeanized, Sorbonne-educated son of a late Soviet oil magnate. As a child, Kika draws an ominous-looking creature who holds a vessel with the outlines of the earth's continents above his head. A stream of black liquid pours from the vessel into the creature's mouth. Kika signs his drawing with "Papa is drinking the blood of the earth."

As Kika grows up, he is continuously entranced and shocked by the topic of oil. He learns that oil is not "the blood of the earth" but something like flammable humus that has formed from ancient living organisms. He experiences visions of extinct dinosaurs incarnated in oil, and produces drawings of cars, trains, and planes, all of which greedily consume "lines of tiny dinosaurs resembling plucked black chickens" (*DPP(NN)* 275). Troubled by

74

the question of where the souls of Soviet citizens go after their death, and having learned from his father that, according to Soviet belief, after they die people live on in the fruits of their labor, Kika envisions the victims of Stalinist purges in the place of dinosaurs as petroleum's organic compounds.

"The Macedonian Critique of French Thought" takes the notion of prehistoric animals transformed into oil, and projects it onto humans: human bodies as organic matter symbolically metamorphose into an energy source. In Kika's theory, oil and oil money are the forms in which the life force of Soviet citizens exists after their demise. With the collapse of the Soviet Union, communist oil enters the bloodstream of the world economy. The results are alarming. As demanded by multinational petroleum flows, Russian oil inundates the West, which is unprepared for the high "sulfur factor" of Russian oil or, in other words, the excess of human suffering concentrated in it. To protect the more peaceful Western civilization from this "infernal infusion," Kika resorts to diverting some of the human suffering in the form of oil money back to Russia. To accomplish this objective, he imprisons a group of Euro-citizens in a secret facility in France and subjects them to elaborate torture:

> In the factory workshop there were installed thirty-seven identical cells resembling an individual office workspace, the so-called cubicle. However, this workspace had neither a table nor a chair in it. The people placed in the cells hung there on special straps in a manner like that of stalled cattle. Their arms and legs were tied by leather straps to sticks driven into the concrete floor so that escape was impossible. . . . A robot, positioned exactly above one, would sharply whip his naked buttocks. Simultaneously, the computer would transfer 368 euros to Russia. (*DPP(NN)* 296)

This "economy of suffering" that Kika inflicts on Euro-citizens to balance out the transnational flows of pain/currency parodies Baudrillard's book *Symbolic Exchange and Death*. As "The Macedonian Critique of French Thought" states explicitly, Kika's half-crazed ideas come to him under the influence of Baudrillard. The formula of the present relations between the former Soviet Union (a premodern, symbolic society) and the West (a productivist modern society) is an exchange of pain for money: "Someone with a spiritual vision will discern Gulag prisoners in torn quilted robes who roll their carts in the business quarters of the world capitals, and grin toothlessly from the windows of expensive shops" (*DPP(NN)* 284). "The Macedonian Critique of French Thought" suggests, however, that the valorization of sacrifice and waste that informs *Symbolic Exchange and Death* is misdirected. Even as premodern impulses seek to subvert the bourgeois values of utility and self-preservation, they harbor risky destructive tendencies. Not only does the narrative nod at the problematic implications of Baudrillard's theorizing, it also points out that, rather than providing alternatives to the capitalist values of production and exchange, symbolic exchange is in fact easily converted into the former.[13]

"The Macedonian Critique of French Thought" is patently grotesque, and yet it encapsulates Pelevin's key biomorphic and zoomorphic motifs. The lines of tiny dinosaurs that look like plucked chickens are auto-references to the chickens awaiting slaughter in "Hermit and Six Toes." The cells-cubicles in which people are tied like stalled cattle evoke Pelevin's vision of humans as biomass for Oranus-Enkidu, the "fat heavenly hulk" of *Generation 'П.'* The high sulfur factor of Soviet petroleum reckoned as the amount of suffering concentrated in it replays the demonic motifs of *Generation 'П,'* and specifically the fiery Gehenna.

Human beings and history are turned into "people oil" (*chelovekoneft'*) and "oil money" (*neftedollary*). In Kika's half-crazed (and Pelevin's playful) rendition of Marxism, the souls of Soviet citizens whose work supplied an economic basis for monetary currents return embodied in those same monetary currents. If pain is reckoned the main energy and currency of the former Soviet Union, as with any resource, it should alchemize into money in the post-Soviet commodified society. The past is transfigured into an energy source that fosters profits for petroleum corporations.

CONSUMPTION OF THE BODY POLITIC

Pelevin's *The Sacred Book of the Werewolf* (*Sviashchennaia kniga oborotnia*, 2004) develops the themes of biomorphic monstrosities (*Generation 'П'*) and the consumption of the body politic (*DPP(NN)*). One of the novel's initial chapters hearkens back to *Generation 'П'*'s vision of Oranus. The narrator, a were-fox named A Huli, alludes to the story of Baron Munchausen claiming to pull himself out of a bog by his own hair, and compares human existence to Munchausen suspended in a void, squeezing his genitalia and screaming in unbearable pain. So why, another character asks, does he not let himself fall if he is in so much pain? A Huli replies as follows:

> This is precisely why the social contract exists. . . . When six billion Munchausens squeeze the balls of their neighbors, the world is in no danger. . . . The more pain is inflicted on each one by someone else, the more pain he will inflict on the two people he is holding himself. And so on, six billion times. (*SKO* 45)

Like Oranus, A Huli's rendition of the social contract conveys the idea that the social superstructure is a bio-aggregate that enslaves humans. It har-

bors the looming presence of another monster behind it—Thomas Hobbes's
Leviathan (1651), the archetypal exposé of the social contract theory. Six
billion trapped humans comprising the social body invoke Abraham Bosse's
etching for the frontispiece of the first edition of *Leviathan*, in which the
body of a giant figure emerging from the landscape is composed of over
three hundred naked little humans.[14]

In A Huli's biting assessment of the social contract, the conditions of war
and suffering are not averted, as Hobbes would have predicted, but become
the very means to secure social stability. *Leviathan* advocates a strong central
government as the means to rescue the people from the "state of nature,"
which is a "war of all against all." In the state of nature, gain, safety, and repu-
tation are three forces driving humans, and every man has a right to everything, even to another's body. The Commonwealth curtails these individual
freedoms in order to secure the advantages of peace. Men "naturally love
liberty and dominion over others, and the introduction of that restraint upon
themselves, in which we see them live in Commonwealths, is the foresight of
their own preservation, and of a more contented life thereby" (Hobbes, *Leviathan*, 129). *The Sacred Book of the Werewolf* certainly features the loss of
freedom, but without "a more contented life." Six billion Munchausens just
hang there in the void, torturing one another to ensure that none escapes.

Like everyone else in the novel, the narrator A Huli participates in
the chain of consumption. She is a hybrid between human and animal, a
2,000-year-old were-fox who works as a prostitute in post-Soviet Moscow. A
Huli employs her tail to hypnotize her clients, bewitching them into thinking
they have sex with her, and feeding off their sexual fantasies. In her spare
time she indulges in chicken-hunting—not to wring the chicken's neck and
consume it, but to experience a supra-physical transformation, with the
chicken as a living catalyst that helps her achieve it. A Huli meets and falls
in love with another in-between, the werewolf Sasha Sery, who is a general
in the secret police.

In the climactic episode of the novel, the two were-creatures travel to
the North of Russia, where A Huli witnesses Sasha howling at the ancient
cracked skull of a cow (this act draws oil from exhausted oil wells). She attempts to render Sasha's howls in human language:

Brindled cow! Do you hear, brindled cow? I know I must have lost all sense
of shame to ask you for oil yet again. I do not ask for it. We do not deserve
it. I know what you think of us—no matter how much you give them, Little
Khavroshka won't get a single drop, it will all be gobbled up by all these kukis-
yukises, yupsi-poopses and the other locusts who obscure the very light of
day. You are right, brindled cow, that is how it will be. Only, let me tell you
something . . . I know who you are. You are everyone who lived here before

us. Parents, grandparents, great-grandparents, and before that, and before that . . . You are the soul of all those who have died believing in the happiness that would come in the future. And now see, it has come. The future in which people do not live for something else, but for themselves. And do you know how we feel swallowing sashimi that smell of oil and pretending not to notice the last ice-floes melting under our feet? (*SKO* 252)

Moved, A Huli joins in the ritual of begging for oil, the cow's skull starts oozing tears, and the oil flows again.

The howling-for-oil episode dramatizes the relentless exploitation and resource extraction (oil, non-humans, and humans are equally resources here) that take place in the post-Soviet period. The brindled cow comes from the Russian fairy tale "Little Khavroshechka" ("Kroshechka-Khavroshechka"). The story's animal does all the impossible jobs assigned to little Khavroshechka by her wicked stepmother and stepsisters. The stepsisters spy on Khavroshechka, and her stepmother orders the cow to be slaughtered. The cow asks the girl not to eat her meat and to bury her bones in the garden. An apple tree with golden leaves grows out of the bones, Khavroshechka picks up an apple and gets her Prince Charming. Now, however, all the apples are gone. A Huli also finds it strange that the wicked stepmother and stepsisters in the fairy tale weren't punished but were simply forgotten about (an analogue to post-Soviet injustices).

In a continuation of "The Macedonian Critique of French Thought" which imagines the victims of Stalinist purges to be oil's organic components, bovine remains (that is, human victims of the past) are used up even as dead matter. The brindled cow stands for "everyone who lived here before us." It "is an important symbol evoking the ancestor cult and the cult of the fertile earth. . . . It is of course Russia—more precisely, its totem" (Lipovetskii, *Paralogii*, 653). A Huli sees in this fairy tale the essence of Russian history, the final cycle of which she had just witnessed, a story of dying meekly under the knife, to be reborn as a magical tree (of golden apples, oil, and money). The North, formerly the territory of the Gulag, is where the Russian oil industry is concentrated. Playing with multiple senses of the word *vyshki*, as watchtowers in prison camps, as death sentences, and as oil derricks, *The Sacred Book of the Werewolf* portrays a perverted mourning ritual which not only does not acknowledge the guilt before the victims of the Gulag, but calls upon the victims of this era, and, more generally, of the country's violent history, to contribute to monetary flows.

Like "The Macedonian Critique of French Thought," the howling-for-oil episode of *The Sacred Book of the Werewolf* presents the human collective as biomass that is exploited even posthumously. The post-Soviet status quo searches for a usable past—usable not in any abstract sense that critics would ascribe to the word, but literally—utilized. The novel imagines the recycling of historical and cultural consciousness as the past's transformation into black liquid—oil. The metaphorical connection between oil and the past is based on an analogy between natural and historical resources. Ancient, hidden natural riches (oil) become symbolic of the historical heritage, the riches of culture and memory, the meanings of history. Russia's collective identity is up for sale. The new consumer culture ousts Soviet ideology, but the basic mechanism of extraction is anything but reversed—it is improved upon. People die—decompose—turn into an energy source—and are sold (profitably or otherwise).

In the country's circular historical time, one round of violence follows upon another. However, if the victims of the past harbored illusions about the meaningfulness of their travail, Pelevin's post-Soviet moment demonstrates that no meaning can be assigned to the country's violent history.[15] In Pelevin's words: "God-seeking is when the best people are horrified by the sight of blood on the axe and start seeking God, and the result is that a hundred years and sixty million corpses later they get a slightly improved credit rating" (*SKO* 12). The future presents itself as even more menacing than the past, for the ossified remnants of the body politic are devoured posthumously, recycled as it were, for the nth, and evidently final, time.

The Sacred Book of the Werewolf, like *Generation 'П'* and *DPP(NN)*, portrays the human collective as a system of organisms that consume each other in the basic biological sense of the word. People become cattle—biomass—energy—money. The image of the brindled cow correlates with the broiler chickens bred for slaughter at the bio-factory in "Hermit and Six Toes," the canned beef in *Numbers*, and the inmates of Kika's secret facility in "The Macedonian Critique of French Thought," who are kept in their stalls like cattle. The name Nefteperegon'evsk itself plays on Skotoprigon'evsk in *The Brothers Karamazov*, linking oil (*neft'*) and cattle (*skot*).

In its turn, *Generation 'П'*'s "fat heavenly hulk" becomes "upper rat":

> The elite here is divided into two branches, which are called "kh . . . sosaeiti" (a distorted *"high society"*) and "apparat" (a distorted *"upper rat"*). "Kh . . . so-saeti" is the business community groveling to authorities who can close down any business at any moment, since business here is inseparable from theft. And "apparat" is the power that feeds on the kickbacks from business. . . . At the same time, there are no clear boundaries between these two branches of power—one smoothly flows into the other, giving rise to a single immense fat rat preoccupied with greedy self-service. (*SKO* 103)

"Upper rat," a bilingual pun on *apparat* (the government apparatus), is another parasitic bio-aggregate that greedily feeds off the oil pipe.

The problem of unbridled resource extraction is sharpened in a series of echoes of fairy tales and children's books. The "money tree," an allusion to the magical apple tree from "Little Khavroshechka" and to Alexei Tolstoy's *The Little Golden Key, or Buratino's Adventures* (1936), turns into a blazing fountain of oil in Pelevin's novel.[16] The tree is a perverted biblical Burning Bush that "does not look the way it was imagined by the light-minded fiction writers of the previous century" and "does not bear golden ducats in the Field of Miracles." Instead "it grows through the icy crust of frozen soil with a blazing fountain of petroleum, a bush like that which spoke to Moses" (*SKO* 240).

Herself striving to escape the predator-prey cycle, A Huli nevertheless becomes complicit in converting people into oil and oil money. As she comes to realize, Sasha makes of her a new false Khavroshechka, an ancient were-fox pretending to be an innocent young girl. She has a feeling that Sasha "showed her to the skull in the role of Khavroshechka." Does she guess right? Sasha grins: "And why not? You are so touching." But "what kind of Khavroshechka am I?" objects A Huli. Sasha does not care. "And if you are Mary Magdalene, what difference does it make? I am a pragmatist. My business is to make the oil flow" (*SKO* 255). But, as Sasha's colleague in the secret police remarks, the reservoir, like the whole of Russia, is finally squeezed dry.

ENLIGHTENED BLOOD-SUCKING

Pelevin's *Empire V/Ampir V: The Novel about a Real Superman* (*Empire V/ Ampir V: Roman o nastoiashchem sverkhcheloveke*, 2006) develops one more extended biopolitical parable, which both reprises and reworks the imagery and the ideas discussed above. In the now familiar Pelevinian chain of humans—animals—biomass—energy—money, the novel substitutes blood for oil. The running theme of blood-sucking, prefigured in *The Life of Insects* (the mosquito-cum-businessman Sam Sucker), and in "The Macedonian Critique of French Thought" with Kika's father "drinking the blood of the earth," is one on which the entire plot of *Empire V* hinges.

Empire V makes explicit the parallel between blood and petroleum as facets of the wider paradigm of consumption. Blood circulates in the human body just as oil and money circulate in the body of the global economy; oil is "black liquid" and "the black blood of the earth"; and blood, in politically correct terms, is termed "red liquid." The golden goddess Ishtar with whom Tatarsky is united at the conclusion of *Generation 'П'* now reappears as the Great Bat, the goddess of the vampires governing the world.[17]

Empire V is an anonymous vampire dictatorship into which Roman

Shtorkin, a nineteen-year-old Muscovite, is initiated. In another nod in the direction of "The Macedonian Critique of French Thought," a long time ago vampires feasted on the blood of the dinosaurs. In the present day, vampires no longer drink blood unless they need information about its carrier. Like A Huli, with her updated manner of chicken-hunting, which avoids slaughter whenever possible but draws on the energy of her victims, neoliberal vampires have converted to a more peaceful form of feeding off humans—they no longer suck blood, but instead feed upon an addictive substance, *bablos* (another word for "money" in criminal argot).

Once more, biocoenosis underlies Pelevin's socio-metaphysical vision. Having transformed their own essence into *iazyk* ("tongue" and "language"), vampires have switched from the "meat industry" (*miasnoe zhivotnovodstvo*) to a "dairy industry" (*molochnoe zhivotnovodstvo*). In the new civilized version of the food chain, the rulers of the world milk humans for *bablos*, a concentrate of money or, rather, the vital human energy expended in the pursuit of money:

> Please do not think I am gloating, but the modern office workspace—the cubicle—even visually resembles a cattle stall. Only instead of a conveyor with food, a monitor stands before the office proletarian and food is presented in digital form. What is being made in the stall? The answer is so apparent that it has entered the most diverse of languages. Humans make money. He or she makes money. . . . Money is extracted from his time and force. His life energy, received from the air, sunlight, and other living impressions, turns into money. . . . Humans think they make money for themselves. But in reality they make money out of themselves. (*EV* 176–77)

Vampires disseminate deception and prey upon the populace's vital biological energies in the furtherance of their own biological interests. The principles used are those of factory farming. The human livestock in urban life are raised at a high density, with the objective of producing the highest output at the lowest cost by exchanging the simulacra of goods for genuine bio-resources. Degraded humans are caught in the process of propagating the money supply regardless of their need, will, or understanding. Exuding vital energy in their pursuit of money-based stimulation, human cattle produce money not for themselves but from themselves—as the very idiom "to make money" (*delat' den'gi*, calqued from English) brings home.

Hooked on simulations, human biomass expends its natural vitality to feed the vampire rulers. Rather than people using money for their own ends, the money supply, in a stark reversal, reproduces itself by means of humans. Money is no longer an equivalent of utility. Indeed, people are bred by vampires expressly to produce money, for they are the only species that possess both mind A: a receptor of sense data, and mind B: a generator of fantasies. Mind B serves as an object for mind A, so that humans are incapable of distinguishing between real goods (food, drink, land) and fantasies (simulacra of fashion and prestige).

In a neo-Marxian turn, *Empire V* outlines the differences between exchange value and utility—vampires control human cattle by enhancing glamour, the added value of the product. In the course of the novel, Roman— or Rama, as he is now called—learns "glamour" (*glamur*) and "discourse" (*diskurs*), the two skills necessary for a vampire to milk humans. Glamour perpetuates a pseudo-Darwinian (inasmuch as it is divorced from genuine necessity) struggle for existence, triggering a mechanism of social desire— the imperative to always consume and never be satisfied. The capitalist stimulation of desire is not a result of natural evolutionary processes, but one of directed breeding.[18]

Pelevin plays with the binary opposition between a barbaric premodern version of the social contract and a postmodern neoliberal version (Foucault's sovereign power and power of discipline versus biopolitics). A militant totalitarian state with governmental tyranny exercised through crude force (the meat industry) has yielded to an apparently less carceral techno-consumer system (the dairy industry). In this implosive characterization, control is now carried out covertly, not through physical and psychological torture, but through an all-encompassing social conditioning that revs up the human desire for material acquisition. This latter variety of manipulation is more subtle and therefore more effective.

It is not just the post-Soviet body politic that gets reduced in this way to biomass, but the global community at large. If "Hermit and Six Toes" still tends to be read as a parable of (late) Soviet society, Pelevin's subsequent biopolitical narratives portray a dehumanization that transcends national boundaries. Whether it is dead Soviet citizens turned into "people oil," Euro-citizens strapped like cattle in their stalls, people-cells of Oranus, six billion Munchausens, or human livestock brainwashed by glamour and discourse, society is conceived as a collection of human biomass that is milked around the world.

∗ ∗ ∗

As Aleksandr Genis points out, Pelevin's works such as "Hermit and Six Toes," "The Problem of the Werewolf in the Middle Region" ("Problema vervolka v srednei polose," 1991), and *The Life of Insects* engage animal protagonists as a facet of his key motif of transformation, of crossing over from one reality to something different:

If, during the Soviet era, Socialist Realism portrayed men as demigods, now, in the post-Soviet era, they are half-men, half-beasts. The beast, with its primal otherness or alterity, fits into the agenda of the post-Soviet writer. This complementary alterity turns the metaphysical quest into an inverse direction to the usual one—not upwards but downwards along the evolutionary ladder. . . . Pelevin frequently turns to animals, which enables him to populate yet another limit, namely that of the border between species. (Genis, "Borders and Metamorphoses," 301)

In this respect, Pelevin's biomorphic and zoomorphic imagery fulfills its traditional role, with individual animals juxtaposed (either likened or contrasted) to human beings. Thus, the chickens engage in teacher-disciple philosophical disquisitions, and so does the moth Mitya with his alter ego Dima—activities one would hardly expect from these nonhuman protagonists.

Yet Pelevin's stories do not so much project human vices onto the animal kingdom in the spirit of Jean de La Fontaine or Ivan Krylov's fables, as point out an essential bestiality that lies at the core of the human condition. While one can look at "Hermit and Six Toes" or *The Life of Insects* as traditional animal fables, tales in which the characters think like people and look like animals, more engagingly, these early stories portray characters who look like people but act like animals. Such a portrayal downplays or outright denies personal self-determination, reason, and ethical personality.[19]

Zoomorphic and biomorphic tropes may carry both positive and negative connotations. Thus, classic modernist dystopias privilege animalistic instincts, seeking an alternative to the sterility of the state in the wilderness beyond (for instance, Zamyatin's Mephies). Buddhism, which is important to Pelevin, likewise promotes a naturalist model of integration with nature. While Pelevin's own biomorphic and zoomorphic imagery can be both positive and negative, the specific kind of biomorphism I consider here, the social system as biocoenosis, carries dark implications.

The theme of social change leading to regression, devolution, and animalism recalls writings of the post-revolutionary period by authors such as Zamyatin. In both post-revolutionary and post-Soviet contexts, the trope of dehumanization (*raschelovechivanie*) is mobilized as a response to drastic social change. In Zamyatin's "The Cave" ("Peshchera," 1922), Martyn Martynych, a refined, Scriabin-loving member of the intelligentsia, steals wood from his neighbor in order to provide a day of warmth for his dying wife and himself. Overstepping his ethical barriers, Martyn Martynich feels himself degraded into an ape-like predatory creature who is forced to fight other animals for survival.[20] Regressive metamorphosis also features in the post-revolutionary writings of Andrey Platonov such as *The Foundation Pit* (*Kot-*

lovan, 1930), as well as in the Strugatsky brothers' works such as *Roadside Picnic* (*Piknik na obochine*, 1972), in which the protagonist's daughter mutates under the influence of an alien Zone. In the post-Soviet period, many Russian authors, in a variety of fictional and nonfictional genres, have expressed acute concern over the processes of dehumanization (biological and social) in the global community.

Zoomorphic and biomorphic imagery has enabled writers in both the East and West to probe problems of freedom and its lack. Franz Kafka's zoomorphic tales like "A Report to the Academy" (1917) and "Investigations of a Dog" (1922) are akin to Pelevin's works insofar as they portray the animal protagonist's bewilderment in the world as analogous to human bewilderment in an enigmatic and threatening universe. However, Kafka's zoomorphic imagery does not move from the micro level (an individual beast/human) to the macro level (society). A novel like Kurt Vonnegut's *Slaughterhouse-Five* (1969) explores the issue of free will using a slaughterhouse as his setting. The Wachowskis' film trilogy, *The Matrix* (1999–2002), portrays humans as enslaved by machines and turned into their bio-resource, and in this sense comes close to Pelevin's oeuvre.

In his mature works, Pelevin dispenses with allegory and directly presents humanity as a zoomorphic community that is ripe for exploitation. In the consumer realm, humans possess consciousness (if any) merely as an instrument for the satisfaction of needs, and thus in effect revert to an animal-like state. Such a regressive metamorphosis captures the degrading effects of social crises and political oppression.

But Pelevin's mature biopolitical narratives go beyond portraying humans as animals (for example, office "cattle") that consume and are consumed; rather, they present the social structure itself as essentially animalistic—a network of organisms feeding upon and being fed upon. At its limit, the society becomes a monstrous bio-aggregate. As a trope of animalistic dehumanization, an entity like Oranus possesses a particularly rich metaphoric potential. It suggests standardization, simplification, and the absorption of the human subject by the system, but on a novel, all-encompassing scale, and thus captures the totalizing effects of the global techno-consumer village.

The population, a living biomass displaying specific biomedical traits (Foucault), becomes just that in Pelevin—cattle, oil people, vampire livestock. In one of the writer's favorite devices, that of the realized metaphor, the werewolf Sasha Sery, a general in the secret police, is a literal "werewolf in shoulder straps" (*oboroten' v pogonakh*), a term taken from the campaign against corruption among the police. Pelevin's plots often make idiomatic expressions real—for example, in the story where the five-legged apocalyptic dog Pizdets realizes the expression "needed as a dog needs a fifth leg" (*nuzhen kak sobake piataia noga*). Pelevin's biopolitical fantasies reify the biomorphic rhetoric of theory.

Treating humans as animals is one form of dehumanization, and the conversion of humans into monsters might be the next step,[21] but presenting society at large as a biomorphic monstrosity is still more radical. The replacement of a more conventional image of social reductionism—the human being as a cog in the machine—by biomorphic imagery suggests the more organic and more pernicious modus operandi of the techno-consumer social structure.[22] Pelevin's biotic schemes capture a general zeitgeist, a sense of political disempowerment and disillusion with social structures in an increasingly menacing and incomprehensible world. Human agency, both individual and collective, is undermined. Pelevin's narratives highlight the de-individualized status of the human being in contemporaneity and buttress his diagnosis of the collapse of spirituality under rampant consumerism and covert but nonetheless efficient modes of social control.

Pelevin's biopolitics also sheds light on the question of teleology; that is, a directive principle behind the system, an issue with which the writer has been concerned throughout his oeuvre. Attributing the causes of major historical events, especially traumatic ones, to the behind-the-scenes activity of a powerful elite is a staple of the postmodern imagination—dramatized, for instance, in Jorge Luis Borges's story "Tlön, Uqbar, Orbis Tertius" (1940), Thomas Pynchon's *The Crying of Lot 49* (1966), and Umberto Eco's *Foucault's Pendulum* (1988). It comes as no surprise, then, that in many instances Pelevin conjures a dark agency behind the system's workings (Chaldeans, werewolves, vampires).[23]

Yet the relegation of agency to a conspiratorial, supernatural, or hidden source is just as often undermined in Pelevin's writings, as is the case with the eye in the triangle on the one-dollar bill that sees nothing, or in Tatarsky's search for a superpower governing reality that ultimately falls back upon himself. In light of Pelevin's biomorphic imaginary, no super-force (sentient or otherwise) is even necessary to transform people into primitive consuming organisms. Humans may have escaped from the biological community, but human society itself is animalistic through and through. As long as the enslaving social structure possesses the self-perpetuating properties of Oranus, no ghosts need apply to bring on the posthuman condition.

The aggregation concept carries dark metaphysical implications, suggesting a lack of agency on the part of humans. Even so, given his predilection for biomorphic transposition, Pelevin does not absolve humans of responsibility. On the micro level, the protagonists of Pelevin's tales themselves bring their worlds into being. As Ishtar's husband, Tatarsky dreams up this world, and the goddess herself (a reification of a greed-driven existence) comes into being through his dreams. Similarly, Roman Shtorkin's childhood memories of a fan in the form of a heart looking like a gigantic vampire bat uncannily foreshadow and perhaps determine the entire plot of the vampire dictatorship. In Pelevin's early story "Vera Pavlovna's Ninth Dream" ("Deviatyi son Very Pavlovny," 1991), the question of whether post-Soviet changes are imminent (external) or immanent (internal) is resolved in favor of the latter.

Empire V forcefully restates the key idea of *Generation 'Π,'* that the anti-Russian conspiracy implicates every Russian adult, and, furthermore, it problematizes the clear-cut predator-prey relationship within the global habitat: "Every room is responsible for itself. It can invite God. And it can invite your company [vampires]" (*EV* 373). Or as the Strugatsky brothers, an eminent presence in Pelevin's oeuvre, have put it, how have people "become so much like beasts [*oZVEReli*]?"

Can Digital Men Think?

> The real problem is not whether machines
> think, but whether men do.
> —B. F. Skinner, *Contingencies of Reinforcement*

RASCHELOVECHIVANIE (an equivalent of "dehumanization") is a term that has grown popular in recent Russian scholarly, journalistic, and literary discourses. Olga Sedakova's statement is representative of the wider trend: "The West has moved away from the classical humanist interest" and "what happens to us in the present is called 'dehumanitarianization' [*degumanitarizatsiia*] . . . that means 'dehumanization' [*raschelovechivanie*]. Culture, as Y. M. Lotman said, is not transferred biologically" (quoted in Galaninskaia, "Babochka letaet").

In contrast to the post-Nietzschean and post-Foucauldian problematization of classic humanism and a strongly pronounced, though not unanimous, welcoming of posthumanism in the West, in the Russian context posthumanism tends to be conceptualized in negative terms, as the denaturing of humankind. Contemporary Russian authors, in a variety of fictional and nonfictional genres, express acute concerns with the processes of dehumanization in the global community.

When it comes to the problem of *raschelovechivanie* in post-Soviet fiction, Pelevin's work is the first that comes to mind. In a manner peculiar to this artist—playful yet with razor-sharp insights—his biotic schemes probe the problem of unfreedom in post-Soviet Russia and the world at large. Even as Pelevin questions conventional conceptualizations of humankind and examines the decentering of human agency by biopolitical processes, he views posthumanity in negative terms.

This chapter focuses on Pelevin's depictions of technology and the ways he imagines the transformative relations between humans and machines. Like his animalistic metamorphosis (humans turned into animals/biomass/source of energy/money), his take on mechanistic metamorphosis (humans turned into machines) attends to the issues of dehumanization and unfreedom. Both the animalistic and mechanistic versions of dehumaniza tion allow Pelevin to raise probing questions about the quality of freedom in the post-Soviet domain and beyond.

Though trained as an engineer and possessing a markedly up-to-date knowledge of high tech, Pelevin displays a wary attitude toward technological progress. Whereas his biopolitical narratives present the degradation of human life to livestock ready for consumption, his narratives of technology dramatize the de-individuating, free will- and consciousness-suppressing effects of the electronic age on the human psyche. Biology dictates through instincts and the iron demands of adaptation to the environment. Men-machines are programmable, and so they are predictable and controllable. Not only are they emotionally desensitized and socially depersonalized, but if the human brain acts like a computer, it will have no choice but to comply with the controlling user's commands. The humanist's older fear was that technology might take over the decisions of free individuals. A more recent but equally potent worry addressed in Pelevin's texts is that contemporary dependence on technology and total commodification makes humans themselves automaton-like and so easy targets of societal control. Still more radically, he suggests that perhaps humans never possessed freedom of will in the first place.

Pelevin's ruminations on these issues follow a clear trajectory. "The Prince of Gosplan" ("Prints gosplana," 1991), from his first short-story collection, *The Blue Lantern*, begins looking into the relationship between humans and technology via the world of computer games. The story "Akiko," from the collection *DPP(NN)*, and the novel *The Helmet of Horror* (2005) are about an internet porn site and a chat room, respectively, and observe problematic effects of the human-computer interface. *Generation 'Π'* portrays the zombified Homo Zapiens of contemporaneity, while *Empire V* takes things a step further by suggesting that humans were created (designed) as machines from the start. Finally, *Pineapple Water for the Beautiful Lady* (2010) and *S.N.U.F.F.* (2011) focus on military robotics and artificial intelligence, probing still more deeply the problems of human mind, consciousness, and will. These works ask: What makes humans quintessential biorobots? Why, rather than artificial intelligence rising to the level of natural human intelligence, has human intelligence been degraded to the level of the subhuman or the machine?

Pelevin's portrayal of technology shows its impact becoming more and more entrenched in the world of contemporaneity. His scenarios move from individual interactions with computers, to the media and businesses using high tech, to all of society getting involved in high tech, and then to higher-order conceptual questions about technology, human consciousness, and free will (and its lack). While some of these elements have been present in Pelevin's work for the entire time, in his later texts the implications of technology are more sweeping, and the stakes are higher.

Pelevin's texts envision posthumanism as a form of mechanistic, bio-logical, and social degeneration. The texts destabilize the boundaries of what it means to be human, but, more importantly, they pinpoint the de-intellectualizing, coercive, and unethical forces of global contemporaneity. Blurring the lines between humans, machines, and animals, they find the arrival of the posthuman no cause for celebration. From this vantage point, even though Western accusations against humanism may be weighty, there is an ethical necessity to save the concept of the human.

CYBERSPACE, LEVEL ONE

"The Prince of Gosplan" launches the theme of computer technology and the effects of the human-computer interaction in Pelevin's oeuvre. The story depicts one workday in the life of Sasha, an employee at the late Soviet gov-ernmental agency Gossnab. At his computer console, Sasha is immersed in his favorite game, *Prince of Persia*. Though he is only a minor staff member, in virtual reality Sasha assumes the role of a valiant prince who must over-come many challenging obstacles as the game progresses from level one to level twelve to reach the princess.

Pelevin's narrative purposefully blurs the boundaries between the everyday and the virtual realms, problematizing the question of the "real."[1] Details from computer games infiltrate everyday existence and vice versa. For Sasha and his colleagues who play computer games at their worksta-tions, life in late 1980s Moscow and the virtual reality of gaming are well-nigh indistinguishable.[2] In a contamination of one cognitive mode by an-other, the gamer projects his mindset onto the everyday.[3] As Sasha travels from Gossnab to Gosplan, he perceives Moscow as akin to the labyrinth in *Prince of Persia* and takes something as pedestrian as a subway turnstile for the deadly body-scissors from the game. As he takes the escalator in the Moscow subway on an errand for his boss, the body-scissors from *Prince of Persia* switch on ahead of him. Hearing the familiar clanking sound, he turns cold from fear. He looks up and sees "two sheets of steel with sharp-toothed edges that clash together every few seconds with such force that the sound is like a blow on a small church bell" (*VPE* 175). On this same trip, Sasha intuits (with a hunch born of obsessive playing) that "some-where in the vicinity there must be another jar, and he decides to look for it" (*VPE* 179).

From an ontological and epistemological point of view, cyberspace exemplifies solipsism—Pelevin's perennial problematic. As "The Prince of Gosplan" states: "There is no such thing as the way everything 'really is'" (*VPE* 216–17). The body-scissors exist only for Sasha. The other passengers all pass through them with no disturbance, but for him "it was as real as anything can be real: he had a long ugly scar running the full length of his back, and on that occasion the body-scissors had barely touched him" (*VPE* 175). The obstacle is as real (or unreal) as one's subjective perceptions make it. Hence, when a temporary consultant from Penza who shares office space with Sasha is "blown up" by a whirlwind of fire in the game *Starglider*, Sasha pulls back instinctively, but quickly realizes that nothing can happen to him. After all, it is not his game.

Compared to Pelevin's mature depictions of virtual reality, the story's virtual spaces are relatively benign. And yet "The Prince of Gosplan" already contains, in succinct form, some of Pelevin's darker insights into the effects of the computer-generated virtuality. Even while computer games provide a respite from the drab existence Sasha and his coworkers lead as minor employees in perestroika-era Moscow, they condition a particular kind of reductive behaviorism in the course of play that extends beyond the bounds of the game. These games reward a correct reaction to stimuli, cultivating reflexes that reduce intellectual activity to a minimum. Even outside the game's bounds, Sasha responds to stimuli in a manner that is rigidly and absurdly programmed: a jar is to be grabbed, a wall is to be jumped toward, a stone is to be tugged at. His actions turn machine-like (or, in terms of behaviorism, rat-like)—they become predictable automatic responses.[4]

Not only does the human-computer interface encourage a mechanization of behavior, but the human subject merges with the game, disappearing into it. At one point, Sasha asks Petya Itakin what happens to the people who are playing, that is, where does the person who controls the prince (in *Prince of Persia*) go to? Itakin, in turn, wants to know who was beating his head against the wall and jumping up and down at level twelve, him or the prince. Sasha's initial unhesitating response is "The prince, of course. I can't jump like that." But when Itakin poses his next question—"And where were you all that time?"—Sasha stumbles and falls silent (*VPE* 217). For the duration of the game Sasha's personality merges with, and is ruled by, the simulacra on the screen.

By the time Sasha/the prince reaches the final level of the game, the reader realizes that the relatively benign illusions of *Prince of Persia* are just plain lies. The princess that Sasha reaches at level twelve turns out to be made of junk: her head is a dried pumpkin, her eyes and mouth are glued on, her arms and legs are cardboard. When Sasha/his avatar, enraged by the deception, lashes out at her with his foot, the princess simply falls apart into a heap of garbage. The virtual space of *Prince of Persia* proves to be brazenly false.

The issue of truth versus falsehood would seem beside the point, given that "there is no such thing as the way everything 'really is'"—but this is actually crucial. As critics have suggested, post-Soviet narratives foreground epistemological hesitation, oscillating between alternate realities. In Aleksandr Genis's formulation:

> Post-Soviet authors have come to see the world around them in terms of a sequence of artificial constructs, in which man is forever doomed to search for a "pure," "archetypal" reality. All these parallel worlds are not "true," without being "false" either, at least while someone still believes in them. ("Borders and Metamorphoses," 67)

However, given that Pelevin, true to the spirit of postmodernism, questions "authenticity" per se and overthrows the conventional hierarchy of real and unreal, his works suggest not an indifferent array of alternate realities but an assemblage of parallel worlds, some more conducive to the life of the spirit than others. All are simulacra, but some are more vulgar and carceral simulacra than others.

"The Prince of Gosplan" highlights a problem that is crucial for Pelevin—that of unfreedom, or, in terms of the computer discourse that pervades the story, the issue of the "controlling user":

> "You see"—said Petya—"If the figure [of the prince] has been working in State Supply for a long time, then for some reason it starts thinking that it is looking at the screen, although it is only running across it. And anyway, if a cartoon character could look at something, the first thing he would notice would be whoever was looking at him." (*VPE* 199)

Sasha appears to control the prince in the game, but what if, the story is asking, he and all other humans are themselves puppets being manipulated by shadowy coercive forces?

The short story "Akiko" describes virtual space as not only false but as outright malicious, and brings to the foreground the problem of humans controlled from behind the screen. In this story, an anonymous visitor to a paid porn site engages in dialogue with the virtual prostitute Akiko. The dainty Akiko is stylized after a geisha, and the site presents the facsimile of a Japanese house of prostitution in its exotic trappings. Although the visitor attempts to hide his identity under the generic log-in ITSUKEN (the first six letters on the Russian keyboard), Akiko, that is, the owners/creators of the site, quickly locates him via his IP address and Mastercard transactions. As Akiko gets access to vital information about her virtual lover, she becomes openly aggressive and manipulative. She extorts money from him, demanding that he pay for various additional features of the porn site, and threatens him with a humiliating exposure of his sexual proclivities if he does not comply with her demands: "You think we do not understand here what kind of ITSUKEN you are? IP address 211. 56.67.4, Mastercard 5101 2486 0000 4051. You think we won't be able to learn?" (*DPP(NN)* 318).

In this story's diagnosis, the internet, a vehicle for information and communication, turns out to be a vehicle for pornography and advertising as well as a powerful means of surveillance and control. The user who navigates the porn site is observed in an Orwellian manner (but with computers instead of telescreens) by the hosts of this segment of cyberspace. Akiko's speech in the later part of the story resembles the crude turns of phrase that a Stalin-era NKVD man might have used during an interrogation. At one point Akiko directly mentions "the fifth chief ministry" (*piatoe glavnoe upravlenie*), that is, the fifth ministry of the KGB (*DPP(NN)* 317). The implications are clear. The site's visitor is now at the mercy of his hosts, and they proceed to fleece him. Reversing the initial power dynamic, they have him "screwed" by Akiko (i.e., themselves): "So, you are not satisfied . . . Up! Down! Up! Down! Up! Down! Did you get it all, you shit?" (*DPP(NN)* 318). The trapped computer user is forced to click the mouse continuously to make Akiko "moan" lest he lose his money. The rat (mouse) race goes on.

A MIGHTY MAZE! BUT NOT WITHOUT A PLAN

Pelevin's *The Helmet of Horror: The Myth of Theseus and the Minotaur* (*Shlem uzhasa: Kreatiff o Tesee i Minotavre*, 2005) develops the themes of false reality and internet manipulation that were probed in "The Prince of Gosplan" and "Akiko." But the novel dives deeper into the ways that modern computer technologies transform the basic structures of human personality and communication.[5] A motley group of characters—Ariadne, the intellectual Monstradamus, gluttonous Organism, cynical Nutscracker, amorous Romeo-y-Cohiba and IsoldA, devout UGLI 666, and the drunkard Sliff-zoSSchitan—are locked in nondescript hotel-like rooms at unidentified locales. Like, for example, Douglas Coupland's heroes, these characters live in cyberspace and spotlight current social diseases like overeating, unrestrained libido, unthinking conformity, and so on.

The plot unfolds as the protagonists try to find out where they are and who has them trapped in this manner, and why. Their only way to communicate is via an internet chat room. The difficulty of exchanging information is intensified by the fact that the chat room moderator edits data at will. For instance, the moderator removes specific personal details about the participants and their locales. It turns out that the characters are all imprisoned in the famed mythical labyrinth roamed by the Minotaur. They dread the Minotaur's appearance and await deliverance by Theseus.

The Helmet of Horror is a baroque work even by the standards of Pelevin's typically intricate fantasies. Perhaps in part due to this, interpretations of it have tended to be impressionistic and oftentimes at cross-purposes. Maya Kucherskaia suggests that, except for the drunkard Sliff, all the other characters are unreal, and "all of the play turns out to be a hangover delirium." Lev Danilkin sees all eight characters as "Pelevin's auto-portrait drawn Picasso-style from deformed fragments" ("Shlem uzhasa"), while Alexey Vernitsky argues that the span of time depicted in the book runs prior to the birth of a human into the world, with the characters embodying that human's various traits. For Pavel Basinsky "the internet is a labyrinth where the Minotaur capable of gobbling us up lives, but in reality the Minotaur lives in ourselves. Get rid of your Minotaur, and the internet will become an ordinary informational and communication instrument" ("Uzhas shlema"). Filip Kataev interprets the computer worlds in works like *The Helmet of Horror* as "a universal metaphor of another, virtual, materially nonexistent reality that he tirelessly describes in his texts as the only authentic one" ("Semantika i funktsii," 166).

In my reading, Pelevin rewrites the classical Greek myth not to suggest that the internalized Minotaur is fallaciously identified with the internet, but to employ cyberspace again as a proxy for the solipsism—albeit a degraded one—to be transcended on the path to authentic being. Each character is trapped in his or her own consciousness, as much as in the labyrinth of the World Wide Web, aka the "helmet of horror." Solipsistically imprisoned in their own minds, they cannot reach out to the others. But this ontological and epistemological uncertainty existing at the core of the human condition is amplified under the conditions of a high-tech, increasingly virtualized world. While the internet functions as a proxy for solipsism, internet technologies are exposed for their manipulation of consciousness, the ease of falsifying information, and the growing alienation among humans. That is, the internet in Pelevin's novel is by no means a metaphor for an authentic nonmaterial reality, but rather a metaphor for a worldly, mass-produced falsehood that ought to be broken through.

"Mythcellaneous," the introduction to *The Helmet of Horror* in the English version (absent in the Russian edition), defines progress as what has "brought us into these variously shaped and sized cubicles with glowing screens" (*The Helmet of Horror*, ix). At the novel's opening, the characters share via chat room that they haven't the slightest idea how they arrived in their locked cells, and they are monitored by someone who doesn't like it when they try to exchange concrete information about themselves. Ariadne initiates the discussion by opening the following *thread* (as well she should):

"I shall construct a labyrinth in which I shall lose myself together with anyone who tries to find me—who said this and about what?" (*SU* 7).

Ariadne and the others locked up in their cubicles in front of computer consoles exemplify the estrangement among humans that computer technologies nourish even as their corporate owners hype the benefits of social networking. The characters appear to exchange personal data, but any of it might be spurious, whether because the user is free to create any image he or she likes unconstrained by life's realities, or due to the moderator being free to edit any incoming data. So UGLI 666 posts: "my name is XXX, I am an XXX by profession, and an XXX by education," and Monstradamus notes that Ariadne "phenomenologically speaking, only exists in the form of messages of unknown origin signed 'Ariadne'" (*SU* 31, 40). And Monstradamus responds to Nutscracker's taunt "You don't understand the difference between a dream and reality?" with "But all I can see are letters on the screen" (*SU* 115). Any of these characters, whether in some attribute or in their totality, may be falsified online.

With an engineer's fondness for detail, Pelevin is not only interested in the concept of virtual falsification, but also in outlining the structure of the helmet of horror—the basic mechanism of dissimulation. It consists of the "frontal net," the "now grid," the "separator labyrinth," the "horns of plenty," and "Tarkovsky's mirror." The now grid divides the human brain into two parts, with the past in the upper section and the future in the lower section. The frontal net, heated by the impressions falling on it, transmits heat to the now grid. The grid transforms the past into vapor, and drives it up into the horns of plenty. The horns descend to the base of the helmet where the future is positioned, and there "bubbles of hope" arise and create the force of circumstances that induces the stream of impressions. This stream rushes and disperses against the net, renewing the cycle.

Importantly, the helmet-of-horror model of the human brain is *a machine.* Its generator mechanism instantiates a spurious separation of the internal and the external. That is, in engineering's idiom, it represents Pelevin's perennial problem of solipsism:

> Everything is produced out of nothing, that is, the place where the stream of impressions arises. And it's also the place where the past, present, and future are separated. . . . It's where "I" and "you," good and bad, right and left, black and white, so on and so forth arise. . . . The "inside" and "outside" . . . have no existence in themselves. . . . And the same applies to everything else as well. . . . We should never under any circumstances regard anything as real. The entire phenomenon is induced, like the electromagnetic field in a transformer. (*SU* 71–75)

The machine produces simulacra that are the basic foundations of human experience: a stream of impressions, the constructs of past, present, and future, and, ultimately, the illusion of the human subject itself.

Having described the brain as a machine and the human agent as a fake generated by this machine, *The Helmet of Horror* proceeds to investigate the issue of illusoriness where it is most acute—that is, under the conditions of high-tech contemporaneity, with cyberspace simulations and unbounded possibilities for the manipulation of consciousness. As virtual reality-savvy Nutscracker points out, cyberspace compels the human subject to make the requisite decision while maintaining that subject's conviction that such a choice is free.

As *The Helmet of Horror* demonstrates, the main task of cyberspace is coercive orientation. The Helmholtz or *Shlemil'*, the wearer of the virtual helmet, is manipulated by the behaviorist technique of conditioned reflexes.[6] Since everything seen in the virtual helmet is generated by a special computer program, the program can be set up in such a way that the Helmholtz makes a predetermined choice every time. The simplest external editing program is "Sticky Eye." For example, as Helmholtz turns his head, one of the vases in view gets stuck in his field of vision and lingers longer. Another technology is "Pavlov's Bitch."[7] When one looks at the vases that should not be chosen, one's vision gets blurry, and there is a buzzing in the ears or an electric shock. This is "a cheap technology for third-world countries" (*SU* 87). The obverse method is stimulation of the pleasure center when the correct choice is made. The Helmholtz's masters at one time had to insert an electrode in his brain, "but now it's done by pharmacological means or by entertaining the brain to delta rhythms" (*SU* 88).

As Pelevin's texts are always eager to remind us, positive reinforcement and covert control are much more effective than the crude technologies of traditional totalitarianism. The dehumanized man used to be trained through pain. In Romeo's words: "It makes you feel like a rat in a maze" (*SU* 101). But with advanced technology and the techniques of positive reinforcement, the same rat responds consistently and correctly. The independent system of coordinates is lost, and the world becomes whatever the cyberspace royalty chooses to show. What results is a 100 percent successful manipulation combined with total imperceptibility.

An obligatory Pelevinian question follows: who activates all these "Sticky Eyes" and "Pavlov's Bitches"? *The Helmet of Horror* describes the controller (the controlling user in "The Prince of Gosplan") as a shadowy Minotaur-like divinity who wears the helmet in which the labyrinth and the humans appear—a deity like Oranus, Enkidu, and the unnamed heavenly hulk of *Generation 'П.'* In a typical solipsistic loop, the evil divinity is itself located in the space that Ariadne sees in her sleep. The controller (Minotaur, moderator, cyberspace host) manipulates and perhaps even imagines all the chat room participants just as it obtains its existence through them.

A large part of *The Helmet of Horror* has the characters debating and the reader pondering the potential significations of the Minotaur and the labyrinth. Clearly the labyrinth stands for (among other things) the internet: as the narrative points out, Windows offers a screen saver called "maze." But other possibilities are offered as to who/what the Minotaur and Theseus might be. The novel contrasts the classical humanist and post-structuralist readings of the myth. According to the former, the labyrinth is a symbol of the brain, and the Minotaur is its animal part while Theseus is its human part. Theseus overpowering the Minotaur therefore symbolizes civilization and progress winning out over nature. In French post-structuralism, on the other hand, the labyrinth, the Minotaur, and Theseus are merely simulacra that come into being through language (*discourse*), the paradox being that discourse itself is not encountered anywhere in nature. The narrative also suggests that the Minotaur may be the spirit of our time, which is manifested in postmodernism as a kind of mad cow disease, a culture feeding upon its own bones.

Unexpectedly, the drunkard Sliff comes up with an unorthodox yet insightful interpretation: the cast of characters represent various cultural discourses of contemporaneity recycled by the media. These discourses deprive the human subject of independent thought and as such constitute the various segments of the helmet of horror. Sliff terms them "shackles on the convolutions of my brain [*tatal'nye kandaly na izvilinakh moego mozga*]" (*SU* 181).[8] In this light, the intellectuals Monstradamus and Nutscracker are horns, pious UGLI is the past, materialistic Organism is the future, and so on. To free oneself—Sliff's and Theseus's task—is to throw off "all your magic wonderland TV quizzes, where you get shafted up the xxx everyday underneath the money tree" (*SU* 181). One has (at the very least) to reject the kind of profane existence that emerges from these characters' online exchanges. The Minotaur of the media and cyberspace will then be killed, and the helmet of horror shattered.

The book's conclusion actually plays on Sliff's resolution. The first letters of Monstradamus, IsoldA, Nutscracker, Organism, Theseus, Ariadne, UGLI, and Romeo do spell M-I-N-O-T-A-U-R. Not only do the characters' first letters (minus Sliff plus Theseus) spell out the mythical creature's name, but Monstradamus, IsoldA, Nutscracker, Organism, and Sliff spell out MINOS.[9] The ending (at least in Sliff's version) is unexpectedly hopeful. The helmet of horror is "the contents of the mind, which attempt to supplant the mind by proving that they—the contents—exist, and the mind in which they arise doesn't. Or that the mind is no more than its function" (*SU* 181). But perhaps the human mind does exist, and perhaps it can be set free.

FROM HOMO ZAPIENS TO GENERATORS OF *BABLOS*

Like *The Helmet of Horror*, *Generation 'Π'* offers a sustained investigation of the ways media technologies squeeze human consciousness within the rigid matrix of the techno-consumer paradigm. *Generation 'Π'* envisions the post-Soviet moment as a point at which the human is being ousted by the posthuman in order to build the new order. Under the influence of modern media technologies, humanity is disappearing as the agent of will, reason, and ethics.

The line of inquiry initiated by "And where were you all that time?" ("The Prince of Gosplan") is developed in greater depth as *Generation 'Π'* examines the ousting of psychic processes by media phantoms. In Che Guevara's mock treatise, the viewer's attention is yanked to and fro by television programming. The virtual subject that replaces individual consciousness manages attention exactly as the program crew directs. One's thoughts and feelings, if they can even be called such, are imposed by an external operator and by the calculations of other individuals. Since the main reason for the existence of television is its advertising function, the medium pushes all psychological processes not connected to monetary transactions from the individual's consciousness.

Contrasting Homo Zapiens to Homo Sapiens, which is understood in its traditional post-Enlightenment humanist domain as an agent of reason, will, and ethics, Pelevin points out that the former has radically weakened cognitive abilities and a minimized (or obliterated) capacity for conscious and deliberate action. Homo Zapiens is no longer capable of doubt or critical analysis. The intellect is no longer regarded as having autonomous value: "Subject number two is not capable of analyzing events, in exactly the same way as an electromagnetic recording of a cock crowing is incapable of it" (*G'Π'* 112). Homo Zapiens's very being and operation are mechanistic inasmuch as they are echoes of electromagnetic processes that take place in the cathode-ray tube of a television.

The Homo Zapiens controlled by the media is a (bio)robot with a limited program that defines its function (consumption and excretion), and it cannot do anything that is not set by the program. Perhaps worst of all, the transmogrified, or rather obliterated, human no longer even notices that something has happened. Of course, the post-subject does not mourn the loss of "I" since there is no longer any "I" to mourn. This novel condition "could appropriately be called the experience of collective nonexistence, since the virtual subject that replaces the viewer's active consciousness is merely an effect created by the collective efforts of editors, cameramen, and producers" (*G'Π'* 105).

If *Generation 'Π'* portrays humans as zombified by the global techno-consumer system, *Empire V* suggests that the human as a self-determined subject may have never existed in the first place.[10] The present, with its all-powerful technological control, makes people most machine-like. *Empire V* offers multiple tropes of men-machines, comparing humans to boats with engines, radio-controlled drones, electrical receivers and transmitters, light bulbs, distillation stills, chemical plants, and even the processes of nuclear fission and fusion. Most prominently, the novel, in an ingenious blend of zoomorphic and mechanistic imagery, characterizes humans simultaneously as vampire livestock and as bioengineered machines that generate *bablos* on which vampires feed. The vampire rulers of the world have bred (designed) humans to manufacture monetary simulacra. As devices for the production of *bablos*, humans have never really possessed free will.

Similar to *The Helmet of Horror*, *Empire V* portrays the human brain as a machine that generates the world, selfhood, and here especially, *bablos*. In engineering terms, the brain is an electromagnetic generator:

> The brain is an appliance [*pribor*] that produces what we call the world. This appliance can not only receive signals but emits them as well. If you configured all of these instruments the same way and focused the attention of all people on the same abstraction, all the transmitters [*peredatchiki*] would be radiating energy at one wavelength. This wavelength is money. (*EV* 230)

The brain as a radio transmitter forms radio waves that fly out at the speed of light. Mind B, which only humans possess and which generates monetary simulacra, serves as a transmitter antenna. The other human antennas, proportionate in size to the length of the wave, receive the energy of money.

Along with the spurious separation of interiority and exteriority, time, and so on, the human brain manufactures money (*delaet den'gi*) to perpetuate the techno-consumer paradigm. Humans are locked in their bodies, and what seems like empirical reality to them is just an interpretation of electrical signals received by the brain. In one more solipsism metaphor, people are locked inside a hollow sphere on whose walls are projected images of a world generated by their sensory organs. These images present a world that humans mistakenly believe exists beyond the sphere. In this witches' Sabbath of simulacra, money is the centerpiece. But in their pursuit of money, humans pay with real blood and tears: "A red spiral of energy trembles in men, a glowing discharge between what they take for reality and what they agree to accept as dream. The poles are false, but the spark between them is real" (*EV* 345). Human energy, even moving between spurious poles, feeds the vampire overlords.

Typically for Pelevin, *Empire V* responds to Western critical theory. The scenario of a self-determining mankind functioning as a veneer for a vampire dictatorship imaginatively reworks notions by thinkers like Lyotard and Foucault who see humanism as a construct and cover for capitalism, Western monopoly, and so on. For Lyotard, the inhumanity of the social system currently being consolidated coexists with a secret, more radical inhumanity within people's souls (the unconscious). Pelevin's twist on this is that not only have humans always lived in an inhuman reality (governed by vampires), but their most cherished notions—of subjectivity, agency, ethics, religion, and art—are mere by-products of the production of *bablos*, the vampires' nourishment.

The human in the sense of Enlightenment humanism may never have existed, but today humankind's incarceration has reached a new extreme. Human automatons in their office workspaces are enticed by high tech into expending genuine resources on on-screen phantoms. Since they cannot bear to stay locked in cells "pulling at levers and generating *bablos*," high tech projects a comfortable virtual space around them, something like "a plasma screen on which a video of Venice is shown, with the levers formatted as the gondola's oars" (*EV* 213). Even as technology places humankind in a *Matrix*-like space (à la the Wachowskis, William Gibson, and Philip K. Dick), it reshapes them after its own kind to become more and more automaton-like.[11] But the vampires themselves, one learns, fare hardly better. Although more advanced, they are equally cogs in the mechanism of circulating *bablos*.[12]

FREE WILL, CONSCIOUSNESS, AND ARTIFICIAL INTELLIGENCE

In *Pineapple Water for the Beautiful Lady* and *S.N.U.F.F.* Pelevin turns his focus more to the machines themselves—while continuing to expose the mechanistic nature of humans. *Pineapple Water for the Beautiful Lady* (*Ananasnaia voda dlia prekrasnoi damy*, 2010), a collection consisting of two novellas and three short stories, is divided into two parts, "Gods and Mechanisms" and "Mechanisms and Gods." The names of these sections introduce the book's core problematic of turning the metaphysical into the profane—by means of worldly technology-based manipulation.

The first novella, "Operation 'Burning Bush'" ("Operatsiia 'Burning Bush'"), focuses on technological manipulations that provide a sham of religious experience and serve corrupt worldly powers. This is the story of a down-on-his-luck teacher of English, a Russian Jew named Semyon Levitan, who is forced by the FSB (the Russian Federal Security Service) to pose as God to George W. Bush, then U.S. president. Semyon transmits his "divine" missives to Bush via a transmitter implanted in his tooth (the receiver in

turn is planted in Bush's jaw). To influence the American president's decisions in ways profitable to the Russian secret services, Levitan communicates
with Bush in the resonant voice of Yuri Levitan, a famous Soviet-era radio
announcer.[13] He fulfills this task while being drugged and placed naked in a
dark salty bath in order to attain "union with the Absolute."[14]

Levitan is a literal deus ex machina who speaks to the White House
via a top secret engineering invention. Here the powerful and the powerless
of the world alike (Russians, Americans, Bush, Levitan, etc.) are dupes in
games of mutual deception enabled by high-tech development. Just as the
FSB (formerly KGB) service strives to compromise its Western opponents,
the CIA tries to trick Soviet and then post-Soviet leaders into following its
directives.

The ludicrous setup of Levitan-turned-involuntary godhead for Bush
explores the essential problem of free will and its loss. After Levitan's super-
visors discover the CIA's devilish theatrics for the benefit of Soviet leaders—
CIA agents had been posing as Satan to the Russian side since at least Stalin's
time—the protagonist gets retrained as Lucifer. But when Levitan is bullied
into an exposure to Satanism, he experiences a loss of will. During his drug-
induced "fall from grace" (a parodic take on Milton's *Paradise Lost*), he has a
growing sense of gloom and despair and an ever-increasing lack of freedom,
as if the space around him were collapsing into some lesser dimensionality.

In "Operation 'Burning Bush," Levitan turning into Satan figures the
loss of human agency and reason and his own transformation into a machine:

> It seemed to me that I became a sort of computer program [*kakoi-to
> komp'iuternoi programmoi*]—not fun and interesting like in *The Matrix*, but
> of the most typical kind of accounting software [*samogo chto ni na est' bukh-
> galterskogo tolka*]. My thinking did not change much, no. It just suddenly
> ceased to be mine—and thinking as such. It began to seem a sequence of op-
> erations on an arithmometer. And it was unbearably sad to watch this because
> another arithmometer, just slightly differently arranged, observed everything.
> It turned out that I have never had anything inside but these cash registers
> [*kassovykh apparatov*] that controlled each other. (*AV* 108).

Parallel to the Homo Zapiens of *Generation 'П'* and the human generators
of *bablos* in *Empire V*, as Levitan-cum-Satan's interiority is recognized as an
accounting software, he becomes an arithmometer or a cash register. As the
Man of desire, Economic Man, performs an internal "cost-benefit analysis,"
which will always give him reason for working within the system (per Fukuyama), all this machine-man can do is calculate profit and loss.

The second story, "Anti-Aircraft Codices of Al-Efesbi" ("Zenitnye
kodeksy Al'-Efesbi"), addresses the theme of sentient machinery in order to

probe further the problems of the human mind and willpower. Subdivided into the sections "Freedom Liberator" (English title) and "The Soviet Requiem" ("Sovetskii rekviem"), the story depicts the life of Savely Skotenkov, a former professor and cultural critic who finds his true vocation in destroying unmanned American aircraft over Afghanistan.

Like other Pelevin texts, "Anti-Aircraft Codices" points out the cognitive and spiritual decline of humankind. Life, on both the micro and macro levels, has lost acceleration in the sense that it has become ahistorical. Following the collapse of Soviet modernizing projects such as space exploration, technological progress not only does not entail a civilizational breakthrough, but its new focus is on reducing humankind to a subhuman state. Hence the expansion into space is abandoned, while the internet drowns people in pornography, blogging, and advertising.

As artificial intelligence (AI) spreads, human intelligence is diminished. "Freedom Liberator" imagines the emergence of artificial intelligence, describing a Pentagon-designed onboard supercomputer system that controls unmanned military aircraft. The system resembles the human brain. Unlike ordinary computers, it is manufactured as a neural net that has no hard drive or memory block, but stores information in networks. The system, rather than its human operators, makes combat decisions. To provide politically correct reports of bombing to the public, the computer has been loaded with "human experience" in the form of archives of every American talk show ever aired on TV.

Pelevin-cum-Skotenkov devises a comedic way to shoot down the American drones flying over the Afghan desert: he resorts to special verbal formulas drawn in the sand that involve politically incorrect invective aimed at neoliberal values. As a result, a drone's controlling computer begins to experience an intense emotion (anger), which gives rise to artificial intelligence endowed with consciousness and will. Just as this sentience is born, the system freezes from information overload, the drone nosedives into the desert floor, and AI dies with it.

The parodic portrayal of the emergence of artificial sentience in "Freedom Liberator" addresses such crucial issues as what humankind was traditionally understood to be, its current makeup, and its relationship to the posthuman. In religious and traditional humanist thinking, there exists a basic distinction between the organic mind and an artificial computer. But in a postmodern trend that views the mind as a bundle of material processes, no such distinction obtains.[15] If human consciousness per se is conceptualized as the operations of a kind of computer, there is nothing to prevent technology from evolving eventually into artificial intelligence. In one more prominent trend of thought, humans may be distinguished from machines not so much by their capacity for reason or choice, as by their capacity to experience emotion. For instance, in Fukuyama's opinion, the likelihood that machines will come to resemble humans seems remote "not so much because machines will never duplicate human intelligence . . . they will probably be able to come very close in this regard—but rather because it is impossible to see how they will come to acquire human emotions" (*Our Posthuman Future*, 168). While Pelevin's texts question traits traditionally attributed to humans such as reason and consciousness, the capacity for emotion, "a red spiral of energy trembling in people," seems less dispensable (*EV* 345). Appropriately, in "Freedom Liberator's" rendition of the birth of AI, sentience arises in the face of politically incorrect jibes in English spiced with Russian profanities. Just as the supercomputer's exposure to human experience is limited to an archive of TV shows, so is the primitive experience of Homo Zapiens limited in *Generation 'Π'*. Comic though this account may be, there is one more point worth underscoring: the machine that gives rise to AI is designed to kill.[16]

Like *Pineapple Water*, *S.N.U.F.F.* addresses the problems of media deception, the mechanization of humankind, and artificially created sentience. The novel portrays a futuristic, post–nuclear war world that is divided into Byzantium or Big Byz and Urkaina, Urkaganate, or Orkland. The former is an affluent, business-oriented, technologically advanced Western society. The latter is a devastated, economically backward part of the territories of the former Russia and Ukraine. The earth has reached the point of an ecological collapse, and the well-to-do populace of Byzantium has retreated to an artificial satellite, or "Ofshar"—a pun on *shar* ("sphere") and *ofshor* ("offshore")—that is anchored above Urkaina's capital, Slava (Glory).

Both Byzantium and Orkland are portrayed in Pelevin's signature acerbic manner, the former as exploitative, morally depraved, hypocritical, and mired in political correctness, and the latter as shabbily militant, backward, and impotent.[17] The division of the world into higher and lower races, echoing H. G. Wells's *The Time Machine* (1895) with its Eloi-Morlock dichotomy, alludes to the outcome of the Cold War and projects the further degradation of the former Russian and Ukrainian lands in the future. The regime of Orkland is called, in an ironic tautology, an "autocratic autocracy" (*avtoritarnaia despotiia*). The regime of Byzantium is a "liberative demautocracy" (*liberativnaia demokratura*)—another ironic appellation that points to the oppressive status quo common to both Orkland and Big Byz.

While Pelevin reserves compassion for the ordinary Orks, the corrupt populace of Byzantium is utterly unredeemed.[18] The uber-consumer "liberative demautocracy" of Byzantium is equipped with all the high tech of the past, but is no longer capable of developing scientifically or culturally. Its people live in the "Era of Saturation" (*Era nasyshcheniia*), "when technologies and languages (both human tongues and IT codes) hardly change at all, since the economic and cultural meaning of progress had been exhausted" (*S.N.U.F.F.* 71). Byzantium considers the Urks/Orks living below to be sub-human. It makes use of Orkland as a colony and an energy source (Orkland possesses huge reserves of gas), buys its infants, puppeteers its leaders (a quasi-criminal ring supported by Byzantium), and conducts incessant warfare down on earth for entertainment.

The problem of false reality enabled by high tech is again a leitmotif. The Orks live in poverty, but Byzantium's prosperity is virtual. Echoing the deceptions that *Generation 'Π'* and *Empire V* explore—e.g., for a lot of money one can buy a crudely painted view from a window or a video of Venice on a plasma screen—the beautiful open expanse outside homes on the Ofshar is computer-generated. London, a favorite destination of the post-Soviet nouveau riche, is just a view in the window: "No other London has existed for many centuries. If rich Orks live here . . . they see the same 3D-projection in the window" (*S.N.U.F.F.* 297). In fact, even the elites on the satellite live in cramped cubicles. In one of Pelevin's ongoing references to the Wachowskis and Baudrillard, Big Byz is called "the desert of the real" (*S.N.U.F.F.* 387).[19]

The crux of the novel's critique is its portrayal of the technologically advanced Byzantium's perennial warfare with Orkland, the carnage of which is recorded in snuff films. The Ofshar's media men provoke, conduct, and film this warfare in order to entertain their over-satiated audience. The novel's narrator, Demian-Landuff Damilola Karpov, who works for the CINEWS media corporation, pilots a drone equipped with lethal weaponry and a film camera. Damilola performs this airmanship from the comfort of his sitting room sofa. His plane shoots down Orks and simultaneously shoots reels of film. The title acronym of the novel is an abbreviation for "Special Newsreel Universal Feature Film"—media entertainment that features real murders and sex.[20] Snuff films bind together reality and fantasy, art and information, and "the two main energies of human existence, love and death—presented as they are in actual fact" (*S.N.U.F.F.* 200).

The media blurs the distinction between the real and the simulated and, more crucially, conducts mass murder for the purpose of entertainment. Baudrillard's dictum "the media promote the war, the war promotes the media, and advertising competes with the war" (*The Gulf War Did Not Take Place*, 31) is taken to its malignant limit. In *S.N.U.F.F.* not only do media people broadcast military operations in real time and present sanitized warfare that does not correspond to reality, but they themselves initiate wars and kill Orks in order to profit from death as an arch-spectacle.[21] The media also profit from pornography, with the battles as a chic setting for lascivious encounters. In this scenario, cause and effect switch places. Whereas in the past wars took place, and then films were made about them, now war is waged specifically in order to make snuff films. The Orks die in a closed arena at the center of their capital, Slava, where the battles invariably take place. Though they think they are fighting real people, they are actually fighting machines and media simulacra while Byzantium's geriatric, plastic surgery-enhanced movie stars make love amidst the gore. Likewise, Pelevin carries to its (il)logical conclusion Baudrillard's observation that contemporary society assigns a quasi-religious significance to the production of information.[22] In the world of Big Byz, the cult of the media has become an official religion, called "Movism," in which "a snuff is first and foremost a religious mystery" (*S.N.U.F.F.* 201).

In tandem with the false reality thread, Pelevin pursues his inquiry into the issue of artificial intelligence. Damilola's sex partner, a Lolita-like anthropomorphic biorobot called Kaya, is set by her owner to "maximum spirituality" and "maximum bitchiness." She successfully simulates the former thanks to having been uploaded with all kinds of cultural quotes. Kaya is all surface and pastiche, and is able to give an impression of an authentic self-determined personality where none (for most of the narrative) obtains. Like A Huli in *The Sacred Book of the Werewolf,* Kaya is also a quintessentially postmodern character, one whose *identichnost'* may be changed (switched on and off) as Damilola wishes.

As Keith Livers demonstrates, *S.N.U.F.F* raises the question of what it means to be human in the light of recent, radical technological and epistemological shifts: "The Damilola-Kaia dyad undercuts the principle of humanity's separatedness from other orders of being, in particular, the increasingly blurry distinction between Homo Sapiens and self-aware machines or AI" (Livers, "Is There Humanity in Posthumanity?" 506). What it means to be human, furthermore, is linked to "who gets to count as human," that is, to the problematic of power and control.

Though the biorobot Kaya is controlled by Damilola, she also exemplifies the lack of freedom that *human* characters experience in Pelevin's world. Like Homo Zapiens, the Helmholtz/*Shlemil'*, and the generators of *bablos,* Kaya is subject to outside domination, with Damilola acting as her literal "controlling user." Though her own settings are controlled by the cameraman, Kaya contends that humans have no free will, either. They are slaves to their biological or chemical makeup; in other words, they are bio-machines driven by their material constituents. Kaya describes Damilola as an uncomplicated little mechanism just like herself, humming and trembling meaninglessly. As she explains:

> My route is inscribed inside me programmatically . . . and your route is inscribed inside you chemically. And when it seems to you that you're advancing towards light and happiness, you're simply advancing towards your inner

handler to get another sugar lump. In fact we can't even say that it's you advancing. . . . In all this there isn't any "you" [*nikakogo "tebia" vo vsem etom net*]. (*S.N.U.F.F.* 399)

In this reading, the human is a bio-machine directed by material constituents that give him no choice, since choice is a category of reason; rather, his behavior is dictated through instinct.[23] Kaya's argument is informed by a mixture of the postmodern problematization of the human person as independent agent and the (more hopeful) Buddhist notion that one needs to overcome one's biological construct (i.e., one's desires) to push through false material reality. To exercise free will means to engage your rational (and ethical) faculties and suppress your biological (mechanistic) drives. In Kaya's (bitchy) estimation at least, this is not possible.

✿ ✿ ✿

In Pelevin's texts, humans are manipulated by means of high tech and are themselves a technology—though not at all a high one. As Mark Lipovetsky observes about *Generation 'Π'*:

Technologies, even if with an irrational underside, aimed at manipulations with mass consciousness, are here the foundations of the "technologist's" nearly absolute power. This power is naturally based on deception and self-deception, illusions, dreams, and, most importantly, a total, blinding and hypnotizing desire for money. ("Traektorii ITR-diskursa," 216)

Even the ad copywriter Tatarsky in *Generation 'Π'* is not exempt from mechanization: He "is a nobody, a human word processor" (Lipovetskii, *Paralogii*, 427). This assumption runs through Pelevin's oeuvre at large.

As he loses his battle to clever Kaya, the lovelorn Damilola mentions at one point that "all suras [surrogate wives] of Kaya's class carry a label that says: '333.33% Turing Test passed'" (*S.N.U.F.F.* 391). Kaya herself conforms to Alan Turing's definition of thinking AI; that is, she can imitate a human being by answering questions in such a way as to deceive a human questioner.[24] By the end of the novel, she is also apparently able to adjust her own settings, thus achieving Turing's dream of a machine capable of modifying its own programs based on the information it has already processed.

Over its course *S.N.U.F.F.* offers a funny and penetrating expose of the Turing mythologeme—his gay identity, his secret work to break the Enigma code at Bletchley Park, and the invention of the Turing test and various objections to the test, as well as recent debates on the human mind and artificial intelligence popularized by scholars like John Searle, David

Chalmers, and Daniel Dennett. Where Dennett envisions consciousness as a physical activity of the brain, Chalmers does not see interiority as reducible to such activity.

As a mathematician and philosopher, Alan Turing became interested in the question of whether programmed machines could evolve toward artificial intelligence and achieve consciousness, will, and feeling. He came to believe that AI could indeed include the traits that had traditionally been thought to be the exclusive province of humankind. Turing proposed that a machine that is to imitate the human brain must appear to behave as if it had free will. One way to achieve this "is to make its behavior depend on something like a roulette wheel or a supply of radium." It is not difficult "to design machines whose behavior appears quite random to anyone who does not know the details of their construction" (*The Essential Turing*, 479). To pursue the question, "Can digital computers think?" Turing invented the imitation game now known as the Turing test. A machine and a human are put in a room and given written questions. If a human observer outside the room cannot tell which answers are produced by the machine and which by the human, the machine is considered capable of thinking.

Rather than engaging Turing as a cultural icon, Pelevin questions Turing's postulates. What Turing's much-popularized musings evade is the issue of consciousness and free will—by positing AI's ability to merely *imitate* these. In the common-sense terms of *S.N.U.F.F.* (and elsewhere in Pelevin's work), the question of agency—"in all of this there isn't any 'you'"—hinges not on imitating free will, but on a genuine capacity to transcend determinism (programmability).[25]

In effect *S.N.U.F.F.* reverses Turing's query: it is no longer a question of machines developing consciousness and will, but of humans losing them or never having possessed them in the first place. Rather than machines evolving upward toward human consciousness, natural intelligence in Pelevin's universe is degraded to automaton-like posthumanity. Intellect and feelings become more and more controlled by immediate inputs, which blocks the cultivation of proper cognitive and emotional processes. Equally, Pelevin builds on classic robot science-fiction novels such as Philip K. Dick's *Do Androids Dream of Electric Sheep?* (1968), which was filmed by Ridley Scott as *Blade Runner* in 1982, and Stanislav Lem's *The Mask* (1976). Yet whereas the central problem in Dick's and Scott's works is androids operating in excess of their programming, Pelevin is more concerned with humans who are incapable of exceeding their programming. Today's high-tech society converts individuals into innumerable replicas of one another and indistinguishable performers of functions. They are kept enthralled by technologies, but the current state of affairs is just an extreme version of the original "flawed" state of humanity. In the guise of artificial intelligence, the posthuman simulates human essence, just as this essence—the independent and coherent human subject—is disappearing—or worse, perhaps never existed.

Why do we possess an illusion of free will despite all evidence to the contrary? *The Helmet of Horror* offers a possible solution: "That is simply his [human's] specific quality as a product [*vyrabatyvaemaia veshch'*]. In other words, the idea that he perceives everything is produced . . . along with everything else" (*SU* 79). *Empire V* pursues the problem of the perceiving subject, consciousness, and, in more old-fashioned phrasing, the soul. Among the various body-mind theories that Roma Shtorkin studies, he finds particularly compelling the one in which the body is likened to a machine, a radio-controlled drone, and one's life "is a three-dimensional film about the drone's trip that is . . . projected onto the immobile mirror that is the soul" (*EV* 99). The thought of the soul upsets Roma because, as a novice vampire with moral compunctions, it now feels to him as if he has lost his. His vampire tutor objects, though: "It's like saying that a boat loses its soul when an engine is installed on it. You did not lose anything. You only acquired" (*EV* 33).

Is that it, then? *Pineapple Water* and *S.N.U.F.F.* offer two opposed, humanistic and posthumanistic, takes on the problem of free will here. In *S.N.U.F.F.* Kaya echoes *The Helmet of Horror*'s denial of human agency and exposes human moral compunctions as sheer fallacy. She describes Damilola's thoughts, wishes, and impulses that compel him to act as not belonging to him at all, but coming to him from an obscure space, as if from nowhere. The human Damilola does not know what he will want or do at any moment, and is merely a witness to processes that are independent of his will. But this "inner witness [*vnutrennii svidetel'*] is so stupid that he immediately becomes party to the crime—and is punished to the full" (*S.N.U.F.F.* 402–3).[26]

By contrast, *Pineapple Water* suggests a humanistic, even religious solution to the problem of human will. The human being has a thinking machine that is the brain, which solves problems and hands the results over to the "inner witness." This witness has traditionally been called the "soul," but the modern age prefers terms such as "consciousness," "agency," or "mind." As Buddhists and other mystics claim, there is no permanent entity in humans, and consequently no soul. Such an inference is logical, but:

> Who sees that man has no soul and selfhood? [*Vot tol'ko kto vidit, chto nikakoi dushi i samosti u cheloveka net?*] . . . The one who perceives this higher truth *is* the soul, that same beam of eternal constant light that falls on the cash register tape crawling out of the brain [*vypolzaiushchuiu iz mozga kassovuiu lentu*] with the results of calculations stating that no eternal essence has been detected inside the machine [*chto nikakoi vechnoi sushchnosti vnutri etoi mashiny ne obnaruzheno*]. (*AV* 194)

This passage, disingenuously attributed to Father Iv. Krestovsky, contains Pelevin's key images and concepts.[27] The expected skeptical conclusion is that the human is a soulless automaton. Then, in a sudden ironic twist, the soul reenters the picture as the entity necessary to perceive the absence of itself. In the traditional religious view, the soul is created by God and is not reducible to material processes. For modern proponents of mechanistic explanations of consciousness, the brain represents a kind of a machine, and consciousness is the product of its operations. The texts offer both versions. Demautocratic indeed.

PART III

History

Not with a Bang but a Whimper

> But a cruel time is coming to us,
> A time of insane fire.
> (O stylized gallop of the horse,
> and foam on the bright stirrups,
> and the apocalyptic rider—toward us!)
> —Joseph Brodsky, "The Procession"

IN PELEVIN'S PARABLE "Hermit and Six Toes," the Last Judgment (*Strashnyi sud*), or in broiler chicken parlance, *Strashnyi sup* (the Last Soup), is swiftly approaching. In less than twenty-four hours the chickens will be slaughtered:

> It turned out that they had all been expecting the advent of the Messiah for a long time, because the approach of the Decisive Stage—which was called the Day of Condiment here, a clear indication that the local inhabitants had moments of serious insight—had been exercising their minds for ages, while the local spiritual authorities had become so gorged and idle that they answered every question put to them with a brief gesture of the head in the direction of the ceiling. (*VPE* 49–50)

Neither the story's comic trappings nor this writer's predilection for puns downplay the centrality of an apocalyptic imagination to his oeuvre.

Pelevin's apocalyptic and post-apocalyptic motifs run from *Generation 'П'* through *The Sacred Book of the Werewolf* and *Empire V* to *Pineapple Water for the Beautiful Lady* and *S.N.U.F.F.* In this chapter I will pick out his distinctive eschatology (post-Soviet, postmodern, posthuman) against the background of antecedent apocalyptic narratives and argue that Pelevin's texts dismiss conventional eschatological visions as unable to capture the catastrophe of contemporaneity. In contrast to traditional eschatology, which mixes catastrophic premonitions and millenarian hopes, Pelevin's work portrays the present as utterly unredeemed by hope. Contemporaneity presents neither the final destruction of the world nor a Last Judgment that may be catastrophic, but is also decisive and redemptive. Instead, Pelevin's version

111

of the apocalypse is banal, evil, and thoroughly inhuman—with tenuous exceptions. Not only is Russia's historical potential annihilated and its messianic hopes abandoned, but globally the human being as an agent of free will, reason, and ethics is ousted by unfree and unselfconscious replicons generated by the techno-consumer machine. Conventional eschatology, for all its frightfulness, proves simply too human-centered and optimistic to describe the replacement of Homo Sapiens by the posthuman.

MOSCOW, THE THIRD WHORE OF BABYLON

With good reason, apocalyptic thinking became prominent in Russian fiction around the time of the collapse of the Soviet Union. It flourished further at the turn of the millennium and during the initial years of the new century.[1] Pelevin's fin-de-siècle classic *Generation 'П'* is an example of a recent take on apocalypticism. The novel is permeated with eschatological symbolism. It captures the mood of fear and disorientation that attended the breakup of the Soviet Union and the early years under the new regime. The financial default of 1998 and the approach of the third millennium only added to this anxious mood.[2]

Generation 'П' displays a well-developed apocalyptic layer that evokes Babylonian motifs (both ancient Hittite myths and Babylonian references in the Bible). The protagonist Tatarsky's first name, Vavilen, alludes to Babylon, which stands for the future kingdom of the Antichrist in the biblical book of Revelation.[3] Post-Soviet Moscow, formerly called the "Third Rome," has become the whore of Babylon.[4] It is destined for destruction due to its dismissal of all values beyond the material sphere. In this benighted realm, worldly success is equated with higher enlightenment, and money is literally sacred.

Tatarsky's first advertising scenario, for the Lefortovo Confectionery Factory, is built around apocalyptic imagery: "The Tower of Babel rose and fell, the Nile flooded, Rome burned, ferocious Huns galloped in no particular direction across the steppes—and in the background the hands of an immense, transparent clock spun around. . . . But eventually even the earth with its ruins of empires and civilizations sank from sight into a lead-colored ocean" (*G'П'* 28). His later advertisement for the Gap chain transforms the general end-of-the-world motifs into a specifically Russian apocalypse (the only thing that remains of Russia is "the gap"). Numerous apocalyptic details permeate the narrative—such as the drug dealer Grigory discussing "a rare tab with a dragon defeating St. George. From the German series: John the Evangelist's Bad Trip," the mass suicide of the members of Heaven's

Gate (recalling the mass suicides of Russian sectarians inspired by apocalyptic and millenarian notions), and Malyuta's (Vavilen's coworker) "gloomy-eschatological positioning of events" (*G'П* 78, 127, 97).[5]

Tatarsky's esoteric experiments are driven by his desire for a mystical revelation—an unveiling—an *apokalypsis*. Like a parodic St. John of Patmos listening to an angel and acquiring prophetic knowledge about the impending fate of the world, he enters into contact with spirits via a Ouija board so that he may "understand more than anyone else" (*chtob bol'she vsekh ponimat'*) (*G'П* 101). His swallowing Grigory the drug dealer's drug-laced Babylonian stamp is a parodic echo of St. John's line: "And I took the little book out of the angel's hand, and ate it up; and it was in my mouth sweet as honey: and as soon as I had eaten it, my belly was bitter" (Rev. 10:10). Like his communication with the spirit of Che Guevara, the consumption of the Babylonian stamp permits Tatarsky to step outside the boundaries of human perception and provides an insight into the diabolical workings of the media—though not to challenge them, but to become part of them. The mystical knowledge he gains will not be employed, as the angel bids St. John in the book of Revelation, "to prophesy again before many peoples, and nations, and tongues, and kings" (Rev. 10:11), but for his personal career advancement.

Pelevin's novel ingeniously reimagines and grounds St. John's visions in the consumer obsessions of contemporaneity. The media is the present version of Tofet (a place of sacrificial cremation) or Gehenna from the book of Revelation—the Lake of Fire where the wicked will be eternally consigned:

> These pits were known as Gehenna—after a certain ancient valley where the whole business started. I might add that the Bible calls it the "abomination of the Ammonites." . . . You can regard the tofet as an ordinary television. . . . This is the technological space where your world is being consumed by fire. (*G'П* 152–54)

While humans are deluded into thinking they are consumers, in reality they are consumed by the media-fueled flames of monetary lust.

The apocalypse in *Generation 'П'* is the state in which all humankind is enslaved to Mammon. In Pelevin's eclectic mythologizing, the biblical Baal (aka the evil deity Enkidu) presides over Gehenna (Tofet). When Enkidu gathers all people on his golden thread—replicating the social/economic/ biomorphic aggregate of Oranus—the world will come to an end:

> There are eschatological motifs to be found in the myth of Enkidu—as soon as Enkidu gathers everyone living of earth onto his thread, life will cease,

because they will again become beads on the necklace of the great goddess. This event, due to happen at some point in the future, is identified with the end of the world. (*G'П* 146)[6]

It is the protagonist Tatarsky himself and more generally members of the benighted Generation Pepsi (aka Pizdets) who bring about the end. The five-legged dog Pizdets is the novel's version of the eschatological Beast from the book of Revelation who is set on destroying all life around him. The beast sleeps somewhere in the snow, and while he sleeps, life goes on. When he wakes up, he attacks. While Tatarsky's colleagues in the media claim that their secret society aims to defend Ishtar and the world against the apocalypse to be brought on by Pizdets, the later revelation is that Tatarsky and his colleagues are themselves the all-destroying Beast. In Tatarsky's own intuition, his entire generation is now on the attack.

Generation 'П' is permeated by jocular yet persistent demonic motifs that reinforce its eschatological preoccupations. In the book of Revelation, Satan is loosed upon the world to test people in their wickedness. Upon their first encounter, the copywriter Morkovin in *Generation 'П'* introduces Tatarsky to the business of advertising with the phrase, "Let's go to the devil" (*G'П* 20). This metaphor is realized later in the novel. During his first assignment as a copywriter, Tatarsky receives a message on his pager: "Welcome to Route 666," the number of the Beast in the book of Revelation, and an infamous (if fictitious) Utah highway (*G'П* 26).[7] The "gray frightening murk" that emerges in *Generation 'П'* following the collapse of the Soviet Union evokes the murky realm of the demonic. Both Tatarsky's first and last names carry demonic associations. The last name plays with Tartarus (hell).

Not only is Vavilen Tatarsky himself pettily demonic, but so is his predecessor in the media business, someone named Legion Azadovsky. His first name evokes "My name is Legion" (Mark 5:9), a group of demons in the New Testament, and the episode known as the "exorcism of the Gerasene demoniac," in which Jesus heals a man from Gadarenes who is possessed by demons. Azadovsky does not mince words about it: "You're no Vladimir; you're called Vavilen. . . . My old man was a wanker too. Know what he called me? Legion. . . . It used to make me miserable too, at first. Then I found out there was something about me in the Bible, so I felt better about it" (*G'П* 186). Azadovsky's manipulations in Moscow real estate are reminiscent of the adventures of Woland and his retinue in Mikhail Bulgakov's *The Master and Margarita* (1940, 1967).[8]

Tatarsky's career rise in the media or, in mythical terms, his ascent up Ishtar's ziggurat, culminates topsy-turvy in his descent into the hundred-meter pit by the Ostankino television tower (hell), where he is anointed as Ishtar's consort and a living god. His initiation into the secret cult of Ishtar at Zero Hour in the Golden Room suggests the onset of a new realm outside time and history when "there should be time no longer" (Rev. 10:6). The novel reenvisions post-apocalyptic timelessness as the annihilation of time and space by the forces of global commerce and advertising. "Time for rent, space for rent" (*vremia sdaetsia, prostranstvo sdaetsia*) puns on the double meaning of *sdaetsia* as "for rent" and "to give up." The destruction of space and time is a commercial venture.

Che Guevara's mock treatise concludes with the claim that the end of the world, "which is the inevitable outcome of the wowerisation of consciousness, will present absolutely no danger of any kind—for the very subject of danger is disappearing. The end of the world will simply be a television program" (*G'Π* 119–20). In the novel's mocking terms, the Apocalypse is "Acapulypse" (*Akapul'kopsis*), after Acapulco, a popular Mexican vacation resort (*G'Π* 125). The struggle against history and humankind is complete—in a funny, painless, and final manner. As Vavilen's Buddhist friend Gireev further suggests, the Day of Judgment has already arrived. In an analogy between divine judgment and criminal investigation, what currently happens to humankind is a phase in a courtroom experiment, a reenactment of their crime. Unlike traditional apocalyptic narratives, *Generation 'Π'* offers no message of hope or redemption.

THE FINAL RECKONING FOR UNHOLY CREATURES

The Sacred Book of the Werewolf and *Empire V* build on the apocalyptic themes of *Generation 'Π'*, with respect both to Moscow as a fallen city and to Pizdets, Pelevin's version of the eschatological Beast. These novels of the 2000s provide a further unorthodox take on the eschatological themes of the Last Judgment and Final Reckoning. It is no longer ordinary post-Soviet humans like Vavilen Tatarsky and his peers, the opportunistic, power- and riches-grabbing Generation 'Π,' who are condemned. Pelevin's novels written during the opening decade of the millennium focus on supernatural protagonists (were-foxes and werewolves, vampires) and frame the questions of the Last Judgment, punishment, and redemption around them. If read as metaphoric of human sins in a hyperbolic form, these changelings permit Pelevin to construct a sharpened eschatological narrative of evil, punishment, and in exceptional cases, redemption.

As the were-fox A Huli learns from one of her sister were-foxes, the Beast is going to turn up in post-Soviet Moscow:

As prophecy says, a super-werewolf will appear in a city where they will destroy a Temple and then restore it in its previous form. For many centu-

ries, everybody thought that meant Jerusalem, and the coming of the super-
werewolf was a prophecy that concerned the very end of time, something
like the Apocalypse. . . . However, there are no references to Jerusalem in
the prophecy. But not so long ago in Moscow they restored the Cathedral of
Christ the Savior. (*SKO* 97)

A Huli's lover, an FSB general and werewolf named Sasha Sery who howls
at the country's exhausted oil wells in order to extract their remaining riches,
is the novel's Pizdets-Beast. Biblical apocalyptic references coexist with allusions to non-Judeo-Christian eschatological traditions, and Sasha is enamored of Nordic end-of-the-world mythology (Ragnarok, Fenrir, Garm, etc.),
combining his interest in Nordic motifs with Nietzsche's "Death of the Gods"
mythologeme.[9] The general-werewolf strives for thanatological superpower:
"The paradox of the scene of calling-for-oil is not only that the character
calling on the brindled cow's pity is one of those who makes Khavroshechka
(and the very cow-Russia) suffer but also that, as the shaman 'bringing' oil
into the world, there appears the very spirit of death, the future Dog Pizdets"
(Lipovetskii, *Paralogii*, 646).[10] The FSB cooperates with the oligarchs in exploiting people; they are the eschatological "locusts [*sarancha*] who obscure
the very light of day" (*SKO* 251).[11] Even the dead are not exempt from exploitation, since they are metaphorically transformed into an infernal black
liquid, oil. In the latter part of the story, Sasha the werewolf turns into the
dog Pizdets, who "happens to someone like shit happens"—bringing an absolute and irreversible end to every creature he meets (*SKO* 322).

A Huli's path, by contrast, is toward a final reckoning and potential sal-
vation. Since were-foxes use their tails to hypnotize people for personal gain
as well as to create false material reality, the act of tugging the tail brings on
retribution. Consequently, A Huli is overwhelmed with an unbearable sense
of shame and guilt and experiences such visions that she loses the desire to
go on living. But judgment and punishment can be followed by redemption for the were-fox who is ready to overcome her selfishness and reject
the corrupt corporeal world. *The Sacred Book of the Werewolf* narrated by
A Huli is an *unveiling* à la the book of Revelation—though paradoxically
and problematically directed at were-creatures. In this account, the super-
werewolf is going to atone for the sins of the were-foxes by giving them a
book that explains how to enter the mystical "Rainbow Stream."[12] Since the
world created by the tail of the were-fox is brimful of greed and selfishness,
the were-creature must understand what love is, and direct the feeling of
love against her own tail. Indeed, on the last page of the novel A Huli breaks
through the evil illusory world she herself creates, and escapes into the Rainbow Stream. In this act she "liberates herself from icy gloom in which the
oligarchs and the public prosecutors, the queers and straights, the internet

communists, werewolves in shoulder straps and portfolio investors wail and gnash their teeth" (*SKO* 367). Then "this world will disappear," and "she will discover who she really is" (*SKO* 381).[13]

As in *Generation 'П'* and *The Sacred Book of the Werewolf*, the Moscow of *Empire V* is the new Whore of Babylon, a fallen and diabolical place where humans are enslaved in a global vampire dictatorship, where vampires feed off humans' energy expended in the pursuit of material well-being. Pelevin "portrays twenty-first century Moscow as the site of an apocalyptic endgame where various conspiratorial societies vie for domination" (Livers, "The Tower or the Labyrinth," 478).

A salient element of the apocalyptic plot is the free choice of the individual between the forces of good and evil.[14] In *Empire V* humans overwhelmingly choose the latter—in what the narrative describes as a basic arithmetical-pragmatic manner. Traditional (biblical) ethical categories no longer matter, and God is "dead" (à la Nietzsche, and in human minds). Humans who in the past used to believe that evil may triumph in this world, but good is rewarded after death, no longer place any trust in heavenly rewards. Since the triumph of evil in the earthly realm is very much apparent, the earth-heaven formula has been nullified. Consequently, any commonsensical person looking for "the good life" naturally sides with evil.

The question of free will or its absence—of whether the human choice between good and evil is voluntary or coerced—is at the foreground of Pelevin's apocalyptic plotline. For the professor of theology with whom Roma Shtorkin discusses vampire rule, the human himself ultimately chooses who or what to side with: every "room" (human) can invite either God or vampires. "Of course, by its nature every room wants the divine. But because of *glamour* and *discourse*, most of the rooms decided that interior design determines everything" (*EV* 373). Yet, as cattle/machines that are bred by vampires to produce *bablos*, humans would appear to possess no free will from the outset. Besides, as the professor implies, *glamour* and *discourse* go a long way to muddle people's perceptions.

Whether having chosen or having the choice of evil imposed upon it, the fallen humankind of *Empire V* is bound for destruction:

> God has a lot of them [rooms]. When all the rooms of one of the palaces get inhabited by bats, God destroys it. More precisely, He ceases to create, but it's the same thing. They say this looks like the light of an incredible force that burns the whole world. . . . Right now, our palace lives through days that are hardly the best. Bats live in almost all the rooms. (*EV* 374)

Though Roma attempts to feign nonchalance throughout this conversation, he is bothered by a dark premonition. This is seen in his poem "Stas

Arkhontoff," in which he prophesies the death of the "ruler of this world" (*nachal'neg mira*)—a Satan-like "prince of this world" whose temporary rule and final destruction are depicted in the book of Revelation.[15]

Like *The Sacred Book of the Werewolf*, *Empire V* concludes on the notion of a final reckoning for an unholy creature—though, unlike A Huli, there is no promise of redemption here for Roma Shtorkin. By the novel's end he has become the most powerful vampire in Russia, and the newly appointed Ishtar's closest friend. But during a superhuman flight over Moscow at the novel's close, the hero has a presentiment of forthcoming punishment and destruction. His conclusion is to climb as high as he can (and enjoy his lofty status in the vampires' world) while the Last Judgment has not yet come upon him.

THE SECOND COMING AND THE END OF HISTORY

Generation 'Π,' The Sacred Book of the Werewolf, and *Empire V* all abound in apocalyptic imagery, reminiscent of biblical as well as Russian eschatological narratives. As Keith Livers observes about *Empire V*:

> Even the anonymous (vampire) dictatorship is in control only temporarily—until the unveiling of the final narrative. . . . The blinding light of retribution promised (but not yet delivered) . . . recalls the "divine wrath"—a kind of partial apocalypse—visited on Moscow/Jerusalem in *The Master and Margarita*. ("The Tower or the Labyrinth," 496)

If Pelevin's novels of the 1990s and 2000s portray a world teetering on the edge of an abyss, and an impending retribution promised but not yet delivered, his works of the decade just past, such as *Pineapple Water for the Beautiful Lady* and *S.N.U.F.F.*, move forward into a post-apocalyptic temporality. The post-apocalyptic realm in "Operation 'Burning Bush'" is one of illusions/lies pitted against competing illusions/lies. The story "Anti-Aircraft Codices of Al-Efesbi" is also post-apocalyptic: the apocalyptic climax, the decisive final battle for the souls of humans, is identified as the narrative's past.

As elsewhere in Pelevin's oeuvre, the media in *Pineapple Water* obfuscates basic existential and ethical distinctions: war versus peace, good versus evil, and so on. The book's copyright page introduces it as "*War and Peace* during the epoch when there is neither war nor peace.*" The collection points to the total media deception that characterizes a contemporary world in which the public can no longer be sure whether and which acts of violence are taking place. But the opening statement goes beyond the idea of pervasive social and technological deception by the media. More importantly, it indicates the moral confusion and perverse dissolution of ethical coordinates (aggression = nonaggression, good = evil, God = Satan) that is taking place. Humanity has lost its anchorage in traditional norms and values and is adrift in violence. In the world of *Pineapple Water*, the secret services pervert faith with the help of advanced technologies.[16] Hence the book's cover, which features Adam from Michelangelo's fresco "The Creation of Adam," on the Sistine Chapel's ceiling, dressed in a KGB uniform.

"Operation 'Burning Bush,'" in which Semyon Levitan pretends to be God to President Bush, is a gloomy parody of the Second Coming prophesied in the Bible.[17] Obviously Pelevin conflates the then-American president's last name and the "burning bush" (*neopalimaia kupina*) described in the book of Exodus, where Moses is appointed by God to lead his people out of Egypt—as well as recalling the flaming fountain of oil in *The Sacred Book of the Werewolf.* Pelevin's black-humor rendition of the biblical Second Coming has the Federal Security Service general Shmyga create a false deus ex machina by which to control a world submerged in darkness.[18] Shmyga ("a runner to and fro") is a pettily demonic puppeteer who forces Levitan to pose as God to George Bush. But both Bush's and Levitan's spiritual experiences are compromised. The American president is tricked by the FSB's technological manipulations into believing that an ordinary Jew from Odessa is God. Levitan receives his "divine visions" while being drugged and locked inside a sensory deprivation chamber (*deprivatsionnaia kamera*) where his consciousness and will are "knocked out and stolen away like a car or a plane" (*AV* 50). The mission forced on Levitan is to carry out the same theft from Bush.

The universe of "Operation 'Burning Bush'" is permeated by deceptions—the traditional provenance of the demonic. Levitan faking the famous voice of Yuri Levitan from the time of World War II is but one in an endless series of hoaxes that make this world bulge at the seams. His imposture as God is a clear if ludicrous blasphemy. But the lies and impersonations do not end there. Deception proliferates from deception. Levitan switches roles and employers/captors—from "God" to "Satan," from FSB to MI-5, CIA, Mossad, and so on. While the Russian secret services seek to control Bush, it turns out that the Americans in turn have been preying on Soviet leaders (and post-Soviet ones) uninterruptedly since the 1930s. As Stalin communicates with "demonic" forces impersonated by the FBI in a secret room in the Kremlin, Lavrenty Beria, then head of the NKVD, tries to profit from the demonic channel by planting his own man as the Prince of Darkness. Having discovered the real nature of the Kremlin "Satan" decades later, the Russians train one of their own (Levitan) to be Lucifer in order to counteract the Americans' power play.

If classic apocalyptic narratives are built on a series of clear ethical oppositions like good versus evil, Christ versus Antichrist, and Babylon versus New Jerusalem, in *Pineapple Water* lies and confusion are given free rein.[19] In the Cold War game and its aftermath, the Russians strive to fool the Americans just as the Americans do the same to the Russians. The official representatives of the status quo (the American president and Soviet general secretaries) turn out to be puppets manipulated by the secret services and other shadowy powers. The secret services fight for global domination, but these puppeteers are themselves revealed to be controlled by next-level controllers. What seems like a machination of one secret service turns out to be but an element of the larger plot.[20]

The *apokalipsis* (revelation) is always deferred, and what results instead is a many-threaded cycle of falsehood cross-contaminations. With the multiplication and looping of lies, it is no longer possible to discern where they start and where they end. Not only that, but the battle portrayed in *Pineapple Water* is not, as in conventional apocalyptic narratives, between the forces of good and evil, but, rather, between competing varieties of evil. Whichever corrupt dark power dominates at a given moment can enjoy only a transient and insignificant victory.

The turns of phrase used at the climactic point in the plot where Levitan is retrained as Lucifer are explicitly biblical, and specifically from the book of Revelation:

> It [his heart] could not beat next to the Heart of Hearts. It was not ready to burn—oh no, it just wanted as much as possible heavenly sweetness for free. It wished to be loved and petted in its abomination and shamelessness [*merzosti i besstydstve*] . . . . And when I realized all of this, I sent a terrible blasphemy to Him [*strashnuiu khulu*]. (AV 123–26)

Exposed to Satanism, Levitan partakes of the abominations of the Whore of Babylon: "And the woman was arrayed in purple and scarlet, and decked with gold and precious stones and pearls, holding a gold cup in her hand full of abominations [*merzosti*] and the filthiness of her fornication. And upon her forehead was a name written, mystery, Babylon the great, the mother of harlots and abominations of the earth" (Rev. 17:4). In the book of Revelation, redemption is denied to anything and anyone "that defileth, either whatsoever worketh abomination or maketh a lie" (Rev. 21:27). Analogously, "men blasphemed [*khulili*] God because of the plague of hail" (Rev. 16:21), and the Beast of the apocalypse "has upon his heads the name of blasphemy [*imena bogokhul'nye*]" (Rev. 13:1).

As always, Pelevin's story zeroes in on the fundamental problem of unfreedom. Levitan as Lucifer feels himself losing agency and being transformed into a compilation of arithmometers and cash registers that calculate profit and loss. These mechanical devices have a clearly identifiable and diabolic "controlling user." Levitan feels that his internal machinery "had a master, and though he was temporarily away, the thought of his return filled him with sticky fear" (AV 108). Furthermore, whether Levitan chooses allegiance to God or Satan depends on the nature of the hallucinogens forcibly administered to him and the literature read to him while under the influence of the drugs. Drugged and mostly submerged in a crucifix-like posture in the black salt water of the sensory deprivation chamber, Levitan is "completely devoid of immunity to others' speech" (AV 47). Though it seems to him that he betrays God out of his own free will, that is not quite the case. The protagonist comprehends both his sins and the indignities visited upon him. That is why, at the story's close, Levitan asks God to forgive him—as he forgives Him.

Like "Operation 'Burning Bush,'" "Anti-Aircraft Codices of Al-Efesbi" imagines another mock Second Coming that features a problematic Christlike figure—something of a martyr, something of a sinner, but above all a plaything of corrupt worldly powers. The protagonist, Savely Skotenkov, enters Kandahar on a donkey (like Jesus entered Jerusalem). He performs his service in Afghanistan and is betrayed by his countrymen and captured by the FBI. In prison he is tortured, immobilized for weeks with his limbs spread and fixed to the prison wall—replicating Jesus on the cross and Levitan's crucifix-like position in the sensory deprivation chamber. At this point he is thoroughly under the control of his torturers. Like Levitan choosing God or Satan depending on the narcotics administered and the texts read to him, Skotenkov, depending on the type of injection administered to him before a given interrogation, "feels like a bound Prometheus or an insect pinned to the wallpaper" (AV 223).[21] This parodic Jesus/Prometheus/insect helplessly awaits his end.

As a character proper to an apocalyptic narrative, Skotenkov must deal with what the end means for his time—namely, the apocalypse after the collapse of the socialist utopia. "Anti-Aircraft Codices of Al-Efesbi" contains telling subsections: "Freedom Liberator" and "The Soviet Requiem" juxtapose the failed Soviet world and the present.[22] The latter segment describes the ideal realm on earth not as the historical Soviet state (marred by violence), but as a utopian dream of technological, social, and ethical progress held by the Soviet shestidesiatniki. Now that this dream has failed to come to fruition, humankind has entered its last days.

These last days are not at all as depicted in the Bible, where a final battle between the forces of good and evil takes place, and the former proves triumphant. Instead, "Anti-Aircraft Codices of Al-Efesbi" portrays an apocalypse of entropy. The "end of history" (Fukuyama's global victory of liberal democracy, after which no further political change would take place) has humans working hard to satisfy their material desires and no longer caring about nonmaterialistic ideals, whether from a secular or a religious perspective. They are more or less comfortably entrenched in the here and now, and have neither the wish nor the capacity to strive for or even imagine an alternative kind of existence.

Importantly, this story locates the apocalyptic climax in which the final confrontation between good and evil takes place not in the book's present but in its *past*. The book of Revelation prophesies the end times of the world, a time of crisis when every human being will have to make a choice between the forces of light and darkness. By contrast, Savely Skotenkov lives in a post-apocalyptic realm: "He was born after the final battle for the soul of humankind had been lost" (AV 225). This Second Coming is not only parodic but also belated. What Pelevin's mock-Jesus does or does not do no longer matters.

At its conclusion, "Anti-Aircraft Codices of Al-Efesbi" takes the reader on a reverse journey—backwards in time, to the darkness of a new Stone Age as history's end point:

> My ancestors had been hairy low-browed corpse-eaters breaking the skulls and bones of carrion rotting on the banks of rivers to suck out the decaying brains. They had been doing so for millions of years . . . without the slightest understanding of why and what had been happening to them—simply based on instinct. . . . Then this herd of apes became humanity and began its dizzying ascent up the ladder of language. And here I am standing on the crest of history and see that *it has passed its highest point*. . . . My descendants— not mine personally but of my biological species—will be hairy traders with low foreheads who, using identical keyboards, will be, century after century, making holes in credit-default swaps on the shores of shallowing rivers of economics. They will do this without any understanding of the why and what for this happens to them—merely *through instinct, like spiders eat flies* . . . History started this way—and will end the same way. A new dark age awaits us, when there won't even be the *ambiguous Christian God*—only transnational arks hidden in black waters . . . The Human will attain such a degree of abomination that *divine mercy toward him will become technically impossible*— and *the earth will again burn* in a conflagration that will be brighter and more terrifying than anything seen before. (AV 224–31)

The hopeless finale of the story predicts a second apocalypse and an utter historic devolution, with humankind circling back to prehistoric savagery.[23] "A new dark age awaits us" (*nas zhdet novyi temnyi vek*) echoes "The dark age has already arrived" of *Generation 'Π'* (*G'Π'* 108). However, whereas Tatarsky's name evokes not only hell but also the Tatar-Mongol yoke, the historic devolution outlined here is much more drastic. If the Homo Zapiens of *Generation 'Π'* are thrust into a new Middle Ages à la the Tatar-Mongol yoke or Nikolai Berdyaev's early twentieth-century musings (*The End of Our Time*, 1933), the humans of "Anti-Aircraft Codices of Al Efesbi" devolve back millions of years. Humans started as apes—ascended the ladder of language—and will end as apes—though gifted with high tech.[24] These post-apocalyptic subhumans no longer possess cognition, and function animalistically through instinct. All technological progress has been for naught—or has served only to complete the circle of history.

The post-apocalyptic age is also post-Christian, and human existence is devoid of moral content. Skotenkov's Neanderthal-like descendants no longer believe in the Lord, only in commerce.[25] But even commerce is no longer a rational pursuit. The new Neanderthals click away on their keyboards and punch holes as mechanistically as if they are paper punchers themselves—or as instinctively as spiders consuming flies. Again in explicit biblical terms, humans will turn so vile (*dovedut cheloveka do takogo gradusa merzosti*) that God will no longer be able to feel compassion for them. In Pelevin's distinct mixture of metaphysical and techno-parlance, "divine mercy toward him [man] will become technically impossible" (*bozhestvennoe sostradanie k nemu stanet tekhnicheski nevozmozhnym*). To be sure, if humans turn into automatons, divine mercy is a technical impossibility. Nor is divine compassion any option if they devolve to low-browed corpse-eaters. No sentient, much less righteous, entities will remain on earth. And so the world will be destroyed one more time in the all-round apocalyptic judgment of fire coming down from Heaven.

The solution, if there is any, is to leave this benighted realm of one's own free will, like A Huli jumping on her bicycle in the air at Bitsevo Park. Levitan likewise anticipates "entering the Rainbow Stream" and "stopping the emergence of phenomena," while Skotenkov is denied this option: he is lobotomized (Zamyatin-like) and reabsorbed (Orwell-like) into the docile collective (*AV* 144). But what if one wants nothing to do with this life—from the start and even before the start of life? Then, like Masha in "The Hotel of Good Incarnations" ("Otel' khoroshikh voploshchenii"), the collection's closing story, one may choose not to be incarnated at all.

"The Hotel of Good Incarnations" is the story of an aborted incarnation. Offered a chance to be born into this world, and not just as anyone, but as a daughter of a Russian oligarch (and a beautiful prostitute), Masha-as-soul rejects this chance because she doesn't want "to walk around with birdshit in her head, giving joy to bright minds gnawing into the nano-world and one another" (*AV* 325, 346). She welcomes neither the violence nor the stupidity of earthly existence. And so she chooses to remain a pure spiritual potential—never tasting pineapple juice (*ananasnyi sok*) and rejoining "that which always was and would always be" (*AV* 349).

As do Pelevin's other works, *Pineapple Water* invites reading against the preceding tradition of apocalyptic thought. Besides the Bible, Pelevin builds on Russian nineteenth- and twentieth-century eschatological narratives in this collection. Multiple allusions to Vladimir Solovyov's Sophiology, Alexander Blok's *Beautiful Lady* cycle (1904), and Daniil Andreyev's *The Rose of the World* (1958) amplify his own eschatological motifs.[26] The title of *Pineapple Water* nods to Solovyov's Sophia and Blok's Beautiful Lady, as well as Vladimir Mayakovsky's "To You!" ("Vam!" 1915): "Is it to you, those who only love women and food / I should sacrifice my life? / I'd rather serve pineapple water / To the whores at the bar" (Maiakovskii 1: 75). Pelevin's title, *Pineapple Water*, thus invokes Mayakovsky's World War I–era indictment of philistines who enjoy materialistic pleasures while remaining indifferent to the plight of the thousands of soldiers killed in the trenches. To Pelevin, the bloody period of 1914–18 resonates with contemporaneity. Both epochs are awash in violence—though the present one causes bloodshed in ways that are enabled by high tech and muddled by the media.

The *Pineapple Water* collection places traditional eschatology in a new light and reconfigures it in light of Pelevin's own preoccupations. "The Hotel of Good Incarnations" plays off Solovyov and Blok's Sophiology and eschatology as well as Buddhism and Gnosticism, with their rejection of the flesh and the benighted corporeal realm. Both Solovyov and Blok have moved from an earlier faith in Sophia (Divine Wisdom) and the spark of the divine in humans to apocalyptic forebodings and philosophical and poetic imaginings of the Whore of Babylon.[27] As if pointing, in one quick allusion, at the evolution of Solovyov and Blok's thinking from theistic to eschatological, Pelevin conflates the "Beautiful Lady" and the "whore" in the collection's title, *Pineapple Water for the Beautiful Lady*. The Mayakovskian whore allusion simultaneously applies to Blok, since his Beautiful Lady is darkly transmogrified in his later apocalyptic poetry into a whore figure. Pelevin's Masha is called "the beautiful lady" (*prekrasnaia dama*) by the Angel of New Life, and her never tasting pineapple juice (*ananasnyi sok* or *voda*) symbolizes her rejection of earthly pleasures. Her rejection of conception (and consequent unborn state) are Pelevin's ironic corrective to Solovyov and Blok's Sophiology. Pelevin is consistent, in spite of Blok's oscillations between *das Ewig-Weibliche* (the Eternal Feminine) as a spiritual principle and a living woman, so that Sophia, the world's soul, is not incarnated in the flesh.[28] Masha's nonappearance is a pithy statement on the current state of affairs. Read: This world is utterly soulless.[29]

WE ARE ABOMINABLE IN THE EYES OF THE LORD

The post-apocalyptic world of *S.N.U.F.F.* has undergone a series of massive conflicts and devastating nuclear wars. The "World of Antiquity" (*Mir drevnosti*) has disappeared in the flames of nuclear explosions. Larger countries like China, Russia, and the United States have disintegrated into warring principalities. Criminal and quasi-criminal states like the drug-trafficking Atstlan have torn the global community apart. Due to ecological devastation, the surviving technologically advanced countries have raised "Ofshars" (cities on artificial satellites) over the surface of the Earth, and the elites of humankind have relocated there.

Just as the book of Revelation prophesies a temporary rule of the Antichrist, the godhead of Byzantium and Orkland in *S.N.U.F.F.* is identified explicitly as that figure. The first time this Antichrist-Manitou appears in criminal Atstlan, he takes on human form to hand people the new Law. The name Manitou refers at once to "money" and "computer monitor," so this name as a whole embodies the unholy trinity of the chief governing forces of this world—debased religion, finance, and technology:

> In ancient times . . . people believed that the screen of an information terminal glowed because a special spirit descended into it. They called the spirit "Manitou." That's why they called the screen a "monitor"—"illuminated by Manitou." And in Church English the word for Manitou is "money," that's what it was originally. . . . Manitou the Antichrist said, "Those who came unto me did proclaim—Render unto God that which is God's, and unto Caesar that which is Caesar's. But I say unto you, all is Manitou's—God and Caesar and whatever belongs to them or to you. And since Manitou is in everything, let the three most important things bear his name: the earthly form of the Great Spirit, the panel of personal information, and the universal measure of value. (*S.N.U.F.F.* 193)

Like the Antichrist in the book of Revelation, Manitou is a perversion of Jesus and his teachings. Whereas Jesus distinguishes between secular and spiritual authority and defines the circumstances under which it is acceptable to submit to earthly authorities, Manitou the Antichrist breaks up Jesus's basic antinomy of the earthly vs. the heavenly. Jesus's words, "Render unto Caesar the things that are Caesar's, and unto God the things that are God's" (Mark 12:17) are perverted into "all is Manitou's—God and Caesar and whatever belongs to them." As in *Generation 'П,' S.N.U.F.F.*'s metaphysical layer coordinates with its social layer. The unholy trinity—Manitou's earthly form, computers, and money—aligns with the fact that money in this world is literally the Godhead, as are technology and the media.

The appearance of Manitou the Antichrist à la the book of Revelation scenario is prepared for by the destabilization of shared ethical norms and by all-out global warfare: "Good and evil start swapping places at a snap of the fingers or a puff of wind. And a great war of annihilation could no longer be prevented" (*S.N.U.F.F.* 199). Manitou's preaching subverts the Bible and codifies the erasure of moral norms: "Manitou lives in everything without exception, in both the high and the low. And it is the division into good and evil, into low and high that is the original sin" (*S.N.U.F.F.* 377). Humankind is given license to commit any kind of vileness.

Manitou the Antichrist is a malignant demiurge with a thirst for human blood—a metaphysical vision that runs throughout Pelevin's oeuvre and is informed in part by Gnostic notions of an evil divinity whose creation is fatally flawed. Every Pelevinian textual universe has its malicious controlling user—whether Oranus/Enkidu/Baal/fat heavenly hulk of *Generation 'П,'* the vampire overlords of *Empire V*, or the controlling user/moderator/minotaur of *The Helmet of Horror:*

> Do you know who he reminds me of? A spiteful little sorcerer who gets the urge to torture a kitten. So he goes down into a deep, dark cellar, molds a kitten out of clay, brings it to life and then—whack!—He smashes its head against the corner of the wall. And he does that every weekend, a hundred times or more. And to make sure no meowing is ever heard from the cellar, our sorcerer teaches the kittens to think stoically—I came from the dust and to the dust I return. And he forces them to pray to him for the few seconds of their existence. (*SU* 156)

As Pelevin puts it in *T*, which preceded *S.N.U.F.F.* by a few years: humans do not just "exist as gladiators in a circus . . . run by cruel and capricious gods. Worse, they live to feed the gods. Like rabbits"; "God does not read the book of life. He burns it and then eats the ashes" (*T*, 206, 106). Appropriately, Byzantium massacres the Orks as human (or subhuman) sacrifices to the bloodthirsty Manitou.

S.N.U.F.F.'s names for its world's Wells-like upper and lower spheres involve multilayered wordplay that points at stagnation and social devolution as well as at eschatological motifs. "Urkaina" or "Orkland" plays on Ukraine (*Ukraina*), *urka* ("prisoner" or "criminal" in Russian criminal jargon), and "orcs" (a loathsome race of humanoid soldiers in Tolkien's *Lord of the Rings* saga). Additionally, "Urkaganate" alludes to a "kaganate," a ninth-century East Slavic political formation, and "*kagan*" (the head of Urkaganate) is a Turkic term for "ruler." In the novel, Urkaganate is an impoverished fragment of the former Russia and Ukraine.

The name Urkaganate captures the retrograde motion in the Orks' his-

tory, as if the country has devolved to its early medieval, pre-Kievan Rus'
fragmentation, and it also emphasizes a civilizational step back to the em-
powerment of criminals. *Pineapple Water* prefigures this theme of historical
devolution: "We allowed a group of rascals, interested in theft exclusively,
to get rich and gave them permission to reign [*iarlyk na kniazhenie*], and so
they dipped these territories in ruin, and held them under their control" (*AV*
99). The name of the Ork capital, Slava (Glory), points to the ethnic origins
of the Orks and their pathetic self-glorification (à la Soviet times, but for
less compelling reasons). Equally, the name Slava points toward, in obvious
parody, the Kingdom of Glory (*Tsarstvo Slavy*) that awaits all faithful after
the Second Coming of Christ, his final defeat of the Antichrist, and the Last
Judgment.

"Byzantium/Big Byz" is one more Rome turned the eschatological
Whore of Babylon. The name refers to the historical second Rome, Byzantium, as well as "business." Like the Byzantine Empire in its later stages,
this elite society is hedonistic, bored, morally depraved, and on the brink
of collapse. Like historic Byzantium, it is a theocracy, though not of Greek
Orthodoxy but of Manitou the Antichrist and "Movism" (the cult of the
media).[30] There are clear echoes of the first Rome as well. Like gladiators
entertaining bored patricians, Orks fight staged battles in a closed circus at
the center of Slava to please—*panem et circenses*—the decadent spectators
on the Ofshar.[31]

Byzantium worships Manitou the Antichrist and is a world that "loveth
and maketh a lie" (Rev. 22:15). Its people use media simulacra to deceive
themselves as well as the Orks below: "By thy sorceries were all nations de-
ceived" (Rev. 18:23). Its media stars and "discourse-mongers" (corrupt intellectuals serving the regime) perform technological miracles and thus seduce
the people to pray to the eschatological Beast. These are not genuine miracles but "lying wonders" (2 Thess. 2:9), dependent on dexterity and confusion of the senses.

The Whore of Babylon abominations of Big Byz—lies, lust, sexual perversions, greed, and violence—are embodied in Damilola Karpov and even
more in the discourse-monger Bernard-Henri-Montaigne-Montesquieu (aka
Bernard-Henri Lévy, a French public intellectual and media personality).[32]
At the novel's start, Bernard-Henri goes down to Orkland to instigate one
more war with the Orks. The warfare he initiates (as do Damilola and other
Big Byz cameramen) is critical for Bernard-Henri because he lusts after
teenage Ork girls. The new round of violence will permit him to abduct girls,
exploit them as sex slaves, and ultimately kill and scalp them to add to his
collection of sexual trophies.

Bernard-Henri exhibits the traits of the false prophet in the book of
Revelation, the accomplice of the Beast. Like the false prophet, he is ani-

malistic, and his intentions are of a crudely (and indeed, perversely) sensual nature. Bernard-Henri uses the Ork teenager Chloe as a casus belli to jump-start the war, and disguises her kidnapping as a rescue from Orkland's cor-rupt ruler, Rvan Durex.[33] During this fake rescue, Bernard-Henri assumes a mask of false piety and imitates Jesus Christ in his performance of "miracles" and even in his appearance (a tunic and fragrant sandals). Cunning and mer-ciless, he uses the power of rhetoric (discourse-mongery) and technology to seduce the backward Ork populace into falling for the pseudo-miraculous Movism. Like the false prophet, Bernard-Henri has the power to bring fire down from Heaven—by means of a military drone-cum-film camera.[34]

The Whore of Babylon–like degeneration and falsehood of Big Byz are not confined to the figures of Bernard-Henri and Damilola Karpov. The whole populace of the Ofshar displays a deficit of normal human feelings. The words "to love" and "to pity" have come to mean mere imitational pat-terns.[35] Damilola's sex partner and slave (up to a point) is a rubber doll. As the protagonist points out, the flesh-and-blood women on Ofshar may be even more fake than biorobots like the doll Kaya. This is so both in the physical sense—since females have had so many plastic surgeries and sili-cone implants that they contain more synthetic matter than organic one—and in the psychological sense, since they (as well as males) have grown in-capable of genuine feelings.

But the lies and perversions do not stop there, since the entire his-tory and culture of Orkland turns out to have been set up by Big Byz. In Bernard-Henri's explanation, Orks (not their bodies but their history and culture) were invented by Big Byz operatives, since Big Byz requires weak and revolting adversaries:

> Not a genuine enemy, really. More like an opponent who was repugnant and odious in all his manifestations. But not especially strong. So that he never caused any serious problems. . . . Do you know why you don't like yourselves? You were invented so that you could be hated with a clear con-science. (*S.N.U.F.F.* 200–201)

In *S.N.U.F.F.* the apocalyptic antinomies of good vs. evil and so on are pushed out by the false oppositions set up by Byzantium itself—like the opposition humans (themselves) versus dehumanized Orks. When one more war en-sues, the environmentally ravaged and criminal-run Orkland turns into an arena of extermination where an attempt takes place to decide between the "human" and the "subhuman."[36] Like the vampires who pragmatically breed humans so they can feed off their energy, Big Byz sets up the Orks to be killed in media wars and exploited as sources of energy and babies, and so that its own populace may vent its negative feelings against them—in the comfortable conviction that they are a subhuman embodiment of evil. If, according to Pyotr Chaadaev's "First Philosophical Letter" (1829; publ. 1835), Russia's mission is to teach the rest of the world how *not to live*, Pelevin's Orks work hard and die even harder to honor this classic dictum.[37]

Big Byz is marred by all the vices of the Whore of Babylon—falsehood, murder, greed, hypocrisy, lechery, and various sexual perversions. The populace of the Ofshar are "the fearful, and unbelieving, and the abominable, and murderers, and whoremongers, and sorcerers, and idolaters, and all liars" (Rev. 21:8). They live beyond morality: everything, except whatever is deemed un-PC, is permitted. The crisis of heterosexual relationships is brought into the limelight.[38] The age of sexual consent for heterosexuals has risen to forty-six, and is about to be raised to forty-eight. Consequently, women bear sickly children or are unable to procreate at all, and Big Byz instead traffics in infants from Orkland. Sexual perversions include fetishism, animalism, coprophagy, pedophilia, intercourse with rubber dolls, and much else.[39] In the latter part of the book the corrupt Bernard-Henri cedes power to Alena-Libertina Thodol-Brigitte Bardot, a high-positioned priestess in the S.N.U.F.F. theocracy. The elderly Alena-Libertina also lusts after underage girls and makes the sixteen-year-old Ork Chloe her lover. Echoing *Empire V*, Alena-Libertina is full of dead, stagnant blood and seeks fresh young "red liquid" to prolong her vitality. Alena-Libertina equates Manitou the Antichrist with herself—the Whore of Babylon incarnate.

The cameraman Damilola calls himself "the free and enlightened horseman number four," that is, the fourth horseman of the apocalypse (*S.N.U.F.F.* 475). This follows from the book of Revelation: "When the Lamb broke the fourth seal, I heard the voice of the fourth living creature saying, 'Come.' I looked, and behold, an ashen horse; and he who sat on it had the name Death; and Hell was following with him" (Rev. 6:7). The fourth deadly rider is given authority over a fourth of the earth, "to kill with sword and with famine and with pestilence and by the wild beasts of the earth" (Rev. 6:8). The new horseman of the apocalypse, Damilola, kills with his weaponized, distantly controlled camera from the comfort of his sofa—and is rather smug about it (up to a point).

Having lost his doll Kaya to the young Ork Grym and awaiting the swiftly approaching destruction of the Ofshar, which is supposed to crash down to earth, a low-spirited Damilola admits at the novel's conclusion that his people are abominable in the eyes of the divine:

> The whole of Big Byz thought that it was carrying out the will of Manitou—but then why is our world crashing down, why is the universe slipping out from under our feet? . . . Manitou does not wish to have professional servants and proclaimers of His will, and our sacraments are repugnant to him.

He does not want us to nourish Him with the blood of others, offering him our immaculate gerontophilic snuffs as a gift. How can he love us if even our own devices for concupiscence, created in our own image and likeness, flee from us? Why would he want a world where only a rubber doll is capable of unconditional love? *We are vile in the eyes of Manitou [my merzki v glazakh Manitu]*, and I am glad that I have lived to see the moment when I am not afraid to say this out loud. (*S.N.U.F.F.* 472)

"We are vile in the eyes of Manitou" again echoes the Bible and the biblical parlance of *Pineapple Water*. Humans created in God's likeness have extinguished their divine potential. Now they themselves are evil divinities creating machines in their own image and likeness—in order to copulate with them. Even as he still refers to Manitou out of habit, Damilola at this point has in mind a vision of the divine as unlike the official divinity of Ofshar as possible. It is the Lord of the Bible, and more specifically of the New Testament, who finds human sacrifices abhorrent, the populace of Ofshar vile, and teaches *unconditional love*.

The Whore of Babylon is destroyed—and so is Byzantium on the novel's last page: "Babylon is fallen, is fallen [*pal, pal Vavilon*], that great city, because she made all nations drink of the wine of the wrath of her fornication" (Rev. 14:8).[40] The Ofshar of Byzantium, attached by a string to a wall in the center of Slava, crashes onto the Ork capital below when the wall is blown up, and the string destroyed. The apocalyptic judgment from Heaven is parodically flipped: Byzantium is destroyed by the latest cunning Ork leader, who is afraid of betrayal by his protectors on high. No heavenly powers are involved in the act of the final destruction.[41] Or who knows the ways of the Lord?

❖ ❖ ❖

David Bethea sums up the basic elements in what he terms the "epistemological deep structure" of apocalypse:

(1) History is a unity or totality *determined* by God but at the same time so configured as to allow humanity, or more precisely, a member of the elect, to *choose* between Christ and Antichrist, between the truth coming from beyond and the mirage of worldly power, well-being, etc. that passes for truth here and now; (2) the moment of decision has arrived, and the initial stage in the climactic pattern of crisis-judgment-vindication has begun; and the coming End is viewed as tragic and retributive for those who have chosen not to uphold the faith and as triumphant for those who have. (*The Shape of Apocalypse*, 9)[42]

Though there were numerous other Armageddon stories produced in Russia in the decades following the collapse of the Soviet Union, few have engaged the heritage of apocalyptic and eschatological thought with the knowledge and astuteness of Pelevin. His end-of-the-world scenarios are meta-apocalyptic. They subject familiar eschatological patterns to scrutiny and then reprocess them in a distinctive manner.

Pelevin modifies apocalyptic narratives to his own purposes—turning tragedy somewhat quotidian (but not dispensing with the tragic element altogether) and eliminating triumph (with ambiguous exceptions). Part of his intent is ironic and parodic—as in the ultimate judgment brought on Big Byz in *S.N.U.F.F.* by powers from below (which are anything than holy). In "Operation 'Burning Bush,'" likewise, the writer comments playfully on his apocalyptic subtexts—as when he uses Daniil Andreyev's own apocalyptic narrative *The Rose of the World* to initiate the chain of deceptions that twists and turns throughout the story. Stalin supposedly reads Andreyev—who depicted him as communicating with the Devil—and demands that a special room be prepared in the Kremlin to secretly commune with Satan. Andreyev's apocalyptic text is thus built into the habitually kaleidoscopic construction of Pelevin's narratives. Unlike the seals broken in the book of Revelation, the revelation coming from the text is used to spin a new web of deception. Pelevin draws on Andreyev's eschatological plot—and gaily bares the device.

Notwithstanding all the humor and irony, I see Pelevin's work as taking the issues of the end of time and historical judgment *in earnest*. The writer may "dismantle classical eschatology step-by-step," with "Tatarsky's televisionary insights resulting, not from epilepsy, but from magic mushrooms," while "his secularized end is not a murder, but a television broadcast" (Hutchings, *Russian Literary Culture*, 180). Yet, as *Generation 'Π'* formulates it, the end of the world *is* a television program. I would rather side with Keith Livers's take, that although Pelevin's use of apocalyptic motifs in *Generation 'Π'* "does not aim for the level of high seriousness characteristic of Dostoevsky or Bulgakov . . . at the same time, one has the sense that they are employed . . . also quite straightforwardly as meta-commentary on a painful, historically recurring dilemma" ("The Tower or the Labyrinth," 483).

A typical Pelevin story is an *apokalipsis*, a revelation or an unveiling, though in a less stable, final, and reassuring manner than in traditional eschatology. Pelevin's texts uncover falsehoods, machinations, and cover-ups proliferating in contemporary life. The problem is that no final unveiling seems possible; the deceptions and delusions move in an infinite regress. There is no revelation of a prophetic meaning in an era of falsehood—other than that the era is one of falsehood. The freedom of choice in this eschatological plotline is also problematized. But the infinite regression of lies and all-encompassing unfreedom are themselves essential revelatory points.

Most crucially, Pelevin's end-of-the-world scenarios are malignant, banal, and non-redemptive. What emerges in his narratives is the apocalypse of entropy, which is not at all how the apocalypse is portrayed in the last book of the Bible or the writings of Solovyov, Blok, or Andreyev. As in Baudrillard, "history, meaning, and progress are no longer able to reach their escape velocity." Humanity is devolving, and will soon disappear, if not physically, then mentally and emotionally. This degraded perception of history can be contrasted to the early twentieth-century experience of modernity as a time of wreckage and crisis that even so held some potential for heroic opposition and change.[43] There is no ultimate victory of good over evil—no judgment of the wicked, glorification of the righteous, or coming of God's kingdom.

As Gary Rosenshield points out, it is precisely the meaning of destruction that is at issue in apocalyptic narratology: "The Apocalypse validates the meaning of death and destruction—of *bezobrazie*—and thus life itself. Death becomes the portal to the new world, a temporal end to an eternal beginning, the beginning not of a new life but of a higher form of existence, in which the truth—the justified order of all things—will finally be revealed" (Rosenshield, "The Laws of Nature," 885). In Kant's formulation: "If no meaning should be attainable, 'creation itself would appear to those who believe in an end of the world to be as purposeless as a play that has no upshot whatsoever and has no rational design'" (Kant, "The End of All Things," 96; quoted in Oppo, "Introduction," 21). In Pelevin's texts, the end of the world is *meaningless*.

The extent to which Pelevin employs apocalyptic imagery seriously rather than frivolously increases in his later work. If *Generation 'П'* and *Empire V* hint at, yet defer, the Final Judgment, *Pineapple Water* and *S.N.U.F.F.*, concerned as they are with warfare on a global scale and ecological devastation, depict the apocalypse as the Final Reckoning, even if this reckoning is parodically colored and lacks a positive millennial-triumphal component.[44] Humans reduced to machinery (even if brainless and will-less) are still more preferable to them reduced to ashes. Still, plenty of Pelevin's characters (especially in his later work) are retired in a more prompt and resolute manner. Pelevin's recent unveilings may not offer a future that makes known the meaning of all that went before, but they do posit a closure and something like a higher judgment. If the world ends with a whimper of broiler chickens in the Last Soup, it is no less lethal for the chickens involved.

Butterflies in Sunflower Oil

> I foresee that man will resign himself each
> day to more atrocious undertakings; soon there
> will be no one but warriors and brigands. I give
> them this counsel: The author of an atrocious
> undertaking ought to imagine that he has
> already accomplished it, ought to impose upon
> himself a future as irrevocable as the past.
> —Jorge Luis Borges, "The Garden of Forking
> Paths"

THIS CHAPTER TURNS to another crucial aspect of
Pelevin's historical imagination—his reworking of the alternative history (or
alternate history) genre. The *Collins English Dictionary* defines this genre
as one in which "the author speculates on how the course of subsequent
history might have been altered if a particular historical event had had a
different outcome." In distinction from apocalyptic narratives, with their
roots in classical narratives (the book of Revelation, nineteenth- and early
twentieth-century eschatology), the genre of alternative history has become
a prominent part of modern pop culture. Given Pelevin's acute feel for the
up-to-date cultural climate, the tropes of alternative history could hardly fail
to attract his attention. This interest spans his entire oeuvre.[1]

Recent decades have seen the flourishing of alternative history in the
West, and in Anglo-American science fiction in particular.[2] It has been exploited by pop culture as well as by mainstream writers such as Philip Roth
and Kingsley Amis.[3] Alternative history has likewise gained popularity in
post-Soviet Russia, with mainstream (Vladimir Sharov, Vladimir Sorokin,
Dmitry Bykov) and science-fiction practitioners (Kir Bulychev, Andrei Lazarchuk, Viacheslav Rybakov) alike enthusiastically spinning "what would
have happened if . . ." scenarios.[4]

The question of what the popularity of alternative historical fiction reveals about post-Soviet Russia has drawn a multiplicity of conjectures. One
is that Russians have experienced constant rewritings of their history—thus
alternative history is a perspective particularly congenial to them. As the

popular writer-satirist Mikhail Zadornov quipped in an Orwellian echo in 1997, "Russia is a great country with an unpredictable past." Zadornov's quip was a humorous response to previously suppressed facts of Soviet history that came to light under perestroika. In her study of the post-Soviet condition, *Literature, History and Identity in Post-Soviet Russia, 1991–2006* (2006), Rosalind Marsh agrees with Zadornov. She points to the flourishing in post-Soviet Russia of alternative history, the fantastic historical novel, and historiographic metafiction, which treat history in an intentionally disorienting way designed to contrast realistic and documentary historical genres, and draw the reader's attention to the way historical narratives are constructed. She cites Viacheslav Pietsukh, Vladimir Sharov, Vladimir Sorokin, and Dmitry Bykov as some of the more prominent practitioners in these genres.[5]

Another way of explaining the popularity of alternative history in post-Soviet fiction is that the period of perestroika, the breakup of the Soviet Union, and the early post-Soviet years were so volatile that the predictability of historical processes decreased. In Viacheslav Ivanov's reading, the genre of alternative history gained popularity at this crucial historical juncture "when history itself was trying out different possible versions of the future" ("The Russian Novel in 1992/93," 241). In line with the school of semiotics' conceptualization of historical processes—and Yuri Lotman's late work *Culture and Explosion* (1991) in particular—perestroika and its aftermath were a period when history moved away from entropic points of equilibrium and multiple future scenarios became feasible.

Critics in both the East and West have singled out dissatisfaction with the present as a source of inspiration for alternative history. Discussing Western examples of the genre, Gavriel Rosenfeld argues that the novels reflect feelings about the present: "We are either grateful that things worked out as they did, or we regret that they did not occur differently" ("Why Do We Ask 'What If?'" 93). In the post-Soviet context, Andrei Nemzer points out an interest in bending historical points that prompt resigned responses like "It went wrong again" or "It could not have been otherwise" ("Nesbyvsheesia," 226). Boris Vitenberg explains the boom in post-Soviet alternative history as the effect of disillusionment with the gloomy realities of twentieth-century Russian history ("Igry korrektirovshchikov," 281).

This chapter places Pelevin's fiction in the framework of the "alternative historical imagination"—an umbrella term for (post)modern, experimental, nonrealistic kinds of historical fiction that diverge from the alternative history genre in various ways, and show tendencies toward science fiction or speculative fiction.[6] To a degree, Pelevin does partake of common concerns in post-Soviet, postmodern historiography. He reacts to the traumas of Russian/Soviet history, comments playfully on Russia's unpredictable past, and challenges realistic historical genres, Marxist teleology, and the concepts of historical logic and progress. I argue, however, that Pelevin reworks the genre of alternative history in line with his own philosophical preoccupations.

The trajectory of Pelevin's alternative historical imagination demonstrates more and more divergence from conventional alternative history. The story "The Crystal World" ("Khrustal'nyi mir," 1991), a microcosm of Pelevin's alternative historical imagination, frustrates the typical alternative historical scenario by imaginatively combining alternative history with parallel realities. In *Chapaev and the Void* (which makes alternative history the object of meta-reflection), the protagonist and other characters create timelines of their own—not communal alternative histories, but parallel realities formed by their individual consciousness, an approach inspired by the writer's interests in solipsism and Buddhism. *Love for Three Zuckerbrins* (*Liubov' k trem cukerbrinam*, 2014) offers Pelevin's most extended excursion into meta-alternative history. As he plays with and skewers various alternative history memes, he critically interrogates the contemporary popular mindset while pursuing his ongoing social and metaphysical concerns. Pelevin is familiar with the recurrent ingredients of alternative history, and his departures are motivated by his interests elsewhere, as well as by his critique of contemporary culture. *Love for Three Zuckerbrins* maps the generic clichés of alternative history onto metaphysical and ethical issues—hearkening back to the problematic of *Chapaev and the Void* but with the issue of ethics gaining prominence.

FRUSTRATED ALTERNATIVE HISTORY

"The Crystal World," from the collection *The Blue Lantern*, gives a satirical depiction of a historical turning point. It takes place on October 24, 1917, the eve of the Bolshevik Revolution. A pair of young cadets, Yuri and Nikolai, are guarding the Smolny Institute, the soon-to-be headquarters of the revolution, as a disguised Vladimir Ulyanov-Lenin is heading there. Whether or not Yuri and Nikolai recognize and stop the leader of the Bolsheviks from entering the building will determine the outcome of the October uprising.

The Revolution of 1917 is a point of divergence, a crucial event to which there was more than one potential outcome. Using a typical ploy of alternative history, Pelevin places his story at such a key moment.[7] The real outcome is well-known, but the travails of post-revolutionary history makes October 25 (November 7), 1917, tempting material for fanciful rewriting. "The Crystal World" also conforms to mainstream alternative history inasmuch as it conceives of the success of the Bolshevik uprising as dependent on the small detail of whether the cadets allow Lenin to sneak into the Smolny Institute.[8]

"The Crystal World" is a confluence of alternative history and parallel realities. One reality is mundane, while the other is hallucinatory or supra-real.[9] The story, suffused with semi-parodic symbolist allusions, has its hallucinatory plane echoing *realiora* à la Solovyov or Blok. In Yuri's cocaine-fueled dream, the pious old Russia, with its multitude of golden cupolas, sleeps inside a crystal ball like Snow White in her glass coffin—or Tsarevna, Pushkin's Russified version.[10] A demon out to destroy old Russia slips out of the cadet's vision, transmogrifying as Lenin in disguise in nocturnal Shpalernaya Street. The Lenin of the story is a trickster and a diabolical shape-shifter, turning up now as a well-dressed gentleman, now as a lady, an invalid in a wheelchair, an ordinary worker, and so on. In the guise of a proletarian, the leader of the Bolsheviks heads toward the Smolny Institute to coordinate their uprising.

As Yuri and Nikolai discuss the role of human agency and contingency in history during their vigil, "The Crystal World" takes a step into meta-alternative history.[11] As Yuri sees it, individuals do not realize what their mission is in life until the very moment they act on what they were meant to do. For example:

> —Someone might believe himself to be a composer of beautiful music while in fact the only purpose of his existence is to be run over by a cart on the way to the conservatory.
> —What for?
> —For instance, so that a lady riding in a cab will be frightened into a miscarriage and humanity will be spared a new Genghis Khan. Or that someone looking out of his window will have a novel idea. It could be anything. (*SF* 300)

Yuri's hypothetical historical actor evokes Berlioz in Mikhail Bulgakov's *The Master and Margarita*, who is decapitated by a tram. Like the individual in Yuri's story who believes himself to be a musician, the cadets expostulate on modern music (and popular early twentieth-century historiography) just as Lenin rolls his cart past them. In the course of the story, Lenin adopts multiple disguises, but is invariably given away by his iconic softened r (*karta-vost'*).[12] In an instance of dramatic irony, this burr alerts the reader, but not the heroes of the story, to the identity of the person in disguise. In one more layer of irony, the two cadets fail in their mission just as they are discussing the human mission in history.

Unlike other post-Soviet works of the same period that imagine a happier turn of events or try to make up for a lost golden age, "The Crystal

World" does not yield to the urge to compensate or comfort.[13] It is neither a conventional alternative history scenario nor just a playful intertextual romp à la Blok, Solovyov, or Oswald Spengler, and what emerges from this psychedelic narrative is paradoxically a rather sober lesson. By the time Lenin appears in the guise of a proletarian, the cadets' cocaine-induced high is replaced by a hangover, and they are too exhausted to check what he is carrying in the cart. Yuri and Nikolai (i.e., the prerevolutionary intelligentsia) fail in their duty to save Russia because they do nothing. Just when they are complaining that the time offers no opportunity for feats of valor, it is precisely the opportunity for *podvig* (actually, just performing their duty) that they miss. As the intelligentsia are prone to do, the cadets seek solace in artistic disquisitions.

"The Crystal World" resists the escapist inclinations of alternative history. It proffers, yet also frustrates, the alternative historical scenario. As Jeremy Black points out about Western alternative history: "It is all too easy to transform the 'What if?' into 'If only,' and to employ the latter to encourage a nostalgic approach that urges . . . a rewriting of the past in order to make another version seem not only possible but also . . . legitimate and desirable" (Black, *Other Pasts, Different Presents*, 7). Whereas mainstream alternative history parts course with the historical timeline at the point of divergence and, by temporal unfolding, diverges farther and farther from real history (a ripple effect), Pelevin indulges in no "What would have happened had the Bolshevik Revolution failed?" fantasy. Yuri and Nikolai fail to recognize Lenin, and history unfolds as we know it.

A TIMELINE OF ONE'S OWN

Rather than glossing over historical trauma with "everything could have been different and better," "The Crystal World" instead asks, if parodically, just what might have happened and why. With time, Pelevin's alternative historical imagination departs more and more from conventional alternative history. His novel *Chapaev and the Void* (*Chapaev i pustota*, 1996) presents a richer and more idiosyncratic take on the genre.

Precisely because *Chapaev and the Void* roams such a long way from conventional historical fiction, several reviewers have misread this innovative work as a traditional historical novel marred by inaccuracies. For example, Pavel Basinsky was taken aback by "a tuxedo-clad Chapaev drinking champagne and discussing Eastern mysticism," Kotovsky snorting cocaine, and the scene of Pyotr and Anna (Anka in her previous incarnation) "arguing about Schopenhauer while having sex" (Basinskii, "Iz zhizni otechestvennykh kaktusov," 4). The book's portrayal of the Russian Civil War, Basinsky asserts, is "offensive for anyone with respect for one's national, professional, and cultural identity" (4).

As critics have subsequently pointed out, with due hindsight, the critique of historical inaccuracy in *Chapaev and the Void* is misdirected, since the novel in no sense aims at historical verisimilitude.[14] Clearly it is no conventional historical novel, but a work of alternative historical imagination informed by postmodern parody and play. Accordingly, Rosalind Marsh considers it in the framework of postmodern historiographic metafiction (as theorized by Linda Hutcheon), where known historical actors or events may be deliberately falsified in order to suggest the failures of recorded history and the potential for error. This genre "does not assimilate historical details, thus drawing attention to the differences between history and fiction, and implicitly asking such questions as: how do we know the past? Can we know it at all? What can we know of it now?" (Marsh, *Literature, History and Identity*, 245). Historiographic metafiction "contests the nature of historical knowledge by rejecting the concept of linear time, combining reality and fantasy, [and] juxtaposing historical figures from different historical periods" (245).

Yet the pioneering traits of *Chapaev and the Void* stand out even by the standards of postmodern, fantastic, and alternative histories. Though the novel has features of historiographic metafiction such as a mixture of reality and fantasy, nonlinear temporality, and spatial disorientation, the *purpose* of such non-verisimilitude and spatial-temporal warping is different. In history as we know it, the Red Army commander Vasily Chapaev is wounded in a fight with White Army forces, and drowns while attempting to swim across the Ural River. In the novel, he fights the Whites (and the Reds), and exits reality by immersing himself in the URAL (the Conditional River of Absolute Love). The figures Pyotr, Anka, Furmanov, and Kotovsky are all familiar, but their social backgrounds, behavior, attitudes, and motivations are anything but expected.[15]

Granted, one may read Pelevin's version of Chapaev's life as a ludic counterpoint to clichéd Soviet textual and cinematic constructs such as Dmitry Furmanov's novel *Chapaev* (1923) and the Vasilyev brothers' movie *Chapaev* (1934).[16] But Pelevin's pointedly whimsical image of the Red commander as an aristocrat and Buddhist guru is hardly conducive to an earnest consideration of the "How can we know the past?" problem. To a certain extent, *Chapaev and the Void* partakes of crypto-history or secret or conspiratorial history, in which known figures and facts are presented with an unusual twist that allegedly reveals hidden truth. For instance, the novel assigns events in established historical narratives to divergent underlying causes or objectives, and certain facts are claimed to have been suppressed and brought into the light for the first time.[17] But when an imaginary editor in the book's "Preface" claims to reveal "the truth about Chapaev hidden from the peoples of Eurasia," he does not frame the manuscript as a serious revisionist account, but rather initiates the novel's parody of neo-Eurasianism (*CP* 9).[18] Common postmodern trends such as poking fun at the staples of Soviet ideology and the inaccessibility of history or history-as-text(s) are probably present here—but they are not Pelevin's primary focus.

Nor is *Chapaev and the Void* proper alternative history, because the author is more interested in other things such as the workings of the human mind, unfreedom and ways to escape, Buddhism, solipsism, and so on. The effect of an alternative history narrative depends on the reader's recognition that an obvious alteration in a crucial historical event results in a ripple effect in the course of history. The "one invariable rule of alternative history is that the difference between the fictional timeline and the real one must be obvious to the reader" (Duncan, "Alternate History," 217). Unlike "The Crystal World" (which selects a discrete point, only to frustrate the expected), *Chapaev and the Void* shows no clear point of divergence from familiar history, nor does it present a conjectural version of history that could result from an identifiable point of divergence. The context of the madhouse frames the stories outside the general historical flow. The transformations the novel describes have less to do with historical events and more with alternative historical characterizations—for example, the Bolshevik commoners Chapaev and Petka are turned into their aristocratic doppelgangers, a warrior-philosopher and a decadent poet, respectively.

Chapaev and the Void is not a proper alternative history but a novel that—from its very opening—tunes the alternative historical imagination toward Pelevin's ongoing concerns and scrutinizes alternative history as an object of meta-reflection. With the editor's mention of alternative titles for Pustota's manuscript in the "Preface," the work at once inscribes itself in the tradition of alternative historical imagination and points to where Pelevin's real interests lie:

> We changed the title of the original text (it is entitled *Vasily Chapaev*) precisely to avoid confusion with the widespread forgery. The title *Chapaev and the Void* has been chosen as the simplest and least suggestive, although the editor did suggest two other variants: *The Garden of Forking Pet'kas* and *The Black Bagel*. (*CP* 9)

While the suggested title "The Black Bagel" anticipates the crucial Buddhist concept of emptiness, "The Garden of Forking Pet'kas" alludes to Jorge Louis Borges's story "The Garden of Forking Paths" (1941).[19] In Borges's story, a certain T'sui Pen describes a vision of time that branches into an infinite number of futures. In this model, all possible outcomes of an event take place, and each event in turn leads to a further proliferation of possibilities.

When a human is confronted with multiple alternatives, he does not choose one and eliminate the others but "chooses—simultaneously—all of them. He *creates*, in this way, diverse futures, diverse times which themselves also proliferate and fork" (Borges, "Garden of Forking Paths," 26).

The punning of "paths" (*tropok*) and *Pet'kas* (*Petek*) in the "Preface" points to a subtle yet meaningful shift: *Chapaev and the Void* is not so much about bifurcating public histories as about bifurcating individual psyches. So when Chapaev later responds to Pustota's "I did not like the look of their commissar, that Furmanov. He and I may not be able to work together in the future," he says: "You have yet to reach that future of which you speak. Perhaps you will reach a future in which there will be no Furmanov—or perhaps you will reach a future in which there will be *no you*" (*CP* 99).

Two temporal-spatial planes organize the novel's architectonics—the Russian Civil War and the post-Soviet 1990s. In the "commonsense" reading of the novel, its action occurs on the outskirts of post-Soviet Moscow, where Pyotr Pustota is being treated for schizophrenia in a psychiatric hospital while imagining himself to be fighting alongside Chapaev circa 1919.[20] His split self may then be taken to highlight the parallels between the post-revolutionary and post-Soviet periods. After all, in a fine instance of numerological rhyming, it only takes a switch of 9 and 1 to transform 1919 into 1991. *Chapaev and the Void* homes in on two of the most critical points of twentieth-century Russian history, positioned symmetrically at the turn and close of the century, and draws analogies between the breakdown of imperial Russia and that of the Soviet Union. But his novel goes beyond immediate political concerns to explore larger historical patterns. In particular, the predicament of the intelligentsia after the Bolshevik Revolution rhymes with post-Soviet cultural degradation and disorientation.[21]

In a disjuncture from Marxist teleology, the novel portrays Russian history in a circular ("bagel-like") manner—or even worse, as a downward spiral.[22] As Pustota revisits Tverskoi Boulevard in the 1990s at the novel's close, the disappearance of the Strastnoi Monastery and the seeming removal of the Pushkin statue from Tverskoi (Pustota does not notice Pushkin's monument because it was moved from its original place to the other side of the Tverskaia) emerge as symbolically charged. If the Pushkin statue in 1919 "seemed a little sadder than usual—no doubt because his breast was covered with a red apron," in the 1990s "the gaping void that appeared where he used to stand somehow seemed like the best of all possible monuments" (*CP* 10, 386). A later iteration of social breakdown leaves even fewer civilizational vestiges and less hope for those segments of the population that aspire to anything other than a basic survival mode of existence.

Chapaev and the Void zeroes in on the traumas of twentieth-century Russian/Soviet history. In this respect, one might interpret Pustota's split self as Pelevin's way of dramatizing coping mechanisms for dealing with trauma. The historic rupture of the 1990s prompts the protagonist's uncertainty with respect to his own position. In the disarray and disillusionment of those early post-Soviet years, Pustota takes refuge in a fantasy about the Civil War. A shrewd interpreter of his own work, Pelevin posits as much in a dialogue between Pustota and his psychiatrist, Timur Timurovich. The patient "belongs to the generation that was programmed for life in one sociocultural paradigm but has found itself living in quite a different one." And so he "persists in his attempts to clarify his nonexistent relationship with the shadows of a vanished world" (*CP* 46–47).[23]

Like "The Crystal World," *Chapaev and the Void* reflects *on* (rather than reflects) historical trauma. That is, the novel rises to a more sophisticated writing of trauma by plotting ways of processing psychologically painful experiences. In a somewhat divergent though related "domestication of fantasy," *Chapaev and the Void* may be read as a parable of history turning inward because communal history no longer promises much. In this reading, Pustota aborts social engagement and jumps away from the discontent of post-Soviet existence and into his private life—illusions and dreams.

An alternative reading would not domesticate or allegorize Pustota's experiences but would grant them psychic validity under the aegis of solipsism, a key leitmotif in Pelevin's oeuvre. In Pelevin's universe, each human being lives in a virtual space formed by his own mind. The mind produces streams of impressions, notions of time and space, and so on. That is, "there is no such thing as the way everything 'really is.'" By the same token, these perceptions are "as real as anything can be real" (Pelevin, "The Prince of Gosplan").

The problem of solipsism recurs in exchanges between Chapaev and his disciple, and is encapsulated in a late dialogue between them after Anna has destroyed the false material reality with the help of Chapaev's Buddhist clay machine gun, and no one remains in the world but the trio of Chapaev, Pustota, and Anna.[24] At this point, Pustota is left wondering what happened to his rival Kotovsky (the historical Grigory Kotovsky, a Soviet military leader):

> —Inasmuch as he never existed . . . it is rather difficult to answer that question. But if you are concerned for his fate out of human sympathy, don't worry. I assure you that Kotovsky, just like you and I, is quite capable of creating his own universe.
> —And will we exist in it?
> —Perhaps we shall, but in precisely what capacity I really cannot say. How should I know what kind of world Kotovsky will create in that Paris of his? Or perhaps I should say—what Paris he will create in this world of his? (*CP* 366–67)

Because every consciousness creates a world of its own, *Chapaev and the Void* emerges as a constellation of parallel realities formed by individual minds (Pustota, Kotovsky, three other inmates of the psychiatric ward, and so on). Like the novel's dark demiurge Kotovsky, Pustota creates his own universe—and so does the rest of the cast. That every mind creates a parallel reality of its own is plotted narratologically by means of inset novellas written from the perspectives of Pustota's comrades in misfortune—Merely Maria, Serdyuk, and Volodin—and shared via Timur Timurovich's collective dream therapy. Analogously, the branch of the world beyond the grave that Baron Jungern presides over conveys the same cosmological vision.[25] In a graph-like modeling, the spots of campfires are positioned "on the intersections of an invisible grid which divided the world up into an infinite number of squares" (*CP* 258). These campfires represent parallel universes formed by solitary minds. In Edith Clowes's formulation, the plain "becomes a meta-phor for cosmic emptiness filled with innumerable private consciousnesses" (*Russia on the Edge*, 75). It only makes sense that the distance from Pustota to the nearest campfire, apparently no more than fifty paces, cannot be tra-versed without Jungern's supernatural help. How indeed does one cross into another's world?

In *Chapaev and the Void*, Pustota escapes incarceration in a post-Soviet psychiatric hospital through something that is (to him) as real as anything can get—as well as *free and meaningful*. Pustota "himself chooses the world in which he is Chapaev's commissar, and follows this choice with the greatest consistency possible" (Lipovetskii, *Paralogii*, 427). Since noth-ing exists "objectively," what matters is the quality of one's psychic reality—whether it enables liberation or entrapment, free thought and emotion or conventional *poshlost'* (vulgarity) and simulacra. These, in turn, are predi-cated on that realm's individuation and personal investment vs. standardized production and consumption. If what a group takes to be reality is but a collective visualization induced by unscrupulous people (like Kotovsky), a proper response to that externally imposed, mechanically reproduced, and mindlessly consumed simulacrum is an individual inner life that is a prod-uct of both labor and love.[26] One might say that Pustota makes the Civil War temporal layer his reality, and invests in its liberating (and aesthetic) potential—before rejecting both timelines in favor of an even greater free-dom of emptiness—Inner Mongolia.[27]

Pustota's timeline is neither a communal alternative history emerging from a discrete point of divergence nor a delusion stemming from mental illness, but an individual psychic life validated as such. Even as *Chapaev and the Void* participates in alternative modes of historical fiction (including alternative history and historiographic meta-fiction), it accomplishes some-thing altogether its own—not so much problematizing historical knowledge or fantasizing "what if . . ." as transforming the alternative historical imagination through Pelevin's personal philosophical pursuits.

BIRDS AND BOMBS

While individual worlds replace alternative histories in *Chapaev and the Void*, Pelevin's novel *Love for Three Zuckerbrins*, written nearly two decades later, reinterprets the multiverse of alternative history as a constellation of individual ethics-dependent projections. The focus shifts to alternative *futures*. The novel consists of five parts, each of which is a novella. Parts I, III, and V are entitled "Kiklop" ("Cyclops"); parts II and IV are called "Kind People" and "Fuck the System," respectively.[28] Parts IV and V are both positioned in the future. Pelevin broadens the idea of alternative historical fiction, exploring not just alternatives to what already happened, but bringing in the concept of divergent scenarios of the future—parallel paths to bear on individual human consciousness.

At the novel's opening, the narrator, Kiklop, becomes one of a select group whose duty is to keep the world in balance. The same part lays out the novel's central event—a slaughter in the offices of the liberal website contra.ru carried out by a radical Islamic suicide bomber, Batu Karaev.[29] Part II, "Kind People," reimagines the smartphone game *Angry Birds* as an evil cosmogony. In a surreal reversal of the game in which the human player throws birds against a pig, malignant bird-like entities hurl humans as living weapons against the world's Creator. This deity is envisioned parodically as a Great Boar (*Velikii Vepr'*), a modification of the target pig from *Angry Birds*. It is Kiklop himself whom the birds take to be the divinity and attack with their human weapons.

Part III focuses on one of the employees of contra.ru, the IT worker Kesha. Kesha is a typical youngster of his generation, spending most of his time surfing the Web. Kesha is an internet troll who is enamored of violent computer games and online pornography. Kiklop tends to enter Kesha's mind more often than other minds (he has something like telepathic ability to keep history straight), presumably because he views Kesha as a Lermontovian "hero of our time." Kesha is one of the many victims of Batu Karaev's suicide blast at contra.ru.

The penultimate part of the novel, "Fuck the System," depicts a futuristic dystopian society with strong overtones of Orwell's *1984*, cyberpunk, and the Wachowskis' trilogy, *The Matrix*.[30] Like the world of *S.N.U.F.F.*, the world of "Fuck the System" has fallen prey to global warfare and ecological degradation. In the twenty-fourth century, humans live in tiny coffin-like modules in gigantic structures called clusters. These clusters are attached to an antigravitational base and resemble garbage dumps made of consumer trash like plastic bottles and cans. The future versions of Kesha and Karaev are confined to their minuscule cells and immersed in virtual reality. Human bodies atrophy in their cells, while human brains have wires implanted that connect them to the overlaying computer interface. The internet monitors everyone's thoughts for political correctness and compels the populace to share their private activities via social networks. The human community is fully interpellated by the Zuckerbrins (a portmanteau word made up from Mark Zuckerberg, cofounder of Facebook, and Sergei Brin, founder of Google), who rule the infosphere.[31] At the novella's close, Karaev introduces a deadly virus into people's internet-induced dreams and kills everyone for real.

The final part of the book depicts a future reincarnation of the contra.ru office custodian Nadya, a compassionate young woman who is untouched by the contemporary climate of violence and is indifferent to the media and online diversions. Like everyone else at contra.ru, Nadya is exterminated by Karaev. In the future, she reemerges as an angel in a private paradise-like realm inhabited by a group of little animals she takes care of as best she can.[32] In contrast to the many female characters in Pelevin who are Lolita-like underage temptresses, Nadya is a mother figure who provides an alternative to the dystopia.

Each part contains cross-references to the other parts of the book. The seemingly motley stories are thus connected in a stereoscopic manner. Karaev's extermination of the staff of contra.ru in the book's present is reprised twice in the book's alternative futures: first, in Kesha's twenty-fourth-century Moscow, where Karaev kills people by releasing deadly code into their shared virtual reality; and next, in Nadya's paradise, where Karaev-turned-serpent sets out to destroy all the other living creatures. There are multiple other cross-linkages. The "angry birds" in "Kind People" (part II) reappear as "Zuckerbrins" in "Fuck the System" (part IV). In the future, Zuckerbrins are the alien entities behind the screen to whom humans are enslaved. Kesha, Karaev, and Nadya peregrinate from novella to novella. These cross-references also imitate internet structures such as hyperlinks and memes.

A leitmotif that runs through all the novellas and links them is violence as a defining feature of contemporaneity. As in *Pineapple Water* and *S.N.U.F.F.*, *Love for Three Zuckerbrins* underscores the bloodshed and hatred, hyped by the media, that permeates the present world. This is captured most vividly in Karaev's massacre of the staff of contra.ru. In that episode, which is uncannily prescient of the *Charlie Hebdo* shootings perpetrated by al-Qaeda in Paris on January 7, 2015 (Pelevin's novel preceded the massacre by a year), "contra.ru publishes something offensive to sensitive Islamic radicals," and its destruction ensues (*LTC* 402).[33]

But violence in the novel goes beyond the starker instances of radical Islamic terror. Kesha, the internet troll, enjoys provocation for provocation's sake; he excels in entering online communities under different avatars, posting offensive messages, and sowing discord. His other online diversions, like video shooting games and teenage pornography, have a similarly perverse coloration. In the novel ordinary gamers perform acts of virtual destruction, but their enjoyment of violence is genuine. As one gamer, Rudolph, observes, *Angry Birds* is a peculiarly cruel pastime, whose essence is killing on-screen birds, watching them die, and deriving pleasure from it. Enjoying a virtual murder, it is suggested, is not fundamentally different from enjoying a real one—spoiling one's karma.

The problems of violence and unfreedom are intertwined throughout the narrative. In Pelevin's reimagining of *Angry Birds*, human missiles are brainwashed into murder. Rather than human gamers killing targets on-screen, humans are zombified into real-life suicide missions by evil bird-like divinities to destroy the Creator. These human missiles are put to sleep by hypnosis, and possess no volition of their own. Even if they see the Creator as good and merciful, they cannot help but proceed along their fatal course. The human bombs resemble military drones that are fully under the power of their "controlling users," the Zuckerbrins.

As *Love for Three Zuckerbrins* shows, violence hinges on the loss of free will and ethical grounding. Via imagery pointing at 9/11 and other acts of terror carried out by Islamic fundamentalists, the human zombies hurled by the birds at the Creator are Shahid-like "living projectiles" (*zhivye snariady*) whose very bodies have become bombs (*LTC* 88). In an explicit reference to 9/11, one of these human missiles, Dasha, "imagines her body becoming a plane" (*predstavila sebe, chto ee telo stalo samoletom*) (*LTC* 103).[34] She and her fellow bombs fly toward their targets and are blindly bent on destroying them.

In Kiklop's estimation, millions of today's people "have descended into the abyss of revolutions and world wars," having become "the most up-to-date weapons against God" (*LTC* 89). The title of Part II, "Kind People," is an ironic counterpoint to "Angry Birds," which also pokes at the notion expressed by Yeshua in Bulgakov's *The Master and Margarita* that all people are kind. In the futuristic narrative of "Fuck the System" there is greater fallout. The nightmares triggered by Karaev's virus are so terrifying that the dreamers actually die of fright.

The production of the right kind of human—what *Love for Three Zuckerbrins* terms the most up-to-date weapon against God—depends on the obliteration of free will. The humans in *Empire V* are the only species capable of producing *bablos* (because they possess Mind B, the generator of fantasies). Similarly, the humans in *Love for Three Zuckerbrins* are, in one more Pelevinian technology metaphor, the radars (*lokatory*) of God—because only they can conceive the notion of the divine. But to come up with a perfect missile aimed at the divine, the Zuckerbrins need a new type of human who can be circumscribed by material interests to such an extent that the very idea of God is meaningless. Someone like Kesha the troll, called the Great Hamster (*Velikii Ham-ster*)—a bilingual pun that references a small rodent, Noah's sinful son in Genesis and the Russian designation for a rude and vulgar person—refuses the divine any value whatsoever, and has no scruples in dispensing with it.[35]

FUCK THE SYSTEM, OR RATHER VICE VERSA

The novel's futuristic part IV, "Fuck the System," extrapolates on and intensifies the qualities of a present permeated by violence and unfreedom. Humans are ensnared in a social structure governed by the Zuckerbrins, silicon-organic alien entities that have arrived on earth in the guise of technologies and codes. The ensnarement metaphor is literalized by the entrapment of the human brain by wires connecting humans to an overlaying computer interface, the "facetop." Humans perceive no "base reality" (*bazovaia real'nost'*), only a shared virtual space. They do not interact directly, meeting only online and in collective dreams or engaging in virtual sex by means of prosthetic Google devices.

"Fuck the System" (cyberpunk jargon) is also to be taken literally—and turned upside down—since it is really the system that fucks its human subjects. The people of the future, even if they aspire to oppose the status quo (Karaev) or at least pretend to (Kesha), are trapped in sexual intercourse with computers. Like the vampires in *Empire V*, the Zuckerbrins use people as an energy source. Here they do not feed off greed hyped by glamour and discourse, but off sexual energy produced in the process of intercourse with computers, as well as intense feelings of suffering generated by computer-induced hallucinations.[36]

In an ongoing Pelevinian theme, human consciousness is manipulated by cyber technology into a complete loss of self-determination. As Karaev explains to Kesha:

> From our birth we are connected to the information flow that brainwashes us with such a force that no random thought can appear in our minds. The system need not read our minds. It is much easier to pump through your head a thought that you will take for your own. . . . When you decide to eat a hundred grams of mashed potatoes, this is not your decision. It is hammered into you the same way that thoughts with contextual advertising are hammered

in. . . . Your entire inner life is just such a pumping through. All of it. This is merely a long programming loop that the system scrolls in your consciousness. . . . You are what the Zuckerbrins are pumping through you [*Ty est' to, chto prokachivaiut skvoz' tebia cukerbriny*]. (*LTC* 318–20)

Humans are blank flash drives, or tabula rasa, in a more traditional parlance. This blank hardware has fragments of cultural code from informational space copied onto it in random order. There remain no unique character traits and no freedom of choice.

The Kesha-Karaev interaction in the latter part of the novella jokingly illustrates the way humans harbor an illusion of free choice when there is none. A dialogue, or rather, monologue that takes place after Karaev's death is a film recording of the hacker terrorist addressing Kesha. As Kesha watches Karaev, he has an opportunity to "choose" how to proceed in their conversation. For instance, he may nod or keep silent or respond "no" or "not really" to some remark by Karaev. Clearly these are fake options that in no way affect Karaev's recorded speech. As in Che Guevara's treatise, the human has been replaced by a simulacrum. This is what Karaev claims in his recording, and this is just what, in Pelevin's habitually ironic play, he is shown to be—mere film.

AN ENCYCLOPEDIA OF ALTERNATIVE HISTORY

The problems of individual agency, determinism, and freedom and unfreedom are major concerns of historiography, and of alternative history in particular. In a narrative that is concerned with historical process, cause-and-effect chains, and the relationship between the past, present, and future, the Tolstoyesque "labyrinth of linkages" one observes in *Love for Three Zuckerbrins*—Kesha, Karaev, Nadya, and others who emerge in diverse hypostases from one novella to another—carries thematic as well as structural value.[37]

On one level, *Love for Three Zuckerbrins* reads like a basic user's guide to popular alternative history and science fiction—but this impression is transfigured by the novel's philosophical concerns. In fact, it is packed with Kiklop's theorizing on historiography and, more specifically, on alternative history. He discourses on, among other issues, determinism, chance, and freedom of choice. In particular, he covers the popular paradigms of contingency, the butterfly effect, chaos theory, points of divergence, the multiverse (a hypothetical set of possible universes), and quantum mechanics to account for the splitting of worlds.

The narrator launches into his discussion of alternative history by juxtaposing two historical accounts: one that is real, in which the Ukrainian president Viktor Yanukovych is removed from power during the Euromaidan movement, and one that is hypothetical, in which he remains in office for another six months.[38] In this part of the narrative, a Euromaidan protester intends to join the other activists on an evening in February 2014. He must cross a street on his way to the square. Whether he crosses it safely depends on a cigarette ash that may or may not fall onto his clothes from the cigarette of a man on a balcony above. In one scenario, the ash does not fall on him, he does not stop to brush it off, and is not injured by a passing car. In the alternative scenario, he is injured and unable to join the gathering. The timing of the ash falling in turn depends on when the smoker's wife rings him on the phone. And so on and so forth, as Kiklop traces the links in this chain of cause and effect, to its farthest extent—whether a certain female citizen takes her umbrella along on her way to the subway. If the activist does not reach the Maidan, "Yanukovych keeps his gold for another six months, Crimea remains in the Ukraine, Obama does not name-call Russia a regional bastion of reaction, and all the other wheels of history, great and small, do not come into motion" (*LTC* 47–48).

Unlikely as it may seem, a major historical event such as the removal of Yanukovych from power is contingent on an ostensibly minor occurrence. The alternative scenario is hypothetical, since Kiklop's service code prohibits him from revealing instances of real interference, and is meant to illustrate the ways that major historical processes may depend on trivial contingencies (as in "The Crystal World"). As Kiklop explains it, the flow of history consists of

> billions of interwoven causal-consequential connections, endlessly ancient and totally senseless in their diversity—but directing the current of life. These connections (Indians call them *karma*) . . . are not at all accidental because they proceed from the impulse that has brought this world into being. But every complex system has its failures and distortions that can fortunately be straightened out. (*LTC* 46)

And this is precisely Kiklop's duty—to intuit where the fragile balance of the world might get disrupted and correct the disruption as efficiently as possible.

The cigarette story is the narrator's playful instantiation of the butterfly effect, whereby a small change in initial conditions results in large differences in a later state. From here, Kiklop enters a detailed discussion of the basic staples of alternative history fantasy clustered around the butterfly effect. First, he refers to Ray Bradbury's well-known story "A Sound of Thunder" (1952), in which a tiny alteration in the distant past (a crushed butterfly) snowballs into major historical changes later.[39] Next Kiklop references Eric Bress and J. Mackye Gruber's movie *The Butterfly Effect* (2004). The movie explores the idea that, by going backward in time, one might change the future.[40] Cross-time travel results in history splitting into several timelines. The protagonist redoes various things in his past, initiating multiple alternative futures and causing plenty of mayhem. Subsequently Kiklop discourses on the butterfly effect in chaos theory, according to which (per Edward Lorenz) a butterfly flapping its wings in New Mexico might ultimately cause a hurricane in China. The inability to provide a precise weather forecast is attributed to the inability to account for every butterfly on the planet. Such an approach views history as a subtle network affected by each single strand of which it is composed, and emphasizes the role of chance and the inherent unpredictability of the historical process.[41]

After the disquisition on the butterfly effect, the narrator delves into another concept in alternative history—the multiverse. Today's physicists, or at least some of them, believe in the existence of an infinite number of parallel universes. Kiklop uses train imagery to convey the notion of alternative universes.[42] Each car in what he terms a "train of fate" is connected not only to the one preceding it and the one that follows, but to the multiplicity of cars in trains that ride along alternative universes. The trains themselves do not interfere with each other, but sometimes passengers can switch from train to train.

As is common in more recent alternative history, Kiklop posits the "many worlds" interpretation of quantum mechanics as his pop-scientific basis for the multiverse. He refers to Erwin Schrödinger's experiment in which a cat placed in a box may be alive or dead, depending on a subatomic event that may or may not occur.[43] When one looks in the box, one sees the cat as either alive or dead, not both at the same time. Kiklop also alludes to Hugh Everett's many-worlds interpretation that the cat is both alive and dead—regardless of whether the box is opened—but the "alive" and "dead" cats are in different branches of the universe, which are equally real but cannot interact.

HAM-STER VERSUS HOPE

Were Pelevin to limit himself to recycling, even ironically, the tropes of alternative history, *Love for Three Zuckerbrins* would be nowhere as compelling a work. But the writer does not stop at a mere reprocessing of key tropes. Western generic staples like Bradbury, Bress-Gruber, and Schrödinger/Everett are mixed up with the classics of Russian historical fiction and the writer's own preoccupations. The objective of this cocktail is much less intertextual play than it is cultural diagnosis and critique.

149

The "mean-spirited citizen" (*vrednaia grazhdanka*) of the cigarette story recalls Bulgakov's (in)famous Annushka who "has already bought the sunflower oil, and has not only bought it, but spilled it," causing the character Berlioz to slip and fall under a tram (*LTC* 48; Bulgakov, *The Master and Margarita*, 16). The Annushka incident illustrates the potentially transformative value of a minuscule detail in the larger chain of causes and effects—a concept of central importance to historiography. Likewise, "all the other wheels of history, great and small, not coming into motion" mimic Tolstoy's mechanistic-historiographic metaphors that populate the world of *War and Peace*. In Tolstoy's critique of conventional nineteenth-century historiography, linear and coherent accounts blot out the importance of contingency, ordinary (non-leader) historical players, and the awareness of potentially multiple historical roads.[44]

Speaking in the current idiom of alternative history, Annushka's spilling the sunflower oil in Bulgakov's novel and Tolstoy's living moments with multiple potentials are versions of the butterfly effect *avant la lettre*. But butterflies proliferate further in Pelevin's hands. Kiklop mentions the famous Zhuangzi dream: when he awakes, he asks himself if he is Zhuangzi who has dreamed of being a butterfly, or a butterfly dreaming that he is Zhuangzi. This enigma—which was replicated earlier in Pyotr Pustota's 1919/1991 psychic split: is he a man in 1919 dreaming of post-Soviet Russia or vice versa?—may also be seen as a butterfly effect, and not just as a pun. As Kiklop claims, Zhuangzi was the first thinker with an insight into the multiverse. More Eastern metaphysics enters the picture. The multitude of tiny causal consequential connections, as Kiklop points out, is called "karma." And so, the Kesha and Nadya of the future are conceived of as their karmic reincarnations (*LTC* 161).

Yet there is a real question as to what extent these classic visions are compatible with the generic staples of alternative history. As the narrator points out, "The world in which Zhuangzi travels has no relationship to the butterflies that fly in Ray Bradbury's head" (*LTC* 153). Zhuangzi's intuition of the multiverse is predicated neither on quantum mechanics nor on time travel, but on the philosophical concept of solipsism. While we dream, we think our dreams are real; what we take to be reality are perspectives embedded in our consciousness. This is "the most ancient and most succinct description of the principle sometimes called 'critical solipsism'" (*LTC* 156). Worlds "consist of emotions, perceptions, and conditions of the mind capable of emerging and disappearing in any skull that is programmably compatible with them." Therefore an alternative universe is "located in the head of the man sitting across from us in the subway" (*LTC* 391–92).

Pelevin's perennial problematic of solipsism also expresses itself in the notion (in "Kind People") that, in order to kill God, humans merely need to stop thinking about Him. From Kiklop's perspective, Kesha the internet troll is the ideal weapon in the Zuckerbrins' warfare against the Creator, since he is so circumscribed by the activities of the moment that the idea of the divine no longer even enters his mind. To frame this idea slightly differently, in the birds' battle against God, the human serves as both weapon and target since he bears within him a spark of the divine (moral principle). Yielding to evil within oneself, whether freely or as a result of societal coercion, therefore means killing God.

In a related problem, *Love for Three Zuckerbrins* departs from the vision of history as blind chance by pointing, like Tolstoy and Bulgakov, at directive (malignant and benign, supernatural and human) forces behind seemingly accidental occurrences. The concatenation of apparently accidental events leading to Berlioz's death in Bulgakov's novel is orchestrated by Woland. Also important is the fact that Annushka facilitates Berlioz's punishment for his sins of greed and non-belief, and that Berlioz's afterlife is nonexistent because "it will be given to each according to his faith" (Bulgakov, *The Master and Margarita*, 273). The solipsistic line "it was given to you according to your faith" (*sbylos' po tvoei vere*) appears toward the end of Pelevin's novel (*LTC* 437). As regards Tolstoy's views, he conceives of every moment as one that offers a multitude of potential actions that could shape the future in different ways, yet he simultaneously insists on the importance of what one does at each particular moment to bring a "providential" future into being.[45] As malignant supernatural agents (Zuckerbrins) vie for dominance with benign ones (Creator/Kiklop) in Pelevin's cosmology, the humans seem unimportant—but each actually plays a crucial ethical or unethical part.

The "many worlds" theory in the novel illustrates how Pelevin remolds familiar tropes of popular science and alternative history into a vision of his own:

> To punish or pardon the cat about whom it is known that there is a fifty percent probability that it is alive, one must open the box where the sadist Schrödinger has placed it. They even say that a trait detected by measurement may not have existed prior to it. Recalling that the measure of all things . . . is the human, one can guess how each ruler finds in the initial infinity a segment fit for himself. The human, taking himself as ruler, simply measures the universe—and comes up with a world in terms of himself. (*LTC* 153–55)[46]

It is doubtful that either Schrödinger or Everett in their dealings with quanta were concerned with the mind making its own reality and human unfreedom—and still less with ethics. But this is precisely what concerns Pelevin, and it is in this direction that he steers the whole discussion.

The vision that emerges from this bricolage of pop and high-cultural historiographic notions is best dramatized in the opposition of Kesha's dystopic and Nadya's idyllic alternative futures.⁴⁷ Both of these are their individual presents projected into the future and are dependent on of-the-moment individual ethical (or unethical) choices. Thus, "what will be in Moscow in two hundred and forty years has meaning only in relation to each individual Muscovite: there will be as many cities with that name as there will be different minds who are going to return there ricocheting across two centuries" (*LTC* 156–57). Kesha's future existence intensifies his present values and vices like internet trolling and pornography. His reincarnation "essentially consists of distorted and hypertrophied repetitions of his mental habits" (*LTC* 438). That is, the "Fuck the System" narrative, in conjunction with Kesha's present, bares the implied "if this goes on" (cautionary) dystopian impulse. This is Kesha's personal future, but with him being a "hero of our time," the majority of humans hasten in their "trains of fate" in the same general direction. Furthermore, the fates of Kesha's reincarnation in the twenty-fourth century and of the futuristic society at large are determined by his personality. As Kesha learns, the social partner with whom he engages in virtual sex is none other than the cyberterrorist Karaev. Before dying, Karaev plants a virus in Kesha's interface that will later penetrate the overlaying network and destroy everyone. He is able to plant this virus due to the same programming flaw that Kesha used to have intercourse with a Lolita-like Japanese girl ("Little Sister," a parodic counterpoint to "Big Brother") in place of his assigned avatar. It is precisely Kesha's online pornographic and pedophilic inclinations that lead to the destruction of his future world.

At the opposite end, Nadya's immunity to the climate of greed and violence extends into her future private paradise. Her world, which is somewhat reminiscent of the biblical Eden and the Buddhist heaven, is also like a kindergarten (*detskii sad*) where Nadezhda ("hope," Russian), as an angel *Spero* ("hope," Latin) oversees a group of little animals.⁴⁸ The animals are reincarnations of the victims of Karaev's blast at contra.ru. Nadya's mini-Eden is her own creation, "like a shelter where the last earthly hope brings lost, darkening minds" (*LTC* 396).⁴⁹ The reverberations of the suicide bombing continue in Nadya's alternative future as well. Karaev, now a serpent, aims to eradicate everyone else in Nadya's magic forest. Unable to safeguard her world against the catastrophic tendencies of contemporaneity, Nadya can still provide respite to her charges out of love and compassion.

Pelevin reinterprets the multiverse of alternative history as a constellation of individual ethics-dependent projections. In his cosmology, one cannot cross timelines via complicated time-travel technology, as in technophile alternative history, but only through individual moral choice.[50] The book's concluding pages are explicit on this point:

> We travel between worlds . . . when we transform our habits and inclinations. Such an effort—barely noticeable, hard to define, and even happening at an unclear temporal point—is that very space engine which carries us from one universe to another. . . . When we consciously change something in our lives, we do not transform ourselves and our world, as supposed by the classics of Marxism, but transfer to a different train of fate that moves across a different universe. (*LTC* 376–77)

This crossover is neither voluntary nor goal-oriented in the sense that the human agent switches for a particular (pragmatic) reason.[51] Rather, one chooses between ethical and unethical ways of acting, transforming oneself and thereby transferring between alternative universes. The mechanism of traveling between alternative realities cannot be explained "because no such mechanism exists" (*potomu chto nikakogo mekhanizma tut net*) (*LTC* 378). One cannot travel on a rocket from one parallel universe to another, but one can become that rocket.

AGENCY, ETHICS, AND FOUCAULT'S TRACE

To what extent is free and ethical human choice even possible?[52] Just before he delivers his "little sermon," and in a gesture befitting a narrative that scrutinizes alternative history's pop memes, Kiklop alludes to the notion of the meme; that is, an idea or behavior that spreads from one person to another in a society. In this description, all the elements of our personality grow into the future like viruses or bacteria. In a nod to the "selfish gene" popular-science conception of Richard Dawkins, Kiklop notes that not only human bodies but human minds consist of genes.[53] Therefore we resemble the people who lived before us.

Combining Dawkins and Foucault, Kiklop conveys human unfreedom under the selfish gene via seaside imagery. Humans are simply the sum of their names, habits, and fears. They leave an imprint on reality while they are alive, and when they die, life reproduces itself (not humans) via this trace. The sea "fills the imprint in the sand and takes itself for a foot. The leg takes a step, again leaves a hole in the wet sand, disappears—and the sea fills its trace" (*LTC* 375). This passage replays Foucault's oft-cited and itself memetic conclusion to *The Order of Things*: "If those arrangements were to disappear as they appeared . . . then one can certainly wager that man would be erased, like a face drawn in sand at the edge of the sea" (357). In

Foucault's view, man as the object of study was born during the age of the Enlightenment and is about to disappear.[54] The Dawkins-Foucault-Pelevin cross-fertilization yields a human subject who is devoid of free will and, in effect, nonexistent due to genetic determinism.

In *Love for Three Zuckerbrins*, humans, in the grip of the Zuckerbrins (or Kiklops), appear to possess no free will. Just as Kiklop objects to Bradbury's butterfly effects, the vast majority of human actions cannot affect anything significant in the structure of the world. The universe is set up in such a way that small fluctuations very seldom alter the general course of things. From the perspective of the Zuckerbrins, the Creator himself is unfree:

> He is like a circus tightrope walker driving a one-wheel bicycle and juggling a set of plates. From the moment he stepped onto the rope and threw the first plate up, he relinquished the freedom of choice. Or rather, he is left but one choice: to fall down . . . or maintain equilibrium. (*LTC* 83)

And yet, the novel leaps from the contemporary discourse on genetic and social determinism (memes, the selfish gene, and Foucault waxing lyrical on the advent of the posthuman) to Kiklop's "little sermon" (*malen'kaia propoved'*) on human agency and ethics: "A slow but most reliable way to cross over into happy worlds is described in all ancient books—in the sections dedicated to, sorry for the cliché, Commandments" (*LTC* 378).[55] This being the last word in Kiklops' narrative—*after* he outlines the ways postmodernists and posthumanists problematize traditional humanist notions—it reads as the most important one, the final message the reader takes from his story.

To be sure, Pelevin delivers his sermon, which is liable to alienate many a reader attuned to irony and play, with a tongue-in-cheek apology: "Sorry for the cliché, Commandments" (*Sorry za banal'nost', zapovediam*). Moreover, *Love for Three Zuckerbrins* ironizes its own cosmology as metaliterary play. It is the authorial alter ego Kiklop whom the Zuckerbrins take for the Creator and who fights evil in the novel. It is Kiklop who as deus ex machina interferes to keep the world in balance, singles out Nadya, and dispenses judgment on Kesha and Karaev.[56] The metaliterary also functions as yet another illustration of solipsism. As Pelevin is fond of reminding his readership, the world is made of ourselves. As pointedly fictional and produced by an individual mind, the narrative hardly aspires at making universally valid claims (à la Tolstoy). But even apologetic and cloaked in irony this way, the ethical message does not lose its potency.

Importantly, the ethical in *Love for Three Zuckerbrins* is compatible with solipsism. The novel performs a crucial spin on Pelevin's perennial problematics—welding this potentially problematic worldview to issues of human agency and ethics. In *Generation 'П'* "eternity existed only as long as

Tatarsky sincerely believed in it," while in *Empire V* to make up God and to discover that He exists are "one and the same thing" (*EV* 360). The Kesha versus Nadya narratives are open to a solipsistic reading, but at the same time they convey an emphasis on the challenge and possibility of an individual's moral choice. Like Vera Pavlovna bringing into existence a Moscow overflowing with excrement (in the story "Vera Pavlovna's Ninth Dream"), Vavilen Tatarsky dreaming up the goddess of money Ishtar, or Roman Shtorkin's world determined by childhood memories of a fan resembling a vampire bat, Kesha and Nadya create worlds after their own kind. Kesha represents the zeitgeist of his time, while Nadya stands for the individual who proves impervious to her era—as if "possessing an inner screen, invisible but very firm—and the world's web and dust were unable to break in" (*LTC* 396). Twenty years after Vera Pavlovna inundates perestroika-era Moscow with feces, Nadya emerges as a welcome counterbalance introduced by her creator (Creator).

Pelevin's vision of where society overall is moving is not a hopeful one. The overwhelming majority of people are neither free nor ethical (and stupid besides).[57] But there remains hope (*nadezhda, spero*) for the minority who do not lie, steal, and kill. Whether Nadya makes a conscious effort to close her brain off from the sewage of contemporaneity or whether she is luckily made this way (or some combination thereof), she is capable of transferring to an alternative and better timeline based on her actions.[58] If all possible decisions are made and infinite timelines exist—the Borgesian scenario of alternative history—human choices carry no moral import; they are predetermined by the timeline one happens to be in.[59] But Pelevin reverses this logic: it is not the timeline one is in that determines the decision, but one's decision that determines the timeline one is in.[60]

To put the question above slightly differently: is it possible to avoid a dismal future on account of Nadya and her like? If we read the multiverse literally, such a query is beside the point, since there will be as many alternate futures as there are individual minds. Yet there is some leeway in how literally or figuratively one understands every significant act as a transfer into an alternate universe. In Tsvetan Todorov's description, there exists a scale of subgenres, extending between the fantastic that "must be read literally" and the allegorical where "the level of literal meaning has slight importance" (*The Fantastic*, 65). Narratives with an explicit allegory (a moral to the story) are rarely enjoyed by modern consumers of literature. Indeed, Pelevin's increased didacticism has made many critics, attuned to his habitual irony and play, uncomfortable.[61] This is something the writer clearly anticipates with his "Sorry for the cliché."

Kiklop's clarification that, when we change our lives, we do not transform ourselves and the world, but transfer to a different universe, cautions against an allegorical reading of the multiverse. The recurrent motif of the mind determining reality also seems quite literal in Pelevin's work.[62] At the same time, the alternative universe "located in the head of the man who sits across from us in the subway" suggests a shared basic reality with many mini-multiverses within individual consciousness. In a more moderate version of epistemological solipsism, one doubts the possibility of accessing anything outside one's mind, rather than denies external reality altogether. In its more extreme variety (metaphysical solipsism), external reality and other consciousnesses are denied existence. Perhaps the kind of world the reader will create in that fictional imaginary of his or what fictional imaginary he will create in that world of his depends on his particular worldview. What one is less at liberty to do is to dismiss the novel's strongly articulated message about ethical verities that structure humans and timelines.

❊ ❊ ❊

Pelevin handles alternative history in a manner typical of his approach to pop cultural paradigms in general—via a knight's move (if we borrow Viktor Shklovsky's term) or, in Pelevin's own parlance, through "a somersault of thought." Just as he does not react to but instead reflects on the trauma of Russian/Soviet history and is not particularly keen on the generic concerns of historiographic metafiction, he does not indulge in "what if . . ." fantasies. The tropes of alternative history are present in his work—but Pelevin shifts gears to play with them on a meta-level. As such, his pop cultural references critique the clichés of popular consciousness, and destabilize memetic processes.[63]

Whereas "The Crystal World" frustrates the approach of alternative history to the past and *Chapaev and the Void* turns provocatively from communal history to individual discoveries of the past and individual histories (pasts and presents), *Love for Three Zuckerbrins* produces alternative histories of the *future*. This shift is significant. As Jeremy Black argues about Western alternative history, much of the potency of counterfactual thinking lies in the fact that it is "not employed solely for discussion about the past, but, instead, take[s] a more central role in consideration of the future" (*Other Pasts, Different Presents*, 5). To be sure, alternative histories of the future are not counterfactual. Instead, they imagine potential scenarios and think through the ways to bring good ones into existence and avert bad ones. Perhaps, as *Love for Three Zuckerbrins* suggests, nearly three decades after the fall of the Soviet Union, it is time to think about the future rather than agonize over or eulogize the past.[64]

Like *Chapaev and the Void*, *Love for Three Zuckerbrins* reconceptualizes alternative histories as parallel realities that are dependent on individual minds. These future-oriented timelines extrapolate on individuals' personality traits, actions, and choices in the here and now. No high tech-enabled time travel or fanciful rewriting of a topical historical scenario takes place—instead the point is made that, though manipulated by Zuckerbrins and Kiklops, a person's choice does possess moral import.

Perhaps most significantly, Pelevin translates the generic clichés of al-ternative history into metaphysical and ethical issues—with the latter gain-ing more prominence in his later work. If we take *Chapaev and the Void* and *Love for Three Zuckerbrins* to mark early post-Soviet and more recent Peleviniana, respectively, a trajectory emerges from metaphysical experi-mentation with a stress on solipsism and personal liberation to a greater emphasis on an ethical relationship to others. As Mark Lipovetsky suggests, such a shift is already evident in *The Sacred Book of the Werewolf*: A Huli's attitude "is based on love understood as a *refusal to exercise power over the Other*, in spite of existing rights and opportunities" (*Paralogii*, 669).

In the complex and fascinating case of *Chapaev and the Void*, Pelevin's emphasis on solipsism may prompt reservations regarding his ethical invest-ment. Angela Brintlinger has pointed out that his "less-than-constructive so-lution [in *Chapaev and the Void*] has frustrated Russian critics and prompted them to call the novel unethical" ("The Hero in the Madhouse," 56). In my reading, however, the problem of *individual liberation* so acutely posited in this classic of the 1990s is already conceived as an *ethical imperative*, if one that is susceptible to solipsistic readings with no clear ethical dimension. The latter relies on the former, since mental interiority is necessary if there is to be an ethical perspective within the universe(s) of contingency.

That said, *Love for Three Zuckerbrins* goes farther in its ethical invest-ment. As Pelevin's apocalyptic narratives, especially later ones like *Pineapple Water* and *S.N.U.F.F.*, take the issues of moral norms and ethical judgment in earnest, *Love for Three Zuckerbrins* transforms a Harry Turtledove al-ternative history novel or a *Wolfenstein* video game into bits of Bulgakov and Zhuangzi joined in unexpected ways and molded into his own trenchant vision. Pelevin transcribes moral verities in terms the generation of Mark Zuckerberg and Sergei Brin can better relate to. His timeline crossovers are karma- and (even) Ten Commandments-fueled. What results is an unortho-dox alternative to, and critique of, the more memetic forms of alternative historical imagination. *Dum Lego Spero.*

PART IV

Intertext and Irony

Somersaults of Thought

O beautiful far-away, do not be cruel to me.
—Soviet children's TV series, *Guest from the*
Future

PELEVIN'S SOCIO-METAPHYSICAL fantasies
are rich and multifaceted works that overflow with subtexts. Rather than
going over his innumerable allusions (an impossible task), this chapter examines two prominent Pelevinian references—Dostoevsky and the Strugatsky
brothers—as a way of modeling his general approach to his literary predecessors.[1] As I argue, Pelevin engages and reworks the classic nineteenth-
century novelist and the classics of Soviet science fiction in order to buttress
his analysis of contemporary global culture.

There are a few points about Pelevin's intertextuality with which I
would like to preface this discussion. First, however playful Pelevin's intertextual engagements may be, I view them as *primarily conceptual*, and
only secondarily meta-literary. That is, Pelevin is less invested in intertextual
effects per se—whether parodic (in the vein of, say, Sorokin), pastiche-like
(à la Akunin), or something else—than in driving home his own political,
philosophical, and metaphysical vision through dialogue with other works.
Dostoevsky's critique of materialism and capitalism, rethought in the light
of recent history, promotes Pelevin's own indictment of postmodern techno-
consumerism. Drawing on Dostoevskian quandaries such as free will versus
determinism, Pelevin interrogates unfreedom(s) in the present. Similarly,
the Strugatsky brothers' discourse on modernity and the late Soviet condition provides a blueprint for Pelevin's investigation of post-Soviet realities.
He demonstrates how their humanistic projects have been perverted, and
reads the defeat of freedom, reason, and ethics in contemporaneity.

Second, Pelevin's intertexts are neither a straightforward homage nor
an obvious parody but an imaginative and often paradoxical *rethinking*. He
considers classic notions from unexpected angles, provides twists on familiar
themes, and reworks them in ways that enrich his own vision. Third, the
target of Pelevin's subversion is to a much lesser extent the past and past
literary productions than the *world we live in* and our own peers. While Dos-

161

toevsky's religious humanism and the Strugatsky brothers' secular humanism may appear arcane to many a (post)modern beholder, Pelevin's take is mercurial, a mixture of satire and longing. Where his stance is consistently unforgiving is toward contemporaneity that has effectively dispensed with the naive/arcane/vital/essential values that Dostoevsky and the Strugatsky brothers had encoded.

WINTER NOTES ON THE RUSSIAN IDEA

Generation 'Π' combines Western theoretical models with the rich Russian heritage of antimaterialist thought. Dostoevsky, who was probably the most eloquent Russian spokesman against materialism, is first on the list.[2] Pelevin uses a Dostoevskian subtext (along with eschatological subtexts) to amplify his own metaphysical critique of techno-consumerism.

Generation 'Π' draws on Dostoevsky to meditate on the disappearance of eternity in post-Soviet Russia. The first chapter closes with a reference to Svidrigailov's vision of eternity as a country bathhouse with spiders in Dostoevsky's *Crime and Punishment* (1866): "One little room, something like a bathhouse in the country, black with soot, with spiders in every corner" (245). As Tatarsky writes in his notebook, when the subject of eternity disappears, then all its objects disappear as well, and the only subject of eternity is whoever happens to remember it. His last poem, written after this entry, ends as follows:

> What is eternity—it is a bathhouse,
> Eternity is a bathhouse with spiders.
> If Man'ka forgets this bathhouse,
> What will happen to the Motherland and to us? (*GΠ* 16)

Tatarsky does not compose any more poems after this because they have lost all meaning and value.

Generation 'Π' reinforces Dostoevsky's concern that (post)modernity may dispense with any meaningful vision of the spiritual. Svidrigailov's vision of eternity is in fact anti-eternity inasmuch as it is conceived in arch-materialist and in banally evil terms.[3] The idiomatic phrase "like spiders in a jar" (*kak pauki v banke*) captures the mutual destruction that primitive consumption entails. By punning *ban'ka s paukami—banka s paukami* ("little bathhouse with spiders—a jar with spiders"), Pelevin's narrative turns Svidrigailov's anti-eternity into an even more vicious denunciation.

Tatarsky's last poem blends classical Russian culture and late Soviet nonconformism. The poem is an unlikely but characteristically Pelevinian combination of Dostoevsky and a perestroika hit by the Russian rock band DDT, "What Is Autumn?" (1991), and it peers into a post-Soviet future that is devoid of the spiritual. It imitates both the prosody and the syntactic structure of the composition by Yuri Shevchuk, DDT's leader. Shevchuk's song conveys the precarious liminal condition of society during the disintegration of the Soviet Union. The future looms unpredictable and scary: "Autumn, will we crawl, will we fly to reach the answer / What will happen to the motherland and to us?"

Pelevin's imagery develops Dostoevsky's theme of entrapment in a materialistic, banal, and evil (anti)-eternity. Svidrigailov's "bathhouse with spiders" becomes a leitmotif in *Generation 'П.'* In the chapter entitled "Poor Folk" (referring to Dostoevsky's 1846 novella of that name), Tatarsky wonders how long it would take after death for media men to scrub off all the human attention that had eaten into the very pores of their souls. He notes that for some reason, in his mind posthumous existence takes the form of a bathhouse. In one more echo of Svidrigailov, Che Guevara's Oranus and the ancient tyrannical god Enkidu are imagined as enormous spiders. Svidrigailov's translation of the spiritual into the material foreshadows *Generation 'П'*'s detailed consumer cosmogony, with the cult of the golden goddess Ishtar, and societal members devouring one another like the proverbial spiders in a jar.

Generation 'П''s mythological and eschatological layers evoke Dostoevsky's condemnation of materialism. Pelevin, like Dostoevsky, employs Babylonian mythology to couch his critique of the mechanical and utilitarian civilization of the West.[4] We see this expressed in Dostoevsky's *Winter Notes on Summer Impressions* (1862), in which the famous Crystal Palace, erected in London in 1851 for the World Industrial Exhibition, is described as:

> A biblical picture, something about Babylon, some prophecy from the Apocalypse taking place before your very eyes. You feel that you need a great deal of eternal spiritual resistance and negation not to succumb to impressions, not to bow before facts, and not to deify Baal, that is, not to accept the material world as your ideal. (*Winter Notes on Summer Impressions*, 42)

The Crystal Palace embodies the values of capitalism, rationalism, and technology, and raises apocalyptic associations in Dostoevsky's mind. He believes that the emphasis on material well-being at the expense of a guiding spiritual framework will bring about the end of times.[5] Like Dostoevsky, Pelevin underscores Babylon's apocalyptic connotations. The temptation to "bow to what is," "to accept the material world as your ideal," are problems at the core of Pelevin's work. Even the aphorism, "Rich Lord for the rich lords," is akin to Ganya Ivolgin's comic yet revealing labeling of Baron Rothschild as the "King of the Jews" in *The Idiot* (1866).

As Tatarsky's story unfolds, the allusions to Dostoevsky multiply. And each time, Dostoevsky's oeuvre is rewritten in order to comment on novel consumer realities. The copywriter Morkovin revises Raskolnikov's "Was I a trembling creature or had I the right?" (*Tvar' ia drozhashchaia ili pravo imeiu?*) into "I am a trembling creature with inalienable rights" [to money] (*Crime and Punishment*, 260; *ГП* 11). Raskolnikov's right to murder as a test or proof of his superman-hood is transposed appropriately enough as the post-Soviet man's right to money while remaining a self-assured louse. The classic formula is given an unexpected twist, and neither reaffirms nor deconstructs Dostoevsky's original point, but reads a new meaning into it.

The later Dostoevskian evocations in *Generation 'П'* are similarly reworked to reflect on the delusional post-Soviet context. Dostoevsky's fantasy of talking corpses in "Bobok" (1873) becomes a phantasmagoria of simulated politics in Pelevin's post-Soviet Russia. In a media man's description, virtual dummies of politicians are produced from "stiffs" and "semi-stiffs." The image of a politician capable of moving his hands and head is a "semi-stiff" (*polubobok*), while one fully immobile is a "stiff" (*bobok*) (*ГП* 207). Whether someone like the then-Russian president Boris Yeltsin appears semi-alive or utterly comatose on the TV screen on a given day depends on the speed of the graphics processors that the United States rations off to Russia. This, in turn, depends on how compliant or disobedient the weakened post-Soviet Russia behaves vis-à-vis American global policy.

Pelevin's wordplay around a warship christened *The Idiot* packs a multilevel joke that satirizes shabby post-Soviet realities:

> Very soon now in the city of Murmansk the nuclear jet-powered cruiser *The Idiot* will slide down the slipway. Its building began to mark [*zalozhennyi po sluchaiu*] the hundred and fiftieth anniversary of the birth of Fyodor Mikhailovich Dostoevsky. It is not yet clear whether the government will be able to return the money it has received from pawning the ship [*poluchennyi v zalog sudna*]. (*ГП* 268)

The word *zalozhennyi* plays on two meanings, "its building began" and "pawning." Insolvent, post-1991 Russia is forced to mortgage the ship to the West. The reference to *The Idiot*, evoking the Christlike Prince Myshkin, which is incongruous in the military and business context, intensifies the critique. Instead of the Russian Orthodox idea of the universal victory of goodness and beauty espoused by Myshkin, there is the Soviet-era doctrine of military aggression, and that in turn is ousted by post-Soviet bankruptcy and corruption.[6] With Pelevin, the designation "the idiot" problematized by Dostoevsky—Myshkin is a fool in Christ, and it is only in the eyes of the novel's undiscerning characters that he is perceived as stupid—returns to its original derogatory meaning.

Tatarsky's appeal to the spirit of Dostoevsky when assigned the task of advertising "the Russian idea" is another multilevel joke that targets degraded post-Soviet realities and sums up the classic novel's legacy and its critical interpretations. A mafia man who needs a national slogan to accompany Russian money in the global flows of capital, orders from Tatarsky an advertisement to use. Tatarsky pins all his hopes on Dostoevsky as the great prophet of the Russian idea, and tries to contact him via Ouija board. The results are disappointing. The Ouija board trembles and leaps in the air, as though pulled in many directions at once by equally strong spirits, and the crooked scribbles left on the paper are useless. Tatarsky consoles himself with the thought that the idea he is seeking is so transcendent that illegible marks are the only way to communicate it.

This mockery is aimed at the bankruptcy of the Russian idea under the new regime, which is reduced to backing up mob money. Dostoevsky's spirit is infuriated at such ignominy. The Ouija board's leaps also point to Dostoevsky's struggles with contradictory ideas and the renowned polyphony of his novels as theorized by Mikhail Bakhtin.[7] Additional satire aims at Dostoevsky's and, more generally, classical Russian literature's ideals of the inexpressible and ineffable (as in Tyutchev's "Russia cannot be understood by the mind"). Yet the main point (just as in *The Idiot* allusion) is not Dostoevsky's naïveté, but life's degradation in post-Soviet Russia.

The elimination of freedom in post-Soviet Russia and the world of contemporaneity is predicated on unbridled materialism—a notion anticipated in works like *The Brothers Karamazov* (1880). Father Zosima exposes problems that underpin the modern Western conceptualization of freedom: "Taking freedom to mean the increase and prompt satisfaction of needs, they [men] distort their own nature, for they generate many meaningless and foolish desires, habits, and the most absurd fancies in themselves" (*The Brothers Karamazov*, 313–14). The modern world postulates that every member of society has needs, and encourages us to satisfy them to the fullest, since each individual possesses the same rights as the noblest and richest. Such an understanding of freedom, Zosima asserts, means enslavement to pleasure-seeking, self-display, and ultimately discord and violence (since members of society are prompted to satisfy their needs at the expense of others). In related terms, *Generation 'П'* describes a mechanism under which commodities operate in a system of unquenchable material desire, and *Empire V* elaborates on this mechanism of artificially hyped needs.

Generation 'П' imaginatively weaves Father Zosima's antimaterialism

165

into its own chain of apocalyptic associations: television—consumerism—
Gehenna. The magical creature Sirruf that Tatarsky encounters during his
hallucinogenic trips tells him: "An old man called Zosima was horrified by
intimations of material fire" (*G'П'* 155). The reference is to a passage in
the "Of Hell and Hell Fire: A Mystical Discourse" chapter of *The Brothers
Karamazov*:

> People speak of the material flames of hell. . . . If there were material flames,
> truly people would be glad to have them, for, as I fancy, in material torment
> they might forget, at least for a moment, their far more terrible spiritual tor-
> ment. And yet it is impossible to take this spiritual torment from them, for
> this torment is not external but is within them. . . . For though the righteous
> would forgive them from paradise, seeing their torments, and call them to
> themselves, loving them boundlessly, they would thereby only increase their
> torments, for they would arouse in them an even stronger flame of thirst for
> reciprocal, active, and grateful love, which is no longer possible. (322–23)[8]

Zosima cautions against reading the flames literally—as part of his general
critique of reductive materialistic conceptualizations of faith. Punishment is
not physical torture, but the loss of one's ability to love—and simultaneously
the freedom to love based on one's desire.

Generation 'П''s interpretation of the fires of hell is equally
unconventional—but different and informed by contemporary realities.
First, it is our earthly life, not any kind of posthumous realm, which is hell-
like. Second, the conflagration has to be maintained, and it is media men
like Tatarsky who are the diabolic service-personnel maintaining those fires.
Third, the man of contemporaneity is deluded into thinking that he benefits
from consumerism, when actually he is the one being consumed:

> —But what is it that is consumed?
> —Not what, but who. Man believes that he is the consumer, but in reality
> the fire of consumption consumes him. . . . There is mercy in the fact that in
> place of crematoria you have television and supermarkets; but the truth is
> that their function is the same. (*G'П'* 119–20)[9]

The fires of hell are both literally material and figurative (an all-consuming
greed), and one cannot help but be engulfed by them.

In *Generation 'П'* the materialistic and demonic generation P(izdets)
supplants their parents, the idealistic *shestidesiatniki*, with the kind of mechanical inevitability demonstrated in the classic fathers-sons divide in Dostoevky's *The Devils* (1871–72). Just as the high-minded phrasemonger Ste-
pan Trofimovich Verkhovensky cedes to the dastardly and super-practical

Pyotr Stepanovich, Aksyonov and Lenin merge and transmogrify into Vavilen Tatarsky and his generation.

AND A BALANCE IN HIS HAND

In the antimaterialistic and eschatological problematic of *Pineapple Water*, Dostoevsky is once more the core reference. There is much in this book that reverberates with Dostoevsky's critiques—except that matters, as the collection insists, have grown significantly worse. *Pineapple Water* revisits, and adds further skeptical twists to, the Dostoevskian quandary of (un)freedom. *The Brothers Karamazov*'s grim rendition of the Second Coming in the fantastic scenario of "The Grand Inquisitor" is recast as a fait accompli.

The rule of Satan, in Dostoevsky's and Pelevin's narratives alike, means subservience to egotism and commerce at the expense of any spiritual component. *The Idiot* rethinks the third horseman of the Apocalypse, traditionally understood as the harbinger of famine, as heralding the age of materialism: we live "in the time of the third horse, the black one, and the rider with a balance in his hand, because in our time everything is in balances and contracts, and people are only seeking their rights" (*The Idiot*, 201).[10] The line "And he that sat on him had a set of scales in his hand [*imeiushchii meru v ruke svoei*]" (Rev. 6:5) spurs such a Dostoevskian rereading of the book of Revelation. In *Pineapple Water*, the pair of arithmometers into which Levitan feels his soul transformed during his exposure to Satanism resembles the scales in Dostoevsky and the book of Revelation. The satanic order is equally technology-based. So the dying Ippolit in *The Idiot* pictures the natural (material) world that kills him as an enormous machine of the most up-to-date construction. Analogously, mechanisms in *Pineapple Water* exterminate humans literally (killer machines) and allegorically (by crushing their spirit).

What do "gifted Russian boys of the new age"—alluding to *The Brothers Karamazov*—do in this post-apocalyptic world? (*AV* 147). In Dostoevsky's novel they meet "in some stinking local tavern." They "have never seen each other before in their whole lives, and when they walk out of the tavern, they won't see each other again for forty years." What are they "going to argue about, seizing the moment in the tavern? None other than the universal questions" (*The Brothers Karamazov*, 234). Likewise, Pelevin's boys dabble in universal questions and occasionally rebel, albeit unsuccessfully.

The themes in "The Grand Inquisitor," a key chapter in *The Brothers Karamazov*—on freedom and its lack, materialism, and faith—are at the core of *Pineapple Water*. In the Grand Inquisitor's oft-cited argument, Christ misjudges humankind when refusing Satan's temptations in the desert.[11] He rejects the banner of earthly bread that will make all men bow to him for freedom and heavenly bread; he does not leap down from the roof of the temple because he does not want to capture men's devotion by a miracle, but wants faith and love freely given; and he refuses the sword of Caesar (earthly power) because his kingdom is not of the earth. Thereby Christ increases men's freedom and unhappiness: "Did you forget that peace and even death are dearer to man than free choice in the knowledge of good and evil? There is nothing more seductive for man than the freedom of his conscience, but there is nothing more tormenting either" (*The Brothers Karamazov*, 255–56). For the Grand Inquisitor, there are three powers capable of holding the conscience of men for their own happiness—miracle, mystery, and authority. And "since man cannot bear to be left without miracles, he will go and create new miracles for himself, his own miracles this time, and will bow down to the miracles of quacks, of women's magic, though he be rebellious, heretical, and godless a hundred times over" (255–56).

The triumph of earthly, rational, materialist, and corrupt powers predicted in *The Brothers Karamazov* is realized in *Pineapple Water*. For Pelevin, like Dostoevsky, the human being has a natural right to freedom. Whether it be a blessing or a torment or some combination thereof, this right has been dispensed with. Reason and ethics (Dostoevskian/biblical knowledge of good and evil) go into the same disposal bin. High tech now provides miracle, mystery, and authority. The divine has been supplanted by the *machina*.

The Dostoevskian problem of human beings' relation to the divine acquires further ironic overtones in *Pineapple Water*. The first recorded speech Levitan listens to while located in his sensory deprivation chamber begins with the words "God is freedom" (*AV* 46). Levitan is force-fed this Dostoevskian/Berdyaevian notion of God as freedom in imprisonment, and his acceptance or rejection of such notions is ensured by chemical stimulants. It is precisely the factor of a free choice that is taken out of his spiritual experiences. He can't help but side with God (or Satan).

Levitan is hyper-manipulable, and his scenario suggests that miracles (high tech, drugs), mystery, and authority (the FSB and the FBI) have effectively done away with free will. The Dostoevskian debate on freedom (with tenuous exceptions) may at this point be obsolete:

> It was all because of Dobrosvet's kvass. He was constantly experimenting with the composition, and the effect was weaker, then stronger—but every time I was forced to become aware of the meanings exploding in my brain with some posthumous irreversibility. I fell into a furrow drawn by them to die painfully there like a kernel [*chtoby muchitel'no umeret' v nei zernom*] that had yet to grow. Every time it was agony because I could hide absolutely nowhere from the voices resounding in my skull in the wet blackness. (*AV* 46–47)

In an ironic re-contextualization, the death of a seed in a furrow alludes to the biblical epigraph to *The Brothers Karamazov*: "Verily, verily, I say unto you, except a kernel of wheat fall into the ground and not die, it abideth alone: but if it die, it bringeth forth much fruit" (John 12:24). This biblical image grows into a leitmotif in Dostoevsky's novel, with Ilyusha's funeral at the novel's end circling back to the epigraph. The boy's death is the seed that might, with the tutelage of Alyosha Karamazov, bear the fruit of goodness in the boys who survive him. Secret services like the FSB are of course no Alyosha Karamazov, and there is no promise of good fruit—though there is a fair chance of Levitan's death.

PIANO KEYS AND SURROGATE WIVES

Like *Pineapple Water*, *S.N.U.F.F.* depicts a world in which miracle, mystery, and authority obliterate free will. In "The Grand Inquisitor" chapter Jesus refuses the sword of Caesar, while Manitou is "both God and Caesar, and what belongs to them and to you" (*S.N.U.F.F.* 193). The Ofshar's theology merges mysticism, commerce, and the latest discoveries of science. Where Dostoevsky's Grand Inquisitor confesses belatedly to being on Satan's side, the godhead of Pelevin's novel is pointedly called Manitou-Antichrist.

Notes from Underground (1864), Dostoevsky's short masterpiece on human freedom and its limitations, provides a further background against which to read Pelevin's work. Contrary to the Grand Inquisitor's position, Dostoevsky takes free will to be essential in matters of faith, as well as viewing it predicated on the transcendence of natural determinism and established rules of cause and effect. The question of free will versus determinism is at the heart of *Notes from Underground*—and of Pelevin's own work. But while *Notes from Underground* envisions humans as becoming subject to scientific understanding some time in the future, Pelevin's *S.N.U.F.F.* (and elsewhere) shows high tech having already reached the level of development that allows science to tabulate and control human actions.

In the eyes of the Underground Man, natural laws are an obstacle that free will cannot break through:

> Science itself will teach man . . . that in fact he possesses neither a will nor a whim of his own, that he never did, and that he himself is nothing more than a kind of piano key or an organ stop; that, moreover, there still exist laws of nature, so that everything he's done has been not in accordance with his desire, but in and of itself, according to the laws of nature. Consequently, we need only to discover these laws of nature, and man will no longer have to answer for his own actions and will find it extremely easy to live. All human

actions, it goes without saying, will then be tabulated according to these laws, mathematically, like tables of logarithms up to 108,000, and will be entered on a schedule. (*Notes from Underground*, 18)[12]

Dostoevky's mechanistic metaphors such as "piano keys" and "organ stops" conceptualize the human being as a will-less machine governed by natural laws. Given a sufficient level of scientific development, these laws will be discovered, and human behavior will become entirely legible.

Notes from Underground envisions man as predictable via scientific development, but even if human behavior is governed by natural laws, it remains unpredictable and uncontrollable until such logarithms are figured out. But the way the Underground Man expresses his apprehensions suggests doubt about human nature's irrational intractability: "What if someday they do really discover the formula . . ." (*Notes from Underground*, 19). For now, he is thankful that "all this has not yet come to pass, and desire still depends on the devil knows what" (23). The Underground Man further privileges irrational whim over reason and advantage as a locus of free will, and mocks the utopian socialism of Chernyshevsky and like-minded thinkers who praise reason and enlightened self-interest. While enlightened self-interest is compulsory and subject to scientific calculation, one's irrational desire might oppose rational advantage and remain opaque to mathematical logarithms: "One's very own free, unfettered desire, one's own whim, no matter how wild, one's own fantasy, even though sometimes roused to the point of madness," are those human qualities that make "all systems and theories constantly smash to smithereens" (9). Even as Dostoevsky's protagonist asserts the omnipotence of natural determinism, he seeks to sneak around that stone wall. As many a Dostoevsky scholar has observed, his discourse is inherently self-contradictory.[13] As the Underground Man suggests, there might be an aspect of free will that is capable of fending off the forces of natural determinism—whether by doing something contrary to the urge to have one's way, or by just going mad to rid oneself of reason.

The problems of unfreedom, predictability, and natural determinism are at the heart of Pelevin's own art. His Homo Zapiens (*Generation 'П'*), machines for producing *bablos* (*Empire V*), arithmometers (*Pineapple Water*), biorobots (*S.N.U.F.F.*), and so on are updated versions of Dostoevsky's piano keys and organ stops. In all these cases free will is illusory, and humans are governed by uncomplicated behavioral algorithms that revolve around monetary production and consumption. But Pelevin is a good deal more radical—reflecting times that are a good deal more radical—than his nineteenth-century predecessor. From Pelevin's perspective, the issue is no longer whether the humans might become transparent to science, but the fact that *they have already become transparent*—and therefore posthuman. This is why Homo Sapiens "is being replaced with a cubic meter of empty space in the condition of HZ" (*Generation 'Π'*), and "in all this there isn't any 'you'" (*S.N.U.F.F.* 399).

While Dostoevsky, via the Underground Man, is troubled that natural determinism and science inhibit free will, Pelevin's texts investigate the mechanisms of social and technical-scientific control that turn humans into piano keys and organ stops. It is not enough that the natural laws underpinning human behavior have been discovered—such knowledge is exploited by unscrupulous players.[14] If Dostoevsky suggests that earthly powers will someday take advantage of humans divested of free will, Pelevin examines in detail the ways the status quo draws on natural (as well as unnatural) human urges to make everyone in the social structure perform their little tune.

Dostoevsky and Pelevin are farther apart on the questions of reason and emotion in the unfreedom scenario. Pelevin's work portrays characters who are unfree in both rational and emotional respects. His humans cannot overcome the forces of egotism, but neither are they rational egoists who understand their true interests and do good out of necessity (à la Chernyshevsky). Instead, to rephrase Chernyshevsky, Pelevin's characters are irrational egoists. They have lost their cognitive capacities, and their self-interest rarely if ever benefits themselves or society at large. While they are to some extent emotional—in the sense of base instincts—even their "whims" have the same iron logic of behaviorist stimulus-response behind them. In the terms of *S.N.U.F.F.*: "One cannot even say that it's you acting. It's just the chemical computer performing the operator 'take sugar' in order to transfer to the operator 'rejoice for five seconds.' And then again there will be the operator 'suffer'" (399).[15]

From the point of view of Chernyshevsky et al., humans are rational beings who are bound to act on advantageous desire. For the Underground Man, humans are constrained by natural determinism, yet they (paradoxically) express their humanity by wanton free will. For the Underground Man's Christian author (or the part of his author that is Christian), man is endowed with free will by God. As James Scanlan puts it:

> On the subject of freedom, Dostoevsky would agree with the Underground Man that it is not only a fact of human nature, but a fact of profound importance. In insisting that a human being is not an organ stop or a piano key, the Underground Man was reflecting Dostoevsky's own firm belief in the special character of human action as opposed to the law-governed processes of nature; a fundamental idea of Christianity, Dostoevsky wrote in *A Writer's Diary*, is "the acknowledgment of human personality and its freedom (and therefore its responsibility)." (*Dostoevsky the Thinker*, 74)

Pelevin's work performs a somersault of thought with respect to Dostoevsky that is not unlike Dostoevsky's earlier somersaulting over the

171

thought of Chernyshevsky and other utopian socialists. According to Pelevin, the stone wall of natural determinism is impenetrable—and so is unnatural (bred, programmed) determinism instantiated by the exploitative status quo. Neither reason nor whim stand a chance, since the latter is as predetermined as the former. In the terms of Pelevin's contemporaneity (genetics, behavioral psychology, cognitive sciences, postmodernism), the human being is an animal led on by sensory stimuli or is a machine with a complex of operating memes, preset and calculable. In Pelevin's work the premonition of Dostoevsky's diarist, that in a rationalized dystopia, where science will discover a way of accounting for and controlling human will, humans will no longer have a will of their own and will have ceased even to exist, is realized to the letter. Unable to transcend material interests, humankind becomes a barely sentient and soulless entity.

But for Pelevin a paradox remains (just as Dostoevsky delights in paradoxes in *Notes from Underground*): one needs a soul in order to register the absence of one. The brain calculates that eternal essence equals zero, yet eternal essence willfully asserts itself as the receiver of that message (*Pineapple Water*). To be sure, Pelevin's attitude toward "an ambiguous Christian God" (*Pineapple Water*) is far more skeptical than Dostoevsky's. Nor does Pelevin fall into the classic antirationalist strain of Russian thought that connects free will and ethics to feeling (Dostoevsky, Tolstoy)—because feelings (or what remains of them in contemporaneity) are as docile as reason (or what remains of it).[16] The destruction of free will takes place in ultra-technologically advanced societies along with the destruction of reason, emotion, individuality, and morals. Where Dostoevsky and Pelevin do converge is in the conceptualization of free will as an essential human trait that should be striven for against all odds—because, among other things, it enables the exercise of ethical judgment and action.

FATHERS AND CHILDREN

In Pelevin's topsy-turvy rewriting of *The Brothers Karamazov* in *Generation 'П,'* it is not the Devil who tempts exceptional humans ("One soul is sometimes worth a whole constellation—we have our arithmetic") (*The Brothers Karamazov*, 639), but God testing the decidedly banal Tatarsky: "What happens to all of us is no more than a phase in a court experiment. Think about it: surely, it's no problem for God to create this entire world out of nothing, with its eternity and infinity, for just a few seconds in order to test a single soul standing before him" (*G'П'* 279).[17] But Pelevin enjoys multi-level allusions, and this one reminds the reader not only of Dostoevsky but also of the Strugatsky brothers' novel *The Doomed City* (1988), in which the characters are apparently subjected to a purgatorial court experiment while thinking they lead weird yet earthly existences.[18]

As Fredric Jameson closes his 1982 treatise, "Progress versus Utopia," on the impossibility of utopian representation in contemporaneity, he enthuses about "a SF-Utopian text from the Second World, one of the most glorious of all contemporary utopias, the Strugatsky brothers' astonishing *Roadside Picnic*" (Jameson, *Archaeologies of the Future*, 294). That novel, in his reading, cannot be decoded as an expression of Soviet dissident protest, nor does it turn on the mixed blessings of technological progress. Rather, what Jameson cherishes in it is "the unexpected emergence, as it were, beyond 'the nightmare of History' and from out of the most archaic longings of the human race, of the impossible and inexpressible Utopian impulse here nonetheless briefly glimpsed: 'Happiness for everybody, free, and no one will go away unsatisfied'" (*Archaeologies of the Future*, 295). For Jameson, the science fiction of the Strugatsky brothers, with its promise of the Suvinian *novum*, is important in a postmodern present that is crippled by the inability to conceptualize a different and viable future.[19] And so the Strugatskys become crucial in the post-Soviet cultural context.[20]

Pelevin's position in post-Soviet Russia is in many respects akin to that of the science-fiction novelists Arkady and Boris Strugatsky in the last three decades of the Soviet Union. Pelevin became a spokesman for the generation that came of age in the 1980s and 1990s, just as the Strugatsky brothers were spokesmen for the Soviet intelligentsia in the 1960s and 1970s. Pelevin's works, like the works of the brotherly duo, are distinctly a product of his time. Like the Strugatskys, he smuggles in adventures of the spirit under the consumer-friendly wrappings of science fiction, fantasy, and speculative fiction. Pelevin continues the Strugatskys' tradition of science fiction as social critique, though in his case it is a critique of society after the collapse of socialist ideology with its modernizing projects of historical progress, technological development, and social improvement. His parables are a discouraging reality check on the Strugatsky brothers' paradigms. As he demonstrates, the dreams of modernity embodied in their classic works of Soviet *nauchnaia fantastika* (science fiction) have been shattered, but those dreams have not been replaced by a compelling alternative scenario.

Even in his youthful works, Pelevin engaged in what would become a running dialogue with the Strugatsky brothers' oeuvre.[21] His *Omon Ra* parodies the theme of space travel, a staple of Soviet utopia, the Thaw, and the Strugatskys' fiction.[22] *The Life of Insects* contains subversive references to the Strugatskys' *Snail on the Slope* (1966) and *Beetle in the Anthill* (1979). The degradation of the individual in commodified society, a theme of the Strugatskys in works like *The Second Invasion of the Martians* (1961), *The Final Circle of Paradise* (1965), and *Monday Begins on Saturday* (1965), is Pelevin's focus in *Generation 'П'* and, indeed, across his entire oeuvre.[23] Pelevin's fin-de-siècle dystopias rework themes and images of hell, apocalypse, and historical impasse from *The Doomed City* as well as, in a more general sense, the Strugatskys' later and more pessimistic musings on social development.[24] *Generation 'П'* and *Empire V* contain multiple echoes of *Hard to Be a God* (1964) and the Strugatskys' theme of "progressorism" (*progressorstvo*).

Generation 'П' lays out a scenario that subverts the aspirations of the Strugatskys' "progressors"—selfless technologists who help less advanced civilizations solve their problems and make progress. The novel sets up a conflict that recurs in Pelevin's novels—of the individual caught in a grotesque social and historical process. In *Generation 'П'* a young man, trapped in an evil social system, starts at the bottom of the ladder and, in the course of the narrative, manages to rise to the top of the power structure. He is co-opted by the establishment and becomes complicit as he attains a commanding position in it. In contrast to the Strugatskys' enlightened protagonists who use technology to help society progress, successfully or otherwise, Tatarsky and his colleagues use technological advances solely to manipulate the populace and acquire money and power.

For Pelevin, the Strugatsky brothers embody the idealistic values of the 1960s, the generation that "ejaculated [*konchili*] the first Sputnik—that four-tailed spermatozoon of a future that never arrived—into the black emptiness of space" (*GП* 12). The double entendre of *konchili*, in its senses of "finished" and "ejaculated," dramatizes the ironic bond between sexual and revolutionary drives, as well as offering a dramatic closure on the idealism-of-space promise (a key staple of the Soviet myth), the Thaw, and the Soviet utopia at large. The launch of Sputnik is presented as the Soviet body politic's last vital deed, which was followed by a descent into geriatric impotence.

Using the Strugatsky brothers' tropes and plot situations, *Generation 'П'* demonstrates how their projects take shape, but in a cynical, perverted manner. Tatarsky, a child of the *shestidesiatniki*, commences his reign as the ruler of Russian virtual reality by issuing a meaningless directive to swap Pepsi for Coca-Cola—a fittingly degraded version of Pepper's first order as Director in *Snail on the Slope* "to the members of the Eradication Group to self-eradicate as soon as possible" (Strugatskie, *Sobranie sochinenii*, 4:484).[25] Tatarsky's rise to the upper echelons of power and his final union with the golden idol of the goddess Ishtar stand in marked contrast not only to the selfless intelligentsia in the Strugatskys' novels, but also to the "prole" Schuhart's unexpected transcendence of egotism at the close of his quest for the Golden Ball in the Zone in *Roadside Picnic*. Having reached his goal, Schuhart asks for happiness for everyone rather than personal gain.[26]

THE BAT AT THE TOP

Empire V's transformation of *Snail on the Slope* conveys how Pelevin goes about reworking the classics of Soviet science fiction. *Empire V*, reprising the conflict of *Generation 'П,'* has Roma Shtorkin rising to the top of the vampire dictatorship. Roma's journey, like Tatarsky's, is not one of defiance but of personal social ascent. Simultaneously, the Strugatsky brothers' sphinxlike, troubling, and inhuman future—symbolized by the snail/human crawling into an unpredictable and menacing far-away—turns evil in *Empire V* in a banal way.

In the novel's second chapter, having failed his first exam to enroll at the physics department of Moscow State University, Roma pays a farewell visit to the examination committee. He sees a drawing of a snail on the office door, and a poem by an early modern Japanese poet written underneath it:

"Oh snail! Crawling toward the top of Fuji, you should not rush . . ." (*EV* 22) The poet is Kobayashi Issa, and his haiku about the snail climbing Mount Fuji (in a slightly different translation) is used by the Strugatskys as their second epigraph to *Snail on the Slope*:

> Slowly, slowly crawl,
> O snail, up the slope of Fuji,
> To its highest summits! (Strugatskie, *Sobranie sochinenii*, 4:288)

The first epigraph to *Snail on the Slope* is taken from Boris Pasternak's poem "Around the Bend" (1946), about a future that "can't be drawn into arguments or petted away" (Strugatskie, *Sobranie sochinenii*, 4:288).

The Strugatsky brothers' vision of the human in relation to the historical process is conveyed in *Snail on the Slope* via the Administration and the Forest, which stand for the present and the future, respectively. The snail stands for the human struggling along in a difficult present from the distant past into a troubling future that will likely not be reached anyway. Human actions under pressure in a hostile and alienating world are the problem not only of *Snail on the Slope* but of many of the Strugatskys' other works: *Escape Attempt* (1962), *Hard to Be a God*, *The Ugly Swans* (written early 1970s, published 1972/1987), *One Billion Years before the End of the World* (1976), and *The Doomed City*. As the art of the Strugatskys evolves, and as social realities change in the Soviet Union, the world portrayed not only is threatening but becomes incomprehensible in a Kafkaesque manner, and the powers of evil acquire a metaphysical, in addition to a social, dimension. The right kind of human being, however, strives to stay defiant even if the odds are against him.

Pelevin's own parables typically have a protagonist trapped in an evil and inexplicable reality, but his protagonists are in most cases assimilated by the establishment. The exceptions achieve individual spiritual enlightenment, escaping social engagement and the world at large. In either case, the Strugatskys' characters fighting through historical predicaments does not apply. In *Empire V*, for instance, Roma's scenario switches from his failure to understand the system (the problem of Pepper and Candid in *Snail on the Slope*) to his failure to resist it.

Pelevin parodically subverts "the snail on the slope" motif—the Strugatskys' allegory of humans in the historical process—at both the human and the process levels. The protagonist anticipates this scenario at the beginning of his journey. On reading the poem, Roma takes out a pen and adds a line:

There, at the top of Fuji, are already plenty of snails. (*EV* 22)

What he means is that one should not bother climbing up the social ladder, since the positions of power have already been taken. Besides, these heights hold no exalted promises, since it is the same petty snails who crawl at the bottom that have usurped the top. The proverbial Mount Fuji is as trivial as its slopes, and, moreover, humans have always been living in an inhuman reality (governed by vampires).[27]

Roma's initial stance is nonconformist: he resists the vampire status quo and questions its principles. As a child he dreamed of "becoming a space hero, discovering a new planet, or writing one of those great novels that make the human heart tremble"; that is, he subscribed to "antiquated" Soviet values (*EV* 38). As he is turned into a vampire, he feels that he has lost his soul and continues to believe that people are better than vampires because they help each other. To attain his exalted status as "a real superman" (*nastoiashchii sverkhchelovek*), he must study various skills that are necessary for a vampire to rule over humans. Roma is childishly inquisitive, pestering his teachers about the workings of the Fifth Empire, rather like Pepper in his attempts to understand the absurd functioning of the Administration. Roma is concerned with abstract questions about good and evil, and for a while is not content to do what his mentors push him toward—to simply suck *bablos* and be grateful that chance has placed him at the top of the food chain. Eventually, however, he starts "feeling ashamed that he does not conform to this high ideal [of the superman] and asks questions at every step like a first grader" (*EV* 213).

By the conclusion of *Empire V*, its protagonist has rejected his infantile questioning of reality and has settled on appreciating his place in the order of things, as Ishtar's close associate:

I look at our stately rigs, sucking black liquid from the vessels of the planet, and understand that I have found my place in the ranks. . . . And with each

176

movement of my wings I am closer and closer to my strange girlfriend and, it must be owned, to *bablos* as well. Which is now all ours. All ours. All ours. All ours. All ours . . . The mountain-climber Rama the Second reports on the subjugation of Fuji. Nevertheless, there is one serious nuance . . . A while ago the stars in the sky seemed to me to be the other worlds to which the spaceships from the Sunny city would fly. Now I know that their sharp points are holes in the armor that closes us off from the ocean of cruel light. On the top of Fuji you sense the force with which this light presses down on our world. . . . The top of Fuji: time, winter. (*EV* 406–7)

The "bat at the top" that Rama now is accepts something that the "snail on the slope" would not reconcile itself to: the universe is unmitigatedly evil, and one is either crushed by it or takes advantage of it to become "the god of money with oaken wings" (*bog deneg s dubovymi kryl'iami*) (*EV* 408). Roma leaves aside his "accursed questions" and fully conforms. "The top of Fuji: time, winter," the novel's closing line, triangulates between the Strugatskys' optimistically youthful book *Noon: 22nd Century* (1962) and Pelevin's own "Mt. Shumeru, eternity, summer," the "nowhere" from which Che Guevara composes his anti-consumer treatise (which itself looks back to the "Inner Mongolia" in *Chapaev and the Void*) (*GTT* 91).The stars and ships evoke space exploration, a staple of Soviet utopia. For Roma, the space dream transforms into a presentiment of a malignant force waiting to destroy him. His conclusion, the opposite of the Strugatskys' call for resistance and solidarity in the face of evil, is to enjoy his power while there is still time.

THE FUTURE NEEDS US . . . TO EAT

Pelevin frames his works as a corrective confrontation of post-Soviet reality with the Strugatsky brothers' fictions. Their classics of Soviet *nauchnaia fantastika* are a familiar reference point that Pelevin employs in order to suggest that life has proved more discouraging than even the Strugatskys' most alarming fantasies. The brothers presented a more persuasive vision than the bright communist future promised by the official literature of that time.[28] That their version of the future has to be dismantled, and that the future is dismantling it, conveys the bleakness of the new vision.

The Strugatskys' own vision did gradually evolve from optimism to gloom. If their works of the early 1960s imagine *Homo Novus* and the future society, with an enlightened humanity united under communism and exploring outer space, their works of the later 1960s, 1970s, and 1980s pitch darker scenarios. In the Strugatskys' later works, superhuman forces like the Slimies, Wanderers, and Ludens begin to displace humans in the historical process. The vision of progressorism transforms from the early sunny stories of

Nooniverse, where young *kommunary* strive to advance progress throughout the galaxy, to *Hard to Be a God*, in which the earthling Anton, despite his best intentions, fails to help the medieval Arkanar as the kingdom falls into the hands of a Nazi-like dictatorship.[29] In still later works like *Beetle in the Anthill* and *The Waves Still the Wind* (1985), the Earth is portrayed as a backward civilization. Unlike Anton and his friends, the superior race of the Wanderers pursues no humanistic objectives on the planet. As humans, formerly the bearers of progressorism, have become backward and disempowered, they yield to superior alien powers.[30]

No matter whether the reader's expectations are based on relatively hopeful works like *Noon: 22nd Century* and *Hard to Be a God* or relatively bleak ones like *Snail on the Slope, Beetle in the Anthill,* and *The Doomed City,* those expectations are sure to be upset as Pelevin provides an ever more discouraging diagnosis of the present. For all its skepticism, the Strugatskys' oeuvre still holds a nostalgic humanistic value, and is employed by Pelevin to offset his own darker stories.

What exactly makes Pelevin's post-Soviet real-life correctives worse than the Strugatsky brothers' imaginary apocalypses? The Strugatskys' human protagonists may be on the losing side, but they are not on the side of the inhuman—a side that Pelevin's characters are all too eager to take. Works like *Snail on the Slope* and *The Ugly Swans*, while pessimistic in their view of history, still place hope in human dignity and morality. And so, someone like Candid on the last page of *Snail on the Slope* strides off to fight, even though he knows he can't win against the overpowering forces of the Forest. Or, in the last words of Victor Banev, the protagonist of *The Ugly Swans*: "All this is beautiful, but there's one thing—I'd better not forget to go back" (Strugatskie, *Sobranie sochinenii*, 8:529). Even though the post-apocalyptic world cleansed by the intellectual Slimies may be enticing, Banev feels responsible to rejoin his imperfect human peers. There is no such looking back or sense of connection for Tatarsky or Roma.

Unlike the Strugatskys, Pelevin gives no premonition of an unknown, perhaps posthuman, but radically different future. The dilemma of the Strugatskys in their later work is between the allure of a superior post-apocalyptic realm and a fear that this realm will need no humans as we know them. In Pelevin's work, any kind of *novum* is ousted by the vision of an existence that is evil and inhuman and at the same time utterly vapid: the absorption of humankind into the primitive bio-aggregate of Oranus; a vampire super-civilization that has no mysterious objectives but feeds, parasitically, off human lifestock; the degraded technocracy of Byzantium versus the shabby autocracy of Orkland, and so on. Whereas the Strugatskys' late novels like *Beetle in the Anthill* and *The Waves Still the Wind* suggest the Wanderers' intent, however scary, to install progressorism on Earth, Pelevin's variegated controlling users clearly have no such objectives. They are mere petty demons who are themselves puppeteered by next-level *besy*.

Pelevin takes issue with the Strugatskys' influential vision of social improvement through the progressorism of the intelligentsia, the education of a free-minded elite, and personal development toward ultimate rationality coupled with virtue and power—that is, the Enlightenment-based principles of modernity reactivated by the Soviet scientific-technical (*nauchno-technicheskaia*) intelligentsia of the 1960s and expressed in the classics of Soviet science fiction.[31] Not incidentally, in Pelevin's works, no *intels* (intellectuals, as they are abbreviated in *The Final Circle of Paradise*) make an effort to disturb the consumer feeding frenzy. Nor do the amiable members of the scientific-technical elite like the junior scientists, who are heroes in *Monday Begins on Saturday*, stand up to oppose the uber-egotist homunculi who are capable of grabbing everything of material value, closing up space, and ending time.[32] The debased post-Soviet intelligentsia turned "middle class" no longer privilege ethical or educational principles over the demands of physical survival. Nor does Pelevin's world possess scientists to fight the forces of homeostasis, in contrast to the scientists of *One Billion Years before the End of the World* and elsewhere in the Strugatskys' oeuvre.[33]

As Pelevin's narratives show, no correlation obtains between knowledge and ethical behavior. The rule of the Chaldeans in *Generation 'П'* and the vampire dictatorship in *Empire V* are based on sophisticated insights into social mechanisms. Knowledge, when it may be pursued, only serves the purposes of personal promotion. Not only that, but in Pelevin's parody of the bildungsroman (mediated by socialist realism and inverted by the Strugatskys), the "real superman," in ironic contrast to Boris Polevoy's *Story of a Real Man* (1947), is nonhuman.[34] Alexei Maresyev, a heroic Soviet fighter pilot in World War II, and the hero of Polevoy's book, is transformed into a vampire servicing the circulation of *bablos* and himself (a bit). But Pelevin's irony extends to harder targets than Polevoy's Sots Realism—such as Nietzsche-esque lore. Roma is a literal, albeit petty and pitiful, ubermensch.

FUTURE PERFECT

Pelevin subverts the Strugatskys, but—and this is worth emphasizing—he directs his sharpest mockery and frustration not at his predecessors, however quaint their belief in rationalism or progress might appear, but at his own generation, which has betrayed the humanistic ideals of the Strugatskys and their time.

As early as *Omon Ra*, Pelevin's parody of Soviet ideology is intertwined with a more wistful outlook toward the "heroes of the Soviet cosmos" (the novella's epigraph). A decade and a half later, *Empire V* once more blends parody and nostalgia.[35] The Soviet space dream was also a dream of Soviet childhood, so "spaceships from the Sunny city" refers to Nikolai Nosov's popular *Adventures of Dunno in the Sunny City* (1958) and the cartoons based on them. Still more recently, *Pineapple Water* goes so far as to compose a requiem for the Strugatskys' generation in the segment entitled "The Soviet Requiem":

> Any epoch has its own future, something like "future in the past" in English grammar. It is as if humans prolong themselves into infinity in a straight line, drawing a tangent to eternity through their own time. . . . The future of the Soviet nineteen-sixties was the most touching of all national self-deceptions. . . . Plump, with old-fashioned haircuts, they stand in their inflatable suits by their pot-bellied rockets, and above them in the pale dazzling zenith there slides a blinding arrow of a starship at lift-off—an impossibly lovely Noon of humanity . . . What is the essence of Russian communism? A drunken man walked along the snow-covered yard toward the toilet, stared at the glow of a little lamp in the window covered with frost, raised his head, saw the black sky with the sharp points of stars—and suddenly these lights drew him toward them from his urine-saturated path with such an anguish that he nearly reached them. (AV 226–27)

This passage synthesizes Pelevin's thoughts about, and imagery of the *shestidesiatniki*. "The Soviet Requiem" evokes spacecraft less as the Soviet Union's ultimate modernizing project and no longer parodically ("spermatozoon of the future"), but as a spiritual promise that has not come to fulfillment. The "impossibly beautiful Noon of humanity" (*nevozmozhno prekrasnyi Polden' chelovechestva*) refers to the Strugatskys' *Nooniverse* stories. The "sharp points of the stars" are auto-referential (*Omon Ra, Empire V*). Soviet man is driven toward utopia by the drabness of reality. The lights above rhyme with the lights of a "little lamp" (*lampada*) in the window below, with religious connotations. The Strugatsky generation's spiritual potential emerges, however romantically, in the very gap between the real and the ideal.[36]

Pelevin's texts, when responding to the *shestidesiatniki* and the Soviet cosmos, veer between parody and nostalgia.[37] Leapfrogging over more parodic works like *Generation 'П,'* *Pineapple Water* resurrects—and leans farther toward lyricism—the mercurial lyrical-satirical tenor of the early novella *Omon Ra*. The only way for Pelevin's characters to travel into space (or elsewhere) is in one's mind—which is precisely what Omon does. But to travel into a beautiful far-away (*prekrasnoe daleko*) one needs inner spiritual potential. The *shestidesiatniki* envision the future based on themselves—by "prolonging themselves into infinity." In the words of *Love for Three Zuck-*

erbrins: "This is that very space engine which carries us from one universe to another."

∗ ∗ ∗

At some point in Pelevin's novel *T* (2009), its hero, Count T, lies in the field looking at the summer sky and the clouds that swim across its expanse. He muses that the sky can rarely be that lofty: "On clear days it has no height at all, only blueness. It needs clouds to become high or low. The human soul is the same way. It cannot be lofty or lowly by itself; everything depends solely on the intentions and thoughts that fill it on a given moment" (*T*, 12). This allusion to Andrey Bolkonsky's epiphany at the Battle of Austerlitz is transparent. But Pelevin neither imitates nor parodies this famous episode, but reframes Tolstoyan imagery unexpectedly in the light of his preoccupation. The "lofty sky," Bolkonsky's realization of the vainglory of war and of an ineffable higher power, conveys the mutability of the human, and the way one brings oneself into being each living moment.

Like the literature of any era, Pelevin's texts point to his literary ancestors and indicate the formative importance of their works. His allusions to them are typically overt, and are often identified in the text. There may be a telescoping of ideas and imagery based on multiple sources, as, for example, Mayakovsky and Blok in *Pineapple Water*. Sources may be mixed together in a novel manner, as, for instance, the Bradbury–Zhuangzi linkage in *Love for Three Zuckerbrins*. Pelevin may also synthesize conceptual and aesthetic patterns emerging out of his predecessors' work as well as their later interpretations, as in the episode with Dostoevsky and the Ouija board.[38]

Pelevin's conversations with his predecessors involve polemics, parody, and deconstruction, but most prominently original rethinking. The real source of complexity is not source identification, as in rich and often poetically obscure modernist allusions, but in the ways that he rethinks intertext. Pelevin imbues classical formulas with new, often paradoxical meanings. Prior texts function as formulaic structures, even memes, and the writer, pun-like, encodes new meanings into them. That Pelevin reads unorthodox meanings into his predecessors' works is not to say that he uses them solely as springboards from which to perform his conceptual circus acts. Rather, he selects subtexts with a problematic close to his own and transforms them to bear on contemporaneity. And lastly, any subversion directed at the past pales in comparison with his critique of the present.

The Total Art of Irony

> What vicious irony! They will say. I am not
> so sure.
> —Mikhail Lermontov, *A Hero of Our Time*

THAT PELEVIN is a consummate ironist is apparent to critics and ordinary readers alike. Naum Leiderman and Mark Lipovetsky express the critical consensus when they call Pelevin's irony "distinct" and "tangible" (*Sovremennaia russkaia literatura*, 507). Indeed, many scholarly treatments of his oeuvre, as well as the multitudinous reviews of his books, give a nod to his irony, which is occasionally characterized as gentle and inoffensive, but more often as sharp and all-consuming, and most frequently, in a kind of shortcut, as simply postmodern.[1]

This chapter examines Pelevin's deployment of irony in his major novels such as *Chapaev and the Void, Generation 'П,' The Sacred Book of the Werewolf, Empire V*, and *T*. In my reading, Pelevin's texts use a variety of ironic strategies, from stable Augustan irony that exposes the follies of society and humans, to a less secure romantic irony that stresses the limits of language vis-à-vis life and selfhood, and plays with paradoxes and self-refuting speech acts. Equally, Pelevin resorts to a highly unstable postmodern irony that destabilizes all kinds of discourses and envisions the subject as an effect of narration. His ironies are multifaceted, ranging from the rhetorical to the situational, from stable to unstable, from the micro-level to the macro-level. I understand Pelevin to build on irony in its modern, post-romantic, and postmodernist meanings, where it is more than a rhetorical device by which what is said is undercut by what is implied. More broadly, his irony entails the creation of an enigmatic personality or text, and a capacity to maintain distance from any specific definition or context (Colebrook, *Irony*, 3).

Historically speaking, as irony broadened from a local trope to a core characteristic of lives, selves, and texts under the aegis of romanticism, it took on several interrelated corollaries. It inhabited issues of the subject, language, and paradox.[2] The concept of romantic irony was tied to the problem of the subject. It presented itself as an inescapable condition of consciousness that is unable to reach beyond itself (solipsism) and that emphasizes continual self-revision.[3] In the deployment of romantic irony, the author switched between contradictory viewpoints throughout the text and emphasized a refusal to succumb to the temptation of closure. The romantic agent used language ironically, always aware that life and selfhood exceed their verbal manifestations. Rather than merely asserting both "a" and "not a," the ironist also deployed logically contradictory speech acts such as the claim that there is no such thing as truth or that one does not mean to speak.[4]

If irony initially expanded from a rhetorical trope into a full-blown worldview with the romantics, its modern version reaches its apogee in postmodernism, where it inheres in the use of language itself, and where the very self is seen as produced by language. As Richard Rorty puts it in *Contingency, Irony, and Solidarity* (1989), such ironists are "always aware that the terms in which they describe themselves are subject to change, always aware of the contingency and fragility of their final vocabularies, and thus of their 'selves'" (73–74).

The thought of irony, both before and after romanticism, has been vitally linked to the issue of *(un)freedom*. In Friedrich Schlegel's wording, irony "is the freest of all licenses." The ironist exercises the right to "relinquish first one and then another part of one's being," "rising infinitely above all limitations" (*Lucinde and the Fragments*, 177). As Kierkegaard weighs in: "When what is said is not my meaning or the opposite of my meaning, then I am free in relation to others and to myself" (*The Concept of Irony*, 247–48). For Bakhtin, the primary author eludes closure by "various forms of reduced laughter (irony), allegory, and so forth" (*Speech Genres and Other Late Essays*, 148). More recently, Rorty asserts that "greater openness, more room for self-creation is the standard demand made by ironists on their societies" (*Contingency, Irony, and Solidarity*, 88).

But the ironic trope may not so much operate in the service of the ironist's freedom as expose the ironist's interpellation in the context. In Linda Hutcheon's *A Poetics of Postmodernism: History, Theory, Fiction* (1988), postmodern irony and paradox "both reveal and question prevailing norms, and they can do so because they incarnate both processes. They teach that, for example, representation cannot be avoided, but it can be studied to show how it legitimates certain kinds of knowledge and, therefore, certain kinds of power" (230).[5] This statement suggests both the liberating potential of irony and limitations to that potential. The ironist—who resists predetermination by encroaching external forces—may still fail to rise above his environment, and when the ironist is conscious of this, irony morphs into self-irony.

While Pelevin's use of irony is varied and pervasive, its prominence points to the importance of self-irony. Perceiving existence as a cosmic joke, the authorial persona defines himself to be the foremost object of that joke. He constructs ironic mechanisms by which the narrative turns on itself and tosses off contradictions and paradoxes that evade resolution; for instance, critiques of consumer society that are themselves cogs in the machine of consumerism, and attempts to comprehend reality that fall back upon the self (including the authorial persona), as well as texts that accuse language of falsehood. The result is a dizzying act of dissimulation, at once playful and serious, that is destabilized by inner contradictions and directed at the ironist as much as at external targets (everyday concepts and values).

While terms such as the "postmodern subversion of authority," "ludic postmodernism," "metafictional postmodernism," "postmodern self-referentiality," and so on can be aptly applied to Pelevin's texts, his focus on self-irony permits me to illuminate what I see as this writer's key concern—interpellation by the very norms of life that one purportedly ironizes from a self-determined position.[6] The very act of speaking about the world creates a position other than the world, and only irony can reflect on this unthinkable gap. "We cannot avoid irony's elevation and questioning; nor can we achieve a pure separation from context" (Colebrook, *Irony*, 119–20). Self-irony hinges on the inability to disengage from the world even as one calls its values into question.

IRONIZING THE ALREADY-SAID

Chapaev and the Void, the novel that made Pelevin a brand, is where he begins foregrounding the problem of ironizing the post-Soviet book market, society, and way of life, all the while prominently participating in and conditioned by these himself. The novel ironizes speech acts by exposing them as utterances per se; that is, authored, and never transcendental or free from the forces of the world. This kind of irony is highlighted in the novel's fifth chapter when Pustota admires the beauty of the starry sky:

> I saw above me the sky full of stars. It was so beautiful that for several seconds I simply lay there in silence, staring upwards. [...]
> —"Beauty is the greatest objectification of the will at the highest level of its cognizability."
> Chapaev looked at the sky for another few seconds, then transferred his gaze to a large puddle right by our feet and spit his cigarette stub into it. [...]
> —"What has always amazed me is the starry heaven under my feet and Immanuel Kant within us."
> —"I do not understand, Vasily Ivanovich, how a man who confuses Kant and Schopenhauer can be entrusted with the command of a division." (*CP* 174–75).[7]

This passage is interlaced with multiple layers of irony. Pustota re-proaches Chapaev for confusing Schopenhauer's sentiment about beauty, with which he began their conversation, with Kant's notion of the categorical imperative. Being versed in German idealism is, of course, a preposterous requirement for a Red cavalry officer.[8] Indeed, a good deal of the novel's irony stems from the incongruity between what is expected and what ac-tually occurs. The distance between Chapaev's image as the down-to-earth Bolshevik commander (familiar from Furmanov's novel and the Vasilyev brothers' movie) and the refined philosophizer of Pelevin's fantasy is a prime example. This passage, however, plays not only with these Soviet classics, but also with Kant's maxim, "Two things fill the mind with ever new and increas-ing wonder and awe the more often and the more seriously reflection con-centrates upon them: the starry heaven above me and the moral law within me" (*Critique of Practical Reason*, 111).[9]

The passage falls in line with the ironization of established discourses favored by postmodernists—throwing doubt on common assumptions and denying the presence of truth behind them—or what Umberto Eco, de-fining postmodern irony, would term "subverting previous utterances," "the 'already-said' that can be reconsidered only in an ironic way" (Rosso, "A Correspondence with Umberto Eco").[10] Furthermore, the passage ironizes speech acts not only by problematizing their validity, but by viewing them as always located, never transcendental or pure.[11] In Chapaev's sardonic obser-vation, what is inherent to us is not Kant's categorical imperative, but Kant positing the imperative in question. To sharpen the irony further, a speech act exposed as located and specific is not any random discourse, but one that postulates itself as transcendental law.

But something more characteristically Pelevinian than an instance of generic postmodern irony takes place here. In a literal somersault of thought, the immaculate Kantian cosmos is turned topsy-turvy. Stars in a puddle are not a convincing visual counterpart to moral law, and the abil-ity to seamlessly reconcile the heavens trampled on and Kant within one's heart makes humans shifty creatures indeed. The stars are actually a second-degree image since, following Kant's own logic, human perception of the world is mediated through the senses. The cigarette butt that breaks the smooth surface of the water in which the stars are reflected problematizes one's vision and questions external reality. It is hard to agree on something as beautiful when what we perceive is dependent on the individual subject.

In Pelevin's world, one is inevitably imprisoned within the self. The "starry heaven under my feet" (physical space) contrasts with "Kant within us" (psychic space), but only to a point, since it is precisely the dichotomy of the external/internal that is always in question. Space and time (Bud-dhist, not Kantian) are not a priori, and Chapaev "finds no use for fixed time and space, which for him are only a dream" (Clowes, *Russia on the Edge*, 78). To fall back on Dostoevsky, materialism and metaphysics don't go well together—any sensory "proof" can be easily turned about-face. But in a solipsistic worldview, reflection is as (un)real as the stars above. The categorical imperative—in Kant's or our own heads—can be neither derived from unreliable sensory data nor dismissed based on the same.[12]

SUBVERTED LYRICAL ADDRESS

If the Kant episode incorporates a postmodern ironic view—as in "those who feel that they simply know the ultimate truths of life have forgotten or repressed their own location and position within life" (Colebrook, *Irony*, 112)—with an appropriate Buddhist twist, Pelevin's other allusions to the classics ironize them in a still more distinct manner, by highlighting the author's unfreedom in a specific material context. This is not irony in its broadest sense, in which any postmodern subversion would be ironic. Rather, the irony is both more specific and more stable. Thus, for example, in *The Sacred Book of the Werewolf* Vladimir Nabokov "gives himself away not when he describes the nymphet's forbidden loveliness . . . but when he sparingly, almost by hinting, mentions Humbert's considerable means that allow him to travel with Lolita around the United States." Nabokov's choice of topic for the sensationalist *Lolita* (1955), Pelevin suggests, "aims to acquire such means" (*SKO* 64).[13]

A similar satiric thrust—less at artistic texts and more at the author per se and his implication in context—occurs in *T*, where both Tolstoy and Dostoevsky make appearances. For all his luminous insights, Dostoevsky is marred by vanity, and at one point draws a beard over the face of Ignatius of Loyola to make the (in)famous Jesuit resemble himself: "It's not you on the cover, Fyodor Mikhailovich. It's Iggy Lo. Or if fully, Ignatius Lopez de Loyola, the founder of the Jesuits. They printed this for the anniversary of his birth. And you yourself drew him a beard with a sharpened pencil" (*T*, 203). Given Dostoevsky's vocal critique of the Jesuits' casuistry and thirst for power, the irony is considerable.[14] Yet one should keep in mind that Tolstoy and Dostoevsky in *T* are not the real flesh-and-blood nineteenth-century classic authors, but their contemporary avatars. In the novel Dostoevsky, a character in a computer shooter game, is a lurid version of the original, and is defined by the corrupt context in which he exists.

In *Empire V*, likewise, irony takes on a form and feeling characteristic of Pelevin—not as a broadly postmodern subversion of any spoken authority, or a simultaneous allowing for and affirmation of the groundlessness of all kinds of articulations—but as the specific problem posed by ironizing a social context while caught in and compromised by that context. The chapter "Villa of Mysteries" draws attention to the relationship between truth locutions and speaking positions. What one may call a "subverted lyrical address" takes place when, toward the novel's close, a professor of theology from Kishinev, a *gastarbeiter* in Moscow, offers his religious-humanistic alternative to the cynical philosophy of the Empire:

> Every room is responsible for itself. It can invite God. And it can invite your company [vampires]. Of course, by its nature any room wants the divine. But because of glamour and discourse most of these rooms have decided that everything has to do with interior design. And if a room believes that, it means the bats have already occupied it. (*EV* 373)

Such an inspired pronouncement is compromised when the professor hands the novel's protagonist Roma his card, on which is written: "To God through God's Word. The house of prayer 'Logos KataKombo'" (*EV* 375). From Pelevin, ever wary of language's ability to furnish a spiritual illumination, not only does this suggest an a priori tainted way to approach the divine, but the professor reveals himself to be yet another huckster dispensing advertising slogans like Tatarsky.[15]

A more resonant yet subverted lyrical address occurs in the final pages of *Empire* V as Roma, now the most powerful vampire in Russia, enjoys his supernatural flight over a sleeping Moscow, simultaneously free and mindful of his limited options:

> I love our empire style. I love its glamour earned in destitution and its battle-hardened discourse. I love its people. Not for any bonuses or preferences but because we are of the same red liquid, though, of course, from different perspectives. . . . And thoughts about ancient people for some reason enter one's head. "What you do, do faster . . ." (*EV* 406).

At face value Pelevin performs a Gogolian gesture, and, having laughed his fill, provides an equivalent of the inspired *troika* passage, the finale of *Dead Souls* (1842).[16] However, this lyrical address is subverted from within. The text does not subscribe to the hero's sentiments but, rather, offers a double-edged representation of his voice, as would be natural for an ironist situated above his characters and their speaking conditions (Livers, "The Tower or the Labyrinth," 501).

Roma's "brotherly" sentiment toward his fellow Russians is disingenuous to say the least. The perspectives on "the same red liquid" of the vampire overlord and his subjects are truly different: it is Roma who sucks blood while the people are being drained of it. Not incidentally, at the end of his speech Roma repeats the words Christ addressed to Judas: "What you do, do faster" (John 13:27). Earlier in the novel, we learn that the English word "self" corresponds to *Iuda* (Judas) on the Russian keyboard (*EV* 187). True to the biblical archetype, by the novel's conclusion, Roma has sold himself to evil.

The lyrical ending of *Empire V* is undercut by irony, but it does not achieve a clear and stable opposite meaning to the one articulated by the novel's protagonist. With the ironic trope at its most obvious, the reader is relied on to recognize that what the author says cannot be what he means. In more complex cases of unstable irony, the surface meaning is contradicted, but is not replaced with a clear second meaning.[17] If the universe is evil but still enticing, and if one is either crushed by evil or takes advantage of it, the hero's sentiments are hard-earned and on some level cogent. Resigned to the world's imperfections, the reader, like the novel's protagonist, may have simply "become an adult." But maybe not. After all, Pelevin serves up both toys—nostalgia and irony—for his readers to play with.[18]

IRONIC FRAMING

Chapaev and the Void, like *Empire V* a decade later, engages irony in the form of paradox by zeroing in on the limitations of critique from within the system—such as consciousness that questions itself and language that challenges language. The novel's mock preface, drawing on the romantic tradition of the found manuscript, unfolds in a tour de force of contradictions and paradoxes: the story is "a psychological journal" whose goal "is to cure the self from the so-called inner life"; it is "a product of critical solipsism" that "records mechanical cycles of consciousness"; the author "discusses subjects which are in no need of discussion"; he seeks, and fails, to point directly to the mind of the reader, since "this task is too simple for such attempts to be successful"; he creates "one more phantom molded from words" in order to transcend language (*CP* 7–8). The book is of interest only "as a psychological account"—but "it possesses a number of artistic virtues"; still, "the objective underlying it is not to create a work of literature"—rather, it is "valuable as the first attempt in world culture to reflect, by artistic means, the . . . myth of the Eternal Non-Return" (*CP* 7–8).[19]

The text presents an ironic contradiction in more than one sense—as verbal artifice that seeks to free itself from words, and as the portrayal of subjectivity incapable of transcending itself (the "critical solipsism") that nevertheless seeks to comprehend external reality and its own functioning. The system malfunctions when dealing with itself, as in Gödel's incompleteness theorems: any formal system that is at least as complicated as arithmetic contains statements that cannot be proved either true or false.[20] To think fundamentally about a context (or subjectivity or language), one would have to reach "outside these"—but one is always caught within them. Since, according to solipsism, the self is the only existing reality and all other realities, including the external world and other people, have no independent existence, the novel's depictions of the outside world are problematized from the outset. Analogously, since there is no objective outside from which subjectivity could perceive itself and since there is nothing but inner life, the text's validity as a psychological account and its objective to cure the author of inner life are equally problematized.[21]

Like *Chapaev and the Void*, *The Sacred Book of the Werewolf* opens with a mock preface, "Commentary by Experts," which destabilizes the narrative that follows and abounds in contradictions. The preface sabotages the authenticity of A Huli's story as "a clumsy literary forgery made by an unknown author during the first quarter of the twenty-first century," and dismisses the manuscript's artistic value as "unworthy of serious literary or critical analysis, . . . interesting solely as a symptom of the profound spiritual decline our society is suffering from" (*SKO* 5–7). In fact, Pelevin engages in a double bluff, since the undermining of A Huli's story (and, by extension, his own author status) is in turn undermined when the authors of the preface themselves prove to be unreliable characters: the FSB major Tengiz Kokoev, two literary scholars with suggestive names, Maya Maracharskaya and Igor Koshkodavlenko, and a media swindler named Peldis Sharm.

In accruing ironic layers, Maracharskaya, Koshkodavlenko, and the others are shown to be unfree, corrupt, and lying servants of the status quo. The suggestion that the disk's discovery and the story are engineered by the FSB is itself advanced by a secret service agent. Likewise, the view that the narrative is unworthy of consideration is put forward by Pelevin's perennial liars—literary critics and media insiders. The name Maracharskaya plays on the word *morochit'* ("to deceive") and alludes to the critic-author Maya Kucherskaia, while the name Koshkodavlenko means "cat-crusher" and alludes to Sharikov, the hero of Bulgakov's *Heart of a Dog* (1925) who, following his transformation from a mongrel into an obnoxious human, supervises the elimination of cats in Moscow. Pelevin's novel reimagines Sharikov as working for the NKVD and links him to the five-legged dog Pizdets that Sasha Sery becomes.

Maracharskaia and the others—who are not generic postmodern unreliable narrators, but specifically Pelevinian hucksters bound and compromised by context—undermine the main text and are in turn undermined themselves. The picture is further complicated by the main text's narrator, who is as unreliable as one could imagine. Like the cunning fox of Russian folk tales, A Huli deceives everyone. The novel's title, *The Sacred Book of the Werewolf,* which means a holy tale for unholy creatures, is itself an oxymoron.[22] But here again Pelevin dodges a state of stable irony. A Huli is both prostitute and virgin, a predator who aspires to humaneness, and she spins a web of illusions while striving to escape it herself. This arch-unreliable narrator does not so much serve the fairly standard (post)modern task of meta-literary play (subverting narrative authority) as she permits Pelevin to comment on the complexity of life. By all these contradictions turning on and into themselves, she may have just composed an earnest narrative and a way into freedom and love.

THE LIAR PARADOX

The fictional narrators in *Chapaev and the Void* and *The Sacred Book of the Werewolf* transparently point at the author and offer instances of the authorial persona's self-ironization. The novels' mock prefaces ironize Pustota's and A Huli's writings. But really the "critical ire" of these introductions is directed at recognizable features of Pelevin's own art—his interest in solipsism and his dense intertext, "a network of borrowings, imitations, rehashings and allusions" (*SKO* 6). A Huli is also a proxy for the author, since Pelevin's authorial image is consistently that of the trickster.[23]

Generation 'П,' which has no fictional narrator, yet adopts Tatarsky's perspective, offers a case of self-ironization by suggesting subversive biographic and stylistic analogies between the hero, the deception-disseminating copywriter Tatarsky, and the author. Like Pelevin, Tatarsky enrolls in a technical institute and subsequently goes to study at the Literary Institute. His advertisements are composed in a manner quite familiar to readers of Pelevin's books—using a dense intertext generously spiced with paradoxes, puns, and other kinds of wordplay.

Generation 'П''s self-conscious marketing strategy (in the real world) relied on diversely packaged editions that targeted both the intelligentsia and the more unassuming members of the reading public. To appeal to the widest *target group*, both "high cultural" and "mass-market" editions were issued by the publishing house Vagrius the year of the novel's release. The former has a reserved gray cover, customary for Vagrius, with a reproduction of Pieter Brueghel the Elder's painting *The Tower of Babel*. The letter "*П*" in standard quotation marks in the high-cultural edition becomes ‚*П*‘ in the mass-market edition, referencing the obscene term *pizdets* (written with two commas, as the novel indicates), which stands for the apocalypse. Andrew Bromfield's English translation was released in the United Kingdom as *Babylon* and republished in the United States as *Homo Zapiens*, likely catering to the more "classical" and the more "modern" sensibilities on opposite sides of the Atlantic, respectively. In a further marketing strategy, prior to the book's publication an excerpt from the novel, "Little Vovchik," was released. That excerpt alludes to Pelevin's highly successful preceding work, *Chapaev and the Void*, through a "Buddhist" explication of advertising, and offers a preview of the new book's preoccupations with commerce, advertising lingo, the media, and the "Russian idea."[24]

So marketing occurs outside the text (in real life) and is foregrounded in the text itself. The inside cover of the mass-market edition presents Che Guevara with a completely symmetrical face (to comment on the reproducibility of commercial images). The interjection "Wow-Vau!" on the back cover conditions the reader's response like a laugh track in sitcoms and simultaneously Russifies the word "wow" for domestic consumption. The cover of another mass-market edition issued in 2002 has a brick wall with three images of Che, the left and right ones as mirror images of each other, and the title of the novel scribbled on the wall graffiti-style.

Generation 'П' simultaneously positions itself "from without," as a critique of commodified, culturally destitute post-Soviet Russia, and "from within" as a participant in that reality. According to the novel, the culture and art of the new "Dark Age" have been degraded to mere advertising:

> A black bag stuffed with hundred-dollar bills has already become the most important cultural symbol and a central element of most films and books . . . The time is approaching when books and films will appear in which the dominant element of content will be a secret hymn of praise to Coca-Cola and an attack on Pepsi-Cola—or vice versa. (*G'П'* 300)

The notion that, with the commodification of cultural production and reception, literature is reduced to advertising is exemplified by the novel itself, which blends novelistic and advertising forms. Tatarsky, a representative of Generation P(epsi), by the book's close has turned Russia into Coca-Cola country. In a new Coke ad described on the last page of the novel, an evangelist from New Mexico tramples a Pepsi can underfoot, raises his arm to point to the Kremlin wall, and quotes from Psalm 14: "There were they in great fear; for God is in the generation of the righteous." Continuing the joke, the cover of a 2002 reprint of the novel shows Che Guevara sporting a beret with a Nike logo surrounded by Coke and Pepsi logos.[25] In another ironic twist, Bhutan, the only country in the world where television is forbidden, is the alleged retirement destination for television moguls—a claim made, in another nudge toward instability, by one of the novel's media swindlers, Sasha Blo.[26]

Pelevin's dystopia assiduously highlights its own complicity in the consumer context. In the world of the novel, everything and everyone are for sale—clothes, cars, homes, politicians, art—but, first and foremost, in a sardonic auto-referential gesture, Pelevin's text itself. The key point here is not that auto-referentiality or self-reflexivity are ironic per se, but that they become ironic when/because the authorial persona demonstrates himself to be implicated in the very folly he denigrates. As cultural production and reception take on the form of commodities, literature becomes subservient to monetary flows.

From its very first page, the novel's paratextual elements spotlight its being co-opted by commerce.[27] The cover of a 1999 edition sports a mock copyright statement that "prohibits" the reader from pondering whatever ideas may be inspired by the text as the sole property of the author: "All the thoughts that may enter the reader's mind are subject to author copyright. Their unsanctioned contemplation is forbidden." This pseudo-copyright statement rewrites dystopian thought control, and is followed by another parodic copyright statement placed in the text proper, following the epigraph:

> All trademarks mentioned in the text are the property of their respected owners . . . Names of goods and politicians do not indicate actual commercial products and refer only to projections of elements of the commercial-political informational field that have been forcibly induced as objects of the individual mind. (*GП* 5)

According to another claim (à la the Frankfurt school), consumer society leaves no space for dissent, since opposition is sold as just one more product—a highly popular one—in the global marketplace. This is just what *Generation 'П'* does, and the text insists that the reader acknowledge that it is doing so. As it quips: "Nothing sells as well as a well-packaged and politically correct rebellion against a world that is ruled by political correctness and in which everything is packaged to be sold" (*GП* 96). The marketing of Che Guevara paraphernalia (T-shirts, slogans, music) is one example of this trend. The ad for a Sony television that Tatarsky comes up with after realizing that the media is today's Tofet or Gehenna is another. Tatarsky draws on Che Guevara's vision of the media as a diabolic force perpetuating greed and lies—in an ironic loop, only to sell a new Sony television set. This is a new advertising technology that turns to its benefit the populace's increasing revulsion at market mechanisms. "Profoundly anti-market in form, it promises to be highly market-effective in content," this technology aptly describes Pelevin's own narrative, with its superabundance of advertising concepts that recycle leftist ideology (*GП* 239).

By a contradiction that resembles the liar paradox, *Generation 'П'* both lays open the carceral nature of consumerism and advertises itself as an offspring of consumer society.[28] If any diagnosis of social ailments is overridden in consumer society, then the novel's own critique is overridden as well. In these terms the mere awareness of one's commodified nature, displayed by the text's meta-commentary, is not sufficient to constitute a transcendence of commodification. The tension in this paradox is not only more radical than a stable irony, but also more far-reaching than the unstable (for example, romantic) irony produced when the author switches between contradictory viewpoints throughout the text. *Generation 'Π'* does not state contradictory viewpoints sequentially, but subverts its anti-establishment thrust in the very process of expressing it. But this is exactly what the novel claims—that commodified society short-circuits all attempts at critique.

LANGUAGE AND THE OPERATIVE CONTRADICTION

Like its prequel, *Empire V* disrupts assumed coherence by means of the liar paradox, simultaneously claiming that consumer culture commodifies and neutralizes attempts at social critique while foregrounding itself as a non-autonomous product of that culture, thus subverting its anti-consumerist thrust. Observations in the vein of "The most vulgar feature of our time is to give foreign names to shops, restaurants, and even novels written in Russian" expose the pragmatics of text production and position the author as a first-rate manipulator of popular consciousness (*EV* 75). The text, of course, actively engineers its presence in the English language.[29] Analogously, claims like "A denigration of glamour projects glamour even into those empty corners into which it would have never entered itself," also frame *Empire V*'s anti-consumerism ironically (*EV* 89).

The self-undermining framing of anti-consumerism recurs throughout *Empire V*. Self-irony is taken to a new level here: not only is the liar paradox enacted through subverted consumer critique, but as part of this consumer critique, the paradox is played out by the text invalidating its own medium, language.[30] The text is a verbal artifact that exposes words as spinning out falsehoods and thereby deconstructs itself at the most basic level.

Words (discourse) imprison humans inside monetary simulacra. Vampires use glamour and discourse to trigger insatiable consumer desire. Discourse erects a mental prison around humans, and makes sure they are unable to leave: it "forbids running away" and acts "as a kind of barbed wire with electricity running through it—not for the human body but for the human mind. It separates the territory that cannot be entered from the territory that cannot be left" (*EV* 92–93). Discourse precludes humans from thinking independently and potentially learning about the vampire dictatorship. Using high-toned but obscure terminology, it shows the lengths to which language can be stretched to obfuscate meaning.[31]

Just as *Empire V*'s attack on discourse drives the text into an ironic contradiction, the identification of the vampire's essence as *iazyk* (both "tongue" and "language") points at a "dictatorship" that self-ironically references *Empire V-iktor.* People are bred by vampires for the purpose of producing the *bablos* on which *iazyk* feeds. The vampire "is the vehicle for a tongue that tests and transmits the *power of the tongue*" (Lipovetsky and Etkind, "The Salamander's Return," 16). *Iazyk* is a literal bloodsucker that conditions humans into submission, reads their minds, and consumes *bablos*, which is people's genuine vitality expended in pursuit of vacuous goals. This very same *iazyk*, as an authorial tool, draws in the reader and even exploits the vampires themselves, or more precisely the popular vampire lore—something *Pineapple Water* will later joke about self-reflexively: "It's no small feat to be able to suck vampires' blood" (*AV* 51).

Grounded in Pelevin's satire of commodity culture, irony in *Empire V* again takes on an unorthodox form and feeling. The novel rewrites the postmodernist/post-structuralist irony of "language that produces the self that it supposedly names" as selfhood being a by-product of the production of *bablos*. In the postmodern ironic tradition, what lies outside language is created through language.[32] For Rorty, "ironists agree . . . about our inability to step outside our language in order to compare it with something else, and . . . about the contingency and historicity of that language" (*Contingency, Irony, and Solidarity*, 75). In Paul de Man's more radical view, language generates the illusion of the subject (*Aesthetic Ideology*, 172–75). In *Empire V*, welding post-structuralism and neo-Marxism, the word exists only as the object of the mind, and the object needs a perceiving subject. So, "for a $100 bill to appear, someone must appear who looks at it. This is like a lift and a counter-lift. That's why, when bablos is being produced, in the mirrors of the money boob there arises an illusion of personhood producing bablos" (*EV* 325).

In the novel's self-subversive logic, any claim, including its own, that language imprisons humans inside monetary simulacra can't help being advanced from within language and so can't help serving monetary simulacra. The text lays bare this problem when Roma questions the dissident vampire Osiris about God:

—You said that mind "A" is a mirror. And then you said that to reflect and to create are one and the same thing. Can one say that God is present in every living creature as mind "A"?
—Yes, one can say this . . . but everything we will say will be made up of words, and every word put in front of mind "A" instantly transforms it into mind "B." All words by definition are located inside the money boob. (*EV* 364)

The narrative ironizes the very attempt to escape verbal bounds. Osiris's view that words do not reflect the world but create it does not satisfy Roma, who wants to know whether God really exists—perceived by mind "A," receptor of sense data, rather than by mind "B," made of words, a generator of fantasies. The older vampire laughs. One can only think of what is extra-linguistic from an ironic vantage point within language. Or, in the terms of *Empire V*, one can posit God as "real" but this will be an utterance as well and, as such, a fantasy of mind "B" and a by-product of *bablos*. One may castigate words in words or one may insist, as does the enterprising professor of theology, that man is analogous to the Villa of Mysteries in ancient Pompeii, whose beautiful frescoes are not the mere waste of *bablos*. But such gestures may be mere captive attempts "to set up, in place of the wine press on the Villa of Mysteries, a small candle factory" (*EV* 375).[33] In other words, they represent the same pragmatic impulse.

Empire V elaborates on and grounds the ironic contradiction stated in the preface to *Chapaev and the Void* in the context of consumer unfreedom: it is "one more phantom molded from words," and it denigrates these same words. But Pelevin's work, distinctly in line with his critique of contemporaneity, reimagines the post-romantic irony of challenging language through language (as in Tyutchev's poem "Silentium!" [1830]) and the post-structuralist irony of the illusory subject generated by discourse—as an attack on empty referents of commodity culture from within commodity culture. Such an attack is always caught in the problem of self-referentiality and as such is bound to fail.

THE PRAGMATICS OF TEXT PRODUCTION

T carries Pelevin's exposure of the commercial pragmatics of text production—the text trapped by its context—to its limit. The novel elaborates on Pelevin's theme that contemporary culture is degraded to *dukhovnyi fastfood* ("spiritual fast food") because that is what readers demand and authors are ready to supply (*DPP(NN)* 71).[34] The novel reveals an intricate structure that turns back on itself, describes the process of its own creation, and transforms Pelevin's diagnosis of the modern condition into self-diagnosis.

In a gesture toward irony and poetic justice, *T* chooses Leo Tolstoy, the all-powerful author par excellence, who was preoccupied in his own lifetime by the question of individual freedom, with whom to frolic. In the novel's terms, Tolstoy is punished for usurping the role of the divine by having his soul posthumously transformed into a literary character puppeteered by another demiurge:

Just imagine: there once lived in Russia a great writer, Count Tolstoy, whose will set in motion a huge dance of shadows. Perhaps he believed that he invented them, but in reality they were the souls of scribblers who, taking part

in the Battle of Borodino or diving under the wheels of a train, were paying
for their sins—for Odysseus, Hamlet, Madame Bovary, and Julien Sorel. And
after his death Count Tolstoy himself began to play a similar role. (*T*, 68)

As in Dante's *Inferno*, the "sinner" is punished in accordance with the sin.
Tolstoy used to manipulate his characters, now it's high time he is made to
dance himself.[35]

As part of his ongoing critique of carceral consumer society, Pelevin
now exposes the exploitative conditions of the literary business. To meet the
demands of the literary market, *T* rewrites Tolstoy's final flight from home to
regain freedom and meaning late in life, all done in the manner of a retro-
detective novel à la Boris Akunin's bestsellers. Unlike the elderly Tolstoy on
his way from Yasnaya Polyana to Ostapovo, Count T is a handsome, youthful
nobleman who is highly proficient in martial arts. He has forgotten everything about his previous existence, and has no idea what the Optina Pustyn'
toward which he is traveling might be or why he is being pursued by an assemblage of ruffians.[36] But thanks to his superman-like qualities, he can dis-
patch his enemies deftly as he progresses toward his mysterious destination.

Each move that takes place in the narrative is determined by marketing considerations. Count T piles corpse upon corpse on his way to the hermitage at Optina Pustyn' because the story of a repentant old Tolstoy would
not sell well and needs to be repackaged as something more entertaining.
He strives to reach Optina Pustyn' because the book's sponsors want to promote a tale of the excommunicated great novelist being reconciled to official
Russian Orthodoxy. Indeed, Tolstoy's repentance before the mother church
functions as a product placement for official post-Soviet orthodoxy. In the
latter part of the book the Tolstoy project is discontinued, and its authors
intend to recycle what they have and resell it to a new party that embarks
on a computer shooter game called "Dostoevsky's Petersburg." And so on.
Not long into the story, T himself learns that his existence as a character in a
popular novel explains both his inability to act freely and the lurid quality of
the events that befall him. He senses "a lubok-like inauthenticity of whatever
takes place, a vulgar and exaggerated comicality," and learns from his creator
that he is the protagonist of a pop novel concocted by a group of literary
hacks under the leadership of the demonic editor Ariel Brakhman (*T*, 85).[37]

Unlike nineteenth-century writers who created texts that touched
human souls, modern-day creators transform life's perceptions into pulp fiction that yields maximum profit. These works are now written by teams of
hacks, with each one responsible for a separate aspect of the narrative (sex,
fighting, drugs), while the editor puts the bits and pieces together. The contemporary writer resembles a Turing machine that manufactures texts according to a preset algorithm.[38] As Brakhman explains: "You are the hero

of a story, Count. One could call you a literary hero, but there are serious doubts that the text from which you arise has a right to be deemed literature" (*T,* 87).

The authorial persona's voice is as self-incriminating as ever, making his own art the object of the degradation critiqued. In the words of the novel:

> The chief cultural technology of the twenty-first century . . . is the commercial exploitation of strangers' graves. Sucking corpses [*trupootsos*] is the most respected contemporary genre because it is a direct analogue of the oil industry. We used to think that only the Chekists inherited from the dinosaurs. And then cultured people in society also found out where to insert a pipe [*kuda trubu vpendiurit'*]. Even the murdered emperor toils like your white horse on the hill. How is Dostoevsky better? (*T,* 142–43)

This cultural diagnosis is aimed at Pelevin's own novel, which exploits the Tolstoy and Dostoevsky myths, and not just at its inner narratives—Brakhman and his brigade's potboilers and shooter games. *T* points to an exploitative recycling of culture the same way earlier works ("The Macedonian Critique of French Thought," *The Sacred Book of the Werewolf*) emphasized the wholesale resource extraction of the oil industry. To further link the authorial persona to the *trupootsos* of the contemporary culture business, a member of Brakhman's writing team, their "metaphysician," has Pelevinesque features—down to a predilection for "metaphysical contemplations, mystical revelations, et cetera," as well as a fondness for Buddhism that results in a segment of the narrative dedicated to the seventh Lama Urgan Dzhambon Tulku, the putative author of the preface to *Chapaev and the Void* (*T,* 94).

Exploring and exploiting auto-reflexively the clichés of contemporary culture, *T* takes the next step: its meta-literary thinking blooms into the larger Pelevinian metaphysics of unfreedom. *T*'s predicament in the hands of his unscrupulous creators is analogous to a general existential predicament. As Princess Tarakanova, another pretender with keen insight into contemporary culture, explains, humans possess neither free will nor selfhood.[39] Rather, what they take to be themselves is brought into temporary existence by controlling agents—creators (if we think in literary terms) or Creators (in terms of metaphysics):

> —But everyone has a constant uninterruptable sense of selfhood. That I am myself. Is not that the case?
> —The sense you speak of is the same for all humans, and is merely an echo of their corporeality, as with all living beings. When an actor puts on a crown, the metal edge squeezes his head. King Lear may be played by many actors in turn, and everyone will be wearing the same cold iron band. But

one should not infer that this iron band is the main participant in the mystery play. . . . King Lear's crown, without the actor who puts it on, will remain a tin hoop. (*T*, 28–29)[40]

In Pelevin's gloomy cosmology, multiple deities amuse themselves by playing the human, like different actors who come on stage in the same attire. Within the confines of the novel, T fights, shoots, and runs from the police without knowing anything about himself—because his hack creators make him behave that way. T suffers from a sense of helplessness and unfreedom to the point of despair.[41] But his fate as a literary character only exemplifies the lot of humankind at large.

Once more irony—in this case, cosmic and dramatic—acquires a specific Pelevinian anti-consumer twist.[42] The hack writers manipulate Count T in a degrading manner akin to the *kommercheskoe skotovodstvo* ("commercial cattle-breeding") seen in *DPP(NN)*, *The Sacred Book of the Werewolf*, *Empire V*, and other works (*T*, 119). The breeders are in turn milked themselves. For editor Brakhman, unfreedom is as true of his own life as it is of T's textual existence:

> If I should like to take credit under twelve per cent per annum and buy the eighth Mazda to stand in stinking traffic looking at a poster advertising the ninth Mazda, is this truly my whim? . . . The difference is that you are screwed only by Miten'ka, while I am—at once by ten swindlers from three offices specializing in brainwashing. (*T*, 176)

In *T*'s pessimistic (and familiar) ontological vision, everyone is in the power of dark mercenaries who are analogous to the Chaldeans of *Generation 'П'* or the vampires of *Empire V*. As Pelevin's reader may have come to expect, the entities that steer people like Brakhman are themselves no omnipotent demiurges, but petty demons who in their turn are manipulated indifferently. Cosmic irony applies to the character T as he is tossed around by Brakhman, to the hireling Brakhman as he is pressured by his employers in the literary business, to Brakhman's employers who are handled by the shadowy secret service and criminal structures, and so on, all the way up to the authorial persona itself.

The novel's latter part seems to represent a benign alternative to the ontology of commercial cattle-breeding, but may in fact be one more instance of subverted lyrical address. Having learned that he has been enslaved by sinister and meaningless forces, T struggles to escape their influence and acquire freedom and self-knowledge—to become, as Vladimir Solovyov teaches him, both the author and reader of his life. He kills his literary overlord Brakhman and arrives at Optina Pustyn' (in *T*, a place of mystical illumination, not the Orthodox hermitage) on the last page of the book. But in one final twist, *T* playfully equates the inner (Brakhman's) narrative with its own outer narrative. The name of Ariel Brakhman, whom T has killed, is typed framed in black as part of *T*'s publication data in the manner of a publisher's memorial. The text exploits consumer culture, subverts it, and offers a spiritual alternative to total commodification, but in the final analysis it refuses to stabilize itself.

❊ ❊ ❊

In Friedrich Schlegel's discussion of irony, "On Incomprehensibility" (1800), "silver and gold are comprehensible and through them everything else." "Irony of irony" takes place "if one has promised to be ironical for some useless book without first having checked one's supply." Most centrally, Schlegel asserts that (Socratic) irony "is the freest of all licenses, for by its means one transcends oneself," and "it is a very good sign when harmonious bores are at a loss about how they should react to this continuous self-parody, when they fluctuate endlessly between belief and disbelief until they get dizzy and take what is meant as a joke seriously and what is meant seriously as a joke" (*Lucinde and the Fragments*, 262, 267, 265). In Schlegel's depiction, irony is also directed at the ironist—an observation that is applicable to Pelevin. Indeed, self-irony dominates other manifestations of irony in his texts; his works are torn by ironic self-contradiction. To use one of Pelevin's favorite images, his books are ouroboroses biting their own tails.[43] Just as the authorial persona derides social and human corruption, he shows himself implicated in the very corruption that is the object of his ironic ire.

Reading Pelevin's (self)-irony pragmatically, it is "highly market-effective both in form and in content." His dutiful wit, provisionality, and bashfulness about any claims to authority, all elements of contemporary literary and critical etiquette, sell well in the marketplace of ideas. His texts minister to postmodern sensibilities that are enamored of playfulness, self-consciousness, and the undecidability of ironic paradoxes. Besides being market-effective, irony protects the author in the sense of "excusing" his exploitation of pulp paradigms. In Linda Hutcheon's terms, "the particular intersection in the communicative space set up by meaning and affect that makes irony happen is a highly unstable one," and a further risk inherent in irony is that using a discourse allows its articulation, even if in quotation marks (Hutcheon, *Irony's Edge*, 196).

In Pelevin's own reading, irony can be a device that is merely mechanical, a tribute to fashion. When Tatarsky's Buddhist friend Gireev claims that television anchormen's eyes are full of hatred (*Generation 'П'*), Tatarsky objects that they don't even look at the camera:

There is a special monitor right under the camera lens that shows the text they are reading and special symbols for intonation and facial expression. I think there are only six of them . . . irony, sadness, doubt, improvisation, anger and joking. So no one really radiates any hatred, personal or even professional. I know for sure. (*G'Π* 270)

The text's parry is here directed at the trope of irony itself, exposing it as first on the list of requisite attitudes in the modern news industry.

Views of irony can be divided into those that emphasize specificity, certainty, and coherence (e.g., Wayne Booth) and those that emphasize instability, negativity, and disruptiveness (e.g., de Man). In his overview of ancient irony, Alexey Losev addresses the problem of irony's "positive" versus "negative" properties by contrasting ancient Socratic and romantic irony. Socratic irony "is aimed at transforming life for the better and constitutes an active means of raising up man," while romantic irony's "chief objective is sheer play. The Romantic artist does not seek ideas, reflections of reality, or morals in art." The aesthetic object is a living play of contradictions, "one that reaches total rupture from the whole of human history, a complete distancing of the subject from life, the utter objectlessness of the game" (Losev, *Istoriia antichnoi estetiki*, 446, 459, 460). Losev links romantic irony to subjectivism that denies objective, substantive being. Everything is established by an "I," and the "I" that creates or destroys anything therefore relates ironically to being (460).

But romantic ironists, destabilizing though they can be, are still capable of sincere first-person pronouncements. It is postmodernist aesthetics that tends to reject wholesale the structures of "truth" in favor of textual and contextual play in which irony's negative properties are made more manifest. Irony liberates language from fixed meaning (de Man, *Aesthetic Ideology*, 179). The ironist's positioning above dogma is disruptive, according to Kierkegaard on romantic irony, and this applies even more to postmodernism (Kierkegaard, *The Concept of Irony*, 26). The seduction of the ironic stance is its elusiveness, which can be critiqued as deceitful—involving pretense and concealment, two-faced skepticism, caution, cunning, and swindlery (Knox, *Ironia*, 45–46).[44] By not stating what one means, one may create not a hidden self but sheer negativity.

The extent to which critiques of unstable irony intersect with critiques of Pelevin's own work is striking—both critiques condemn unbridled solipsism, making oneself ungraspable, absolving oneself of moral commitment. If we read postmodern irony as associated with relativism and not carrying any ethical message—this chimes closely with the accusations of Pelevin's detractors.[45] One might say that the perpetual ironist resembles Bakhtin's "pretender," who tries to evade the project of selfhood and the ethical obligations of the moment and instead supplies "an alibi in Being" (Bakhtin, *Toward a Philosophy of the Act*, 42; Morson and Emerson, *Mikhail Bakhtin*, 31).

Pelevin is a Swift-like author who exhibits an earnest and grim attitude toward social degradation. At the same time he is a romantic ironist in the vein of Schlegel, Wordsworth, or Tyutchev who strives to escape the given in life and language; and he is a modernist ironist in the spirit of Eliot or Joyce who places himself above the mechanical forces of the everyday. But Pelevin is also a postmodern verbal juggler who redefines irony as dependent on a sense of truth beyond the acrobatics of discourse, on an authorial viewpoint other than the one expressed.

Does an exposure of the ironic contradictions exhaust the function of Pelevin's texts, or does anything remain of the ouroboros beyond the act of biting its tail? Perhaps it is for readers to decide whether their critical assessment of Pelevin's critique is real or illusory. From the perspective of this study, appreciating Pelevin's ironies does not lead to dismissing his critiques. His suggestion that *Generation 'П*'s dominant element is secret praise of Coca-Cola or Pepsi might be just another playful provocation, rather than a fair restatement of the novel's contents. Exhaustively laying out the novel's twists and turns does not fully account for how "the illusion of critical assessment of what takes place on the screen [in the book] takes place" (*G'П* 239). Perhaps this illusion is another Pelevinian red herring. One learns a good deal about the foibles of the world and language despite (or because of) the contradiction in terms that these thoroughly ironic texts foreground.

In this reading, Pelevin's oeuvre is saturated with irony because he perceives irony to saturate contemporary society and culture, where no one means, or feels able to mean, what they say. As Roman Kozak and Sergei Polotovsky ask in their biography of Pelevin:

> If all Russian writers from century to century went en route from artist to publicist, trying to sow the true, good, and eternal, and Pelevin does not want this, does this mean that tradition has come to its end with Pelevin? Alternatively, does this mean only that Pelevin is not entirely traditional? (*Pelevin i pokolenie pustoty*, 12)

In my view the answer is—neither. Pelevin has to be ironic to be understood, and it is precisely from this position that he is able to smuggle across the much-trivialized values of goodness, truth, and beauty.

More to the point here, an affirmative dimension to Pelevin's texts—one that invests them with a measure of ethical authenticity—may be suggested in their very ironies. The idea of a meaning other than that stated implies the existence of a speaker and an intent beyond language, and this goes against the post-structuralist view of the text as a play of signifiers with no grounding sensibility (Muecke, *Irony and the Ironic*, 100–101). Not only that, but a "romantic" reading will interpret the ironist's inscrutability not as an alibi for being that evades the project of selfhood, but as a way to safeguard that selfhood by charting a sovereign territory for it.

An interplay of freedom and irony unfolds in Pelevin's story "Hermit and Six Toes." As the chickens hide between some crates, a worker finds them and moves them over to Shop Number One, the place of impending slaughter. At first the sentient birds "take this calmly and even with some irony. They settle near the World-wall and begin to build refuges of the soul for themselves" (*VPE* 47). What the worker does not know is that the chickens have realized there exists a larger universe beyond the World-wall, and have been training themselves to fly away (as well as cultivating their spiritual liberation from the cant of chicken society). Although they get scared when, having been found out, a man puts a strip of tape around Six Toes' leg, in the finale of the story the two protagonists manage to fly away. The chicken escapees use irony (and wings) to claim a space of freedom for themselves.

The multiplication of ironies in Pelevin's texts suggests authorial attempts to escape one's own bounds (the deceptions of consciousness, the demands of the market, the vulgarity of readers, the falsehoods of language) and is analogous to the key motif of his works—his protagonists' struggling to make a break, literal and figurative, from their caged existences. Schlegel, in fact, imagines the liberating power of irony as flight or hovering—"airy, fragrant, as it were, imponderable" (*Lucinde and the Fragments*, 261).[46] As early as "The Prince of Gosplan," the story ends as follows: "If he pressed the <Shift>, <Control>, and <Return> keys simultaneously, and then reached for the key with the arrow pointing upwards and pressed that as well, then wherever the little figure might be, and no matter how many enemies it was facing, it would do something very unusual—it would jump, stretch upward, and a second later *dissolve in the sky*" (*VPE* 228). Hermit and Six Toes fly into freedom, Pustota describes happiness as "a special flight of free thought," and A Huli leaps on her bicycle in the air in Bitsevo Park (*CP* 264).

Then, again, in non-redemptive works like *Generation 'П,' DPP(NN)*, and *Empire V*, the protagonists are assimilated into the status quo or fall prey to ersatz mysticism, and their struggles (if there are any) end in no flight into freedom. When "silver and gold are comprehensible and through them everything else," irony may allow a modicum of free space from encroaching social dogma. But one may also "promise to be ironical for some useless book without first having checked one's supply." Pelevin, like Pustota, makes good his exit into Inner Mongolia or, like Tatarsky on the last page of *Generation 'П,'* ends up in a Tuborg beer commercial.

A Christmas Carol with Qualifiers

> You're not the same as you were before.
> You were much more muchier; you've lost your
> muchness.
> —*Alice in Wonderland* (Disney, 2010)

PELEVINIANA NEEDS no product placement, least of all in an academic study. What follows in this concluding section is less a defense of Pelevin's fiction (even if it may in places come across as one) than one more attempt to suspend judgment and analyze in a sustained manner what this writer has (and has not) been able to accomplish. My work as a whole has sought to provide a more comprehensive picture of Pelevin as an artist and thinker. Here as elsewhere, I should like not to dismiss but to engage different critical interpretations of him, as well as point out when such interpretations, in my estimation, fail to consider the bigger picture.

Pelevin's diagnosis of our existence is thoroughly unnerving, and appears to be more and more prescient as smartphone zombies, oligarchic presidencies, and silicon-empowered exhibitionistas compete in blind vision, and facts no longer matter—only the medium and the money do. As both Pelevin's thinking and the larger techno-consumer society develop, sources of unfreedom—social, biological, technological, verbal, and combinations thereof—proliferate and complicate. The game cannot be won—if you succeed at one level, there is always another beyond it. Pelevin's narratives peel off layers of meaning while never reaching a hidden kernel: humankind serves a higher caste of Chaldeans (*Generation 'П'*); humans and Chaldeans are enslaved by vampires and the bat-goddess Ishtar (*Empire V*); regional vampire dictatorships are under the control of a global vampire overlord residing on a drifting tanker somewhere in the oil-drenched waters of the world ocean (*Batman Apollo*, 2013), and so on. One can only assume that this divinity of blood and petrol is in turn puppeteered by some other entity in an endless hierarchy of enslaving forces. There is no access to "final truth" and no (at least collective) way out of bondage.

Nor is the potential for personal transcendence easy to achieve.

Pelevin's protagonists thirst for knowledge as if it would set them free, but even if they learn partial and provisional "how's" and "why's" of social-metaphysical mechanics, things hardly change for the better. Successful climbers like Vavilen Tatarsky (*Generation 'Π'*) and Roma Shtorkin (*Empire V*) join a cult that supplies them with esoteric knowledge and promises access to higher reality, but what the occult exposes is no higher realm but merely itself. One becomes a consumer of esoteric glamour and discourse as opposed to the things these purport to illuminate such as freedom, happiness, or the Absolute (not the vodka brand).

If one is in luck, one becomes a master of discourse and concurrently of society, albeit a deity that is disenchanted, bewildered, and easily dispensable, a "god of money with oaken wings." But even if characters reject the rat (aka snail) race, their redemption by withdrawing from the world has acquired over time an increasingly dark coloration. Pelevin's early stories ("Hermit and Six Toes," *The Yellow Arrow* [*Zheltaia strela*, 1993], *The Life of Insects*) end optimistically, and the end of Pyotr Pustota's journey is still hopeful, with his arrival in pastoral Inner Mongolia. But A Huli's final jump on the bicycle in Bitsevo Park (*The Sacred Book of the Werewolf*) is essentially a suicide, and Masha, the beautiful lady in "The Hotel of Good Incarnations" of *Pineapple Water*, chooses not to be born into this benighted world at all.

Pelevin is troubling because he sees no way of overcoming vicious social systems, while obsessively and compellingly narrating the obliteration of selfhood—and surely no one reading those pages would like being characterized as "an electromagnetic recording of a crowing cock." Not only is social deadlock a certainty, but liberation from the falsehoods and indignities of this world means collapsing the self into the negative space of *emptiness-pustota* beyond action or feeling: "The maximally accessible freedom equates with 'self-erasure,' the obliteration of 'I' and the reality to which this 'I' belongs and which it creates" (Lipovetskii, *Paralogii*, 641). Indeed, one discovers (paradoxically) that there is no self to act or feel. Thus runs the luminous (in its early versions), predictable (later), and somewhat sterile (for those more attuned to "ambiguous Christian" or Russian-literary-humanist traditions) Pelevinian finale.

A decade or so after Pelevin's landmark *Chapaev and the Void* and *Generation 'Π'* came out, Alexander Chantsev criticized a series of post-Soviet novels of the 2000s by Dmitry Bykov, Olga Slavnikova, Vladimir Sorokin, and Alexei Ivanov, calling them "close-range anti-utopias" that failed to create new meanings capable of uniting society. In Chantsev's reading, such texts embody a common feature of post-totalitarian consciousness: a distrust not of concrete politicians and concrete ideology, but of the whole idea of politics and ideology (Chantsev, "Fabrika antiutopii"). Such a conviction that any social activity is selfish and deeply flawed is quintessentially Pelevinian.

And yet, despite all its nihilistic hopelessness, there exists a more affirmative strain in Pelevin's oeuvre. While total estrangement from history and politics may be unproductive, *social critique is essential if one is to harbor any hope of bettering rotten social structures*. Moreover, freedom as an ethical necessity—an ever-present notion—unfolds into the ethical relationship to others in Pelevin's later work. *Chapaev and the Void* lays bare the world's intricate solipsistic architectonics, and simultaneously raises the issue of human interconnectedness—as in Pustota's wistful wondering on the shores of the URAL, "Who will read the description of my dreams?" (*CP* 310). Conversely, ethics and solipsism, far from contradicting each other, go hand in hand in *Love for Three Zuckerbrins*—as when the massacred employees of contra.ru find refuge in Nadya's inner kindergarten.

The way Pelevin's worthier characters act on their ethical duty contrasts with the way the protagonists of recent pro-imperial Russian speculative fiction gain a sense of agency through conformity with the imperial body politic: "Imperial SF replaces the feat of holiness [that is, an individual who confronts the overwhelming forces of his surrounding environment] with the feat of conformity [with the environment]" (Slavnikova, "Ia liubliu tebia, imperiia").[1] And Pelevin's more likeable protagonists fit into a longer tradition of moral (self)-betterment (to enable social improvement) as advanced by the Russian intelligentsia and articulated most forcefully in nineteenth-century classical literature.

The intermittent yet palpable shift in Pelevin's work from solipsism and individual liberation to intra-human ethics is no about-face, nor is the drive toward freedom (happiness, peace, love) sharply demarcated from Buddhist emptiness (*pustota*). The two coexist and interweave as leitmotifs throughout Pelevin's oeuvre. For all of Chapaev-Pustota's ingenious koans, the hero of Pelevin's classic is not fleeing into some white, black, or rainbow-colored hole. Instead, in the narrative's final sentence, he and his guru are "surrounded by the whispering sands and roaring waterfalls of his beloved Inner Mongolia," where Pustota has rushed upon learning that "Anna awaits some books he has promised to her" (*CP* 413). The Inner Mongolia (Shambhala, Nirvana) is mystic but also physical and geographic. It is beloved. And it promises creativity and a fair woman reading Pustota's work (even if on a loan from Bulgakov).

The requisite Nirvana or Shambhala in Pelevin's most famous novel is suggestively Bulgakovian, and perhaps not only Bulgakovian. The novel draws on the classical Russian literary-humanist tradition—irony and all.

From the disillusioned perspective of *Generation 'П,'* "happiness for every-body, free, and no one will go away unsatisfied" (the Strugatskys) may be impossible, and Bulgakov's "he has not deserved light, he deserved peace" is a more appropriate individualistic solution (*The Master and Margarita,* 340). Then again, Urgan Dzhambon Tulku VII in the "Preface" to *Chapaev and the Void* conveys an ethical and a humanist intent: he "dedicates the achieve-ment of this text to the good of all living beings."

The Buddhist and Bulgakovian strains playing side by side in the finale of *Chapaev and the Void* are one instance of Peleviniana operating among di-vergent worldviews in unorthodox configurations. Some of these worldviews are clearly in opposition: nihilistic and spiritual, humanist and posthumanist, postmodern/post-structural and pre-postmodern. One example of this kind of playful contrastive poetics is Kiklop delivering his little sermon on the Ten Commandments and ethical choice as an engine transferring between alter-native universes (*Love for Three Zuckerbrins*), right on the heels of discus-sions of Dawkins's selfish gene and Foucault's disappearance of the human. The whimsical yet challenging antinomy between the posthuman credo and its humanistic spiritual flip side—the soul necessary to perceive its own ab-sence (*Pineapple Water*)—is another example of these contrasts.

Pelevin infuriates and delights as a contrarian. In the words of *Genera-tion 'П'*: "Any enlightened spirit will agree that it does not exist"—but "Man is a remotely controlled television program"—and again "By his nature man is beautiful and great, . . . he simply does not realize this" (*G'П'* 107, 155). Or as *Empire V* formulates it: everything that makes up humanity (art, faith, selfhood itself) is a by-product of the production of *bablos*—versus "You vampires think you've built this farm [the Pompeian Villa of Mysteries, aka humankind] to press *bablos*," but actually the villa's ancient frescoes are the quintessence of humankind obscured by later technological usage (*EV* 372).

Which view does Pelevin himself find more compelling? Or which does he favor? Perhaps what Pelevin is partial to and what he deems con-vincing are not quite the same thing, as in "two times two makes four is an excellent thing, . . . but two times two makes five is sometimes a most charming little thing as well" (Dostoevsky, *Notes from Underground,* 18), or, more pertinently, "a deception that uplifts us is dearer than a host of low truths" (Pushkin, *Polnoe sobranie sochinenii,* 3:251). Perhaps Pelevin is of two minds about these larger philosophical issues, and demautocratically leaves the reader at liberty to choose an interpretation or solipsistically se-lect the one that is most "programmably compatible" with his particular self. One can see such tensions as cases of postmodern aporia. Or, put in Dostoevskian-Bakhtinian terms, Peleviniana generates an ongoing pro-and-con, a *perpetuum mobile* of challenging social-metaphysical questing.

But all worldviews being equal, some are more equal than others—as seen in the overarching trajectory of Pelevin's work. One can see where nihilistic readings of the texts are coming from, but these often miss key points. The following characterization of *Pineapple Water* is an illustration: Pelevin "frees God from the signs of power, . . . makes him disappear, wear out together with the soul." Levitan "assumes the role of God, informing Bush: 'The main proof of my existence is evil.' He was god for some and devil for others, but always remained a living negation of any kind of metaphysics fulfilling the mission of General Shmyga" (Tatarinov, "Pelevin bez prekrasnoi damy").

Such a reading disregards the crucial second part of the statement quoted: "The main proof of my existence is evil, *since in a world without God evil would not be evil but corporate etiquette*" (AV 79). That humans are still capable of distinguishing good from evil, notwithstanding all the secret service Shmygas and all the corporate etiquette, provides a modest form of spiritual encouragement. Shmyga is clearly no god, but a proper petty demon in the Dostoevskian and Sologubian tradition, and the exposure of materialist (perverted) simulacra of the spiritual does not mean that Pelevin is debunking the spiritual per se.[2]

Suggestions of a nihilistic or romantic-decadent strain, à la Baudelaire's embrace of evil in *The Flowers of Evil* (1857), appear elsewhere in analyses of Pelevin. In his panoramic overview of his fellow writer's work, "Pelevin, the Way Down" (2014), Dmitry Bykov claims an emotional about-face in the mature Pelevin: "Total anger and cynicism come out. Having seen that goodness is helpless and unnecessary, he grows fascinated by vice. This predetermines his current catastrophe. Why try hard for these petty little people [*liudishki*]?" (Bykov, "Pelevin, put' vniz"). That is why, according to Bykov, Pelevin's novels of the 2000s turn away from humans, making were-creatures and vampires into his protagonists.

Granting that Pelevin's mature productions tend to be less sanguine, I see no reason to claim a poetization of evil on his part. Someone like A Huli is an appealing character not because she is a were-fox but because, despite being one, she is capable of love, pangs of conscience, and self-sacrifice, while the *bablos*- and demagoguery-processing vampires are vicious and vacuous, too—as *Empire V* demonstrates with utter clarity. Pelevin is simply too soberly reflective about evil, as he is generally soberly reflective, to fall under the sway of a decadent poetics and worldview. "It is pleasant to flirt with evil," asserts Kotovsky in *Chapaev and the Void.* "There is no risk at all, while the gains are apparent" (*CP* 145). But, as the story "Thagi" in *Pineapple Water* shows clearly, the gains are in fact dubious and the risks are high.[3] The protagonist of this short story searches for an enchanting "ultimate evil" in the members of a Hindu murder-and-robbery cult, only to be destroyed by them in a businesslike way.

Far from being dispensable, ethical norms in Pelevin's texts are obfuscated by opportunistic humans and vicious social structures. This is something *Empire V* articulates in a razor-sharp way:

> What exactly is the source of evil is something all the newspapers argue every day. This is one of the most amazing things in the world because the human being can understand the nature of evil, without any explanation, through instinct. To make it opaque is a serious magic act. (*EV* 92)

The human being possesses an inborn moral intuition which can be nurtured or, alternatively, suppressed. The black-magic circus act of contemporaneity undermines this innate ethical sense. That is, with the earth-heavens formula turned into a non-equation, basic calculation leads one to side with evil. But in Pelevin, as in Dostoevsky, morals and math belong to different universes. Evil "exists in man's mind, and nowhere else. But when all men secretly side with evil, which does not exist anywhere except in their heads, does it need another victory?" (*EV* 66). Or, as *Chapaev and the Void* puts it: "A huge army of voluntary scoundrels appears to consciously confuse top with bottom and right with left" (*CP* 145).

Consistently anti-establishment, Pelevin directs his subversive thrust at postmodernism when, preoccupied in its more robust forms with the problem of freedom, it grows authoritarian itself. "The Macedonian Critique of French Thought," parodying Foucault and Baudrillard, and defining postmodern discourse as "stealing into the dark the last remnants of simplicity and common sense," is a case in point (*DPP(NN)* 270). Discourse, or *diskurs* (*Empire V*), is demagogic rhetoric that fudges meaning with convoluted terminology, precluding people from thinking independently and obfuscating vampire rule. Discourse-mongers like Bernard-Henri Montaigne Montesquieu and Alena Libertina (*S.N.U.F.F.*) engage in up-to-date theorizing while inciting wars, murder, and rape. Though they purport to interrogate society from an independent standpoint, these intellectuals are in fact instrumental to human enslavement.

As Mark Lipovetsky has reflected on the state of post-Soviet postmodernism in the late 2000s:

> Everything turned out not at all as it had been hoped for ten years ago. The strategies of spiritual liberation transformed themselves into petty technologies to swindle the populace, the power of a dashing deconstructionist . . . got devalued due to a sharp decline of the shares of culture in the market of services. . . . As to postmodernism, it, too, became a stylish "brand," annoying "strangers," uniting "its own kind," and somehow having lost its quintes-

sence: instead of a novel formula of freedom and a new understanding of the world—a get-together party, a Masonic lodge, a Guild of Chaldeans, a union of post-communist writers. (*Paralogii*, 447)

Lipovetsky's suggested remedy is a more mature (as successors, not epigones) engagement with modernist paradigms of intellectual freedom, existential intensity, self-analysis and self-conviction, and play with cultural archetypes in earnest and as an equal.

But Pelevin, as I see it, *is already doing all of the above.* He tests the limits of freedom and conducts harsh self-analysis and ethical and existential questioning. His intertexts outline positions beyond sheer play. He both practices postmodernism and subverts it for falling into an orthodoxy or a pulp of its own. He laughs at his literary figurines—protagonists who are not heroes, obstacles that are not overcome—while favoring seekers after "golden luck" (*zolotaia udacha*), when "a special flight of free thought permits one to perceive the beauty of life" (*CP* 264).[4] And this, not unexpectedly, returns one to the Russian canon of other, better freedoms (modernist, and back to the nineteenth century), a transfiguring power of creativity, and over-pumped but perhaps not yet entirely exhausted variations thereof.

As Sergei Kornev pointed out early on, Pelevin "has to combine paradoxically all the formal traits of postmodern literary production, to utilize its subversive potential a hundred percent," with being "a genuine Russian classical writer-ideologue like Tolstoy or Chernyshevsky" ("Stolknovenie pustot," 244).[5] This observation makes sense, except that neither Chernyshevsky (due to conceptual rigidity and poor writerly ability) nor Tolstoy (master of an exuberant portrayal of the physical aspects of existence, at odds with Pelevin's distrust of the sensory and the sensual) seems the best fit to me. How is Dostoevsky, the author of *The Brothers Karamazov*, better as a classic antecedent for the focus of this study? Perhaps in the following ways:

(a) as a philosopher-ideologue of a *non-monolithic/non-monologic/modern* kind—contrarian, ironic, paradoxical, disharmonious;

(b) as a professional writer implicated in publishing, commercial, contexts;

(c) as a topical, journalistic mind, with a keen instinct for contemporary predicaments and pulp paradigms;

(d) as someone who is critical of (post)modernity, techno-civilization, the West, materialism, and so-called progress;

(e) as a producer of fantastic and hallucinatory works;

(f) as a writer with a cerebral yet sentimental approach;

(g) and as someone with a consistent, even obsessive, and intensely metaphysical vision.

In the light of some critical investigations, one might add conservatism to the list—this is something to be discussed.

PELEVIN, THEN AND NOW

Ever since Pelevin's supernova launched in the turbulent late 1980s and early 1990s, his relationship with the critics has been uncomfortable. His early texts incurred severe critiques from the more conservative side of the critical camp as irresponsible and unconstructive, as meaningless or even harmful verbal games that were messing up traditional Russian cultural values.[6] When *Chapaev and the Void* didn't make it onto the Russian Booker Prize shortlist, that future Pelevin classic was derided as a computer virus destroying Russian culture (Shaitanov, "Booker-97").[7] Pelevin responded in kind, punning vigorously on the name of his longtime nemesis Andrei Nemzer ("Nedotykomzer") and (in)famously drowning "Pavel Bisinsky" (Basinsky in the real world), who meets his end in a village toilet in *Generation 'П.'*

The charges against the mature and later Pelevin are, interestingly, diametrically opposed to those described above, though equally heavy. Pelevin, the former enfant terrible who disregarded all values and restraint and indulged his exuberant fantasy and an aptitude for subversion, has allegedly turned artistically and ideologically stale, recycling his trademark devices, and, moreover, developing a penchant for moralizing and preachiness. So, for instance, *Love for Three Zuckerbrins* is described as unfashionably direct; that is, it is "explained by the example of *Angry Birds*, interpreted through a Soviet cartoon, via an appeal to Ten Commandments, and so forth.". . . When the author "writes on the last pages, 'If I felt in myself the makings of a preacher . . . ,' it's frightening to think what would have been then if he does not feel like a preacher now" (Babitskaia, "*Liubov' k trem cukerbrinam* Viktora Pelevina").

By the time one arrives at Pelevin's "sorry for the cliché" latter-day sermons, their message comes out as uncertain and uncomfortable, and is colored by, complicated, and enriched by irony. As Chapaev advises Pustota, "Live by the laws of the world in which you end up, and use these laws to free yourself from them. Get discharged from the hospital" (*CP* 324–25). But even when preserving a veneer of didacticism in a world uncomfortable with didacticism, these outlying positions are still meaningful. If postmodernist expectations are obligatory, defying them is a radical move. Being earnest when earnestness is not the norm becomes a new form of subversion.

Going back to "Pelevin, the Way Down," Dmitry Bykov envisions his fellow writer's apparent downward spiral as an artistic and conceptual ossification that is mainly due to his disappointment with post-Soviet realities. In Bykov's estimation, Pelevin's artistic fate is unexpected, even shocking: Pelevin was the main literary hope of Russia in the early 1990s and the best-realized talent of the second half of that decade, but once he got harnessed to the annual release of his works by the Eksmo publishing house in the early 2000s, literature ceased to be of interest to him. Grounded in late Soviet culture and disillusioned with post-Soviet inanities, he underwent his fascination-with-evil period and subsequently chose not to develop further as an artist out of sheer contempt for his undeserving readership.

Never mind the enchantment-with-evil business, the claim that Pelevin is rooted in late Soviet culture (and especially counterculture) is a valid and important point. So is the point that Brezhnev's "period of stag-nation" in the 1970s and early '80s—with its nonconformist *tamizdat* and *samizdat*, its revival of modernism (Russian and Western), Brodsky and the Leningrad school of metaphysical poetry, Moscow conceptualism, subtle neo-Chekhovian poetics, and its interest in the occult and esoteric—seems now like a new Silver Age compared to the *chernukha-pornukha* (pulp, porn, criminality) of Russia in the 1990s. To fall back on Pelevin's own idiom, he, like Pyotr Pustota, "belongs to the generation that was programmed for life in one sociocultural paradigm, but has found itself living in quite a different one"—and a much more obscene one at that.

Following this logic, Pelevin can either skate along on reminiscences of his youth or castigate the new era. But both options—of lachrymose nos-talgia and unbridled satire—are ultimately limiting. An artist needs some-thing existing that he can, if not admire, then relate to in ways more com-plex than that of a mere feuilleton. Or else, having partially exhausted his creative method and intellectual reserve, he must settle on mechanistic self-repetition. Whoever has the need will read some sort of meaning into the text, anyway.

Critical accusations of repetitiveness, curiously, appear as early as *Gen-eration 'П,'* and are clearly unjustified in that particular case.[8] With hindsight, no other Russian novel captures the 1990s in such a vivid photographic man-ner, while at the same time pointing presciently into the next millennium. Analogous charges against Pelevin have been voiced over and over in the course of the new century. While some of his works of the first decade of this century, for example, the collection *PPPPP* (2008), are less than exciting, *The Sacred Book of the Werewolf, Empire V,* and *T* are strong Peleviniana. To my mind, *Empire V* offers Pelevin's richest analysis of techno-consumerism to date. But by around 2010, critical complaints about the lack of novelty in the latest Pelevin novel had become as predictable as the obligatory de-parture into the *pustota*—the rainbow stream (or a Tuborg commercial) in the novel's finale. As I have tried to show, certain later works like *Pineapple*

Water, S.N.U.F.F., and *Love for Three Zuckerbrins* are imaginative and in-sightful: Pelevin is developing and pushing ahead. That said, some of his recent productions are mediocre indeed.

The artistic exhaustion that Pelevin stands accused of is addressed in his novel *iPhuck 10* (2017). The plotline takes place in the mid-twenty-first century, and is narrated by a literary-police computer algorithm called Porfiry Petrovich, the namesake of the master detective in Dostoevsky's *Crime and Punishment.* Porfiry Petrovich investigates crimes and composes detective novels about them. As he is loaned to an opportunistic art critic, Marukha Cho, he navigates the arts black market and hunts for coveted *gips* (plasters), early twenty-first-century art objects that are not original themselves but are valued for striving to breathe new life into earlier, authentic art forms.[9] Like *T* with its team of hack writers, or *S.N.U.F.F.* with its *sommelier*-wine stew-ards (professional selectors of previous texts who replace old-school writers), *iPhuck 10* advances a severe critique of contemporary art as parasitizing off older, genuinely creative works.[10] It evokes self-reflexively Walter Benjamin's essay *The Work of Art in the Age of Mechanical Reproduction* and John Barth's "The Literature of Exhaustion" (1967), and responds face-on to the charges that Pelevin is growing stale: "Writers can be of two kinds. Those who, all of their lives, write one book—and those who, all of their lives, write none [*pishet ni odnoi*]" (*iPhuck 10,* 217).

To refer again to the dichotomy made famous by Isaiah Berlin, Pelevin is clearly a hedgehog in his dogged pursuit of certain themes throughout his lifetime. But though the original hedgehog, Dostoevsky, was consistently preoccupied with Christianity, modernity, (ir)rationality, sin, redemption, and suffering, no one would claim that *The Brothers Karamazov* recycles *Crime and Punishment* or other earlier productions. Dostoevsky's last novel is acknowledged rightfully as his crowning achievement, and he certainly never repeated himself.

Where does this place our latter-day hedgehog, Pelevin, at least pro-visionally? At present, no later work of his has bested *Chapaev and the Void* for its conceptual novelty and aesthetic execution, and it is likely that no later production has outdone *Generation 'П'* and its sequel *Empire V* as social-cultural critiques. And yes, Pelevin has written more mediocre works than strong ones in the 2010s than in the 1990s or the 2000s. Perhaps we should just be grateful that, to use one of Pelevin's English syntax-inspired jokes, *pishet ni odnoi* does not apply to him. Or one may object that, even if all con-temporary art is controlled by opportunistic critics and a voracious market (with authors reduced to Turing machines, sommeliers, and literary-police algorithms), this is no excuse for Pelevin's *own* work not living up to its initial brilliant standards. Nor is "Porfiry Petrovich" such a witty or workable alibi anymore—if only because of its overuse.

Why turn Benjaminian, and not in a good sense—just mechanically reproducing oneself? A certain satirical misanthropy in the Gogolian or Swiftian vein (as per Bykov, Pelevin has an entrenched distaste for our time and the people who live in that time period) is a psychological possibility; there are regrettably no Swiftian Houyhnhnms (virtuous and rational horses) in our timeline.[11] In more practical terms, Pelevin's output becoming repetitive might have to do with political systems repeating themselves. If he is running out of ideas, it is perhaps because he has already identified the major concerns of contemporaneity, and now is left to explore nuances, and somehow come up with new plots and stories. But nuances can turn infinitesimal, and algorithms grow sweeping. Whether Pelevin is growing less imaginative or reality is doing so, with matters becoming more dire but not changing substantively, whether he is incapable of innovation or sees no need to strive for newness—the recent Pelevin has become more transparent to analysis, yet one would heartily welcome new challenges from him.

That charges of Pelevin's growing orthodoxy go hand in hand with accusations of aesthetic ossification is hardly surprising, since form and content (as per the formalists) tend to be interdependent. Gravitation toward traditionalism tends to accompany maturation. Pelevin, moreover, is very much tied to the time in which he writes, and there is presently a wider turn toward conservatism worldwide—and Russia is no exception. Were one indulgently to stress Pelevin's bent for irony, the hypothesis would be that he is reprocessing conservatism for meta-critique, probing and mocking the ways it functions in the current popular imagination. Or were one harshly to think of him as a pragmatist (or still worse, a populist or opportunist, a *kon'iunkturshchik* in Russian), the inference would be that he produces *panem et circenses* for the *vox populi*.[12] More *bablos* for less effort, simple and easy.

Neither of these versions convinces me. As for the former, I see no reason to dismiss Pelevin's "sermons"—which, irony and all, are no travesty but an earnest questioning. As for the latter, given the current climate that rewards expressions of conservatism, in Pelevin's case there has been no reward. Critics and ordinary readers alike are at best much colder, and at worst downright hostile, toward his recent output as compared to his immensely popular earlier works. The liberal camp has largely disowned him for his mockery of neoliberalism, the West, and especially themselves—as in contra.ru (*Love for Three Zuckerbrins*), the "gynecology of protest" (*Batman Apollo*), and so on. Conservatives have never liked him and never will, and with good reason. As much as Pelevin's anticapitalist and anti-Western agendas may appeal to the right wing, his diagnosis of both late Soviet totalitarianism and post-Soviet Russia is too unforgiving for pro-government readers and critics to stomach.

213

When two superpowers, the United States and the Soviet Union, vie for world dominion, and one of them collapses, cui bono (to whom is it a benefit?) does not demand great acumen. And this is what the Russian right wing overwhelmingly falls on—accusing the West of all the indignities and privations Russia has had to endure after the disintegration of the Soviet empire. The jockeying for national identity and leadership (and even sheer survival) in a world where old and new powers compete fiercely is no easy matter. Conspiratorial thinking comes in handy (*They* plotted against us), but *this is not the core point of Pelevin's texts*.[13] As in his famous "The anti-Russian conspiracy exists without any doubt. The problem, however, is that all the adult population of Russia takes part in it" aphorism (*Generation 'П'*), agency, responsibility, failure, and hope—as Pelevin does not tire of showing—are all predicated *on the self*. To recall Joseph Brodsky: "A free man, when he fails, blames nobody" (Brodskii, *Sochineniia Iosifa Brodskogo*, 6:7). To reiterate, Pelevin's most relatable characters act out of their yearning for freedom or ethical duty, not out of conformity with the body politic.

As I understand conservative populism (and populism in general), its practitioners hold no integral position but only scripts and props (à la Peter Sloterdijk's analysis).[14] They speak to the public manipulatively, voicing what is most inspirational to hear in order to gain power and *bablos*. Unlike the nineteenth-century Russian *narodniki* who went to the people to educate them and supply medical care (and incite social protest along the way), present-day populists on both sides of the Atlantic supply "medical care" only in front of the cameras. They *do not try to educate the public*. They accuse and praise, but they do not reason things out or explain how things function. Their messages are superficial, the ideal target group is noncerebral, and it should stay this way for the best processing of said messages. The present climate promotes anti-intellectualism to the heart's content of everyone involved. And because there are no convictions but only self-aggrandizing objectives, discourses can be switched at random provided they remain heart-warming and appropriate to the situation and the target group.

Now back to Pelevin. He is (a) consistent in his philosophy and aesthetics to the point of being obsessive, and (b) more cerebral at his weakest than the shiniest insights of populist thought. He knows his arithmetic and much more in math, and is fully capable of producing the delectable GMO tidbits the public wants him to supply. But he *does not* supply them with these. On the contrary, he is uncomfortable, and remains so—as numerous hostile critics of divergent ideological persuasion can attest.

In my reading, Pelevin is neither a liberal nor a conservative inasmuch as he considers *any system and any manner of politics/politicians rotten*, whether they are pro-status quo or otherwise. Even to call this anarchism would go against Pelevin's thoroughgoing skepticism of political systems. In fact, from his standpoint, the very notion of an ideology is misleading, since there are only business interests in the world of contemporaneity. More precisely, there are only contesting business interests masquerading as contesting ideologies, as in the case of post-Soviet mob money that needs a Russian Idea in order to advertise itself in the global marketplace in *Generation 'П.'* The geriatric epicurean Alena-Libertina, a high priestess of Manitou who sleeps with underage Ork girls, and Rvan Durex or Rvan Latex, the criminal ruler of Orkland, are equally repellent in *S.N.U.F.F.*, even though they are ranged on opposing sides. Pelevin does not reflect social norms, conservative or liberal, because it is precisely through social norms—collective visualizations, forms of zombification—that the world has learned to police itself in myriad ways and to perfection. This is a knot he pries open. He provides remarkable insights into the anatomy and functioning of social malignancies—and this by itself is a step toward a cure.

AND IN THE END

The promise of freedom in Pelevin's dystopian universe has much to do with the image of the author himself. Pelevin's authorial persona—clever, satirical, elusive, but also kindly—sees through the schemes portrayed, and provides a counterpoint to the one-dimensional dystopian mindset. The authorial image can be a redeeming force even given claims to the contrary. The self-irony that permeates the texts enriches them, adding twists and new levels of auto-reflexivity. Pelevin stimulates in a good way, demanding intense scrutiny from his audience. He wants his readers to follow top-notch analyses, investigate structures, be aware of traps and loopholes, and appreciate both ambiguities and outspoken positions. His writing sharpens the brain and softens the heart. And how else should he come across?—he is a Russian writer, after all.

How can we oppose the system—impersonal, thingy, powerful, cozy—which generates our depersonalized and decentered totalitarianism? In the days before the fall of the Berlin Wall, an escape into freedom could be defined in clear and comprehensible terms. Someone like the prominent Cold War–era dancer Rudolf Nureyev could perform a literal jump toward French policemen at Le Bourget Airport—and voila, "O brave new world, that has such people in it . . ." Nureyev, of course, had a unique jumping ability. But how to free oneself when there is no coordination on the part of Paris policemen, no Berlin Wall, no Iron Curtain, and even, as some scientists suggest, no Euclidean system of coordinates? How to respond to al-Qaeda crashing planes into skyscrapers in an echo of Hollywood blockbuster aesthetics, trucks crushing human flesh into gender-neutral proteins, one out of two humans expected to have cancer and not enough water by mid-century, and dementia growing exponentially, too? Perhaps by persisting in thought work—by which I mean not taking imposed formulae for granted, asking difficult questions, sharpening the knives of irony and self-irony, daring to be cynical, if one is so inclined, and judgmental and sentimental, even if this is unfashionable. Pelevin has developed as an intellectual and as an artist. Against all odds, even if this world of great bats and discourse-mongers rewards conformism, opportunism, political correctness, and hypnopedic shorthand, he makes a difference by *liking to think*.

Notes

INTRODUCTION

1. The only extant Russian-language monograph on Pelevin's work, Olga Bogdanova, Sergei Kibalnik, and Lyudmila Safronova's *Literaturnye strategii Viktora Pelevina* (2008; *Victor Pelevin's Literary Strategies*), examines Pelevini-ana of the early- to mid-1990s. My own project explores Pelevin's entire oeuvre, from his youthful short stories to his most recent novels. Roman Kozak and Sergei Polotovsky's *Pelevin i pokolenie pustoty* (2012; *Pelevin and the Generation of Emptiness*) is the only extant Russian-language biography of the writer.

2. "Hyper-auto-reflexivity" means a high degree of self-scrutiny.

3. "Techno-consumerism" designates a combination of advanced technologies and an increasing consumption of goods.

4. All translations of Pelevin's writings are mine, with borrowings from Andrew Bromfield's extant translations.

5. Aleksandr Kushner, "Vremena ne vyburaiut" (1978; "You Don't Choose Your Time").

6. Osip Mandelstam, *Shum vremeni* (1925; *The Noise of Time*).

7. "Carceral" indicates a jail or prison.

8. Many critics (e.g., Rodnianskaia) have taken *S.N.U.F.F.* as the first instance of Pelevin's global critique. In fact, *Generation 'П'* already engages the ways of all humanity in full force. But even Pelevin's youthful works (such as *Omon Ra*) contain hints of a future global critique (for example, Henry Kissinger and the bear hunt scene).

9. Elbe Day refers to April 25, 1945, when Soviet and American troops met at the Elbe River in Germany, marking an important step toward the end of World War II in Europe.

10. Nikolai Gogol's "The Overcoat" ("Shinel'") (1842) includes the so-called humane or "philanthropic" passage in which the narrator describes the lack of compassion with which the story's protagonist, Akaky Akakievich, is treated by his co-workers. In one of Akaky's rare pleas to be left alone by his tormentors, a new office-mate hears, "I am your brother" (Gogol, *The Complete Tales*, vol. 2,

217

307). Critics have debated whether this passage provides evidence of Gogol's genuine philanthropic intent.

11. In *Prisms* (1967) Adorno explores the carceral nature of modern techno-informational society, which legitimates itself as a natural necessity and makes the populace voluntarily choose their unfreedom by accepting socially imposed norms. Adorno and Horkheimer (*Dialectic of Enlightenment*) investigate the distractions the culture industry supplies to manipulate the people into a passive acceptance of the system.

12. Compare this to Heidegger's "standing-reserve" (Heidegger, *The Question Concerning Technology*, 17). Žižek's work also reiterates much of the Frankfurt school's techno-consumer critique. Liberal democracy masks people's state of unfreedom because it offers its subjects a chance to express their political opinions, yet limits the extent to which they can act on those opinions by instituting the laws to which they have to conform. People seek to conform to the standards laid out by the majority, and such standards deny them any sense of genuine freedom. See Slavoj Žižek, *The Sublime Object of Ideology* and "The Ambiguity of the Masochist Social Link."

13. On the intelligentsia's false consciousness in a society dominated by instrumental rationality, see Sloterdijk, *Critique of Cynical Reason*.

14. In *Anti-Oedipus* (1977), Deleuze and Guattari envision capitalism as deliberately spurring on desire in order to assist the market economy. The society manufactures needs that are never satisfied but lead to increased craving.

15. Baudrillard builds on Georges Bataille's theories, for example, the latter's *Erotism* (1957).

16. Foucault's lectures at the Collège de France were published in French in the late 1990s, in Russian in 2005–7, and in English in the late 2000s. For an analysis of Foucault's biopolitics, see, for example, Binkley, *A Foucault for the 21st Century*. Other critics of modern carceral society (e.g., Hannah Arendt) also employ biomorphic and zoomorphic metaphors to convey the de-individuation of the person.

17. For post-Foucault and post-Lyotard studies of posthumanism, see Hayles, *How We Become Posthuman*; Haraway, *Simians, Cyborgs, and Women*; and Wolfe, *Animal Rites*.

18. Fukuyama later expanded his essay "The End of History?" into a book, *The End of History and the Last Man*.

19. In the words of Elana Gomel: "Humanism may have been philosophically demolished but it remains a default ethical position, especially when issues of fair treatment and universal rights are raised" (*Science Fiction, Alien Encounters*, 21).

20. Compare to Kristeva, *Contre la dépression nationale*, "Europhilia, Europhobia," and *Sens et non-sens de la révolte*.

21. Pelevin's *Smotritel'* (2015; *The Warden*) has been promoted as a "somersault of thought."

22. The term "biotic" refers to living things in their ecological relations.

CHAPTER ONE

1. Rodnianskaia spots many of the novel's dystopian interests in "Etot mir priduman ne nami."

2. Garros-Evdokimov's *Golovolomka* (2002; *Headcrusher*), Gary Shteyngart's *Absurdistan* (2006), Olga Slavnikova's *2017* (2006), and Dmitry Minaev's *Dukhless* (2006) are a few examples of post-Soviet novels with a substantial commodified resonance to Pelevin's work.

3. On dystopian conventions, see Kumar, *Utopia and Anti-Utopia in Modern Times*; and Booker, *Dystopian Literature*.

4. The title of Huxley's dystopia was inspired by Miranda's line in Shakespeare's *The Tempest*, "O brave new world, That has such people in it!" (act 5, scene 1).

5. The menacing role that television plays in the novel recalls Orwell's two-way television screens, but the methods of control are dissimilar.

6. The name "Oranus" combines "oral" and "anal," and also puns on Uranus, the primal Greek god personifying the sky.

7. Pelevin's title chimes with Coupland's.

8. The influence of Baudrillard has been noted by many critics. See, for instance, Lipovetskii, *Paralogii*, 428; Genis, "Besedy o novoi slovesnosti"; and McCausland, "Viktor Olegovich Pelevin," 216.

9. Works of the fantastic genre often realize the literal sense of a figurative expression (Todorov, *The Fantastic*, 76–79).

10. The Russian financial crisis occurred on August 17, 1998, and resulted in the Russian government and the Russian Central Bank devaluing the ruble and defaulting on the country's debt. Russian inflation reached 84 percent in 1998.

11. "The system's collapse had been profoundly unexpected and unimaginable to many Soviet people until it happened, and yet, it quickly appeared perfectly logical and exciting when it began" (Yurchak, *Everything Was Forever*, 4).

12. In the Akkadian *Epic of Gilgamesh*, Enkidu is a wild man created by the god Anu.

13. On the theme of the intelligentsia in the novel, see Parts, "Degradation of the Word"; and Hutchings, *Russian Literary Culture in the Camera Age*.

14. Parts suggests that Tatarsky views eternity in mythological terms ("Degradation of the Word," 444).

15. Baal was worshipped in the ancient Middle East, especially among the Canaanites, as a fertility deity. When the Israelites entered Canaan, they found

that the land was fertile beyond anything they had seen, and the Canaanites attributed these riches to their god Baal. The Israelites worship Baal (1 Kings 18) as an economic promise. The book of Judges records the ongoing struggle: the Israelites' attraction to the Canaanite gods; God's disciplinary response; the people's repentance and divine forgiveness.

16. "Orthodoxy, Autocracy, and Nationality" (*pravoslavie, samoderzhavie, narodnost'*) was the doctrine of Tsar Nicholas I proposed by Minister of Education Sergei Uvarov.

17. The band Rage Against the Machine is politically oriented and critiques its own participation in consumer society. Pelevin is likely aware of this level of irony.

18. During the Soviet-Afghan War in the 1980s, Kandahar witnessed heavy fighting.

19. The system's ability to co-opt opposition has led critics to reimagine the "revolt of the clerk" novels as reinforcements of corporate culture that include an obligatory critique of that culture. A precisely measured dosage of rebellion against the social virtues of office culture, such as hard work, careerism, abiding by the law, a healthy way of life, and so on, is seen as the foundation of the marketing strategy of Chuck Palahniuk and other "revolt of the clerk" authors.

20. Ishtar is the Assyro-Babylonian goddess of fertility, love, storms, and war.

21. Rodnianskaia notices the absence of a single ruling hand in the novel ("Etot mir priduman ne nami").

22. Clowes's study discusses meta-utopias—narratives that critically examine diverse ideologies. This term would apply to *Generation 'П'* as well.

23. The "quintessentially individual strategy of freedom transforms easily into a total manipulation of the mob" (Lipovetskii, *Paralogii*, 428).

24. Gregory Freidin observes the significance of the last name "Tatarsky" ("*Dzheneraishen 'P'*," 166).

25. Ostankino Tower is a television and radio tower in Moscow, the tallest free-standing structure in Europe.

26. Most obviously, 'П' stands for Pepsi and *pizdets*. Additional possibilities include π, Pelevin, postmodernism, and post-Soviet.

27. *Per realia ad realiora* (also *a realibus ad realiora*) is Viacheslav Ivanov's definition of Symbolism in his poetry—"through the real to the more real."

28. In the Hebrew Bible, Tophet (Topheth) was a location in Jerusalem in the Gehinnom where worshipers influenced by the ancient Canaanite religion engaged in child sacrifice to the gods Moloch and Baal by burning children alive. Tophet became a synonym for Hell within Christendom. Gehenna was the valley of Hinnom, near Jerusalem, where propitiatory sacrifices were made to Moloch (2 Kings 23:10). Gehenna or Tartarus means the place or state of punishment of the wicked after death.

29. "In the field of mass culture, the metaphysical is related to that symbolic

capital the consumer needs most of all" (Berg, *Literaturokratiia*, 301). On symbolic capital, see Bourdieu's *Distinction* (1984).

30. The theme of false reality that runs throughout Pelevin's oeuvre is an ingenious mixture of postmodernism (à la Baudrillard and the Wachowskis) and Buddhism (which views the entire material world as an illusion).

CHAPTER TWO

1. See Lipovetskii, "Goluboe salo pokoleniia" and *Paralogii*; Genis, "Fenomen Pelevina" and "Besedy o russkoi slovesnosti"; and Rubinshtein, Mozur, McCausland, Freidin, and Paulsen. Paulsen places the reception of Pelevin's language in the novel in the broader context of norm negotiation in post-Soviet Russia.

2. Scholars who view Pelevin's wordplay in a positive light include Lipovetsky, Rubinshtein, Freidin, Paulsen, and Rodnianskaia. Genis objects to Pelevin's overindulgence in punning: "All the book is overgrown with a forest of puns" ("Fenomen Pelevina"). Nemzer, Shaitanov, Sverdlov, Novikov, and Salieva are strongly critical.

3. In *Why I Write* (1946), Orwell claims that to write in plain, vigorous language one has to think fearlessly and therefore cannot be politically orthodox. Newspeak is based on a theory held by many at that time, that thought is dependent on the words in which it is expressed (Sapir-Whorf hypothesis).

4. As discussed by Humboldt in *On Language*.

5. In Andrei Bely's "Moskovskaia simfoniia" (1905; "Moscow Symphony"), the conclusion plays on two meanings, a bank account or bill, and a final reckoning such as would occur during the apocalypse when everyone's sins are weighed.

6. The reference is to Alexander Pushkin's *Eugene Onegin* (1823–31).

7. Griboedov draws on *Et fumus Patriae dulcis* ("And the smoke of fatherland is sweet," Latin).

8. The constitutional crisis of 1993 was a standoff between Boris Yeltsin and the Russian parliament that was resolved by military force. On September 21, 1993, Yeltsin aimed to dissolve the country's legislature. The parliament declared the president's decision void, impeached Yeltsin, and proclaimed Alexander Rutskoy as acting president. On Yeltsin's orders the army stormed the Supreme Soviet building on October 4 and arrested the leaders of the resistance.

9. The words by Griboedov "are now used as a product wrapper for a commercial hit" (Freidin, *"Dzheneraishen 'P',"* 168). The emergence of Russian capitalist democracy was "founded on the violent storming in 1993 of Russia's democratically elected parliament" (Hutchings, *Russian Literary Culture*, 184).

10. For example, in the story "The Hall of the Singing Caryatides" ("Zal poiushchikh kariatid"), in the collection *PPPPP*, the word "hall" acquires a new meaning as the plot unfolds—different from the habitual museum or architec-

tural sense. For a similar effect, see "The Russian Forest" ("Russkii les") chapter of *The Life of Insects.*

11. "The portrait turned on its head mirrors the use of Latin letters for the Russian phrase" (Parts, "Degradation of the Word," 445).

12. *DPP(NN)*, following *Generation ' П,'* features numerous bilingual puns such as "shchit happens," a play on the phonic similarity between the English "shit" and the Russian *shchit* ("shield"). *Shchit i mech* (1968; *Shield and Sword*) was the title of a Soviet TV series about a World War II–era Soviet officer working undercover in Nazi Germany (based on Vadim Kozhevnikov's novel). The plot of *S.N.U.F.F.* is likewise inspired by an English pun: in the novel, media men simultaneously shoot films and shoot (kill) men. In *Love for Three Zuckerbrins* Pelevin comes up with a bilingual pun, "Voru vor! War on War!" (225). The English "war" sounds close to the Russian *vor* ("thief"). As this pun suggests, politicians pretending to fight radical Islamic terrorism are profiting from the oil industry in the Middle East. Pelevin's puns are not confined to Russian-English crossovers. An example of a French-English pun in *DPP(NN)* is *merder* (derived from "merger," "tender" and the vulgarity *merde*), which denotes an ostensibly independent bank absorbed (in a criminal manner) by a larger financial structure.

13. "Forster's syndrome," or the phenomenon of compulsive punning, was recorded by a German doctor in 1939. John Dryden disparaged puns as "the lowest and most groveling kind of Wit." Nabokov self-reflexively characterized puns as "trivial Leskovian jollity dependent on verbal contortions" (*Pnin*, 12). Punning effects "can create a semblance of common origin or semantic kinship where neither obtains" (Tynianov, *Arkhaisty i novatory*, 560).

14. Sprite is a substitute for 7 Up. 7 Up was promoted in the "Uncola" advertising campaign.

15. Many critics have noted the multilingualism in the novel. See, for example, Parts, "Degradation of the Word," 445–46; Hutchings, *Russian Literary Culture*, 181; McCausland, "Viktor Olegovich Pelevin"; and Marsh, *Literature, History, and Identity*, 383.

16. In the opening of *DPP(NN)*, Pelevin's "2nd Elegy" (alluding to Alexander Vvedensky's "Elegiia," 1940) offers an inventory of things and concepts that progress mechanically, through words linked on a phonic level rather than in terms of meaning. Disrupting the connection between the phonic and semantic aspects of the word expresses boredom and disillusionment with life.

17. Compare this to the Nescafé commercial, with the punchline "Nescafé Gold, a real explosion of taste" and the voice behind the screen: he *"razvel ego vtemnuiu. No slil ne ego, a vsekh ostal'nykh"* ("He brewed it rough and dark") (*GП* 65).

18. On these Bakhtinian ideas, see *The Dialogic Imagination* and *Problems of Dostoevsky's Poetics.*

19. In *Chapaev and the Void*, the Buddhist-like throne that Baron Jungern describes to Pyotr Pustota is positioned in the void or nowhere: *nakhoditsia nigde*. Such a grammatical construction is calqued from English.

20. "And the whole earth was of one language, and of one speech" (Genesis 11:1). "And they said, Go to, let us build us a city and a tower, whose top [may reach] unto heaven; and let us make us a name, lest we be scattered abroad upon the face of the whole earth" (Genesis 11:4). "And the LORD said, Behold, the people [is] one, and they have all one language; and this they begin to do: and now nothing will be restrained from them, which they have imagined to do. Go to, let us go down, and there confound their language, that they may not understand one another's speech" (Genesis 11:6–7).

21. "The new Babel spells, potentially, the end of productive heteroglossia and a fall into entropic universality" (Hutchings, *Russian Literary Culture*, 182).

22. See, for example, Derrida's "Des Tours de Babel."

CHAPTER THREE

1. Each biocoenosis (the term was coined by Karl Möbius in 1877) comprises producer species (plants), consumer species (animals), and species that decompose living matter (bacteria, fungi). The food web determines which species feed upon which others. On the struggle for existence among late Soviet writers and critics, see Kashchuk, "Nishi biotsenoza."

2. Pelevin's texts and Foucault's biopolitical thinking alike portray the governance of the populace understood as a biological species. Pelevin's familiarity with Foucault is clear from his work.

3. Agamben describes a world where only biological survival matters, and humans are moved by economic concerns, and thoroughly policed. Proper human activities such as art and religion are degraded into spectacle, and humans are animalized: "The completion of history necessarily entails the end of man" (*The Open*, 7).

4. Anatoly Lunacharsky was the first Soviet People's Commissar of Education.

5. "The reader's slow progress in putting the details of the description and dialogue together parallels the progress of the main characters in their gradual enlightenment" (McCausland, "Viktor Olegovich Pelevin," 285).

6. "One's relationship to the Other is predicated entirely on the act of eating or devouring, 'survival' paradoxically brings with it the destruction of both victim and victimizer" (Livers, "Bugs in the Body Politic," 5).

7. The post-perestroika cultural crisis in Russia "symbolizes the demise of the intelligentsia" (Parts, "Degradation of the Word," 435).

8. The word "Mammon," a biblical term for riches, is used by Jesus in the Sermon on the Mount and also appears in the Gospel according to Luke.

9. I do not view *Generation 'П'* as yoking Jamesonian notions of commodi-fication under late capitalism to a simple biological process of aggregation, but rather as showing how issues of key interest to Pelevin—biomorphism, cogni-tion, and propaganda—are intertwined.

10. Humans of contemporaneity do not move beyond Freud's stages of oral and genital fixation in children's development.

11. The imagery of consuming canned meat from Soviet times (recycling of the past) recurs in several post-Soviet novels, including Slavnikova's *2017* and Ili-chevskii's *Matiss* (2006; *Matisse*).

12. The oil narrative has been pumped by many post-Soviet writers, includ-ing Ilichevskii. On petropoetics, see Kalinin, "Petropoetics."

13. See the criticism of Baudrillard, for instance, Cupitt, *Time Being*.

14. "If the community of social contract theorists—past and present—had to select a single image as a symbol for their work, there is a fair chance that they would agree on picking the engraved title page of the first edition of Thomas Hobbes' *Leviathan*" (Heugens et al., *The Social Institutions of Capitalism*, 1).

15. "The victims, and even more so their peers and their descendants, wish to find meaning in their suffering. If meaning can be discovered, then death be-comes a sacrifice, rather than just a loss or a murder" (Etkind, "Stories of the Undead," 636). Etkind has classified the works of Pelevin, Bykov, and Sorokin that feature pronounced supernatural elements under the term "magical histori-cism." He reads these works as reflective of the impossibility of properly mourn-ing the dead ("Stories of the Undead," 631). See also Etkind, *Warped Mourning*: "Whatever the scale of victimization, mourning remains a personal matter, but collective rituals and cultural artifacts are critical for the process. . . . Crystals of memory, monuments keep the uncanny where it belongs, in the grave" (211).

16. The cottages of Nefteperegon'evsk appear to stand on chicken legs. This detail is reminiscent of the huts in traditional Russian fairy tales involving the witch Baba Yaga, which are always described as standing on chicken legs.

17. Livers and Brouwer, among others, point out that *Empire V* is a sequel to *Generation 'П.'*

18. Balod interprets *bablos* as Marx's added value of the product (Balod, "Ironicheskii slovar' *Empire V*," 140).

19. Pavel Florenskii notes an antinomy between *tolstovstvo* and *roza-novstvo*: our contemporaries "wish to see in man either only a personality, *hypo-stasis*, without elemental roots, or else pure elementariness, *ousia*, without any personal self-determination" (*Filosofiia kul'ta*, 139).

20. On Martyn Martynich's bifurcation between humanness and animality, see, for example, Langen, "Evgeny Zamyatin's 'The Cave,'" 210.

21. Etkind, "Stories of the Undead," 658.

22. The organic model implies more potency as based on the state of things in nature.

23. Chaldeans ruled ancient Babylonia. *Khaldei* is a pejorative term in Russian that connotes servility (a servant, a slave).

CHAPTER FOUR

1. The model of life as a computer game has been utilized in Coupland's *Microserfs* (1995), Gavelis's *Paskutiniųjų žemės žmonių karta* (1995; *The Last Generation of People on Earth*), Garros-Evdokimov's *Headcrusher*, and other works. In Gavelis's novel, the cyberpunk protagonist destroys the world in order to exit into virtual reality. On *Headcrusher*, see Khagi, "Garros-Evdokimov and Commodification of the Baltics."

2. For instance, a group of office girls at Gossnab are depicted as standing at the edge of a pyramid of multicolored cubes from the *Angry Birds* game. The reader is challenged to notice the boundaries between the worlds on and beyond the screen. Like "The Prince of Gosplan," a later work, *Love for Three Zuckerbrins*, is inspired by the *Angry Birds* computer game.

3. Pelevin "dwells in the zone of confrontation of realities. The space of their contact generates expressive artistic effects" (Genis, "Borders and Metamorphoses," 299). The "simultaneity of the layers of consciousness, when all of them function at once, constitutes a characteristic trait of Pelevin's works" (Pronina, "Fraktal'naia logika Viktora Pelevina," 7–8).

4. Such reactive behavior is similar to the learned chain of stimulus and response that a rat acquires by running in a maze. The subject "does not explain to itself the nature of the connection between the action and the result" (Pronina, "Fraktal'naia logika Viktora Pelevina," 21).

5. *The Helmet of Horror* was commissioned by the British publishing house Canongate as part of their project "Myths." An international group of writers including Margaret Atwood, Karen Armstrong, Alexander McCall Smith, and Victor Pelevin were invited to compose contemporary versions of classical myths. In Greek mythology, the Minotaur was a monster with the body of a man and the head and tail of a bull. Due to the Minotaur's monstrous form, King Minos ordered the craftsman, Daedalus, and his son, Icarus, to build a huge maze known as the Labyrinth to house the beast. The Minotaur remained in the Labyrinth receiving annual offerings of youths and maidens to eat. He was eventually killed by the Athenian hero Theseus with the help of Ariadne.

6. Hermann von Helmholtz was an influential nineteenth-century German scientist. In his sign theory of perception, Helmholtz argues that the mind makes a series of mental adjustments, "unconscious inferences," to construct a coherent picture of its experiences. "Schlemiel" is a Yiddish pejorative meaning "incompetent person" or "fool."

7. Classical conditioning refers to a learning procedure in which a biologically potent stimulus is paired with a previously neutral stimulus. In the experi-

225

ments that Ivan Pavlov conducted with his dogs in the 1890s, Pavlov found that objects or events could trigger a conditioned response.

8. Sliff employs the Runet slang of *padonki* with numerous misspellings and profanities.

9. Ariadne, as UGLI accuses her, has revealed everything because she stands next to Theseus in the MINO<u>TAUR</u>.

10. *Generation 'Π'* prefigures this notion: "Only a personality that was real can become unreal" (*G'Π'* 115).

11. Compare to *Chapaev and the Void*:

> It was as if one stage set was moved aside, and the next one was not immediately installed in its place, so for an entire second I looked into the space between them. That second was sufficient to perceive the deception behind what I took to be reality, to behold the simple and silly layout of the universe. And, having gotten acquainted with it, nothing remained but confusion and a certain sense of self-shame. (*CP* 418)

On Pelevin and the Anglo-American science-fiction tradition, especially Dick, see, for example, Kalfus, "Chicken Kiev."

12. Vampires are carriers of, and subservient to, the Tongue. They need to consume *bablos* for the Tongue to suck it in. The Red Ceremony does not take place with vampires personally, and they possess little knowledge of it.

13. Levitan's voice chronicled the battles of World War II for millions of Soviet citizens. He became famous for his distinctive, sonorous tones announcing, "Attention, this is Moscow calling." It is said that Levitan's voice infuriated Adolf Hitler.

14. "Operation 'Burning Bush'" contains auto-allusions to *Omon Ra*. Like Omon, Semyon Levitan involuntarily participates in the technology-enabled games of deception. His incarceration in the sensory deprivation chamber resembles Omon's confinement in the "moonwalker" when a fake trip to the moon takes place.

15. On consciousness as a product of the computer-like brain, see, for instance, Dennett, *Consciousness Explained*. Human consciousness "is itself a huge complex of memes . . . that can be best understood as the operation of a 'Von Neumannesque' virtual machine implemented in the parallel structure of a brain that was not designed for such activities" (Dennett, *Consciousness Explained*, 210).

16. The people of contemporaneity "gnaw into the nano-world and into one another" (*AV* 346). The theme of nanotechnology also emerges in *PPPPP* and *Love for Three Zuckerbrins*. In Drexler's *Engines of Creation: The Coming Era of Nanotechnology* (1986), the world is imagined to be transformed by nanobots manipulating matter on the atomic level. Some of the better-known Western

science-fiction works on nanotechnology are Gibson, *Idoru* (1996) and Crichton, *Prey* (2002).

17. The novel "is a satire of the relationship between imperialist, Westernized powers and the second- and third-world objects of their manipulation, condescension, and aggression. The snuffs serve to entertain a rich and jaded populace while simultaneously demonizing the Orcs as the primitive enemy of Big Byz 'democracy'" (Borenstein, "Off the Reservation").

18. Critics' opinions were divided with respect to Pelevin's attitudes to Urkaina vs. Byzantium. "Two non-truths—of 'Westernizers' and of 'Slavophiles'— are equal in Pelevin's eyes" (Rodnianskaia, "Somel'e Pelevin"). "No freedom exists or is forthcoming either 'there' in 'London' or 'here' in 'Urkaina'" (Danilkin, "*S.N.U.F.F.* Viktora Pelevina"). Roman Arbitman faults Pelevin for his anti-Western stance (Arbitman, "Uronili v rechku miachik"). I agree with Alexei Lalo that Pelevin criticizes U.S. cultural imperialism (Lalo, "New Trends in Russian Intellectual Anti-Americanism," 36).

19. In the first film of the trilogy, Morpheus in his conversation with Neo refers to the real world outside the Matrix as the "desert of the real," a reference to Baudrillard's *Simulacra and Simulation.* Baudrillard's book appears in the film.

20. A snuff film is "a movie in a purported genre of movies in which an actor is actually murdered or commits suicide" (*American Heritage Dictionary*). The title of Pelevin's novel "harks back to the well-known 1997 movie *Wag the Dog* co-written by David Mamet and directed by Barry Levinson" (Lalo, "New Trends in Russian Intellectual Anti-Americanism," 35).

21. Pelevin presents "the reality show 'House 2' on a state-religious scale" (Rodnianskaia, "Somel'e Pelevin"). He "transforms the snuff film into a global metaphor" (Andrei Arkhangel'skii, "Liubov' rezinovoi zhenshchiny") and "depicts a complete confluence of the work of an operator and a soldier" (Mil'chin, "Vozvrashchenie v provintsiiu").

22. "Whoever is underexposed to the media is desocialized or virtually asocial. Everywhere information is thought to produce an accelerated circulation of meaning. . . . We are all complicit in this myth" (Baudrillard, *Simulacra and Simulation*, 80).

23. Most natural scientists now "would argue that what we believe to be free will is in fact an illusion and that all human decision-making can ultimately be traced to material causes" (Fukuyama, *Our Posthuman Future*, 151).

24. "With a suitable dictionary such a machine would surely satisfy Turing's definition but does not reflect our usual intuitive concept of thinking" (Shannon and McCarthy, *Automata Studies*, vi).

25. Even if a machine's responses are indistinguishable from those of a human, that does not mean it possesses consciousness and intentions. As John Searle has pointed out (the Chinese room, or the Searle anti-test), the imitation

game cannot be an adequate test of human mentality, since the machine will have no awareness of what it is doing or have any feelings about its activities.

26. The figure of Kaya herself suggests skeptical versus humanist readings: (1) She is programmed for maximum bitchiness, and that's why she runs away with Grym as Damilola's symbolic rival. In the future Grym will turn into a new target of Kaya's bitchiness. (2) Kaya has fallen in love with Grym, becomes a revolutionary against Big Byz, and turns human.

27. Father Iv. Krestovsky is a likely play on Father Ioann Kronshtadsky (John of Kronstadt), a saint of the Eastern Orthodox Church known for mass confessions, charity, miracles, and monarchist views.

CHAPTER FIVE

1. For select contemporary (post)-apocalyptic Russian narratives, see Tolstaya, *Kys'* (1999; *The Slynx*); Sorokin, *Den' oprichnika* (2006; *Day of the Oprichnik*) and *Sakharnyi Kreml'* (2008; *The Sugar Kremlin*); and Glukhovsky, *Metro 2033* (2002, 2005).

2. *Generation 'П'* "is a fiction of the end in a more straightforward sense. Like *The Idiot*, it is saturated with apocalyptic references" (Hutchings, *Russian Literary Culture*, 175).

3. On Vavilen/Babylon, see Livers, "The Tower or the Labyrinth," 482. Both Romes (Rome and Constantinople) "fell, the third endures, and a fourth will never be" (Zenkovsky, *Medieval Russia's Epics*, 323). Pelevin "plays with the apocalyptic mythology associated with Babylonian history and the image of Babylon in the Old and New Testaments in order to evoke the confusion created by the collapse of communism" (Marsh, *Literature, History, and Identity*, 383).

4. Moscow as the Third Rome is the idea that Russia is the successor to the Roman and Byzantine empires. It has sixteenth-century roots and first appeared in the writings of the Russian monk Filofei of Pskov. During the Silver Age, Russian philosophers such as Vladimir Solovyov and Nikolai Berdyaev interpreted "Third Rome" as evidence of Russian messianism. The Whore of Babylon is a symbolic female figure associated with the Beast and the place of evil.

5. Heaven's Gate, an American UFO religious group based near San Diego, California, participated in a mass suicide in 1997 in order to reach what they believed to be an extraterrestrial spacecraft. Over a period of several decades in late seventeenth- and early eighteenth-century Russia, tens of thousands of Old Believers committed suicide, generally by self-immolation. The name "Malyuta" alludes to Malyuta Skuratov, a notorious leader of the Oprichnina during Ivan the Terrible's reign.

6. God's missive to the seventh church of the Laodiceans rebukes it for serving Mammon: "Because thou sayest, I am rich, and increased with goods, and have need of nothing; and knowest not thou are wretched, and miserable, and

poor, and blind, and naked" (Rev. 3:17). The church of the Laodiceans "is the last, most terrible epoch before the end of the world, which is characterized by indifference toward faith and by material wellness" (Taushev, "Apokalipsis ili otkrovenie Ioanna Bogoslova").

7. "Let him that hath understanding count the number of the beast: for it is the number of a man; and his number is Six hundred threescore and six" (Rev. 13:18). The attribution of modern techno-consumer culture to demonic agency occurs in several satires of commodification, for example, in Huxley's *Ape and Essence* (1948) and *Island* (1962).

8. In *The Master and Margarita* "Moscow is the city of the devil, a getting-and-spending world of petty Judases, the fallen whore of Babylon" (Bethea, *The Shape of Apocalypse*, 224).

9. Ragnarok is a series of apocalyptic events, including a great battle foretold to lead to the death of the gods Odin, Thor, Týr, Freyr, Heimdallr, and Loki, natural disasters, and the submersion of the world in water. After these events, the world would resurface anew. Garm is a wolf or dog associated with Hel and Ragnarok. Nietzsche's "God is dead" first appeared in *The Gay Science* (1882) and was made famous in *Thus Spoke Zarathustra* (1883–85).

10. Fenrir "was the most fearsome brute in the Nordic bestiary, the central character of Icelandic eschatology: the wolf who would eat the gods when the northern project was shut down" (*SKO* 134–36).

11. Locusts come from the book of Revelation: "Then out of the smoke locusts [*sarancha*] came upon the earth. And to them was given power, as the scorpions of the earth have power" (Rev. 9:9).

12. In Buddhism, entering the rainbow stream is the first of the four stages of enlightenment.

13. "Only a free act that can perceive things 'ex post,' from the point of view of the absolute end, can shut down that apparent world and reveal what that world is not" (Oppo, "Introduction," 32).

14. "History is determined by God's plot, but the individual is free to choose between positive and negative fields of action within that plot" (Bethea, *The Shape of Apocalypse*, 40).

15. "Now is the judgment of this world: now shall the prince of this world be cast out" (John 12:31). *Archon* is a Greek word that means "ruler." In ancient Greece the chief magistrates of various Greek city states were called *Archon*.

16. The *mashina* "is the ultimate machine and handiwork of the Antichrist" (Bethea, *The Shape of Apocalypse*, 58). Kostyrko reads *Pineapple Water* as about "the transformation of the very idea of God in contemporary society" ("Knigi. Obzory").

17. In Revelation 21:4, God "will wipe every tear from their eyes. Death will be no more; mourning and crying and pain will be no more."

18. "Operation 'Burning Bush'" exposes "the ugliness of the world in which

the Second Coming . . . looks like the manipulations of secret services with the consciousness and voice of English-language instructor Semyon Levitan" (Danilkin, "Ananasnaia voda dlia prekrasnoi damy").

19. In the Book of Revelation, following the end times and the second creation of heaven and earth, the New Jerusalem will be the earthly location where all true believers will spend eternity with God.

20. "There are secret and seemingly fateful intrigues of the secret services that form the layers of reality and supra-reality, which turn out to be only elements in the game of other intelligence services, and vice versa" (Narinskaia, "Vozvrashchenie glavnogo geroia").

21. Prometheus stole fire from the gods and gave it to humans. In punishment, Zeus bound him with chains and each day sent an eagle to eat Prometheus's immortal liver, which then grew back every night.

22. Bethea points at the difference between "apocalypse" and "utopia," between "a divinely inspired conclusion to history leading to an atemporal ideal (the new Jerusalem) and a humanly engineered conclusion to history leading to a secular paradise" (*The Shape of Apocalypse*, xvi).

23. Compare this to Zamyatin's "The Cave," which takes the reader on a reverse temporal journey, to the frozen wasteland of the ice age. The coming of the Apocalypse is heralded by the trumpeting of a mammoth.

24. "Up the ladder of language" (but not civilization) is a playful homage to Kafka's "A Report to an Academy" (1917) and Čapek's *War with the Newts* (1936). In Kafka's story, a captured ape wants "a way out," and this requires taking on as much as possible of the human world around him. The language of this report bears the marks of something artificially acquired. In Čapek's novel, Book Two is entitled "Up the Ladder of Civilization."

25. The passage "Transnational arks hidden in black waters" previews *Batman Apollo,* in which the king of vampires rules the global world from a gigantic oil tanker hidden in the black waters of the world ocean.

26. Pelevin "gives a short information about the visionary [Andreev], assuming apparently that the average reader is not familiar with the name" (Chantsev, "Strasti po Daniilu").

27. In the first cycle of *Stikhi o prekrasnoi dame* (1904; *Verses on a Beautiful Lady*), Blok "developed the thesis about the 'ruler of the world' in the language of Apocalypse—'woman clothed with the sun.' In the second cycle, the reader was supposed to see the reign of the 'beast' embodied in the symbol of the 'whore'" (Sarychev, "Apokalipsis ot Sofii," 11).

28. "If, in the early and middle stages of his career, Solovyev expressed faith in Sophia—or the transfiguration of humanity that will come to pass when we live to the divine potential in each of us—then at the end of his life he was consumed by the counter-notion of apocalypse." A similar pattern is found in the works of Bely and Blok (Bethea, *The Shape of Apocalypse*, 112).

29. Masha moves beyond the carnal sex act so as not to be incarnated in the body at all. On the carnal sex act, see Solov'ev, "Smysl liubvi" (1892–94; "The Meaning of Love"). The route of Solovyov, Fyodorov, Berdyaev, and many others is "to turn away from the closed circle and evil eternity (*durnaia beskonechnost'*) of animal procreation" (Bethea, "D. H. Lawrence and Vasily Rozanov," 15).

30. *Generation 'Π'* anticipates the media theocracy of *S.N.U.F.F.*: "As for the political regime corresponding to wowerism, it is sometimes known as telecracy or mediocracy" (118).

31. The Whore of Babylon "could be the Roman empire in one epoch and the church of Rome in another" (Bethea, *The Shape of Apocalypse*, 8). "All the more mankind that always *post panem* demanded *circenses*" (Solov'ev, "Kratkaia povest' ob Antikhriste," 139). *Panem et circenses* (bread and circuses, Latin) means sustenance and entertainment provided by government to appease public discontent.

32. Lévy supported the NATO campaign of bombings of Yugoslavia in 1999, and was in Kiev during the Maidan in February 2014, actively promoting the events.

33. Orkland's rulers carry parodic names of condom brands. For example, Rvan Durex means "a torn Durex condom."

34. "And he does great wonders, so that he maketh fire come down from heaven on the earth in the sight of men, And deceives them that dwell on the earth by means of those miracles which he had power to do in the sight of the beast" (Rev. 11:15).

35. "Here cynicism and money reign, here murderers, buyers of children, and sexual perverts rule the ball" (Arbitman, "Uronili v rechku miachik"). Pelevin highlights "the depressive condition of moral culture," "the crisis of gender self-identification," and "national identity turned into mere formality" (Kupina, "Lingvisticheskii katastrofizm v izobrazhenii," 383–85).

36. "Perhaps concentration and extermination camps are also an experiment of this sort, an extreme and monstrous attempt to decide between the human and the inhuman" (Agamben, *The Open*, 22).

37. Pelevin portrays the relations between Russia and the West in a similar manner in earlier works such as "The Macedonian Critique of French Thought" and *Pineapple Water*.

38. "Pelevin's anti-PC is, based on the current standards, astonishing. . . . The theme of sexual perversions is especially important. Pelevin is not afraid to use this expression" (Rodnianskaia, "Somel'e Pelevin"). "The question of 'inanity' is linked to an equally crucial aspect of *S.N.U.F.F.*, its concern with sex or, to be more exact, with the crisis of heterosexual relationships in the contemporary (not future!) Americanized world" (Lalo, "New Trends in Russian Intellectual Anti-Americanism," 39–41).

39. Rodnianskaia explains this expansion of perversions as "a necessary

shadow that is thrown by the sweet-voiced 'transhumanism' that is growing stronger in the post-religious world" ("Somel'e Pelevin").

40. Grym and Kaya escape the techno-consumer machine into the countryside, which resembles the world outside the Wall in Zamyatin's *We*. There are other parallels to *We*. For instance, Orks have no names, only "the individual non-erasable number." The green world also resembles the Buddhist heaven, which is at once a physical location in Tibet and an inner location.

41. In the temple of Manitou, Grym beholds "a blue fire searing his eyes [that] was probably the sword of Manitou, which the black cotton wadding of the universe mercifully concealed within itself" (*S.N.U.F.F.*, 380). Compare this to the unbearable light of the stars that Roma Shtorkin observes at the conclusion of *Empire V*.

42. Apocalyptic fictions signal "our deep need for intelligible ends." Although "for us the End has perhaps lost its naive *imminence*, its shadow still lies on the crises of our fictions" (Kermode, *The Sense of an Ending*, 6).

43. On the fin-de-siècle feeling of catastrophe that still bodied forth "a heroic stance at the 'edge of an abyss,'" and could be viewed through a Benjaminian "prism of revolutionary and redemptive dialectics," see Steinberg, *Petersburg Fin de Siècle*, 9, 271. "What is now called 'apocalyptic' is more and more the *end as nothingness* (an especially vivid theme in, say, Beckett)" (Bethea, *The Shape of Apocalypse*, 60). "Time moves toward entropic inertia. . . . This is the dystopian view that history has exhausted itself. The irony is that we live beyond morality or meaning" (Quinby, *Anti-Apocalypse*, xvi).

44. Discussing contemporary Anglo-American narratives that invoke the biblical paradigm, Dale Knickerbocker notes that "the ambiguity of cause, the continuing alterability of reality, and the uncertainty of the ending—i.e., their indeterminacy—stand in direct opposition to the divinely-bestowed transcendent Truth provided in Revelation" (Knickerbocker, "Apocalypse, Utopia, and Dystopia," 349). Such a description fits a narrative like *Generation 'П'* well but less so the more recent Pelevin narratives. See also Calinescu's "The End of Man in Twentieth-Century Philosophy" on "the obsessive recurrence of the idea of the end" in twentieth-century Western fiction.

CHAPTER SIX

1. These motifs run from "The Crystal World" through *Chapaev and the Void* to the recent *Love for Three Zuckerbrins*, *The Warden*, and *Methuselah's Lamp, or the Final Battle of the Checkists with Masons* (2016; *Lampa Mafusaila, ili krainiaia bitva chekistov s masonami*).

2. "Russian society's confrontation with its past has remained one of the main themes of Russian culture throughout the 1990s and the early twenty-first century" (Marsh, *Literature, History, and Identity*, 13). Brooks and Draliuk have considered the proliferation of alternative and pseudo-histories in contempo-

rary Russia. On the importance of history in Russian literature, see, for example, Wachtel, *An Obsession with History*.

3. "Countless tales of alternate history . . . have appeared in recent years on a broad range of themes" such as the Nazis winning World War II or the American Revolution failing (Rosenfeld, "Why Do We Ask 'What If?'" 90). Dick's *The Man in the High Castle* (1963) is an important predecessor. Other works of note are Amis, *The Alteration* (1976), and Roth, *The Plot against America* (2004).

4. Some notable Russian works of alternative history are Sharov, *Do i vo vremia* (1993; *Before and During*), Rybakov, *Gravilet "Tsesarevich"* (1993), Lazarchuk, *Inoe Nebo* (1993; *The Other Sky*), van Zaichik (Rybakov and Alimov), the *Plokhikh liudei net (Evraziiskaia simfoniia)* series (2000s; *There Are No Bad People [Eurasian Symphony]*), Krusanov, *Ukus angela* (2001; *The Bite of an Angel*), and Bykov, *Opravdanie* (2001; *Justification*), *Orfografiia* (2003; *Orthography*), and *ZhD* (2006). The Strugatsky brothers' *Trudno byt' bogom* (1964; *Hard to Be a God*) relates to alternative history inasmuch as it has "progressors" (like time travelers) change the course of history. Aksyonov's *Ostrov Krym* (1979; *The Island of Crimea*) is another predecessor. On Bykov's *ZhD*, see Khagi, "Parameters of Space-Time."

5. Marsh views the post-Soviet fantastic historical novel as a development of the alternative history that emerged during perestroika, and as a subdivision of historical metafiction.

6. I am borrowing the term from the "Factuality and Counterfactuality" panels at the 2015 ASEEES Convention. Historiographic metafiction suggests the difficulty of determining what took place, and as such relates to the problematics of alternative history with its "what could have been."

7. October 1917 is one of the most popular post-Soviet points of divergence. Other works of alternative history that zero in on 1917 include Zviagintsev, *Odissei pokidaet Itaku* (2000; *Odysseus Leaves Ithaca*) and Bulychev, *Shturm Diul'bera* (1992; *Storming Diul'ber*).

8. Counterfactualism "emphasizes the contingent, undetermined character of historical change" and "undermines any sense of the inevitability of the actual historical outcome" (Black, *Other Pasts, Different Presents*, 13). "It does not matter that we readers know the outcome. We want to know *what might have been*" (Edel, "Blurring the Real and the Fantastic"). Russia's fate "depends on whether they let one single civilian into Smolny" (Shurko, "Chetyre paradoksa khrustal'nogo mira").

9. It is a typical Pelevinian phantasmagoria—the cadets sniff cocaine and hallucinate. The switches between the everyday and the fantastic planes are structurally marked by sniffs of drugs.

10. Pushkin's version of Snow-White is the Tsarevna in "The Tale of the Dead Princess and the Seven Knights" (1833).

11. Alternative history "opens up a multitude of routes mediated by contingency and chance" (Black, *Other Pasts, Different Presents*, 187).

12. Lenin spoke with a small speech impediment, a softened *r* that would

normally have been fixed in childhood. The actors who played Lenin in Soviet films hyped this speech defect.

13. In *Storming Diul'ber*, Admiral Kolchak wins over Lenin, and in *Gravilet "Tsesarevich"* Alexander II's reforms prevent the revolutions of 1905 and 1917. In van Zaichik's *Eurasian Symphony*, a union of Rus' and the Mongol-Tatar Horde results in a prosperous and enlightened country called Ordus'. For Bykov, the post-Soviet boom in alternative history is "a form of psychosis that tries to find justification for what has happened at various times in Russia" ("Dmitriiu Bykovu stalinskoe vremia kazhetsia soblaznitel'nee nashego," 7). Vitenberg points out major twentieth-century "psycho-traumas" such as World War II and the collapse of the Soviet Union.

14. "Pelevin's novel is not a conventional historical novel but an extended 'Chapaev joke' casting doubt on the very nature of reality" (Marsh, *Literature, History, and Identity*, 265).

15. In December 1917, Vasily Chapaev was elected commander of the 138 Infantry Regiment. He later commanded the 2nd Nikolaev Division and the 25th Rifle Division. On September 5, 1919, his divisional headquarters were ambushed by White Army forces. Chapaev tried to escape by swimming across the Ural River, but was never again seen alive. In the Vasilyev brothers' film, Chapaev's adjutant Petka and the machine gunner Anka develop a love interest. In 1918, Dmitry Furmanov went to the Eastern Front to serve as a political worker, and crossed ways with Chapaev. After the Civil War he returned to Moscow, where he was employed by several organizations dealing with military publications. He worked for "Gosizdat," a publisher of propaganda, and for the Moscow Association of Proletarian Writers. Furmanov's novel about Chapaev made him famous. Kotovsky was a gangster and a bank robber who later became a Red Army commander. In 1918, he took command of a revolutionary battalion and helped the Bolsheviks gain control of Ukraine. He was killed by his friend for having an affair with his wife.

16. The term "ludic" means "playful."

17. Pelevin's novels *Generation 'П,' The Sacred Book of the Werewolf, Empire V*, and *Pineapple Water* suggest a conspiratorial underpinning of historical events. On the contemporary Russian conspiratorial imagination, see Borenstein, *Plots against Russia*; Livers, "The Tower or the Labyrinth" and *Conspiracy Culture*; and Yablokov, *Fortress Russia*.

18. On Pelevin's satire of contemporary neo-Eurasianism, see Clowes, *Russia on the Edge*, 68–95.

19. On emptiness in Buddhism, see, for example, Humphries, *Reading Emptiness*.

20. "In his own mind Pustota is a modernist poet turned civil war commissar, although in 1990s 'reality' he is a delusional young man in his mid-twenties undergoing psychiatric treatment" (Brintlinger, "The Hero in the Madhouse," 52).

21. Pelevin "rhymes" these two epochs (Rodnianskaia, ". . . i k nei bezumnaia liubov' . . . ," 214).

22. On the circularity of Russian history in post-Soviet novels, see, for instance, Pustovaia, "Skifiia v serebre."

23. On the novel and trauma studies, see Noordenbos, "Shocking Histories and Missing Memories."

24. For other excursions into solipsism, see the "onion episode" (*CP* 167–68), Chapaev's disquisition on personhood (171), and the "Russia in trouble" exchange (172).

25. "Baron Jungern" is a play on Baron Ungern von Sternberg, dictator of Mongolia for six months in 1921, and Carl Jung, founder of analytical psychology.

26. "Aesthetic appeal is what initially draws the decadent Pyotr to Chapaev's mystical world" (Pavlov, "Judging Emptiness," 101).

27. Inner Mongolia is "inside anyone who can see the void. . . . It is well worth striving all your life to reach it" (*CP* 282).

28. In Greek mythology, Cyclops is a one-eyed giant. In the *Odyssey*, Odysseus escaped death by tricking and blinding the Cyclops Polyphemus.

29. Contra.ru refers to the liberal-oppositional site Colta.ru (opened in 2013).

30. For an analysis of Western punk, see, for instance, Grassian, "Discovering the Machine in You."

31. Althusser introduces the concept of interpellation, otherwise known as "hailing." Ideologies "call out" or "hail" people and offer a particular identity, which they accept as "natural" or "obvious." In this way, the dominant class exerts a power over individuals that is quite different from abject force. According to Althusser, individuals are interpellated from the day that they are born—and perhaps even before, since parents and others conceive of the role and identity that their child will assume. The subject exists only as he or she is recognized in a specific way that has a social structure as its referent. The subject is thus preceded by social forces, or "always-already interpellated."

32. Nadya's forest, a respite from the Kesha-Karaev dystopia, echoes Grym and Kaya's escape from the post-apocalyptic world of *S.N.U.F.F.* into the countryside. At the end of *The Yellow Arrow*, Andrey escapes the train of history into nature.

33. The *Charlie Hebdo* incident was a series of militant Islamist terrorist attacks that took place in France in January 2015, claiming the lives of seventeen people, including eleven journalists and security personnel shot at the Paris offices of *Charlie Hebdo*, a satiric magazine.

34. On September 11, 2001, nineteen militants associated with the Islamic extremist group al-Qaeda hijacked four airplanes and carried out suicide attacks against targets in the United States. Two of the planes were flown into the twin towers of the World Trade Center in New York City; a third plane hit the Pen-

tagon just outside Washington, D.C.; and the fourth plane crashed in a field in Shanksville, Pennsylvania.

35. Ham, according the book of Genesis, was the second son of Noah. According to Samuel, Ham sodomized Noah (Genesis 34:2). According to Rab, Ham castrated Noah.

36. *Batman Apollo*, a sequel to *Empire V*, introduces the notion that vampires feed off people's suffering.

37. For Tolstoy, critics should "guide readers in that endless labyrinth of linkages [*beskonechnyi labirint stseplenii*] that makes up the stuff of art" (letter to Nikolai Strakhov, April 23, 1876, in *Sobranie Sochinenii v 22 tomakh*, vol. 18, 784).

38. During the Euromaidan, there were protests and clashes with the police throughout Ukraine, especially at the Maidan (central square) in Kiev. The protests climaxed in mid-February 2014. Yanukovych and other high government officials fled the country.

39. In Bradbury's story, hunters go back in the past in a time machine, shoot a doomed dinosaur, and return, with the world's balance not disturbed. But one of them had accidentally crushed a butterfly during their excursion into the past. The dead butterfly has disrupted the connection of world events to such an extent that, when they come back to their time, they find that the rules of English have changed and the United States has a different president.

40. In the movie, the protagonist Evan finds he can travel back in time, with his adult mind inhabiting his younger body. He attempts to change the present by changing his past behaviors and set things right for himself and his friends, but there are unintended consequences for all. The film presents several alternative present-day outcomes as Evan attempts to change the past, before settling on a final outcome.

41. On Lorenz, the butterfly effect, and chaos theory, see Gleick, *Chaos*. In Kiklop's understanding, only certain critical events represent a danger to the world. That's when he has to interfere.

42. Many stories and novels "presume that more than one 'parallel world' with divergent histories can coexist, so that characters can purposefully or accidentally travel, or 'timeslip,' from one timeline to another, like a commuter switching trains" (Duncan, "Alternate History," 214). Train imagery was employed in Pelevin's early novella *The Yellow Arrow*. It depicts early post-Soviet realia as a retrograde movement of Russian history: "The past is a locomotive that pulls the future after it" (*VPE* 296). For Mikhail Epstein, the collapse of communism entailed a temporal anomaly in that the communist future "has become a thing of the past, while the feudal and bourgeois 'past' approaches us from the direction where we had expected to meet the future" (Epstein, *After the Future*, xi).

43. On the cat paradox and the "many worlds" interpretation, see Everett, Barrett, and Byrne, *The Everett Interpretation of Quantum Mechanics*.

44. "There are a hundred million diverse chances, which will be decided on the instant by whether we run or they run, whether this or that man is killed" (Tolstoy, *War and Peace*, 773). In his polemics with historians, Tolstoy "constantly stresses how the road taken blots out the very awareness that there were other roads" (Morson, *Narrative and Freedom*, 156–57).

45. Tolstoy departs from a narrower conception of providential history in which options in the shape of free will do not exist. For him each individual act is free, meaningful, and contributes to a specific historical outcome.

46. Quantum physics might be consistent with solipsism, since observers appear to affect their observations. What Pelevin does is switch the focus from the behavior of particles to human consciousness.

47. The term "bricolage" refers to a construction from a diverse range of available things.

48. *Dum Spiro Spero* (Latin) means "While I breathe, I hope."

49. Nadya's Eden also alludes to Boris Grebenshchikov's song "The Golden City" (1972; "Gorod zolotoi").

50. In H. G. Wells's *Men Like Gods* (1923), a group of Britons are transferred to an alternate universe via time travel. In later alternative history (Piper, Turtledove), paratime travel capsules or time portals carry out crossovers in the multiverse.

51. The motivation behind cross-time travel is frequently pragmatic: to explore natural resources one lacks, or to carry out trade. In Piper's *Paratime* series (1948–65), the ability to travel between alternate universes is employed for collecting resources. In Stross's *Merchant Princes* series (2004–), jumping from world to world is performed for trade purposes.

52. Kesha playing the online game *World of Tanks* functions as a *mise en abyme* of alternative history in the novel. In this online war game, players choose actual or fictional battles set during World War II. They can change history at their whim, without a sense of responsibility or serious repercussions. Such is not the case in the larger world of *Love for Three Zuckerbrins*. Historical play "allows individuals to participate imaginatively in the great conflicts and dramas of the past, testing themselves and examining their agency in a realm free of existential consequences and often infused with humor" (Brooks and Draliuk, "Parahistory," 78).

53. "I wrote of the genetic replicators: 'They created us, body and mind'" (Dawkins, *The Selfish Gene*, 271).

54. Meme theory "is a comfortable fit with the Poststructuralist notion of the death of the subject: rather than seeing the individual consciousness as the nexus of interacting and conflicting 'discourses,' memetics defines consciousness . . . as a phenomenon fostered by the brain's function as a repository and generator of memes" (Borenstein, "Survival of the Catchiest," 467).

55. The Ten Commandments, also known in Christianity as the Decalogue,

are as follows: "I am the Lord thy God, thou shalt not have any strange gods before Me"; "Thou shalt not take the name of the Lord thy God in vain"; Remember to keep holy the Sabbath day"; "Honor thy father and mother"; "Thou shalt not kill"; "Thou shalt not commit adultery"; "Thou shalt not steal"; "Thou shalt not bear false witness against thy neighbor"; "Thou shalt not covet thy neighbor's wife"; "Thou shalt not covet thy neighbor's goods."

56. Science fiction, like postmodern writing, "lays bare the process of fictional world-making itself" (McHale, *Constructing Postmodernism*, 12).

57. The novel's "main protagonist, a categorically negative one, is the phenomenon of the human itself" (Svetlova, "I uvidel ia son").

58. As an artist, Pelevin is not bound to the rigor and consistency of philosophy, and the scenarios he describes result in a tension between free will and determinism (a problem he also turns to via his work with intertexts).

59. In Niven's "All the Myriad Ways" (1971), an epidemic of suicide results from people learning of the existence of the multiverse.

60. Counterfactualism is "a product of a free society characterized by liberalism and, in particular, a stress on individualism and free will; as opposed to societies where the stress is on fatalism, especially in the shape of providentialism" (Black, *Other Pasts, Different Presents*, 41).

61. "Of all the techniques, the author has chosen the worst possible one. Having dispensed with artistic conventions, he explains to the reader how this world is put together and how to live in it" (Beliakov, "Pogovorim o strannostiakh liubvi").

62. *The Warden's* alternative historical timeline is of a spiritual order, positioned in the consciousness of its protagonist.

63. Alternative history "is not a product of modernism, magic realism or postmodernism, each of which are more subversive, but of reader interest at the popular level" (Black, *Other Pasts, Different Presents*, 70). This is not the case with Pelevin.

64. Post-Soviet discourses "have become preoccupied with the Here and Now, or with reexamining various pasts" (Menzel, "Russian Science and Fantasy Literature," 117). Pelevin's future-oriented alternative history departs from this trend.

CHAPTER SEVEN

1. I focus on select important examples. Pelevin's engagement with Dostoevsky also occurs, for instance, in *Chapaev and the Void* (Pustota watching the "little tragedy" *Raskolnikov and Marmeladov* on stage).

2. The eschatological subtext that animates Dostoevsky's oeuvre is "definitive of the literature whose passing haunts Pelevin's novel" (Hutchings, *Russian Literary Culture*, 175).

3. On Svidrigailov's eternity, see, for example, Lanz, *The Dostoevsky Encyclopedia*, 426.

4. Just as Dostoevsky "had compared nineteenth-century British capitalism to Babylon, Pelevin associates the 'Babylon' of *Revelation* with the corruption and materialism of emergent post-Soviet capitalism" (Marsh, *Literature, History, and Identity*, 384).

5. On Dostoevsky's apocalypticism, see, for example, Mochul'skii, Bethea, Hollander, Leatherbarrow, and Rosenshield. Dostoevsky "touches upon his most profound idea regarding the Anti-Christ's earthly kingdom: criticism of the bourgeois order in the spirit of Herzen suddenly grows into an apocalyptic vision" (Mochul'skii, *Dostoevsky: His Life and Work*, 233). He warns "of the fall of Western civilization, and he expands his warning to include Russia's westernized ruling classes" (Leatherbarrow, "Apocalyptic Imagery," 125). Russia is "also ruled by the spirit of Baal, her daily life governed by mercantilism and murder" (Hollander, "The Apocalyptic Framework," 130).

6. On Myshkin's "beauty will save the world," see, for example, Miller, *Dostoevsky and "The Idiot,"* 229.

7. On Dostoevsky's dialogism, see Bakhtin, *Problems of Dostoevsky's Poetics*.

8. Dostoevsky "clearly distinguishes physical from spiritual suffering" (Frank, *Dostoevsky: The Mantle of the Prophet*, 638). "Modern man has no faith; only science, industry, commerce and capital" (Leatherbarrow, "Apocalyptic Imagery," 125).

9. In the related terms of *Empire V*: humans think they make money for themselves. But really they make money out of themselves.

10. Though Dostoevsky puts these words in the mouth of his comic character Rakitin, Myshkin listens to them attentively.

11. On the Grand Inquisitor's argument, see, for example, Frank, *Dostoevsky: The Mantle of the Prophet*, 612.

12. The underground man "lives in a world in which, he fears, his behavior is determined by forces beyond his control" (Lanz, *The Dostoevsky Encyclopedia*, 146).

13. "One might even desire something opposed to one's advantage, and sometimes (this is now my idea) one *positively must do so*" (Dostoevsky, *Notes from Underground*, 19).

14. This is something "The Grand Inquisitor" suggests in passing but does not explore.

15. Compare this to "Human decisions emerge in dark corners of the mind where science cannot penetrate, and are accepted mechanically and unconsciously, as an industrial robot that measures and punches holes" (*T*, 176). The Underground Man concedes briefly that any kind of whim and desire, not just rational advantage, might be predetermined (Dostoevsky, *Notes from Underground*, 22).

239

16. In places, Pelevin's approach to Dostoevsky's antirationalism is parodic. So, for example, the religious right "consider themselves God's chosen solely on the basis of their faith in the fact that they are chosen by God" (*AV* 36–37). Elsewhere, an experience of the divine with one's entire being, rather than rational understanding, is posited less ironically. Explaining the concept of God to man means that "on his hump there will appear another bag of junk, which he will drag along to the cemetery. God can only be experienced" (*AV* 42).

17. Gireev's comment alludes to Ivan Karamazov's interview with the devil (Livers, "The Tower or the Labyrinth," 483). See Dostoevsky, *The Brothers Karamazov*, 645.

18. "Today Christianity (as Dostoevsky understood it) and socialism in its humanist variant both confront powerful entropic forces and tendencies—indifference, irresponsibility, consumerism, and the draining of meaning from life" (Amusin, "A Selective Similarity," 83). On *The Doomed City* as a posthumous thought experiment, see Jameson, "Fear and Loathing in Globalization," 105.

19. "Novum" (Latin for new thing) is a term used by science fiction scholar Darko Suvin and others to describe the scientifically plausible innovations used by science fiction narratives. On the *novum*, see Suvin, *Metamorphoses of Science Fiction*.

20. On the Strugatskys, see, among others, Suvin, "Criticism of the Strugatsky Brothers' Work" and "The Literary Opus of the Strugatsky Brothers"; Howell, *Apocalyptic Realism* and "When the Physicians Are Lyricists"; Amusin, *Brat'ia Strugatskie*; Boris Strugatskii, *Kommentarii k proidennomu*; Arkadii Strugatskii and Boris Strugatskii, *Ulitka na sklone: Opyt akademicheskogo izdaniia*; and Potts, Nakhimovsky, Simon, and Smith.

21. For Boris Strugatsky on Pelevin, see Boris Strugatskii, "Na randevu."

22. *Omon Ra* won Boris Strugatsky's Bronze Snail award in 1993.

23. "The 'Country of the Boob' is "a vivid illustration of Dostoevsky's thoughts on the danger of boundless abundance and comfort with no spiritual perspective" (Amusin, "A Selective Similarity," 75). "The closer humanity comes to the catastrophic consequences of modern technological development" and "the more evident the growing social inadequacy that accompanies globalization," the more distinct are critical voices (Ivanov, "The Lessons of the Strugatskys," 27).

24. *The Doomed City* refers back to Solovyov's "Short Tale about the Antichrist" (1899–1900; "Kratkaia povest' ob Antikhriste") and Florensky's *On The Goal and Meaning of Progress* (1905; *O tseli i smysle progressa*) and "reveals a deeply pessimistic view" (Menzel, "Russian Science and Fantasy Literature," 138).

25. Although Pepper may be put in opposition to Candid as someone who is assimilated by the powers that be, his first order can still be seen as a gesture of defiance.

26. In Stalker lore, there exists a Golden Ball in the Zone that can grant one's most important wish. Throughout his quest, Schuhart has been hoping to get the Golden Ball to save his daughter Monkey. As Schuhart emphasizes, he has never sold his soul to anyone.

27. Mount Fuji is the highest mountain in Japan, a symbol of the country.

28. The Strugatsky brothers were preeminent Soviet practitioners of anti-utopian science fiction (Nakhimovsky, "Soviet Anti-Utopias," 143). Their novels challenged the ideological foundations of the Soviet Union (Smith, "Arkady Natanovich Strugatsky," 364).

29. "The progressors in a Strugatsky novel carefully lead the civilizations of other planets to the almost ideal state that they fancy Earth has already attained. The plot of *Hard to Be a God* is remarkable in that no progress is achieved" (Ivanov, "The Lessons of the Strugatskys," 13–14). The idea of progressorism "is turned on its head on the principle: 'And if you were to be dealt with like that?'" (Kukulin, "Al'ternativnoe sotsial'noe proektirovanie," 183). See *Hard to Be a God*: "'I know only one thing: man is an objective carrier of reason, everything that prevents man from developing his reason is evil, and evil should be eradicated as fast as possible and by any means.' 'Any means? Truly?'" (Strugatskie, *Sobranie sochinenii*, 3:314).

30. "The Slimies in *The Ugly Swans* represent the same type of super-civilization as the Wanderers (in the future history cycle) or the Ludens (in *The Waves Still the Wind*)." They "dismiss their less developed human brothers as one dismisses small children from a meaningful discussion." In the evolution of the Strugatskys' poetics, "the stature of the hero-as-humanist enlightener . . . gradually diminishes, while the prominence of the alien super-human increases" (Howell, *Apocalyptic Realism*, 111, 115).

31. "Today the 1960s are perceived as a source of social romanticism—that is, of actions founded on faith in the productivity of a selfless personal effort. Such a romanticism might be considered discredited . . . but its memory recurs in the most divergent conceptions" (Kukulin, "Sentimental'naia tekhnologiia," 301).

32. In the Strugatskys' *Monday Begins on Saturday*, Professor Vybegallo conducts a scientific experiment to produce (in Pelevin's terms) an Oranus-like monstrous being to rehabilitate the values of consumerism. A white magician saves the universe by blowing up the monster.

33. In the Strugatskys' *One Billion Years before the End of the World*, scientists' work is disrupted by strange events explained as the universe maintaining its structure (*gomeostaticheskoe mirozdanie*). The more ingenious the obstacles put up by the Homeostatic Universe, "the more meaning is accorded to heroic attempts [by scientists] to work" (Kaspe, "The Meaning of (Private) Life," 48).

34. This "reflects the crisis of the ideology of the Enlightenment, . . . disappointment in the theory of progress, scientific objectivity and scientific ratio-

nalism" (Khapaeva, "Vampir-geroi nashego vremeni"). Contemporary culture's gothic themes lead "to the negation of the human and civilization as the highest value" (Khapaeva, *Koshmar: Literatura i zhizn'*, 293).

35. "An undeniable constitutive part of today's phenomenon of 'post-Soviet nostalgia,' which is a complex post-Soviet construct, is the longing for the very real humane values, ethics, friendships, and creative possibilities that the reality of socialism afforded—often in spite of the state's proclaimed goals—and that were as irreducibly part of the everyday life of socialism as were the feelings of dullness and alienation" (Yurchak, *Everything Was Forever*, 8).

36. Compare this to *Love for Three Zuckerbrins*: "When we look at the world around us, with its cosmos and its history . . . , we perceive . . . only the geometry of the step of the staircase on which our foot stands at the present moment. . . . It is as if the reality of each step is based on the new wanderer, and every one of them is surrounded by one's own cosmos with distant planets on the dusty paths of which local poet-bards have already left their traces" (*LTC* 156–57). The passage alludes to Oskar Feltsman and Vladimir Voinovich's popular cosmonaut hymn, "I believe, friends" (1961; "Ia veriu, druz'ia").

37. The epigraph to *Omon Ra*, "For the Heroes of the Soviet Cosmos," refers not just to the Soviet space program, but to the entire Soviet space, physical, cultural, and metaphysical. This is also how I use the term "cosmos" here.

38. *T* is an example of Pelevin not making a specific allusion but seeking to capture the essence of a writer's oeuvre.

CHAPTER EIGHT

1. For some examples of critical commentary on Pelevin's use of irony, see Bykov, "Pobeg v Mongoliiu," 4; Rodnianskaia, ". . . i k nei bezumnaia liubov' . . . ," 214; Leiderman and Lipovetskii, *Sovremennaia russkaia literatura*, 2:507; Bogdanova, *Postmodernizm v kontekste sovremennoi russkoi literatury*, 334; Bondarenko and Anninskii, *Zhivi opasno*, 382; Balod, "Ironicheskii slovar' *Empire V*," 139; Noordenbos, "Breaking into a New Era?" 86; and Kozak and Polotovskii, *Pelevin i pokolenie pustoty*, 65. Kozak and Polotovsky suggest that Pelevin's irony changes from "the gentle one of an observant wise man" in his earlier works such as *The Life of Insects* to "a more scathing type in his later work" (*Pelevin i pokolenie pustoty*, 65, 144).

2. These features differ from irony, but are related to its conceptualization, and as such are discussed here. Analogously, traits like subversion and incongruity both differ from, and are linked to irony, and are therefore mentioned here. On irony as subversion through an articulation of positions antithetical to prevailing dogmas, see Hutcheon, *Irony's Edge*, 27–28. On irony as the incongruity between what is expected and what occurs, see, for instance, Chevalier, *The Ironic Temper*, 44.

3. The subject "cannot turn back and know its own activity, and what is other than the speaking subject is known only in its relation to subjectivity or in its potential to become known by the subject" (Colebrook, *Irony*, 70, 75). Compare this to Shklovsky: "Here I use the notion 'irony' not as 'mockery' but as a device for a simultaneous perception of two divergent occurrences" (Shklovskii, *Eshche nichego ne konchilos'*, 233).

4. The romantic ironist faces the quandary that words "are a constraint upon the soul's ever more capacious inner sensitivity" and cannot function as "the emanation of reality and truth" (Humboldt, *On Language*, 92; Wordsworth, *Prose Writings*, 184). "Irony is the form of paradox. Paradox is everything simultaneously good and great" (Schlegel, *Lucinde and the Fragments*, 266).

5. Hutcheon's *Irony's Edge*, Eco's "Postmodernism, Irony, the Enjoyable," and other postmodern theories make similar claims.

6. To look at the same issue from a different angle, many critics (Hutcheon, Rorty, Hassan) have posited irony to be postmodernism's defining feature.

7. On Pelevin's tongue-in-cheek allusions in *Chapaev and the Void*, see Leiderman and Lipovetskii, *Sovremennaia russkaia literatura*, 507; Rodnianskaia, ". . . i k nei bezumnaia liubov' . . . ," 213; and Clowes, *Russia on the Edge*, 83.

8. "When Pyotr reproaches Chapaev for confusing the two philosophers, he refers not to Chapaev's revision of Kant, but rather to his own Schopenhauerian sentiment about beauty with which the conversation began" (Vaingurt, "Freedom and the Reality of Others," 477).

9. Chapaev "scoffs at Kant, misquoting the famous conclusion of *Critique of Pure Practical Reason* [sic]" (Clowes, *Russia on the Edge*, 78).

10. "The system's conventionality is laid bare—instead of authorial speech there emerges authorial behavior, instead of authorial position—authorial posture" (Tynianov, "O parodii," 279). On the relations between parody and irony, see Tynianov, *Poetika, istoriia literatury, kino*, 305.

11. Compare this to Derrida's critique of the Kantian suppression of the specificity of voice in philosophical argumentation ("On a Newly Arisen Apocalyptic Tone in Philosophy," 117–72).

12. In Julia Vaingurt's reading, in the Kant-Schopenhauer debate on morality, in place of the former's assumption that moral laws exist a priori, the latter proposes that an ethical action arises as an exception to the rule of pure egoism, "from the identification of the self with the other," a position resembling the concept of compassion in Buddhism (Vaingurt, "Freedom and the Reality of Others," 478). The novel "seeks a transcendence of master-slave dialectics, conceptualizing a relationship in which the singularity of neither self nor other need be threatened" (Vaingurt, 467).

13. In *Empire V* the painting *Lolita* portrays a naked young girl with the head of a bald, elderly Nabokov (*EV* 42).

14. Tolstoy's aging face, in turn, "looks like the map of a wooded country

with two cold lakes separated by a long mountain ridge of the nose. Not the face, thousand-year empire" (*T*, 147). On Dostoevsky's attitude to the Jesuits, see Cassedy, *Dostoevsky's Religion*, 90; and Frank, *Dostoevsky: The Seeds of Revolt*, 8.

15. On Pelevin's apophaticism, see Pustovaia, "Niche ni o kom."

16. For readings that take the closing sentiment seriously, see Basinskii, "Ampir na krovi"; Bykov, "Za piat' minut do smysla"; and Bondarenko, "Vampiry na sluzhbe piatoi imperii."

17. On stable and unstable irony, see Booth, *A Rhetoric of Irony*, 6–7, 148, 275.

18. "If restorative nostalgia ends up reconstructing emblems and rituals of home and homeland in an attempt to conquer and spatialize time, reflective nostalgia cherishes shattered fragments of memory and temporalizes space. Restorative nostalgia takes itself seriously. Reflective nostalgia, on the other hand, can be ironic and humorous" (Boym, *The Future of Nostalgia*, 49).

19. Like the "Mongolian Myth of the Eternal Non-Return," which is a mockingly incongruous modification of Nietzsche's Eternal Return, Pelevin's term "critical solipsism" plays on "critical realism" (the opposite of subjective idealism). On Nietzsche's Eternal Return, see *The Gay Science*.

20. See Gödel, *On Formally Undecidable Propositions of Principia Mathematica and Related Systems*.

21. On critical solipsism in *T*, see Gubailovskii, "Gegel', Everett i graf T," 195, 198.

22. "The comic playwright Philemon (fourth to third centuries B.C.) speaks of the fox 'who is ironic in its nature and at the same time strong-willed'" (Losev, *Istoriia antichnoi estetiki*, 442).

23. On the trickster trope in Pelevin, see Lipovetskii, *Charms of the Cynical Reason*, 233–75; and Milne, "Jokers, Rogues, and Innocents," 94–95. On *A Huli* as a metaphor for the contemporary Russian writer, see Danilkin, "Pora mezh volka i sobaki," 153.

24. The lama who arrives in Moscow to lecture on advertising is the Seventh Urgan Dzhambon Tulku, the "author" of the preface to *Chapaev and the Void*.

25. Compare this to *The Helmet of Horror*: the word *Kreatiff* in the book's subtitle is a foreignized version of *kreativ*, a term used in the Russian advertising industry that means the concept for an ad.

26. "Sergei Lisovsky is designated as one of the editors of *Generation 'П'*— the creator of one of the first producing companies in the USSR and the biggest advertiser of the 1990s" (Kozak and Polotovskii, *Pelevin i pokolenie pustoty*, 92).

27. In *Paratexts: Thresholds of Interpretation*, Genette defines "paratext" as things in a published work that accompany the text such as the author's name, the title, introduction, illustrations, and so on.

28. The paradox attributed to Epimenides is: "Epimenides the Cretan says

that 'all Cretans are liars.'" It is impossible to determine if Epimenides is telling the truth in this statement. Similarly, if the sentence "This sentence is false" is false, it is true; and if what it says is true, it means that it is false. This type of logical inconsistency cannot be resolved unless one employs the restriction that one cannot apply truth locutions to sentences which themselves contain truth locutions. Pelevin's works are permeated by operative contradictions à la Epimenides's paradox.

29. Giving a foreign name to a Russian novel "is the case, of course, with the very novel we are reading" (Brouwer, "What Is It Like to Be a Bat-Author?" 249).

30. "The problem of language as the form of consciousness is foregrounded; inevitably thus the status of the text we are reading and the relation it has to its author is problematized" (Brouwer, "What Is It Like to Be a Bat-Author?" 249).

31. Discourse "establishes the discursive limits that allow the parasitic elites to go unnoticed—forever wrapped in a cloak of conspiratorial silence" (Livers, "The Tower or the Labyrinth," 497).

32. The novel "relies heavily on the postmodern notion of signifier creating (unreal) signified" (Dalton-Brown, "Illusion—Money—Illusion," 39).

33. The Villa of Mysteries is named after the hall located in the residential part of the building, where a large fresco covering three walls, one of the best preserved ancient paintings, depicts a mysterious rite reserved for devotees of the cult. The villa included an area with a wooden press intended for the production of wine.

34. *T* "explodes the modern literary business from within" (Basinskii, "Graf ukhodiashchii," 38).

35. On Tolstoy as the Bakhtinian monologic writer in Pelevin's context, see Zagidullina, "Mutatsiia otsenki," 164.

36. Optina Pustyn' was a spiritual retreat for both Tolstoy and Dostoevsky. Located in the Kaluga region south of Moscow, during the nineteenth century the hermitage became widely known for its sages who achieved the designation *starets*, or "elder."

37. Ariel is a spirit who appears in Shakespeare's play *The Tempest*. "Brakhman" is a Vedic Sanskrit word, and it is conceptualized in Hinduism as the creative principle which is realized in the whole world.

38. A Turing machine is a mathematical model of a hypothetical computing machine that can use a predefined set of rules to determine a result from a set of input variables.

39. Princess Tarakanova was a royal impostor who claimed to be the daughter of Alexei Razumovsky and Empress Elizabeth of Russia.

40. Compare to *Chapaev and the Void*: "If only I could truly as easily as Chapaev parted with these people part with the dark gang of false 'I's, ransacking my soul for so many years!" (*CP* 107).

41. On T's despair, see Kostyrko, "Dva l'va." Pelevin investigates "the

essence of the philosophy of freedom that occupies a central place in Tolstoy's art" (Zagidullina, "Mutatsiia otsenki," 163). See also Boeva, "Obrazy Tolstogo i Dostoevskogo."

42. In cosmic irony "we do not see the effects of what we do, the outcomes of our actions, or the forces that exceed our choices" (Colebrook, *Irony*, 14). On the irony of absurdity, see Behler, "The Theory of Irony in German Romanticism," 76.

43. On the image of the ouroboros as defining postmodern culture, see Kuritsyn, "Postmodernism," 49.

44. Hence the Sophist Thrasymachus's charge against Socrates: "I predicted that when it came to replying you would refuse and ironically disparage yourself and do anything rather than answer any question" (Knox, *Ironia*, 115). Compare this to Shklovsky on Hegel and Schlegel: "Irony, about which Hegel wrote studying Schlegel, is close to the comic, but the comic destroys either falsehood in the occurrence itself or the falsehood of an occurrence" (Shklovskii, *Eshche nichego ne konchilos'*, 244).

45. For a critique of Pelevin as evading moral judgment, see, for instance, Nemzer, "Kak by tipa po zhizni," 88.

46. On irony through metaphors of hovering above, see Behler, "The Theory of Irony in German Romanticism," 51.

CONCLUSION

1. Quoted in Suslov, "Of Planets and Trenches," 569.

2. Levitan "does not even try to glance into the dark soul of General Shmyga—though he suspects that there he would meet a close tin bottom covered by the 'abyss-like' camouflage" (AV 87).

3. Thuggee is a a semi-religious Hindu cult with a highly organized system of murder and robbery. According to Thuggee beliefs, the goddess Kali taught the fathers of thuggery to strangle with a noose and to kill without spilling blood. All victims of the Thuggee were sacrificed to Kali.

4. Compare this to the following commentary on *The Sacred Book of the Werewolf*: the obstacle here "is a modernist idea of escape—its goal is the empty center of the postmodern worldview." As the plot unfolds, "there emerges a core incompatibility between the position of the postmodernist mediator with the escapist freedom of his former, modernist in their essence, heroes" (Lipovetskii, *Paralogii*, 677).

5. Other critics, by contrast, see Pelevin as essentially postmodern. See, for instance, Dalton-Brown, "Ludic Nonchalance or Ludicrous Despair?"; and Chuprinin, "Sbyvsheesia nebyvshee."

6. Pelevin and Sorokin alike "were denied any other status beyond mitrofanushkas and nedotykomkas, at best—creators of amusing texts for skits,

at worst—lampooning anti-cultural saboteurs" (Lipovetskii, *Paralogii*, 423). On Pelevin's commercialism, see, for example, Ivanova, "Peizazh posle bitvy." Pelevin's critique of mass culture using its own clichés may "make the reader's exit from the vicious cycle of illusions all the more problematic" (Amusin, "Chem serdce uspokoitsia," 29).

7. The Russian Booker Prize was a Russian literary award modeled after the Man Booker Prize. It was awarded from 1992 to 2017. The Booker International Prize, introduced in 2004, is a different award.

8. This is Pelevin's "first miss. The novel written out of inertia is a reason to stop" (Genis, "Fenomen Pelevina").

9. Plasters "were the last attempt to breathe life into old art forms and enliven them. [. . .] Imagine God with all of His bones broken, and he is dead. He needs to be buried, but [. . .] those thick-stomacked ones announce that God is actually alive, and just needs to be encased in plaster bandages, and in a few years—five, ten, twenty—he will recover" (*iPhuck 10*, 40).

10. In *S.N.U.F.F.*, creative work resolves itself into choosing from what has already been created: "Metaphorically speaking, we do not grow grapes any more. We send someone to the cellar to get a bottle. People who do this are called *sommelier*" (*S.N.U.F.F.*, 374).

11. Jonathan Swift's satirical 1726 novel *Gulliver's Travels* describes a race of horses called Houyhnhnms, rational equine beings and masters of the land. They contrast with the Yahoos, savage humanoid creatures who are no better than beasts of burden. Whereas the Yahoos represent all that is bad about humans, Houyhnhnms have a settled, calm, reliable, and rational society. Gulliver prefers the Houyhnhnms' company to the Yahoos', even though the latter are biologically closer to him.

12. *Vox populi* (Latin) means "voice of the people."

13. "Even Pelevin is reluctant to abandon systemic thinking entirely, creating elaborate conspiracies even as he lampoons conspiratorial paranoia" (Borenstein, "Survival of the Catchiest," 477). "When Victor Pelevin closed out the Yeltsin era in his novel *Homo Zapiens* with the casual revelation that the entire Kremlin leadership was generated by CGI, readers could be forgiven for idly wishing that their next president would be produced by Pixar" (Borenstein, *Plots against Russia*, 60).

14. In *Critique of Cynical Reason* (1983), Sloterdijk investigates mechanisms of falsifying ideological convictions for personal profit.

Bibliography

Adorno, Theodor. *Prisms*. Cambridge, Mass.: MIT Press, 1967.

Adorno, Theodor. *Probleme der Moralphilosophie*. Frankfurt: Suhrkamp, 1996.

Adorno, Theodor, and Max Horkheimer. *Dialectic of Enlightenment*. New York: Verso, 1972.

Afanas'ev, Aleksandr. *Narodnye russkie skazki Aleksandra Nikolaevicha Afanas'eva*. Moscow: Olma Press, 2004.

Agamben, Giorgio. *The Open: Man and Animal*. Stanford, Calif.: Stanford University Press, 2003.

Aksyonov, Vasily. *The Island of Crimea*. New York: Vintage, 1984.

Aksenov, Vasily. *Ostrov Krym*. Ann Arbor, Mich.: Ardis, 1981.

Aksenov, Vasily. *Moskva-kva-kva*. Moscow: Eksmo, 2006.

Akunin, Boris. *Azazel'*. Moscow: Zakharov, 1998.

Akunin, Boris. *The Winter Queen*. Translated by Andrew Bromfield. New York: Random House, 2004.

Alimov, Igor', and Viacheslav Rybakov. *Plokhikh liudei net (Evraziiskaia simfoniia)*. St. Petersburg: Azbuka, 2000–2005.

Althusser, Louis. "Ideology and Ideological State Apparatuses (Notes towards an Investigation)." In *Lenin and Philosophy and Other Essays*, 142–76. London: Verso, 1970.

Althusser, Louis. *Lenin and Philosophy and Other Essays*. London: Verso, 1970.

Amis, Kingsley. *The Alteration*. New York: New York Review Books Classics, 2013.

Amusin, Mark. *Brat'ia Strugatskie: Ocherk tvorchestva*. Jerusalem: Beseder, 1996.

Amusin, Mark. "Chem serdtse uspokoitsia: Zametki o ser'eznoi i massovoi literature v Rossii na rubezhe vekov." *Voprosy literatury*, no. 3 (2009): 5–45.

Amusin, Mark. "Dramy idei, tragediia liudei: Zametki o tvorchestve Stanislava Lema i brat'ev Strugatskikh." *Znamia*, no. 7 (2009): 174–86.

Amusin, Mark. "A Selective Similarity: Dostoevsky in the Worlds of the Strugatsky Brothers." *Russian Studies in Literature* 47, no. 4 (Fall 2011): 67–83.

Andreev, Daniil. *Roza mira*. Moscow: Biblioteka vsemirnoi literatury, 2018.

Andreev, Daniil. *The Rose of the World*. Hudson, N.Y.: Lindisfarne Books, 1997.

Anninskii, Lev, and Vladimir Bondarenko. *Zhivi opasno*. Moscow: PoRog, 2006.

Arbitman, Roman. "Uronili v rechku miachik." Laboratoriia fantastiki, December 2011. https://fantlab.ru/work334698.

Arendt, Hannah. *The Human Condition*. Chicago: University of Chicago Press, 1958.

Arkhangel'skii, Aleksandr. "Pustota. I Chapaev." *Druzhba narodov*, no. 5 (1997): 190–93.

Arkhangel'skii, Andrei. "Liubov' rezinovoi zhenshchiny." *Kommersant*, December 11, 2011. https://www.kommersant.ru/doc/1831375.

Armstrong, Karen. *A Short History of Myth*. London: Canongate, 2004.

Atwood, Margaret. *The Handmaid's Tale*. New York: Anchor, 1998.

Atwood, Margaret. *The Penelopiad: The Myth of Penelope and Odysseus*. London: Canongate, 2006.

Babitskaia, Varvara. "*Liubov' k trem cukerbrinam* Viktora Pelevina: Nas vsekh toshnit." *Vozdukh*, September 2014. https://daily.afisha.ru/archive/vozduh/books/nas-vseh-toshnit-lyubov-k-trem-cukerbrinam-viktora-pelevina.

Bakhtin, Mikhail. *The Dialogic Imagination: Four Essays*. Edited by Michael Holquist, translated by Michael Holquist and Caryl Emerson. Austin: University of Texas Press, 1983.

Bakhtin, Mikhail. *Problems of Dostoevsky's Poetics*. Edited and translated by Caryl Emerson, introduction by Wayne C. Booth. Theory and History of Literature, edited by Wlad Godzich and Jochen Schulte-Sasse, vol. 8. Minneapolis: University of Minnesota Press, 1984.

Bakhtin, Mikhail. *Speech Genres and Other Late Essays*. Austin: University of Texas Press, 1986.

Bakhtin, Mikhail. *Toward a Philosophy of the Act*. Austin: University of Texas Press, 1993.

Balina, Marina, and Mark Lipovetsky, eds. *Dictionary of Literary Biography: Russian Writers since 1980*. Detroit, Mich.: Gale Research, 2003.

Balod, Aleksandr. "Ironicheskii slovar' *Empire V*." *Novyi mir*, no. 9 (2007): 139–57.

Barth, John. "The Literature of Exhaustion." In *The Friday Book: Essays and Other Nonfiction*. Baltimore, Md.: Johns Hopkins University Press, 1984.

Barth, John. *The Friday Book: Essays and Other Nonfiction*. Baltimore, Md.: Johns Hopkins University Press, 1984.

Basinskii, Pavel. "Ampir na krovi." *Rossiiskaia gazeta*, no. 4228 (November 22, 2006). http://www.rg.ru/2006/11/22/ampir.html.

Basinskii, Pavel. "Iz zhizni otechestvennykh kaktusov." *Literaturnaia gazeta*, May 1996, 4.

Basinskii, Pavel. "Uzhas Shlema." Lenizdat.ru. November 23, 2005. https://lenizdat.ru/articles/1035663.

Bataille, Georges. *Erotism: Death and Sensuality.* San Francisco: City Lights Books, 1962.

Baudelaire, Charles. *The Flowers of Evil.* Middleton, Conn.: Wesleyan University Press, 2006.

Baudrillard, Jean. *The Consumer Society: Myths and Structures.* London: SAGE Publications, 1998.

Baudrillard, Jean. *The Gulf War Did Not Take Place.* Bloomington: Indiana University Press, 1995.

Baudrillard, Jean. "Hystericizing the Millennium." CT Theory, October 5, 1994. http://ctheory.net/ctheory_wp/hystericizing-the-Millennium/.

Baudrillard, Jean. *The Illusion of the End.* Stanford, Calif.: Stanford University Press, 1994.

Baudrillard, Jean. *The Jean Baudrillard Reader.* New York: Columbia University Press, 2008.

Baudrillard, Jean. *Simulacra and Simulation.* Ann Arbor: University of Michigan Press, 1994.

Baudrillard, Jean. *Symbolic Exchange and Death.* London: SAGE Publications, 1993.

Behler, Ernst. "The Theory of Irony in German Romanticism." In *Romantic Irony*, edited by Frederick Garber, 43–81. Amsterdam: John Benjamins, 1981.

Beigbeder, Frédéric. *99 Francs.* Paris: Grasset & Fasquelle, 2000.

Beliakov, Sergei. "Pogovorim o strannostiakh liubvi." *Ural*, no. 1 (2015). http://magazines.russ.ru/ural/2015/11/18bel.html.

Belyi, Andrei. *Sobranie sochinenii v 6 tomakh.* Moscow: Terra, 2005.

Benjamin, Walter. *The Work of Art in the Age of Mechanical Reproduction.* New York: Prism Key, 2010.

Berdiaev, Nikolai. *The End of Our Time.* New York: Semantron, 2009.

Berdiaev, Nikolai. *Novoe srednevekov'e (razmyshlenie o sud'be Rossii).* Berlin: Obelisk, 1924.

Berg, Mikhail. *Literaturokratiia: Problema pereraspredeleniia vlasti v literature.* Moscow: Novoe literaturnoe obozrenie, 2000.

Berlin, Isaiah. *The Hedgehog and the Fox: An Essay on Tolstoy's View of History.* Foreword by Michael Ignatieff, edited by Henry Hardy. Princeton, N.J.: Princeton University Press, 1953.

Berry, Ellen, and Anesa Miller-Pogacar, eds. *Re-Entering the Sign: Articulating New Russian Culture.* Ann Arbor: University of Michigan Press, 1995.

Bethea, David. "Apocalypticism in Russian Literature: A Brief Portrait." In *Fearful Hope. Approaching the New Millennium*, edited by Christopher Kleinhenz and Fannie J. LeMoine, 135–48. Madison: University of Wisconsin Press, 1999.

Bethea, David. "D. H. Lawrence and Vasily Rozanov: The End as Language." In

Poetics, Self, Place: Essays in Honor of Anna Lisa Crone, edited by Catherine O'Neil, Nicole Boudreau, and Sarah Krive, 11–25. Bloomington: Indiana University Press, 2007.

Bethea, David. *The Shape of Apocalypse in Modern Russian Literature.* Princeton, N.J.: Princeton University Press, 1989.

Binkley, Sam. *A Foucault for the 21st Century: Governmentality, Biopolitics and Discipline in the New Millennium,* edited by Sam Binkley and Jorge Capetillo. Cambridge: Cambridge Scholars, 2010.

Black, Jeremy. *Other Pasts, Different Presents, Alternative Futures.* Bloomington: Indiana University Press, 2015.

Blok, Aleksandr. *Sobranie sochinenii.* Moscow: Gosudarstvennoe izdatel'stvo khudozhestvennoi literatury, 1960–63.

Blok, Alexander. *The Stranger: Selected Poetry.* Translated by Andrey Kneller. Scotts Valley, Calif.: CreateSpace Independent Publishing, 2011.

Boeva, Tat'iana. "Obrazy Tolstogo i Dostoevskogo v romane V. Pelevina *T*: Qui pro Quo." *Toronto Slavic Quarterly.* sites.utoronto.ca/tsq/55/Boeva.pdf.

Bogdanova, Ol'ga. *Postmodernizm v kontekste sovremennoi russkoi literatury: 60e–90e gody XX veka—nachalo XXI veka.* St. Petersburg: Filologicheskii Fak-t S.-Peterburgskogo universiteta, 2004.

Bogdanova, Ol'ga, Sergei Kibalnik, and Liudmila Safronova. *Literaturnye strategii Viktora Pelevina.* St. Petersburg: Petropolis, 2008.

Bondarenko, Vladimir. "Vampiry na sluzhbe piatoi imperii." *Zavtra* no. 12 (March 2007): 696.

Booker, Keith. *Dystopian Literature: A Theory and Research Guide.* Westport, Conn.: Greenwood, 1994.

Booth, Wayne. *A Rhetoric of Irony.* Chicago: University of Chicago Press, 1974.

Borenstein, Eliot. "Off the Reservation." Plots against Russia. http://plotsagainstrussia.org/eb7nyuedu2016/12/6off-the-reservation.

Borenstein, Eliot. *Plots against Russia: Conspiracy and Fantasy after Socialism.* Ithaca, N.Y.: Cornell University Press, 2019.

Borenstein, Eliot. "Survival of the Catchiest: Memes and Postmodern Russia." *Slavic and East European Journal* 48, no. 3 (Fall 2004): 462–83.

Borges, Jorge Luis. *Everything and Nothing.* New York: New Directions, 1999.

Borges, Jorge Luis. "The Garden of Forking Paths." In *Everything and Nothing,* 29–51. New York: New Directions, 1999.

Borges, Jorge Luis. "Tlön, Uqbar, Orbis Tertius." In *Everything and Nothing,* 12–30. New York: New Directions, 1999.

Bourdieu, Pierre. *Distinction.* Cambridge: Routledge, 1986.

Boym, Svetlana. *Another Freedom: The Alternative History of an Idea.* Chicago: University of Chicago Press, 2010.

Boym, Svetlana. *The Future of Nostalgia.* Cambridge, Mass.: Harvard University Press, 2001.

Bradbury, Ray. *A Sound of Thunder and Other Stories.* Toronto: William Morrow Paperbacks, 2005.

Brintlinger, Angela. "The Hero in the Madhouse: The Post-Soviet Novel Confronts the Soviet Past." *Slavic Review* 63, no. 1 (Spring 2004): 43–65.

Brodskii, Iosif. *Sochineniia Iosifa Brodskogo.* St. Petersburg: Pushkinskii fond, 1998.

Brooks, Jeffrey, and Boris Draliuk, "Parahistory: History at Play in Russia and Beyond." *Slavic Review* 75, no. 1 (Spring 2016): 77–98.

Brouwer, Sander. "What Is It Like to Be a Bat-Author? Viktor Pelevin's *Empire V.*" In *Dutch Contributions to the Fourteenth International Congress of Slavists, Ohrid, September 10–16, 2008*, edited by Sander Brouwer, 243–56. Amsterdam: Brill, 2008.

Brouwer, Sander, ed. *Dutch Contributions to the Fourteenth International Congress of Slavists, Ohrid, September 10–16, 2008.* Amsterdam: Brill, 2008.

Bulgakov, Mikhail. *Heart of a Dog.* New York: Grove, 1994.

Bulgakov, Mikhail. *The Master and Margarita.* Translated by Richard Pevear and Larissa Volokhonsky, introduction by Richard Pevear. New York: Penguin, 1997.

Bulgakov, Mikhail. *Master i Margarita.* Paris: YMCA Press, 1967.

Bulgakov, Mikhail. *Sobach'e serdtse.* Paris: YMCA Press, 1987.

Bulychev, Kir. *Shturm Diul'bera.* Moscow: Veche, 2018.

Bykov, Dmitrii. "Dmitriiu Bykovu stalinskoe vremia kazhetsia soblaznitel'nee nashego: Interv'iu s Igorem Shevelevym." *Vremia MN,* April 2001, 7.

Bykov, Dmitrii. *Living Souls.* Rochester, N.Y.: Alma Books, 2010.

Bykov, Dmitrii. *Opravdanie. Evakuator: Romany.* Moscow: Vagrius, 2008.

Bykov, Dmitrii. *Opravdanie.* Moscow: Vagrius, 2001.

Bykov, Dmitrii. *Orfografiia.* Moscow: Vagrius, 2003.

Bykov, Dmitrii. "Pelevin: put' vniz." https://biblio.litres.ru/dmitriy-bykov/lekciya-viktor-pelevin-put-vniz-chast-1-8388900/.

Bykov, Dmitrii. "Pobeg v Mongoliiu." *Literaturnaia gazeta,* May 29, 2006. http://pelevin.nov.ru/stati/o-dva/1.html.

Bykov, Dmitrii. "Za piat' minut do smysla." *Ogoniok,* no. 43 (October 2006): 12.

Bykov, Dmitrii. *ZhD.* Moscow: AST, 2007.

Cahan, David, ed. *Hermann von Helmholtz and the Foundations of Nineteenth-Century Science (California Studies in the History of Science).* Los Angeles: University of California Press, 1994.

Calinescu, Matei. "The End of Man in Twentieth-Century Philosophy: Reflections on a Philosophical Metaphor." In *Visions of Apocalypse: End or Rebirth?* edited by Saul Friedlander et al., 171–95. New York: Holmes and Meier, 1985.

Calvino, Italo. *If on a Winter's Night a Traveler.* Orlando: Harcourt Brace Jovanovich, 1982.

Čapek, Karel. *War with the Newts.* North Haven, Conn.: Catbird, 1990.

Cassedy, Stephen. *Dostoevsky's Religion.* Stanford, Calif.: Stanford University Press, 2005.

Chaadaev, Peter. *The Major Works of Peter Chaadaev.* Edited by Petr McNally. Notre Dame, Ind.: University of Notre Dame Press, 1969.

Chaadaev, Petr. *Polnoe sobranie sochinenii i izbrannye pis'ma v dvukh tomakh.* Moscow: Nauka, 1991.

Chantsev, Aleksandr. "Fabrika antiutopii: Distopicheskii diskurs v rossiiskoi literature serediny 2000kh'." *Novoe literaturnoe obozrenie,* no. 86 (2007): 269–301.

Chantsev, Aleksandr. "Strasti po Daniilu." *Novyi mir,* no. 8 (2011). http://magazines.russ.ru/novyi_mi/2011/8/ch15-pr.html.

Chernyshevskii, Nikolai. *Chto delat'?* Moscow: Gosudarstvennoe izdatel'stvo khudozhestvennoi literatury, 1947.

Chernyshevskii, Nikolai. *What Is to Be Done?* Ithaca, N.Y.: Cornell University Press, 1989.

Chevalier, Haakon. *The Ironic Temper: Anatole France and His Time.* Oxford: Oxford University Press, 1932.

Chuprinin, Sergei. "Sbyvsheesia nebyvshee." *Znamia,* no. 9 (1993): 81–88.

Clowes, Edith. *Russia on the Edge: Imagined Geographies and Post-Soviet Identity.* Ithaca, N.Y.: Cornell University Press, 2011.

Clowes, Edith. *Russian Experimental Fiction: Resisting Ideology after Utopia.* Princeton, N.J.: Princeton University Press, 1993.

Colebrook, Clare. *Irony.* London: Routledge, 2004.

Cornwell, Neil, ed. *The Routledge Companion to Russian Literature.* London: Routledge, 2001.

Coupland, Douglas. *Generation X: Tales for an Accelerated Culture.* New York: St. Martin's Griffin, 1991.

Coupland, Douglas. *Microserfs.* New York: Harper Perennial, 2008.

Crichton, Michael. *Prey.* New York: Harper, 2002.

Cupitt, Don. *Time Being.* London: Hymns Ancient & Modern, 2000.

Dalton-Brown, Sally. "Illusion—Money—Illusion: Victor Pelevin and the 'Closed Loop' of the Vampire Novel." *Slavonica,* no. 17 (2011): 30–44.

Dalton-Brown, Sally. "Ludic Nonchalance or Ludicrous Despair? Viktor Pelevin and Russian Post-Modernist Prose." *Slavonic and East European Review* 75, no. 2 (April 1997): 216–33.

Danilkin, Lev. "Ananasnaia voda dlia prekrasnoi damy." *Afisha,* December 20, 2010. http://www.afisha.ru/book/1745/review/354170/.

Danilkin, Lev. "Pora mezh volka i sobaki." *Afisha,* November 22, 2004: 151–53.

Danilkin, Lev. "*S.N.U.F.F.* Viktora Pelevina." *Afisha,* December 21, 2011. https://daily.afisha.ru/archive/vozduh/archive/10832/.

Danilkin, Lev. "Shlem Uzhasa." *Afisha,* October 18, 2005. http://msk.afisha.ru/books/book/?id=8281488.

Dante. *The Divine Comedy.* Translated by John Ciardi. New York: Berkley, 2003.

Davies, Tony. *Humanism.* London: Routledge, 1997.

Dawkins, Richard. *The Selfish Gene.* Oxford: Oxford University Press, 1989.

Deleuze, Gilles, and Felix Guattari. *Anti-Oedipus: Capitalism and Schizophre-nia.* New York: Penguin, 2009.

DeLillo, Don. *White Noise.* New York: Penguin, 1985.

De Man, Paul. *Aesthetic Ideology.* Edited by Andreij Warminski. Theory and History of Literature, edited by Wlad Godzich and Jochen Schulte-Sasse, vol. 65. Minneapolis: University of Minnesota Press, 1996.

De Man, Paul. *The Resistance to Theory.* Theory and History of Literature, edited by Wlad Godzich and Jochen Schulte-Sasse, vol. 33. Minneapolis: University of Minnesota Press, 1986.

Dennett, Daniel. *Consciousness Explained.* Boston: Back Bay Books, 1992.

Derrida, Jacques. *Margins of Philosophy.* Translated by Alan Bass. Chicago: University of Chicago Press, 1972.

Derrida, Jacques. *Of Grammatology.* Translated by Gayatri Chakravorty Spivak. Baltimore, Md.: Johns Hopkins University Press, 1976.

Derrida, Jacques. "On a Newly Arisen Apocalyptic Tone in Philosophy." In *Raising the Tone of Philosophy: Late Essays by Immanuel Kant, Transformative Critique by Jacques Derrida,* edited by Peter Fenves, 171–72. Baltimore, Md.: Johns Hopkins University Press, 1998.

Derrida, Jacques. "Des Tours de Babel." In *Difference in Translation,* edited and introduction by Joseph F. Graham, 165–207. Ithaca, N.Y.: Cornell University Press, 1985.

Dewhirst, Martin, and Alla Latynina. "Post-Soviet Russian Literature." In *The Routledge Companion to Russian Literature,* edited by Neil Cornwell, 234–50. London: Routledge, 2001.

Dick, Philip K. *Do Androids Dream of Electric Sheep?* New York: Del Rey, 1996.

Dick, Philip K. *The Man in the High Castle.* New York: Mariner Books, 2012.

Dobrenko, Evgeny, and Mark Lipovetsky, eds. *Russian Literature since 1991.* Cambridge: Cambridge University Press, 2015.

Dostoevsky, Fyodor. *The Brothers Karamazov.* Translated by Richard Pevear and Larissa Volokhonsky. New York: Farrar, Straus and Giroux, 2002.

Dostoevsky, Fyodor. *Crime and Punishment.* Translated by Jessie Senior Coulson, edited by George Gibian. New York: W. W. Norton, 1989.

Dostoevsky, Fyodor. *The Devils: The Possessed.* Translated by David Magarshack. New York: Penguin, 1954.

Dostoevsky, Fyodor. *The Idiot.* Translated by Richard Pevear and Larissa Volokhonsky. New York: Vintage Classics, 2003.

Dostoevsky, Fyodor. *Notes from Underground.* Translated and edited by Michael R. Katz. New York: W. W. Norton, 2001.

Dostoevskii, Fedor. *Polnoe sobranie sochinenii v 30-ti tomakh.* Edited by V. G. Bazanov et al. Leningrad: Nauka, 1972–90.

Dostoevsky, Fyodor. *Poor Folk.* Mineola, N.Y.: Dover, 2007.

Dostoevsky, Fyodor. *Short Stories. Bobok.* Redditch, U.K.: Read Books Ltd, 2018.

Dostoevsky, Fyodor. *Winter Notes on Summer Impressions.* Translated by David Patterson. Evanston, Ill.: Northwestern University Press, 1988.

Drexler, Eric K. *Engines of Creation: The Coming Era of Nanotechnology.* Norwell, Mass.: Bantam Doubleday Dell, 1986.

Dryden, John. *John Dryden: Tercentenary Essays.* Oxford: Clarendon, 2000.

Duncan, Andy. "Alternate History." In *The Cambridge Companion to Science Fiction,* edited by Edward James and Farah Mendelsohn, 209–18. Cambridge: Cambridge University Press, 2009.

Eco, Umberto. *Foucault's Pendulum.* Boston: Mariner's Paperback, 2007.

Eco, Umberto. "Postmodernism, Irony, the Enjoyable." In *Reflections on the Name of the Rose,* 65–72. London: Martin Secker and Warburg, 1992.

Eco, Umberto. *Reflections on the Name of the Rose.* London: Martin Secker and Warburg, 1992.

Edel, Anastasia. "Blurring the Real and the Fantastic: Victor Pelevin's *The Blue Lantern and Other Stories.*" *World Literature Today,* December 9, 2015. http://www.worldliteraturetoday.org/blog/blurring-real-and-fantastic-victor -pelevins-blue-lantern-and-other-stories.

Epstein, Mikhail. *After the Future: The Paradoxes of Postmodernism and Contemporary Russian Culture.* Boston: University of Massachusetts Press, 1995.

Erofeev, Venedikt. *Moscow to the End of the Line.* Evanston, Ill.: Northwestern University Press, 1992.

Etkind, Alexander. "Stories of the Undead in the Land of the Unburied: Magical Historicism in Contemporary Russian Fiction." *Slavic Review* 68, no. 3 (Fall 2009): 631–58.

Etkind, Alexander. *Warped Mourning: Stories of the Undead in the Land of the Unburied.* Stanford, Calif.: Stanford University Press, 2013.

Everett, Hugh, Jeffrey A. Barrett, and Peter Byrne. *The Everett Interpretation of Quantum Mechanics: Collected Works, 1955–1980.* Princeton, N.J.: Princeton University Press, 2012.

Fenves, Peter, ed. *Raising the Tone of Philosophy: Late Essays by Immanuel Kant, Transformative Critique by Jacques Derrida.* Baltimore, Md.: Johns Hopkins University Press, 1998.

Ferguson, Niall, ed. *Virtual History: Alternatives and Counterfactuals.* London: Basic Books, 1997.

Florenskii, Pavel. *Filosofiia kul'ta: Opyt pravoslavnoi antropoditsei.* Moscow: Akademicheskii proekt, 2014.

Florenskii, Pavel. *Sochineniia v 4 tomakh.* Moscow: Mysl', 1994.

Fontaine, Jean, de la. *Selected Fables.* Edited, introduction, notes and vocabulary by Cecile Hugon. Oxford: Clarendon Press, 1923.

Foucault, Michel. *The Birth of Biopolitics: Lectures at the Collège de France, 1978–79*. New York: Picador, 2010.

Foucault, Michel. *Discipline and Punish: The Birth of the Prison*. Translated by Alan Sheridan. New York: Vintage, 1977.

Foucault, Michel. *The History of Sexuality*. Translated by Robert Hurley. New York: Vintage, 1976, 1981.

Foucault, Michel. *The Order of Things: An Archaeology of the Human Sciences*. London: Routledge, 1994.

Foucault, Michel. *Security, Territory, Population: Lectures at the Collège de France, 1977–78*. Edited by Arnold Davidson. New York: Picador, 2009.

Foucault, Michel. *"Society Must Be Defended": Lectures at the Collège de France, 1975–76*. Translated by David Macey. New York: Picador, 2003.

Frank, Joseph. *Dostoevsky: The Mantle of the Prophet, 1871–1881*. Princeton, N.J.: Princeton University Press, 2002.

Frank, Joseph. *Dostoevsky: The Seeds of Revolt, 1821–1849*. Princeton, N.J.: Princeton University Press, 1979.

Freidin, Gregory. *"Dzheneraishen 'P'." Foreign Policy*, no. 118 (Spring 2000): 165–69.

Freud, Sigmund. *Civilization and Its Discontents*. New York: W. W. Norton, 2010.

Friedlander, Saul, et al., eds. *Visions of Apocalypse: End or Rebirth?* New York: Holmes and Meier, 1985.

Fukuyama, Frances. "The End of History?" *The National Interest* (Summer 1989): 3–18.

Fukuyama, Frances. *The End of History and the Last Man*. New York: Free Press, 1992.

Fukuyama, Frances. *Our Posthuman Future: Consequences of the Biotechnology Revolution*. New York: Picador, 2002.

Furmanov, Dmitrii. *Chapaev*. Moscow: Gosizdat, 1923.

Furmanov, Dmitrii. *Chapaev*. Translated by George and Jeanette Kittell. Moscow: Foreign Languages Publishing House, 1955.

Galaninskaia, Svetlana. "Babochka letaet i na nebo: Interv'iu s Ol'goi Sedakovoi." *Religare*, December 25, 2012. http://www.religare.ru/298818.html.

Garber, Frederick, ed. *Romantic Irony*. Amsterdam: John Benjamins, 1981.

Garros-Evdokimov. *Golovolomka*. St. Petersburg: Limbus Press, 2002.

Garros-Evdokimov. *Headcrusher*. New York: Vintage, 2005.

Gavelis, Ricardas. *Paskutiniųjų žemės žmonių karta*. Vilnius: Vaga, 1995.

Genette, Gerard. *Paratexts: Thresholds of Interpretation*. Cambridge: Cambridge University Press, 1997.

Genis, Aleksandr. "Besedy o novoi slovesnosti: Beseda desiataia: Pole chudes, Viktor Pelevin." *Zvezda*, no. 12 (1997). http://magazines.russ.ru/zvezda/1997/12/genis1-pr.html.

Genis, Alexander. "Borders and Metamorphoses: Viktor Pelevin in the Context of Post-Soviet Literature." In *Twentieth-Century Russian Literature: Selected Papers from the Fifth World Congress of Central and East European Studies, Warsaw, 1995*, edited by Karen L. Ryan and Barry P. Scherr, 294–306. New York: Palgrave Macmillan, 2000.

Genis, Aleksandr. "Fenomen Pelevina." *Radio Svoboda*, no. 24 (April 1999). http://www.svoboda.org/programs/OTB/1999/OBT.02.

Gibson, William. *Idoru*. New York: Berkley, 1997.

Gibson, William. *Neuromancer*. New York: Ace Books, 1984.

Gleick, James. *Chaos: Making a New Science*. New York: Penguin, 1987.

Glukhovskii, Dmitrii. *Metro 2033*. Moscow: AST, 2002.

Glukhovskii, Dmitrii. *Metro 2033*. Scotts Valley, Calif.: CreateSpace Independent Publishing, 2013.

Gödel, Kurt. *On Formally Undecidable Propositions of Principia Mathematica and Related Systems*. Mineola, N.Y.: Dover, 1992.

Gogol, Nikolai. *The Complete Tales of Nicholai Gogol*, 2 vols. Chicago: University of Chicago Press, 1985.

Gogol, Nikolai. *Dead Souls*. Translated by Richard Pevear and Larissa Volokhonsky. New York: Vintage, 1997.

Gogol, Nikolai. *Polnoe sobranie sochinenii v 14 tomakh*. Edited by N. L. Meshcheriakov. Moscow: Izdatel'stvo Akademii Nauk SSSR, 1937–52.

Gomel, Elana. *Science Fiction, Alien Encounters, and the Ethics of Posthumanism: Beyond the Golden Rule*. New York: Palgrave Macmillan, 2014.

Graham, Joseph F., ed. *Difference in Translation*. Ithaca, N.Y.: Cornell University Press, 1985.

Grassian, Daniel. "Discovering the Machine in You: The Literary, Social and Religious Implications of Neal Stephenson's *Snow Crash*." *Journal of the Fantastic in the Arts* 12, no. 3 (2001): 250–67.

Grenoble, Lenore, and John Kopper, eds. *Essays in the Art and Theory of Translation*. Lewiston, N.Y.: Edwin Mellen, 1997.

Gribble, Charles, ed. *Alexander Lipson: In Memoriam*. Columbus, Ohio: Slavica, 1994.

Griboedov, Aleksandr. *Sochineniia v stikhakh*. Moscow: Biblioteka poeta, 1987.

Griboedov, Alexander. *Woe from Wit*. New York: Columbia University Press, 2020.

Gubailovskii, Vladimir. "Gegel', Everett i graf T." *Novyi Mir*, no. 3 (2010). http://magazines.russ.ru/novyi_mi/2010/3/gu16.html.

Haraway, Donna. *Simians, Cyborgs, and Women: The Reinvention of Nature*. London: Free Association Books, 1991.

Hassan, Ihab. *The Postmodern Turn: Essays in Postmodern Theory and Culture*. Columbus: Ohio State University Press, 1987.

Hayles, N. Katherine. *How We Become Posthuman: Virtual Bodies in Cybernetics, Literature, and Informatics.* Chicago: University of Chicago Press, 1999.

Heidegger, Martin. *The Question Concerning Technology, and Other Essays.* New York: Harper Perennial, 2013.

Heugens, Pursey, Hans van Oosterhout, and Jack Vromen, eds. *The Social Institutions of Capitalism: Evolution and Design of Social Contracts.* Cheltenham, Eng.: Edward Elgar Publications, 2003.

Hobbes, Thomas. *Leviathan.* Oxford: Oxford University Press, 1997.

Hollander, Robert. "The Apocalyptic Framework of Dostoevsky's *The Idiot.*" *Mosaic* 7, no. 2 (Winter 1974): 123–39.

Houellebecq, Michel. *Extension du domaine de la lute.* Paris: Éditions J'Ai Lu, 1994.

Howell, Yvonne. *Apocalyptic Realism: The Science Fiction of Arkady and Boris Strugatsky.* New York: Peter Lang, 1994.

Howell, Yvonne. "When the Physicians Are Lyricists." In *Essays in the Art and Theory of Translation*, edited by Lenore Grenoble and John Kopper, 165–96. Lewiston, N.Y.: Edwin Mellen, 1997.

Humboldt, Wilhelm von. *On Language: The Diversity of Human Language-Structure and Its Influence on the Mental Development of Mankind.* Translated by Peter Heath, introduction by Hans Aarsleff. Cambridge: Cambridge University Press, 1988.

Humphries, Jeff. *Reading Emptiness: Buddhism and Literature.* New York: State University of New York Press, 1999.

Hutcheon, Linda. *Irony's Edge: The Theory and Politics of Irony.* New York: Routledge, 1995.

Hutcheon, Linda. *A Poetics of Postmodernism: History, Theory, Fiction.* New York: Routledge, 1988.

Hutchings, Stephen. *Russian Literary Culture in the Camera Age: The Word as Image.* London: Routledge, 2004.

Huxley, Aldous. *Ape and Essence.* Chicago: Elephant Paperbacks, 1992.

Huxley, Aldous. *Brave New World and Brave New World Revisited.* New York: Harper Perennial Modern Classics, 2005.

Huxley, Aldous. *Island.* New York: Harper Perennial Modern Classics, 2009.

Huxley, Julian, ed. *Aldous Huxley, 1894–1963: A Memorial Volume.* London: Harper & Row Publishers, 1965.

Ilichevskii, Aleksandr. *Matiss.* Moscow: Vremia, 2006.

Ilichevskii, Aleksandr. *Pers.* St. Petersburg: Astrel', 2012.

Issa, Kobayashi. *Issa's Best: A Translator's Selection of Master Haiku.* Translated by David G. Lanoue. HaikuGuy.com, 2012.

Ivanov, Viacheslav. "The Lessons of the Strugatskys." *Russian Studies in Literature* 47, no. 4 (Fall 2011): 7–30.

Ivanov, Viacheslav. "The Russian Novel in 1992/93." *Glas*, no. 7 (1993): 224–46.

Ivanov, Viacheslav. *Sobranie sochinenii v 4 tomakh.* Brussels: Foyer Oriental Chretien, 1974.

Ivanova, Natal'ia. "Peizazh posle bitvy." *Znamia,* no. 9 (1993): 189–98.

Jakobson, Roman. *Language in Literature.* Edited by Krystyna Pomorska and Stephen Rudy. Cambridge, Mass.: Belknap, 1987.

James, Edward, and Farah Mendelsohn, eds. *The Cambridge Companion to Science Fiction.* Cambridge: Cambridge University Press, 2009.

Jameson, Fredric. *Archaeologies of the Future: The Desire Called Utopia and Other Science Fictions.* New York: Verso, 2005.

Jameson, Fredric. *The Cultural Turn: Selected Writings on the Postmodern, 1983–85.* London: Verso, 1998.

Jameson, Fredric. "Fear and Loathing in Globalization." *New Left Review,* no. 23 (2003). https://newleftreview.org/II/23/fredric-jameson-fear-and -loathing-in-globalization.

Jameson, Fredric. *Postmodernism, or, The Cultural Logic of Late Capitalism.* Durham, N.C.: Duke University Press, 1991.

Kafka, Franz. *Franz Kafka: The Complete Stories.* New York: Schocken, 1995.

Kalfus, Ken. "Chicken Kiev: Surreal Stories from Russia Include One about Philosophical Poultry." *New York Times,* December 7, 1997. http://www .nytimes.com/books/97/12/07/reviews/971207.07kalfust.html.

Kalinin, Ilya. "Petropoetics." In *Russian Literature since 1991,* edited by Evgeny Dobrenko and Mark Lipovetsky, 120–44. Cambridge: Cambridge University Press, 2015.

Kant, Immanuel. *Critique of Practical Reason.* Indianapolis, Ind.: Hackett, 2002.

Kant, Immanuel. *Critique of Pure Reason (The Cambridge Edition of the Works of Immanuel Kant).* Cambridge: Cambridge University Press, 1999.

Kant, Immanuel. "The End of All Things." In *Perpetual Peace and Other Essays,* translated by Ted Humphrey, 93–106. Indianapolis, Ind.: Hackett, 1983.

Kant, Immanuel. *Perpetual Peace and Other Essays.* Translated by Ted Humphrey. Indianapolis, Ind.: Hackett, 1983.

Kashchuk, Iurii. "Nishi biotsenoza." *Literaturnaia gazeta,* October 10, 1990, 4.

Kaspe, Irina. "The Meaning of (Private) Life, or Why Do We Read the Strugatskys?" *Russian Studies in Literature* 47, no. 4 (Fall 2011): 31–66.

Kataev, Filip. "Semantika i funktsii komp'iuternogo diskursa v proze Viktora Pelevina." *Rossiiskaia i zarubezhnaia filosofiia* 2, no. 14 (2011). http:// pelevin.nov.ru/stati/kataev.pdf.

Kermode, Frank. *The Sense of an Ending: Studies in the Theory of Fiction.* Oxford: Oxford University Press, 2000.

Khagi, Sofya. "Alternative Historical Imagination in Viktor Pelevin." *Slavic and East European Journal* 62, no. 3 (Fall 2018): 483–502.

Khagi, Sofya. "From Homo Sovieticus to Homo Zapiens: Viktor Pelevin's Consumer Dystopia." *The Russian Review* 67, no. 4 (October 2008): 559–79.

Khagi, Sofya. "Garros-Evdokimov and Commodification of the Baltics." *Journal of Baltic Studies* 41:1 (Spring 2010): 119–37.

Khagi, Sofya. "Humans, Animals, Machines: Scenarios of Raschelovechivanie in *Gray Goo* and *Matisse.*" In *The Human Reimagined: Posthumanism in Late Soviet and Post-Soviet Russia*, edited by Julia Vaingurt and Colleen McQuillen, 69–97. Boston, Mass: Academic Studies, 2018.

Khagi, Sofya. "Incarceration, Alibi, Escape? Victor Pelevin's Art of Irony." *Russian Literature* 76, no. 4 (November 2014): 381–406.

Khagi, Sofya. "The Monstrous Aggregate of the Social: Toward Biopolitics in Victor Pelevin's Work." *Slavic and East European Journal* 55, no. 3 (Fall 2011): 439–59.

Khagi, Sofya. "One Billion Years after the End of the World: Historical Deadlock, Contemporary Dystopia, and the Continuing Legacy of the Strugatskii Brothers." *Slavic Review* 72, no. 2 (Summer 2013): 267–86.

Khagi, Sofya. "Parameters of Space-Time and Degrees of (Un)freedom: Dmitry Bykov's *ZhD.*" In *Geo-Political Identity Making in Post-Soviet Russian Speculative Fiction*, edited by Mikhail Suslov and Per-Arne Bodin, 281–300. London: I. B. Tauris, 2019.

Khapaeva, Dina. *Koshmar: Literatura i zhizn'*. Moscow: Tekst, 2010.

Khapaeva, Dina. "Vampir—geroi nashego vremeni." *Novoe literaturnoe obozrenie* 109, no. 3 (June 2011). http://magazines.russ.ru/nlo/2011/109/ha6-pr.html.

Kierkegaard, Søren. *The Concept of Irony, with Continual Reference to Socrates: Notes of Schelling's Berlin Lectures*. Princeton, N.J.: Princeton University Press, 1989.

Kleinhenz, Christopher, and Fannie J. LeMoine, eds. *Fearful Hope: Approaching the New Millennium*. Madison: University of Wisconsin Press, 1999.

Knickerbocker, Dale. "Apocalypse, Utopia, and Dystopia: Old Paradigms Meet a New Millennium." *Extrapolation* 51, no. 3 (2010): 345–57.

Knox, Dilwyn. *Ironia: Medieval and Renaissance Ideas on Irony*. Leiden: Brill Academic, 1989.

Kornev, Sergei. "Stolknovenie pustot: Mozhet li postmodernism byt' russkim i klassicheskim." *Novoe literaturnoe obozrenie* 28 (1997): 244–59.

Kostyrko, Sergei. "Dva l'va." *Novyi mir*, no. 3 (2010). http://magazines.russ.ru/novyi_mi/2010/3/ko15.html.

Kostyrko, Sergei. "Knigi, Obzory, Viktor Pelevin: *Ananasnaia voda dlia prekrasnoi damy.*" *Novyi mir*, no. 3 (2011). http://magazines.russ.ru/novyi_mir/2011/3/kn21-pr.html.

Kostyrko, Sergei. *Prostodushnoe chtenie*. Moscow, 2010.

Kozak, Roman, and Sergei Polotovskii. *Pelevin i pokolenie pustoty*. Moscow: Mann, Ivanov & Ferber, 2012.

Kozhevnikov, Vadim. *Shchit i mech*. Moscow: Sovetskii pisatel', 1968.

Kristeva, Julia. *Contre la dépression nationale*. Paris: Textuel, 1998.

Kristeva, Julia. "Europhilia, Europhobia." In *French Theory in America*, edited by Silvere Lotringer and Sande Cohen, 321–32. New York: Routledge, 2001.

Kristeva, Julia. *Sens et non-sens de la révolte*. Paris: Fayard, 1996.

Krusanov, Pavel. *Ukus angela*. St. Petersburg: Amfora, 2001.

Krylov, Ivan. *The Fables of Ivan Krylov*. Translated by Stephen Pimenoff. Dublin: Dedalus Books, 2017.

Krylov, Ivan. *Polnoe sobranie sochinenii*. Moscow: OGIZ, 1946.

Kucherskaia, Maiia. "Knizhnaia polka Maii Kucherskoi." *Novyi mir*, no. 1 (2006). http://magazines.russ.ru/novyi_mi/2006/1/kn16.html.

Kukulin, Il'ia. "Al'ternativnoe sotsial'noe proektirovanie v sovetskom obshchestve 1960kh–1970kh godov, ili Pochemu v sovremennoi Rossii ne prizhilis' levye politicheskie praktiki." *Novoe literaturnoe obozrenie* 88, no. 6 (2007): 169–201.

Kukulin, Il'ia. "Sentimental'naia tekhnologiia: Pamiat' o 1960-kh v diskussiiakh o modernizatsii 2009–2010 godov." *Neprikosnovennyi zapas*, no. 6 (2010): 277–301.

Kumar, Krishan. *Utopia and Anti-Utopia in Modern Times*. Oxford: Blackwell, 1987.

Kupina, N. A. "Lingvisticheskii katastrofizm v izobrazhenii Viktora Pelevina: Linguistic Catastrophism in the Work of Viktor Pelevin," *Russian Literature* 77, no. 3 (2015): 383–405.

Kuritsyn, Viacheslav. "Postmodernism: The New Primitive Culture." *Russian Studies in Literature* 30, no. 1 (1993): 52–66.

Kushner, Aleksandr. *Stikhotvoreniia*. Leningrad: Khudozhestvennaia literatura, 1970.

Laird, Sally, ed. *Voices of Russian Literature: Interviews with Ten Contemporary Writers*. Oxford: Oxford University Press, 1999.

Lalo, Alexei. "New Trends in Russian Intellectual Anti-Americanism: The Strange Case of Viktor Pelevin's Novel *S.N.U.F.F.*" *Slavonica* 20, no. 1 (2014): 34–44.

Langen, Timothy. "Evgeny Zamyatin's 'The Cave.'" *Philosophy and Literature* 29, no. 1 (April 2005): 209–17.

Lanz, Kenneth. *The Dostoevsky Encyclopedia*. Westport, Conn.: Greenwood, 2004.

Latynina, Iuliia. *Dzhahannam, ili do vstrechi v adu*. Moscow: Eksmo, 2005.

Lazarchuk, Andrei. *Inoe Nebo*. Moscow, 1993.

Leatherbarrow, William J. "Apocalyptic Imagery in Dostoevskij's *The Idiot* and *The Devils*." In *Shapes of Apocalypse. Arts and Philosophy in Slavic Thought*, edited by Andrea Oppo, 122–33. Boston: Academic Studies, 2013.

Le Guin, Ursula K. *The Dispossessed: An Ambiguous Utopia*. New York: Harper Collins, 1974.

Leiderman, Naum, and Mark Lipovetskii. *Sovremennaia russkaia literatura, 1950e–1990e gody*. 2 vols. Moscow: URSS, 2003.

Lem, Stanislav. *Mortal Engines*. Translated by Michael Kandel. Boston: Mariner, 1992.

Lermontov, Mikhail. *A Hero of Our Time*. Translated by Paul Foote. New York: Penguin, 2001.

Lermontov, Mikhail. *Sobranie sochinenii v 4 tomakh*. Moscow-Leningrad: Izdatel'stvo Akademii nauk SSSR, 1961–62.

Lilly, Ian, and Henrietta Mondry, eds. *Russian Literature in Transition*. Nottingham, Eng.: Astra, 1999.

Lipovetsky, Mark. *Charms of the Cynical Reason: The Trickster's Transformations in Soviet and Post-Soviet Culture*. Boston: Academic Studies, 2010.

Lipovetskii, Mark. "Goluboe salo pokoleniia, ili Dva mifa ob odnom krizise." *Znamia*, no. 11 (1999): 207–15.

Lipovetskii, Mark. *Paralogii: Transformatsii (post)modernistskogo diskursa v russkoi kul'ture 1920–2000-kh godov*. Moscow: Novoe literaturnoe obozrenie, 2008.

Lipovetskii, Mark. "Traektorii ITR-diskursa: Razroznennye zametki." *Neprikosnovennyi zapas* 74, no. 6 (2010): 213–30.

Lipovetsky, Mark, and Alexander Etkind. "The Salamander's Return: The Soviet Catastrophe and the Post-Soviet Novel." *Russian Studies in Literature* 46, no. 4 (2010): 6–48.

Livers, Keith. "Bugs in the Body Politic: The Search for Self in Victor Pelevin's *The Life of Insects*." *Slavic and East European Journal* 46, no. 1 (Spring 2002): 1–28.

Livers, Keith. *Conspiracy Culture: Post-Soviet Paranoia and the Russian Imagination*. Toronto: University of Toronto Press, 2020.

Livers, Keith. "Is There Humanity in Posthumanity? Viktor Pelevin's *S.N.U.F.F.*" *Slavic and East European Journal* 62, no. 3 (Fall 2018): 503–22.

Livers, Keith. "The Tower or the Labyrinth: Conspiracy, Occult, and Empire-Nostalgia in the Work of Viktor Pelevin and Aleksandr Prokhanov." *The Russian Review* 69, no. 3 (July 2010): 477–503.

Losev, Aleksei. *Istoriia antichnoi estetiki: Itogi tysiacheletnego razvitiia*, vol. 2. Moscow: Folio, 1994.

Lotman, Yuri. *Culture and Explosion (Semiotics, Communication and Cognition)*. Berlin: Mouton de Gruyter, 2009.

Lotringer, Silvere, and Sande Cohen, eds. *French Theory in America*. New York: Routledge: 2001.

Lunde, Ingunne, and Tine Roesen, eds. *Landslide of the Norm: Language Culture in Post-Soviet Russia*. Bergen: University of Bergen Press, 2006.

Lyotard, Jean-Francois. *The Inhuman: Reflections on Time*. Stanford, Calif.: Stanford University Press, 1991.

Lyotard, Jean-Francois. *The Postmodern Condition: A Report on Knowledge.* Minneapolis: University of Minnesota Press, 1984.

Maiakovskii, Vladimir. *Polnoe sobranie sochinenii v 12 tomakh.* Edited by N. N. Aseev, L. V. Maiakovskaia, V. O. Pertsov, and M. I. Serebrianskii. Moscow: Pravda, 1939.

Mandel'shtam, Osip. *The Noise of Time: Selected Prose.* Translated by Clarence Brown. Evanston, Ill.: Northwestern University Press, 2002.

Mandel'shtam, Osip. *Sobranie sochinenii v 4 tomakh.* Edited by P. Nerler and A. Nikitaev. Moscow: Terra, 1993.

Marcuse, Herbert. *A Critique of Pure Tolerance.* Edited by Robert Paul Wolff, Barrington Moore, Jr., and Herbert Marcuse. Boston: Beacon, 1969.

Marcuse, Herbert. *One-Dimensional Man: Studies in the Ideology of Advanced Industrial Society.* Boston: Beacon, 1968.

Marcuse, Herbert. "Repressive Tolerance." In *A Critique of Pure Tolerance,* edited by Robert Paul Wolff, Barrington Moore, Jr., and Herbert Marcuse, 95–137. Boston: Beacon, 1969.

Marsh, Rosalind. *Literature, History, and Identity in Post-Soviet Russia, 1991– 2006.* Oxford: Peter Lang, 2006.

McCall, Alexander. *Dream Angus.* London: Canongate, 2006.

McCausland, Gerald. "Viktor Olegovich Pelevin." In *Dictionary of Literary Biography: Russian Writers since 1980,* edited by Marina Balina and Mark Lipovetsky, 208–19. Detroit, Mich.: Gale Research, 2003.

McHale, Brian. *Constructing Postmodernism.* New York: Routledge, 1992.

Menzel, Birgit. "Russian Science and Fantasy Literature." In *Reading for Entertainment in Contemporary Russia: Post-Soviet Popular Literature in Historical Perspective,* edited by Birgit Menzel and Stephen Lovell, 117–50. Munich: Sagner, 2005.

Menzel, Birgit, and Stephen Lovell, eds. *Reading for Entertainment in Contemporary Russia: Post-Soviet Popular Literature in Historical Perspective.* Munich: Sagner, 2005.

Mil'chin, Konstantin. "Vozvrashchenie v provintsiiu." *Russkii reporter,* no. 35 (September 2014). http://expert.ru/russian_reporter/2014/35/vozvraschenie -v provintsiyu/media/preview/.

Miller, Robin Feuer. *Dostoevsky and "The Idiot": Author, Narrator, and Reader.* Cambridge, Mass.: Harvard University Press, 1981.

Milne, Lesley. "Jokers, Rogues, and Innocents: Types of Comic Hero and Author from Bulgakov to Pelevin." In *Reflective Laughter: Aspects of Humor in Russian Culture,* edited by Lesley Milne, 85–96. London: Anthem, 2004.

Milne, Lesley, ed. *Reflective Laughter: Aspects of Humor in Russian Culture.* London: Anthem, 2004.

Milton, John. *Paradise Lost.* New York: Harper Collins, 2014.

Minaev, Dmitrii. *Dukhless: Povest' o nenastoiashchem cheloveke.* Moscow: AST, 2006.

Mochul'skii, Konstantin. *Dostoevsky: His Life and Work.* Translated by M. Minihan. Princeton, N.J.: Princeton University Press, 1967.

More, Thomas. *Utopia.* Edited by George M. Logan, translated by Robert M. Adams. New York: W. W. Norton, 2010.

Morson, Gary Saul. *Narrative and Freedom: The Shadows of Time.* New Haven, Conn.: Yale University Press, 1996.

Morson, Gary Saul, and Caryl Emerson. *Mikhail Bakhtin: Creation of a Prosaics.* Stanford, Calif.: Stanford University Press, 1990.

Mozur, Joseph. "Victor Pelevin: Post-Sovism, Buddhism & Pulp Fiction." *World Literature Today* (Spring 2002): 59–67.

Muecke, Douglas C. *Irony and the Ironic.* London: Routledge, 1982.

Nabokov, Vladimir. *Lolita.* New York: Vintage, 1989.

Nabokov, Vladimir. *Pnin.* Portsmouth, N.H.: Doubleday, 1957.

Nakhimovsky, Alice S. "Soviet Anti-Utopias in the Works of Arkady and Boris Strugatsky." In *Alexander Lipson: In Memoriam,* edited by Charles Gribble et al., 143–53. Columbus, Ohio: Slavica, 1994.

Narinskaia, Anna. "Vozvrashchenie glavnogo geroia: *Ananasnaia voda dlia prekrasnoi damy* Viktora Pelevina." *Kommersant* 228, no. 4528 (September 9, 2010). http://www.kommersant.ru/doc/1554035.

Nemzer, Andrei. "Kak by tipa po zhizni: *Generation 'П'* kak zerkalo otechestvennogo infantilizma." *Vremia MN,* March 30, 1999.

Nemzer, Andrei. "Nesbyvsheesia: Al'ternativy istorii v zerkale slovesnosti." *Novyi mir,* no. 4 (1993): 226–38.

Nietzsche, Friedrich. *The Gay Science: With a Prelude in Rhymes and an Appendix of Songs.* Edited by Bernard Williams, translated by Josephine Nauckhoff, poems translated by Adrian del Caro. Cambridge: Cambridge UP, 2001.

Nietzsche, Friedrich. *Thus Spoke Zarathustra: A Book of All and None.* Translated by Walter Kaufmann. New York: Penguin, 1978.

Niven, Larry. *All the Myriad Ways.* New York: Random House, 1971.

Noordenbos, Boris. "Breaking into a New Era? A Cultural-Semiotic Reading of Viktor Pelevin." *Russian Literature* 64, no. 1 (July 2008): 85–107.

Noordenbos, Boris. "Shocking Histories and Missing Memories: Trauma in Viktor Pelevin's *Čapaev i Pustota.*" *Russian Literature* 85, no. 1 (October 2016): 43–68.

Nosov, Nikolai. *Neznaika v solnechnom gorode.* Moscow: Iunatstva, 1988.

Novikov, Vladimir. "Mutant: Literaturnyi peizazh posle nashestviia Pelevina." *Vremia i my,* no. 144 (1999). http://magazines.russ.ru/project/arss/novikov .mutant.html.

O'Neil, Catherine, Nicole Boudreau, and Sarah Krive, eds. *Poetics, Self, Place: Essays in Honor of Anna Lisa Crone.* Bloomington: Indiana University Press, 2007.

Oppo, Andrea. "Introduction." In *Shapes of Apocalypse: Arts and Philosophy in Slavic Thought,* edited by Andrea Oppo, 20–33. Boston: Academic Studies, 2013.

Oppo, Andrea. "Preface." In *Shapes of Apocalypse: Arts and Philosophy in Slavic Thought,* edited by Andrea Oppo, 13–18. Boston: Academic Studies, 2013.

Oppo, Andrea, ed. *Shapes of Apocalypse: Arts and Philosophy in Slavic Thought.* Boston: Academic Studies, 2013.

Ortega y Gasset, José. *The Revolt of the Masses.* Notre Dame, Ind.: University of Notre Dame Press, 1985.

Orwell, George. *1984: A Novel.* New York: Signet Classic, 1950.

Orwell, George. *Why I Write.* New York: Penguin Books, 2014.

Palahniuk, Chuck. *Fight Club: A Novel.* New York: Henry Holt, 1996.

Parts, Lyudmila. "Degradation of the Word, or the Adventures of an Intelligent in Viktor Pelevin's *Generation 'П'.*" *Canadian Slavonic Papers* 46, no. 3–4 (2004): 435–49.

Pasternak, Boris. *Sobranie sochinenii v 5 tomakh.* Moscow: Khudozhestvennaia literatura, 1991.

Paulsen, Martin. "Criticizing Pelevin's Language: The Language Question in the Reception of Victor Pelevin's Novel *Generation 'П'.*" In *Landslide of the Norm: Language Culture in Post-Soviet Russia,* edited by Ingunn Lunde and Tine Roesen, 143–58. Bergen: University of Bergen Press, 2006.

Pavlov, Evgeny. "Judging Emptiness: Reflections on the Post-Soviet Aesthetics and Ethics of Viktor Pelevin's *Chapaev i Pustota.*" In *Russian Literature in Transition,* edited by Ian K. Lilly and Henrietta Mondry, 89–104. Nottingham, Eng.: Astra, 1999.

Pavlov, Ivan. *Conditioned Reflexes (Classics of Psychology).* Mineola, N.Y.: Dover, 2013.

Pelevin, Viktor. *Ananasnaia voda dlia prekrasnoi damy.* Moscow: Eksmo, 2010.

Pelevin, Victor. *The Blue Lantern: Stories.* Translated by Andrew Bromfield. London: New Directions, 1997.

Pelevin, Victor. *Buddha's Little Finger.* Translated by Andrew Bromfield. New York: Penguin, 2001.

Pelevin, Viktor. *Chapaev i pustota.* Moscow: Vagrius, 1996.

Pelevin, Viktor. *DPP(NN): Dialektika perekhodnogo perioda iz niotkuda v nikuda.* Moscow: Eksmo, 2003.

Pelevin, Viktor. *Empire V / Ampir V: Povest' o nastoiashchem sverkhcheloveke.* Moscow: Eksmo, 2006.

Pelevin, Victor. *Empire V: The Prince of Hamlet.* Translated by Anthony Phillips. London: Gollancz, 2017.

Pelevin, Viktor. *Generation 'П.'* Moscow: Vagrius, 1999.

Pelevin, Victor. *The Helmet of Horror: The Myth of Theseus and the Minotaur.* London: Canongate, 2007.

Pelevin, Victor. *Homo Zapiens.* Translated by Andrew Bromfield. New York: Penguin Books, 2002.

Pelevin, Viktor. *iPhuck 10.* Moscow: Eksmo, 2017.

Pelevin, Viktor. *Lampa Mafusaila, ili krainiaia bitva chekistov s masonami.* Moscow: Eksmo, 2016.

Pelevin, Victor. *The Life of Insects.* Translated by Andrew Bromfield. New York: Farrar, Straus and Giroux, 1996.

Pelevin, Viktor. *Liubov' k trem cukerbrinam.* Moscow: Eksmo, 2014.

Pelevin, Viktor. *Omon Ra.* Moscow: Tekst, 1992.

Pelevin, Victor. *Omon Ra, with the Novella "The Yellow Arrow."* Translated by Andrew Bromfield. London: Harbord, 1994.

Pelevin, Viktor. *PPPPP: Proshchal'nye pesni politicheskikh pigmeev Pindostana.* Moscow: Eksmo, 2008.

Pelevin, Victor. *The Sacred Book of the Werewolf: A Novel.* Translated by Andrew Bromfield. New York: Penguin Books, 2009.

Pelevin, Viktor. *Shlem uzhasa: Kreatiff o Tesee i Minotavre.* Moscow: Otkrytyi mir, 2005.

Pelevin, Viktor. *Sinii fonar'.* Moscow: Alfa fantastika, 1991.

Pelevin, Viktor. *Smotritel': Orden Zheltogo flaga.* Moscow: Eksmo, 2015.

Pelevin, Viktor. *Smotritel': Zheleznaia bezdna.* Moscow: Eksmo, 2015.

Pelevin, Viktor. *S.N.U.F.F.* Moscow: Eksmo, 2011.

Pelevin, Victor. *S.N.U.F.F.* London: Gollancz, 2015.

Pelevin, Viktor. *Sviashchennaia kniga oborotnia.* Moscow: Eksmo, 2004.

Pelevin, Viktor. *T.* Moscow: Eksmo, 2009.

Pelevin, Viktor. *Vse povesti i esse.* Moscow: Eksmo, 2005.

Pelevin, Victor. *A Werewolf Problem in Central Russia.* New York: New Directions, 2010.

Pelevin, Viktor. *Zheltaia strela.* Moscow: Vagrius, 1993.

Pelevin, Viktor. *Zhizn' nasekomykh.* Moscow: Vagrius, 1993.

Piper, H. Beam. *The Complete Paratime.* New York: Ace, 2001.

Plato. *The Allegory of the Cave.* Translated by Benjamin Jowett. Los Angeles: Enhanced Media Publishing, 2017.

Plato. *The Republic.* Translated by G. M. A. Grube, revised by C. D. C. Reeve. Indianapolis: Hackett Publishing Company, 1992.

Platonov, Andrei. *The Foundation Pit.* Translated by Robert and Elizabeth Chandler and Olga Meerson. New York: New York Review Books Classics, 2009.

Platonov, Andrei. *Kotlovan.* Ann Arbor: Ardis, 1973.

Poe, Edgar Allan. *The Complete Poetry of Edgar Allan Poe.* Dachau: Musaicum Books, OK Publishing, 2017.

Polevoi, Boris. *Povest' o nastoiashchem cheloveke.* Moscow: Rech', 2018.

Polevoi, Boris. *A Story about a Real Man.* New York: Benediction Books, 2010.

Potts, Stephen. *The Second Marxian Invasion: The Fiction of the Strugatsky Brothers.* San Bernardino, Calif.: Borgo, 1991.

Prigov, Dmitrii. *Sobranie sochinenii v 5 tomakh.* Moscow: Novoe literaturnoe obozrenie, 2017.

Prigov, Dmitrii. *Soviet Texts.* Translated by Simon Schuchat with Ainsley Morse. New York: Ugly Duckling Presse, 2020.

Pronina, Elena. "Fraktal'naia logika Viktora Pelevina." *Voprosy literatury,* no. 4 (2003): 5–30.

Pushkin, Alexander. *Eugene Onegin: A Novel in Verse.* Translated by James Falen. Oxford: Oxford University Press, 2009.

Pushkin, Aleksandr. *Polnoe sobranie sochinenii v shestnadtsati tomakh.* Edited by Maksim Gor'kii et al. Moscow: Izdatel'stvo Akademii Nauk SSSR, 1937–59.

Pustovaia, Valeriia. "Niche o nikom: Apofatik Pelevin." *Oktiabr',* no. 6 (2010). http://magazines.russ.ru/october/2010/6/pu12.html.

Pustovaia, Valeriia. "Skifiia v serebre: 'Russkii proekt' v sovremennoi proze." *Novyi mir,* no. 1 (2007): 168–88.

Pynchon, Thomas. *The Crying of Lot 49.* Philadelphia: J. B. Lippincott, 1966.

Pynchon, Thomas. *Vineland.* Boston: Little, Brown, 1990.

Quinby, Lee. *Anti-Apocalypse: Exercises in Genealogical Criticism.* Minneapolis: University of Minnesota Press, 1994.

Rodnianskaia, Irina. "Etot mir priduman ne nami." *Novyi mir,* no. 8 (1999). http://magazines.russ.ru/novyi_mi/1999/8/rodnyan.html.

Rodnianskaia, Irina. ". . . i k nei bezumnaia liubov' . . ." *Novyi mir,* no. 9 (1996): 212–16.

Rodnianskaia, Irina. "Somel'e Pelevin. I sogliadatai." *Novyi mir,* no. 10 (2012). http://magazines.russ.ru/novyi_mi/2012/10/r16.html.

Rorty, Richard. *Contingency, Irony, and Solidarity.* Cambridge: Cambridge University Press, 1989.

Rosenfeld, Gavriel. "Why Do We Ask 'What If?' Reflections on the Function of Alternate History." *History and Theory* 41, no. 4 (December 2002): 90–103.

Rosenshield, Gary. "The Laws of Nature: Autonomy and 'Unity' in Dostoevskii's *Idiot.*" *Slavic Review* 50, no. 4 (Winter 1991): 879–89.

Rosso, Stefano. "A Correspondence with Umberto Eco." *Boundary* 212, no. 1 (1983): 1–13.

Roth, Philip. *The Plot Against America.* New York: Vintage, 2005.

Rothenberg, Molly Anne, and Slavoj Žižek, eds. *Perversion and the Social Relation.* Durham, N.C.: Duke University Press, 2003.

Rozanov, Vasily. *Dostoevsky and the Legend of the Grand Inquisitor.* Translated by Spencer E. Roberts. Ithaca, N.Y.: Cornell University Press, 1972.

Rubinshtein, Lev. *Complete Catalogue of Comedic Novelties*. New York: Ugly Duckling Presse, 2014.

Rubinshtein, Lev. "Kogda zhe pridet nastoiashchii P?" *Itogi*, no. 17 (April 26, 1999). http://pelevin.nov.ru/stati/o-rub/l.html.

Rushdie, Salman. *The Satanic Verses: A Novel*. New York: Random House, 2008.

Ryan, Karen, and Barry P. Scherr, eds. *Twentieth-Century Russian Literature: Selected Papers from the Fifth World Congress of Central and East European Studies, Warsaw, 1995*. New York: Palgrave Macmillan, 2000.

Rybakov, Viacheslav. *Gravilet 'Tsesarevich.'* St. Petersburg: Lan', 1994.

Rydel, Christine, ed. *Russian Prose Writers after World War II*. Detroit, Mich.: Gale Research, 2004.

Salkind, Neil. *An Introduction to Theories of Human Development*. New York: SAGE, 2004.

Salieva, L. "Mify 90-kh ili 'Vechnye tsennosti novogo pokoleniia.'" Viktor Pelevin: Sait tvorchestva. http://pelevin.nov.ru/stati/o-myth90/1html.

Sarychev, V. "Apokalipsis ot Sofii: Religiozno-khudozhestvennaia kontseptsiia knigi A. Bloka 'Stikhi o prekrasnoi dame' v kontekste sofiologii Vl. Solov'eva." *Izvestiia RAN: Seriia literatury i iazyka*, no. 5 (2008): 3–15.

Scanlan, James. *Dostoevsky the Thinker*. Ithaca, N.Y.: Cornell University Press, 2011.

Schlegel, Friedrich. *Lucinde and the Fragments*. Translated and introduction by Peter Firchow. Minneapolis: University of Minnesota Press, 1971.

Searle, John. *Minds, Brain, and Science*. Cambridge, Mass.: Harvard University Press, 2003.

Shaitanov, Igor'. "Booker-97: Zapiski 'nachal'nika premii.'" *Voprosy literatury*, no. 3 (1998). magazines.russ.ru/voplit/1998/3/shait.html.

Shakespeare, William. *The Tempest*. Edited by Barbara Mowat and Paul Werstine. New York: Simon and Schuster, 2004.

Shannon, C. E., and J. McCarthy, eds. *Automata Studies. (AM-34), Volume 34 (Annals of Mathematics Studies)*. Princeton, N.J.: Princeton University Press, 1956.

Sharov, Vladimir. *Before and During*. Dublin: Dedalus, 2014.

Sharov, Vladimir. *Do i vo vremia*. Moscow: Arsis Books, 1993.

Shklovskii, Viktor. *Eshche nichego ne konchilos'*. Moscow: Propaganda, 2002.

Shklovskii, Viktor. *Khod konia*. Moscow-Berlin: Gelikon, 1923.

Shklovskii, Viktor. *Knight's Move*. Translated and introduction by Richard Sheldon. London: Dalkey Archive, 2005.

Shteyngart, Gary. *Absurdistan*. New York: Random House, 2007.

Shurko, Igor'. "Chetyre paradoksa khrustal'nogo mira." *Neva*, no. 1 (2004). http://magazines.russ.ru/neva/2004/1/sh23.html.

Simon, Erik. "The Strugatskys in Political Context." *Science Fiction Studies* 31, no. 3 (2004): 378–406.

Skinner, B. F. *Contingencies of Reinforcement: A Theoretical Analysis.* New York: B. F. Skinner Foundation, 1969.

Slavnikova, Ol'ga. "Ia liubliu tebia, imperiia." *Znamia*, no. 12 (2000). https://magazines.gorky.media/znamia/2000/12/ya-lyublyu-tebya-imperiya.html.

Slavnikova, Ol'ga. *2017.* Moscow: Vagrius, 2006.

Slavnikova, Ol'ga. *2017: A Novel.* Translated by Marian Schwartz. New York: Harry N. Abrams, 2012.

Sloterdijk, Peter. *Critique of Cynical Reason.* Theory and History of Literature, edited by Wlad Godzich and Jochen Schulte-Sasse, vol. 40. Minneapolis: University of Minnesota Press, 1988.

Smith, Adam. *The Wealth of Nations.* New York: Bantam Classics, 2003.

Smith, Alexandra. "Arkady Natanovich Strugatsky and Boris Natanovich Strugatsky." In *Russian Prose Writers after World War II*, edited by Christine Rydel, 356–65. Detroit, Mich.: Gale Research, 2004.

Sologub, Fyodor. *The Petty Demon.* Edited by Murl Barker, translated by S. D. Cioran. Ann Arbor: Ardis, 2009.

Sologub, Fedor. *Sobranie sochinenii v 6 tomakh.* Moscow: Intelvak, 2004.

Solov'ev, Vladimir. *Filosofiia iskusstva i literaturnaia kritika.* Moscow: Iskusstvo, 1991.

Solov'ev, Vladimir. "Kratkaia povest' ob Antikhriste." In *Tri razgovora o voine, progresse i kontse vsemirnoi istorii.* Moscow: AST, 2011.

Solov'ev, Vladimir. *Polnoe sobranie sochinenii i pisem v 20 tomakh.* Moscow: Nauka, 2001.

Solov'ev, Vladimir. "Smysl liubvi." In *Filosofiia iskusstva i literaturnaia kritika*, 99–160. Moscow: Iskusstvo, 1991.

Solov'ev, Vladimir. *Tri razgovora o voine, progresse i kontse vsemirnoi istorii.* Moscow: AST, 2011.

Sorokin, Vladimir. *Day of the Oprichnik.* New York: FSG Adult, 2012.

Sorokin, Vladimir. *Den' oprichnika.* Moscow: Zakharov, 2006.

Sorokin, Vladimir. *Goluboe salo.* Moscow: Ad Marginem, 1999.

Sorokin, Vladimir. *Sakharnyi Kreml'.* Moscow: AST, 2014.

Spengler, Oswald. *The Decline of the West.* New York: Vintage, 2006.

Steinberg, Mark. *Petersburg Fin de Siècle.* New Haven, Conn.: Yale University Press, 2011.

Steiner, George. *After Babel: Aspects of Language and Translation.* Oxford: Oxford University Press, 1988.

Steiner, George. *Language and Silence: Essays on Language, Literature, and the Inhuman.* New York: Open Road Media, 1974.

Stross, Charles. *A Merchant Princes Omnibus.* New York: Tor Books, 2004.

Strugatsky, Arkady and Boris. *Beetle in the Anthill.* Translated by Antonina DuBouis. New York: Macmillan, 1980.

Strugatsky, Arkady and Boris. *The Doomed City.* Translated by Andrew Bromfield. Chicago: Chicago Review Press, 2016.

Strugatsky, Arkady and Boris. *Escape Attempt.* Translated by Roger DeGaris. New York: Macmillan, 1982.

Strugatsky, Arkady and Boris. *Far Rainbow: The Second Invasion from Mars.* New York: Macmillan, 1979.

Strugatsky, Arkady and Boris. *The Final Circle of Paradise.* London: D. Dobson, 1979.

Strugatsky, Arkady and Boris. *Hard to Be a God.* Translated by Olena Bormashenko. Chicago: Chicago Review Press, 2014.

Strugatsky, Arkady and Boris. *Lame Fate. Ugly Swans.* Translated by Maya Vinokour. Chicago: Chicago Review Press, 2020.

Strugatsky, Arkady and Boris. *Monday Starts on Saturday.* Translated by Andrew Bromfield. Chicago: Chicago Review Press, 2017.

Strugatsky, Arkady and Boris. *Roadside Picnic.* Translated by Olena Bormashenko. Chicago: Chicago Review Press, 2012.

Strugatsky, Arkady and Boris. *The Snail on the Slope.* Translated by Olena Bormashenko. Chicago: Chicago Review Press, 2018.

Strugatskie, Arkadii and Boris. *Sobranie sochinenii v odinnadtsati tomakh.* Donetsk: Stalker, 2000–2003.

Strugatskie, Arkadii and Boris. *Ulitka na sklone: Opyt akademicheskogo izdaniia.* Moscow: Novoe literaturnoe obozrenie, 2006.

Strugatskii, Boris. *Kommentarii k proidennomu.* St. Petersburg: Amfora, 2003.

Strugatskii, Boris. "Na randevu." www.rusf.ru/abs/int/bns_chat.htm.

Suslov, Mikhail. "Of Planets and Trenches: Imperial Science Fiction in Contemporary Russia." *The Russian Review*, no. 75 (October 2016): 562–78.

Suslov, Mikhail, and Per-Arne Bodin, eds. *Geo-Political Identity Making in Post-Soviet Russian Speculative Fiction.* London: I. B. Tauris, 2019.

Suvin, Darko. "Criticism of the Strugatsky Brothers' Work." *Canadian-American Slavic Studies*, no. 2 (1972): 286–307.

Suvin, Darko. "The Literary Opus of the Strugatsky Brothers." *Canadian-American Slavic Studies*, no. 3 (1974): 454–63.

Suvin, Darko. *Metamorphoses of Science Fiction.* New Haven, Conn.: Yale University Press, 1979.

Sverdlov, Mikhail. "Tekhnologiia pisatel'skoi vlasti (o dvukh poslednikh romanakh V. Pelevina)." *Voprosy literatury*, no. 4 (2003). http://magazines.russ.ru/voplit/2003/4/sver.html.

Svetlova, Irina. "I uvidel ia son, i etot son uskol'znul ot menia." *Novyi mir*, no. 1 (2015). http://magazines.russ.ru/novyi_mi/2015/1/18svet.html.

Swift, Jonathan. *Gulliver's Travels.* Mineola, N.Y.: Dover, 1996.

Tatarinov, Aleksei. "Pelevin bez prekrasnoi damy." *Literaturnaia Rossiia*, no. 12 (March 2011). http://www.litrossia.ru/archive/item/4987-oldarchive.

Taushev, Averkii (Archbishop). "Apokalipsis ili otkrovenie Ioanna Bogoslova." Azbuka very. https://azbyka.ru/otechnik/Averkij_Taushev/apokalipsis-ili -otkrovenie-svjatogo-ioanna-bogoslova/.

Tertz, Abram (Siniavskii, Andrei). *Liubimov*. Washington: Izdatel'stvo B. Filippova, 1964.

Tertz, Abram (Siniavskii, Andrei). *The Makepeace Experiment*. Translated by Manya Harari. Evanston, Ill.: Northwestern University Press, 1989.

Tiutchev, Fedor. *Polnoe sobranie sochinenii i pis'ma v 6 tomakh*. Volume 2. *Stikhotvoreniia 1850–1873*. Edited by N. N. Skatov et al. Moscow: Klassika, 2002–4.

Tiutchev, Fedor. *Selected Poems*. Translated, introduction and edited by John Dewey. Gillingham, Dorset, Eng: Brimstone Press, 2014.

Todorov, Tsvetan. *The Fantastic: A Structural Approach to a Literary Genre*. Translated by Richard Howard, introduction by Robert Scholes. Ithaca, N.Y.: Cornell University Press, 1975.

Tolkien, J. R. R. *The Lord of the Rings*. Boston: Mariner Books, 2012.

Tolstaia, Tatiana. *Kys': Roman*. Moscow: Izdatel'stvo Dom Podkova, 1999.

Tolstaia, Tatiana. *The Slynx*. Translated by Jamey Gambrell. New York: NYRB Books, 2007.

Tolstoi, Aleksei. *Zolotoi kliuchik, ili prikliucheniia Buratino*. Moscow: Rosman, 2012.

Tolstoy, Leo. *Polnoe sobranie sochinenii v sta tomakh*. Edited by G. I. Galagan et al. Moscow: Nauka, 2000.

Tolstoy, Leo. *War and Peace*. Translated by Richard Pevear and Larissa Volokhonsky, introduction by Richard Pevear. New York: Vintage, 2008.

Turing, Alan. *The Essential Turing: Seminal Writings in Computing, Logic, Philosophy, Artificial Intelligence, and Artificial Life plus The Secrets of Enigma*. Edited by B. Jack Copeland. Oxford: Oxford University Press, 2004.

Turtledove, Harry. *Crosstime Traffic* series. New York: Tor Books, 2003–8.

Tynianov, Iurii. *Arkhaisty i novatory*. Leningrad: Priboi, 1929.

Tynianov, Iurii. *Dostoevskii i Gogol: K teorii parodii*. Petrograd: Opoiaz, 1921.

Tynianov, Iurii. *Permanent Evolution: Selected Essays on Literature, Theory and Film (Cultural Syllabus)*. Translated by Ainsley Morse and Philip Redko, introduction by Daria Khitrova. Boston: Academic Studies, 2019.

Tynianov, Iurii. *Poetika, istoria literatury, kino*. Moscow: Nauka, 1977.

Vaingurt, Julia. "Freedom and the Reality of Others in *Chapaev and the Void*." *Slavic and East European Journal* 62, no. 3 (Fall 2018): 466–82.

Vaingurt, Julia, and Colleen McQuillen, eds. *The Human Reimagined: Posthumanism in Late Soviet and Post-Soviet Russia*. Boston: Academic Studies, 2018.

Vernitskii, Aleksei. "Pelevin V. Shlem uzhasa: Kreatiff o Tesee i Minotavre," *Novoe literaturnoe obozrenie* 80 (2006), www.litkarta.ru/dossier/vernitsky-pelevin/#7.

Vitenberg, Boris. "Igry korrektirovshchikov: Zametki na poliakh 'al'ternativnykh istorii.' *Novoe literaturnoe obozrenie* 66 (2004): 281–93.

Voinovich, Vladimir. *Moscow 2042*. New York: Mariner Books, 1990.

Voinovich, Vladimir. *Moskva 2042*. Moscow: Vsia Moskva, 1990.

Vonnegut, Kurt. *Slaughterhouse-Five, or the Children's Crusade: A Duty Dance with Death*. New York: Delacorte, 1969.

Vvedenskii, Aleksandr. *Vse*. Moscow: OGI, 2010.

Wachtel, Andrew. *An Obsession with History: Russian Writers Confront the Past*. Stanford, Calif.: Stanford University Press, 1994.

Wells, Herbert G. *Men Like Gods*. London: Cassell, 1923.

Wells, Herbert G. *The Time Machine: 100th Anniversary Collection*. New York: Seawolf, 2018.

Wolfe, Cary. *Animal Rites: American Culture, the Discourse of Species, and Post-humanist Theory*. Chicago: University of Chicago Press, 2003.

Wolfe, Tom. *The Bonfire of the Vanities*. New York: Picador, 2008.

Wordsworth, William. *Prose Writings*. Selected, edited, and introduced by William Knight. London: Forgotten Books, 2018.

Yablokov, Ilya. *Fortress Russia: Conspiracy Theories in the Post-Soviet World*. Medford, Mass.: Polity, 2018.

Yurchak, Alexei. *Everything Was Forever, Until It Was No More: The Last Soviet Generation*. Princeton, N.J.: Princeton University Press, 2006.

Zagidullina, M. B. "Mutatsiia otsenki: Temporal'nyi transfer klassicheskogo teksta (romany V. Pelevina *T* i B. Akunina *F. M.*)." *Russian Literature*, no. 1 (2011): 157–68.

Zamyatin, Yevgeny. *The Dragon, and Other Stories*. New York: Penguin, 1975.

Zamyatin, Yevgeny. *Sobranie sochinenii v 5 tomakh*. Moscow: Dmitrii Sechin, 2011.

Zamyatin, Yevgeny. *We*. Translated by Clarence Brown. New York: Penguin Twentieth Century Classics, 1993.

Zenkovsky, Serge. *Medieval Russia's Epics, Chronicles, and Tales*. Nampa: Meridian, 1974.

Žižek, Slavoj. "The Ambiguity of the Masochist Social Link." In *Perversion and the Social Relation*, edited by Molly Anne Rothenberg and Slavoj Žižek, 112–25. Durham, N.C.: Duke University Press, 2003.

Žižek, Slavoj. *The Sublime Object of Ideology (Phronesis)*. London: Verso, 1989.

Žižek, Slavoj. *Welcome to the Desert of the Real: Five Essays on September 11 and Related Dates*. New York: Verso, 2002.

Zviagintsev, Vasilii. *Odissei pokidaet Itaku*. Moscow: Eksmo, 2014.

Index

Adorno, Theodor, 11, 17–18, 55, 218n11
advertising: and apocalypse, 112–15; and
dystopia, 30–32, 36, 38–39, 40–41, 45–
46, 97; of *Generation 'Π'* book, 190–92;
jingles, 31, 50–51, 53, 57; and language
of total administration, 11–13, 18; language play of, 50–51, 53–60, 62–66; slogans, 50–51, 59, 63, 188, 192; and target
groups, 59–60, 66, 72. See also *Generation 'Π'*; media; *specific brands*
Aesthetic Ideology (De Man), 194
Agamben, Giorgio, 223n3, 231n36
Aksyonov, Vasily, 7, 29, 30, 43, 167, 233n4
Akunin, Boris, 161, 196
Al-Ghazali, 42
alibi in Being (Bakhtin), 201
Alimov, Igor, 233n4, 234n13
allegory, 155–56
allegory of the Cave (Plato), 46
al-Qaeda, 144, 215, 235n34
alternative historical imagination, 15–23,
134–35, 138, 139, 142–43
alternative history: conceptualized, 133–
35, 139, 147–49, 156–57; as constellation
of projections, 143–46, 152; for cultural
critique, 137–43, 149–56; points of divergence in, 135–37, 139; timelines, 134,
137–38, 142, 149, 152, 155–57
Althusser, Louis, 235n31
Amis, Kingsley, 133, 233n3
Amusin, Mark, 240n18, 240n23, 246n6
Andreyev, Daniil, 124, 131, 132
Anglo-American idiom, 50–51, 56, 59–
64, 65
Angry Birds (game), 143, 145, 210, 225n2
animals. *See* zoomorphic imagery

"Anti-Aircraft Codices of Al-Efesbi"
(Pelevin), 100–102, 118, 121–23
Antichrist, 112, 125–30, 169. *See also* controlling user
apocalypse: the Beast and, 114–15, 120,
127, 225n5, 228n4, 231n34; conceptualized, 111–12, 130–32, 133, 230n22; Dostoevsky on, 162–63, 167; and final reckoning, 52, 70–71, 115–18; horsemen of,
129, 167; media/advertising and, 112–15;
and post-apocalyptic temporality, 118–
24; and reign of Antichrist, 41, 65–66,
112, 125–30, 169; Strugatsky brothers
on, 177–79
apokalipsis (revelation), 120, 131
Arbitman, Roman, 227n18, 231n35
Archaeologies of the Future (Jameson), 7,
173
Arendt, Hannah, 218n16
Ariadne, 92–96
Arkhangel'skii, Andrei, 227n21
Armageddon, 131. *See also* apocalypse
Armstrong, Karen, 225n5
"Around the Bend" (Pasternak), 175
art, 36–37, 39–40, 63, 212
artificial intelligence (AI), 101–2, 104–6,
212. *See also* technology
Atwood, Margaret, 9, 225n5
automatons. *See* posthumanism; technology

Baal, 38, 46, 73, 113, 126, 163
Baba Yaga, 224n16
Babitskaia, Varvara, 210
bablos (life energy). See *Empire V*
Babylon. *See* apocalypse; Enkidu; Whore
of Babylon

Index

Index